Speech carries info about the
structure and organisation of language.

LAD. pg 23

The Discovery of
Spoken Language

Language, Speech, and Communication

The Discovery of
Spoken Language

Peter W. Jusczyk

A Bradford Book
The MIT Press
Cambridge, Massachusetts
London, England

This book was set in Times Roman on the Monotype "Prism Plus" PostScript Imagesetter by Asco Trade Typesetting Ltd., Hong Kong.

Printed and bound in the United States of America.

Library of Congress Cataloging-in-Publication Data

Jusczyk, Peter W.
  The discovery of spoken language / Peter W. Jusczyk.
    p. cm. — (Language, speech, and communication)
  "A Bradford book."
  Includes bibliographical references and index.
  ISBN 0-262-10058-4 (hc)
  1. Speech perception in infants. 2. Speech perception in newborn infants.
3. Language acquisition. 4. Psycholinguistics.
  I. Title. II. Series.
BF720.S67J87   1997
401'.93—dc20   96-29015
                                                        CIP

To Ann Marie, the real saint in our household

If a man can keep alert and imaginative,
an error is a possibility, a chance at something new;
to him, wandering and wondering are part of the same process,
and he is most mistaken, most in error,
whenever he quits exploring.

—William Least Heat-Moon, *Blue Highways*

Contents

Acknowledgments

I had been intending to write a book of this sort for a number of years—just as soon as I could get through the stack of things to do that always seemed more pressing. Finally, several years ago, Anne Cutler got me to agree to undertake this project, and she and Pim Levelt made me an offer I could not refuse by inviting me to the Max Planck Institute for Psycholinguistics. This provided me with the necessary distraction from the "stack," and the supportive environment to begin writing this book. I am deeply indebted to them, to the staff of the MPI, and to a thoughtful and quiet officemate—Pieter Joordens—for all the encouragement they gave me. I am also grateful to the National Institutes of Child Health and Human Development (NICHD) and the National Institutes of Deafness and Other Communication Disorders (NIDCD) for the financial support for many of the research studies that are reported in this book. Without this help, there would not have been much for me to write about.

I would also like to take this opportunity to thank a number of people who have helped shape my thinking about many of the issues discussed in this book. I have been very fortunate to have had some wonderful teachers and colleagues who have helped me along the way. I am especially indebted to Father Patrick Walsh, C.S.C., Peter Eimas, Einar Siqueland, Rochel Gelman, Harris Savin, Lila and Henry Gleitman, Burt Rosner, David Pisoni, Jacques Mehler, Josiane Bertoncini, Ranka Bijeljac-Babic, Benedicte de Boysson-Bardies, Tom Bever, Doug Hintzman, Dick Aslin, Robert Remez, LouAnn Gerken, Jim Sawusch, Paul Luce, and above all, Deborah Kemler Nelson—my Intro Psych Lab Instructor, my Ph.D. supervisor, and my close colleague.

My family also has been a real source of strength to me throughout my career, and particularly while writing this book. So, I want to thank my parents, Eleanor and Walter; my wife, Ann Marie; and my children,

Karla and Tad for their encouragement, their support, and their great patience with me.

I received many helpful suggestions on earlier drafts of this book from LouAnn Gerken, Robert Remez, Deborah Kemler Nelson, Mark Seidenberg, Lynn Santelmann, Michael Tucker, Rochelle Newman, Michele Shady, Mara Goodman, Derek Houston, Ruth Tincoff, Ann Marie Jusczyk, Amy Pierce, Peter Eimas, and two anonymous reviewers. Their comments and questions undoubtedly made this a better book. Needless to say, they are not responsible for advice not followed, nor for any remaining errors in the book.

Chapter 1
Surveying the Terrain

Language involves a duality of patterning, as Hockett (1954) has noted. On the one hand, there are patterns that pertain to the way that sounds are organized; on the other, there are patterns that relate to how meanings are organized. Although language use involves dealing with patterns at both levels, it often seems as though the two are studied in relative isolation of one another. This seems especially true with respect to the study of language acquisition. Peruse a typical textbook in the field, and you are apt to find that only a relatively small portion of the book is concerned with the development of speech perception and speech production. There are several possible reasons for this. It could be the case that there is simply a lot less known about the way speech perception and production capacities develop. Another possibility is that research on perception and production makes relatively little contact with the rest of the research on language acquisition.

Historically, there is support for both of these contentions. Although investigations documenting the growth of speech production have a relatively long history in diary studies (Ament 1899; Gregoire 1933, 1937; Leopold 1939, 1947; Scupin and Scupin 1907; Stern and Stern 1928), extensive research on infant speech perception had its inception during the last quarter century. Thus, with respect to how the receptive side of speech processing develops, there really was not a great deal of information available until fairly recently. However, the same cannot be said for developmental studies of speech production. Even the early diarists took pains to record some of the changes in pronunciation that occurred in the child's early words, although to be sure, the accuracy and reliability of phonetic transcriptions have improved enormously with the advent of the tape recorder and more sophisticated technology for analyzing speech production. Hence, to fully explain the separation between speech and the rest of language research, we also have to consider the second alternative—that the two domains have made little contact with each other. The fact that speech researchers typically receive very specialized training does have something to do with this. Not every linguist is trained to do, or is well-experienced in doing, phonetic transcriptions. Furthermore, speech perception researchers are trained in the basics of acoustics and signal processing. The kinds of analyses that they perform, the dimensions they examine, and even the terminologies they employ are pretty foreign to the rest of linguistics. Perhaps, then, it is not surprising that speech research has not been better integrated with psycholinguistic research in general and with language acquisition research in particular.

There was also another factor that helped encourage the separation of speech research from other aspects of language acquisition. This had to do with the way research in linguistics was conducted during the 1960s and 1970s. Generative grammarians such as Chomsky (1965; Chomsky and Halle 1968) and his colleagues held that each level of linguistic organization could be studied more or less independently from other levels. In fact, according to this view, one could best capture the correct generalizations about the organization of some component of language, such as syntax, by studying it in isolation from the other components. Only when the structures of each component were understood would it be possible to examine the integration and interaction of the various components.

Finally, there was still another factor that likely played a role in limiting the integration of infant speech-perception studies into language acquisition studies overall. Many of the early investigations demonstrated that even very young infants (i.e., 2- to 3-month-olds) apparently have well-developed speech perception capacities. These findings may have helped give rise to the belief that all the basics for speech perception are already in place well before the bulk of language learning even begins. Hence, those investigating how the child's semantic and syntactic development occurs could just assume that the child had already succeeded in segmenting words from fluent speech. In part, then, language researchers did not need to worry about developmental changes in speech perception capacities because there did not appear to be any real changes.

This picture has begun to change during the past decade, and it has done so for a variety of reasons. First, the general zeitgeist with respect to whether components of language should be studied separately or not has changed. More and more research is being devoted to the way different linguistic levels interact during the course of language production and comprehension (Bates and MacWhinney 1989; Marslen-Wilson and Welsh 1978; McClelland and Elman 1986; Seidenberg and McClelland 1989; Tanenhaus et al. 1993). Second, we have a much clearer picture of the basic speech perception and production capacities of infants. This picture, in turn, has provided investigators with a backdrop for viewing developmental changes in these capacities. Moreover, it has become evident that many changes to speech perception and production capacities are occurring within the first year of life and that these capacities are very much influenced by the kind of input to which infants have been exposed. Third, speech researchers themselves have begun to make efforts toward relating their findings to other findings in psycholinguistic and language acquisition research. In fact, this book is one such attempt to situate the findings of infant speech-perception research more squarely within the field of language acquisition.

Some Characteristics of Speech Perception

For the average adult, there is little mystery in speech perception. It is just a matter of hearing the words in the order in which they are spoken. Aside from the times in which interfering noises are present, the whole process of speech perception seems rather effortless. One simply hears the sounds and grasps the meanings that they stand for. In fact, the transition from sound to meaning is so seamless that we commenly hear right through the sounds directly to their meanings. The whole process is so fluid that, other than learning which sound patterns go with which meanings, it is hard to believe that learning plays much of a role in speech perception. Yet, this process of going from sound patterns to meanings, which is so easily accomplished by humans, still has not been successfully implemented on machines (Marcus 1984; Reddy 1976; Waibel 1986). Among the impediments to successful machine recognition of speech, boundaries between successive words are not clearly marked in the speech stream (Cole and Jakimik 1980; Klatt 1979, 1989), and the acoustic shapes of words are frequently affected by the nature of the words in the surrounding context (Liberman and Studdert-Kennedy 1978; Mills 1980). Hence, speech researchers are well aware of the fact that the perception of fluent speech is a lot more complex than it first appears.

There are moments when we do appreciate some of the complexities in speech perception that we overcame when learning to speak and understand a language. For instance, when we are with people speaking an

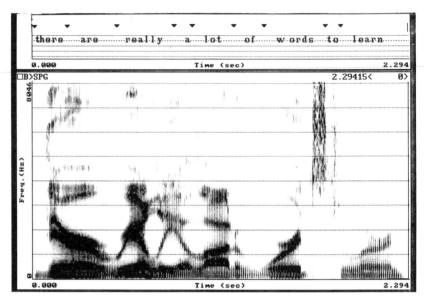

Figure 1.1
A sound spectrogram of the utterance, "There are really a lot of words to learn."
Frequency is plotted on the ordinate; each horizontal line indicates a 1 kHz
increase in frequency. Arrows at the top indicate the approximate locations of the
word boundaries in the utterance. Notice that these boundaries are not always
clearly marked by pauses and that some pauses actually occur in the middle of
words.

unfamiliar language, we often realize that comprehension is difficult not
only because we do not know what the words actually mean but also
because it is difficult to determine what the words are. We find it hard to
tell when one word begins and another one ends. Why is this the case?
Native English speakers typically have the impression that speakers of
foreign languages talk faster than we do in English. However, this is an
illusion. Native speakers of other languages tend to voice the same kinds
of complaints about English speakers.

A major reason it is difficult to perceive boundaries between words in a
foreign language has to do with the way words are typically produced,
that is, with the nature of the acoustic signal that must be decoded. Figure
1.1 shows a sound spectrogram (a time by frequency analysis) of the
English sentence "There are really a lot of words to learn." Notice that
there are a number of discontinuities in the spectrogram. A first guess

about these discontinuities might be that they correspond to boundaries between words. However, as the word boundary markers in the figure show, not all word boundaries show up as breaks in the speech wave, and not all breaks in the speech wave correspond to boundaries between words. Thus, unlike the printed words on this page, there are no clear spaces between spoken words. Rather, words in spoken language are usually run into one another. This absence of clearly defined breaks between successive words is commonly a consequence of what speech researchers refer to as *coarticulation* (e.g., Liberman et al. 1967). Coarticulation occurs because speech production involves moving our articulators (e.g., vocal folds, tongue, lips, jaw, etc.) from one configuration to another in a very short time span. Because it takes time to move the articulators into the proper position for each sound, the articulatory apparatus is forced to find a compromise solution that involves starting the articulatory gestures for one segment prior to finishing the gestures relevant to a preceding segment. This causes the segments to overlap as speech is produced. For this reason, a given slice of the speech wave includes information about the articulation of several different sounds in the utterance. Coarticulation most commonly occurs between successive segments within words, but as speaking rates increase, the likelihood of coarticulation across word boundaries also increases. Consequently, undoing the effects of coarticulation is a part of what is involved in segmenting fluent speech into strings of discrete words.

Since coarticulation occurs in all human languages, why are the solutions to the problem in one's native language not also effective with other languages? The answer is that languages differ in their organizations of sound patterns of utterances, both within words and between different words. The cues that point to the location of word boundaries in the speech stream are apt to be closely tuned to the underlying organization of the sound patterns for a particular language. These cues differ from language to language. Moreover, a given acoustic cue can serve more than a single linguistic function. For instance, vowel lengthening in English is related to syllable stress, voicing differences, word boundaries, and clause boundaries (Klatt 1975, 1976). Consequently, among the things that one has to learn in order to speak and understand a native language is what the correct cues are for segmenting words from fluent speech in that language.

To this point, we have been viewing the segmentation problem from an adult's perspective. The adult is already an experienced perceiver of speech and, presumably, has acquired considerable knowledge of how at least one language works, including knowledge of some cues that could signal word boundaries. In principle, this knowledge and experience should be more helpful than hurtful in learning to segment words in another language (although one might argue that such an individual will also have to "unlearn" some habits that work for the native language, but not for the nonnative one).

We suspect that newborn infants are even worse off than adults when it comes to perceiving fluent speech. Along with the other problems that stand in the way of speaking and understanding a native language, they must solve the segmentation problem for the first time. Moreover, they must do so with information-processing and memory resources that are less well developed than those of adults. Yet, since the overwhelming majority of infants learn to speak and understand a native language, they obviously do solve the segmentation problem and surmount all the other obstacles connected with learning a language. How do they accomplish this within a relatively short period of time, and what resources do they rely on?

The objective of this book is to examine the origins of language acquisition in relation to the development of speech perception. In particular, the focus is on the sound structure of the native language and how the infant's perceptual capacities are developed and optimized for perceiving fluent speech in the native language. The development of speech perception capacities is viewed in the broader context of acquiring fluency in a native language. Consequently, I not only review what is known about infant speech-perception capacities and their development, but I also consider the role that these capacities play in the acquisition of language. This is not to say that infants rely only on their speech-perception capacities to acquire language. Clearly there are multiple sources of information and many different abilities that are involved in acquiring a native language. The infant learning to decode the speech stream is also an infant who is learning about the structure of objects and events in the world. Hence, this infant is engaged in acquiring the conceptual structure that underlies the semantic component of language. At the same time, the infant is a participant in a range of social activities that certainly affect the content of his or her communications. Information about semantic properties of the input may prove helpful in learning about its syntactic organization (Pinker 1984, 1989, 1994) just as knowledge of syntactic properties might play a role in discerning some semantic features of new words (Fisher

et al. 1994). My intent is not to discount the role that these other sources of information play in language acquisition. Rather, it is to explore how speech perception capacities evolve and how, at various points in development, they might provide learners with information that facilitates the acquisition of a native language.

A first consideration is to provide a better picture of the nature and range of the perceptual capacities that we will be concerned with. I have already discussed one of the critical problems that language learners need to solve, namely, segmenting words from fluent speech. Thus some of the capacities that are considered are ones that underlie word segmentation. However, there are many other abilities required in order to be a successful perceiver of fluent speech. The language learner has to have, or acquire, some proficiency in all of these. Let us consider further what some of the abilities are that the learner must master to become a fluent listener.

Dealing with Variability in the Speech Signal

Speech is produced by people of many different shapes and sizes. Although different talkers generally use the same types of articulators in producing sounds, the size and shapes of their vocal tracts differ considerably. These vocal tract differences have an impact on the acoustic characteristics of speech. The length and mass of the vocal folds, as well as the overall length of the vocal tract, affect the typical fundamental frequency (or pitch) of one's speaking voice. Greater length and mass of the vocal folds and longer vocal tracts are associated with lower-pitched voices. Men generally have longer vocal tracts than women, and adults have longer vocal tracts than infants and young children. Moreover, the vocal tracts of different talkers differ in other ways that affect how sounds are articulated, such as whether or not teeth are missing, the characteristic shape and flexibility of the tongue, the state of the vocal folds, and so on. These factors, too, affect the acoustic characteristics of the speech that is produced. Consequently, the acoustic characteristics of the same word produced by different talkers may vary considerably. Worse yet, the acoustic characteristics of a word produced by one talker may actually more closely resemble the acoustic characteristics of a different word (as opposed to the same word) produced by another talker. This factor presents a perceptual constancy problem of major proportions for any

automatic speech-recognition device, and it might be particularly difficult
for infants learning words in cases in which they derive perceptual representations that are actually nonwords. However, adult human listeners
seem to have little difficulty in adjusting to pronunciations by different
talkers of the same dialect.

In addition to the variability in speech production among different
talkers, there are also differences that occur within a particular talker. The
most obvious differences have to do with changes in speaking rate. Distinctions among speech sounds that are cued by temporal differences
(such as the stop/glide distinction between [b] and [w]) are known to be
affected by changes in speaking rate (Liberman et al. 1956; Miller and
Liberman 1979). Similarly, changes in speech register to produce infant-
directed speech or whispered speech will affect the acoustic characteristics
of particular words. Once again, this kind of variability presents no undue
hardship for experienced normal listeners of a particular language.

Another factor that influences the production of particular speech
sounds is the other sounds with which they occur—that is, their phonetic
contexts. For example, English, unlike French or Polish, does not include
a distinction between oral and nasal vowels. In French, the oral versus
nasal vowel distinction conveys a meaningful difference between words
such as "beau" ([bo]) and "bon" ([bõ]). By comparison, there is no meaningful distinction among English words that is conveyed solely by a difference between the presence of a nasal vowel versus an oral vowel. However,
vowels in English are nasalized, to some degree, when they occur with
nasal consonants (such as [n] or [m]). Hence, in fluent speech, the English
words "cat" ([kæt]) and "can't" ([kæ̃t]) are primarily distinguished by the
fact that the vowel is nasalized in the latter case. Furthermore, because of
coarticulation, the production, and consequently the acoustic characteristics, of most consonants is influenced by which vowels and which consonants they occur with. This kind of acoustic variation does not pose a
serious problem to experienced listeners.

As these kinds of examples indicate, successful speech perception cannot depend upon responding to any absolute set of acoustic properties.
Rather, because the production of speech is so variable, the critical distinctions must take into account such factors as speaking rate, speech
register, talker's voice, and phonetic context. Becoming a fluent perceiver
of a particular language requires an ability to handle these sources of
variability in the speech signal.

Learning Elementary Sound Units and Their Orderings

Languages differ in which sets of phones they use and, further, on how these phones are grouped to form meaningful distinctions among words in the language. For example, English includes both the phones [ð], the first sound of "the," and [θ], the first sound of "think." Moreover, both sounds form minimal pairs (i.e., meaningful distinctions) with other sounds in the language. For example, the distinction between the English words, "thin" and "din" is conveyed by the occurrence of [θ] or [d], respectively, as the initial consonant sound. Similarly, the words "lathe" and "laid" are distinguished by the occurrence of either [ð] or [d] as the final consonant. Neither [ð] nor [θ] occurs in French words. However, French has a phonemic vowel distinction between [y], as in "tu," and [u], as in "tous," that does not occur in English. Consequently, one of the things that language learners must discover about the sound patterns of their native language is just what phones serve as elementary sound units for forming words in the language.

However, merely taking stock of what sounds occur in native language utterances will not ensure that the infant arrives at the set of meaningful sound distinctions in the language. This is because not every difference between phones signals a difference in meaning between words. For example, English includes a number of variants (or allophones) for its phoneme [t]. Thus, when [t] occurs at the beginning of a word like "tap," the phone produced, [tʰ], is aspirated. However, when [t] occurs in the final position of a word like "pat," the phone that appears, [t], is unaspirated. Although both the phones [tʰ] and [t] occur in English, they are not used to distinguish between words. That is, for English speakers, pronouncing the word "tap" as [tæp], instead of [tʰæp], conveys no meaningful distinction. In another language, such as Thai, which also includes both of these phones, words *are* distinguished solely on this basis. Consequently, it is not enough to know which sounds appear in words in one's native language; one also has to discover which differences among these sounds are relevant for conveying distinctions in meaning.

Languages differ in their sound patterns not only in terms of which sounds they use to form words but in other ways as well. One such difference has to do with the kinds of restrictions that are imposed on how phones can be ordered to form words or syllables. Phonologists refer to this property of language sound patterns as *phonotactics*. For example, in English words, the phone [ŋ] can occur at the ends of syllables such as the word "rang" (i.e., [ræŋ]), but it cannot occur at the beginning of a sylla-ble. Other languages that include the sound [ŋ] , such as Vietnamese, do allow this sound to occur in syllable-initial position. Similarly, it is not permissible to begin English words with a cluster of two stop consonants (e.g., [db]). However, stop consonant clusters of this sort do occur regu-larly in words in Polish (e.g., "dba"). Hence, to master the sound patterns of a language, one needs to learn the phonotactic organization of the language.

The sound patterns of languages also differ in the characteristic rhyth-mic patterns that they use. Some languages, such as Czech and Polish, are very regular with regard to which syllables in words receive most stress (initial syllables in Czech, penultimate syllables in Polish); other languages, such as Russian, show considerable variation with respect to word stress. In French, the rhythmic organization of the language appears to center upon the syllable (Cutler et al. 1983), whereas in Japanese, the mora is the pivotal unit of rhythmic organization (Otake et al. 1993). Comparable kinds of differences are found with respect to the tonal structure of dif-ferent languages. For instance, although many African and East Asian languages are said to have well-developed tonal organizations, the inven-tory of tone levels and shapes tends to be larger and the distribution of tones within utterances is freer in East Asian languages (Kenstowicz 1994). In English, new words are derived from old words by the addition of suffixes and prefixes to the root form of the word (e.g., "use," "useful," "reusable," etc.), whereas in some languages, such as Arabic, infixes are added to the root of the word.

These, then, are some of the organizational properties of language sound patterns that learners must discover about their own native lan-guage in order to speak and understand it fluently.

Learning Words and Building a Lexicon

At some point in development, the learner must begin the process of storing information about the specific words of a language. These are the elements needed for communication with other speakers of the language. It seems likely that some ability to segment fluent speech is required to build an effective vocabulary in a language. Even when mothers are explicitly instructed to teach their children new words, they only present them as single-word utterances about 20 percent of the time (Woodward and Aslin 1990). Thus, most of the time, the infants must find the new words in utterances that include other words. Moreover, some words such as functors, like "the," "of," and "at" in English, are unlikely to ever be presented as isolated words.

One aspect of word learning involves storing some information about the sound pattern of a word that allows its meaning to be accessed during speech comprehension. Clearly, for comprehension to be successful, whatever is stored about the sound pattern of a particular word must be sufficient to distinguish it from other words in the lexicon. Storing the word "phone" as any consonant C plus [on] would be misleading when someone suggests giving the dog a "bone." Furthermore, whatever information is stored about the sound patterns of words has to allow for the kind of variability that is evident in speech production. That is, changes in talker's voice, speech register, and speaking rates should not prevent the retrieval of the correct meaning.

There are many unknowns about the way the lexicon develops: When do infants start storing words in the lexicon? What are the earliest lexical items? How are items added to the lexicon? For instance, do infants ever store incomplete entries (i.e., meanings without associated sound patterns, or sound patterns without meanings)? To what extent are entries that are made early in development only partial entries (i.e., ones that only include a partial specification of either the sound patterns or the meanings of the words)? How, if at all, might lexical entries be reorganized as new words are added to the lexicon? How abstract are the representations of the sound patterns of words? What kinds of information about the sound structures of words are actually encoded, and do these representations change during the course of development? Is there a single lexicon that serves both production and perception? If so, how might the demands associated with speech production influence the organization of the lexicon? If, on the other hand, there are separate lexicons for perception and production, are there any influences of one on the other? Are there any substantial difference in the structure of lexical entries and the organization of the lexicon before and after children acquire the phonology of their native language? These are some of the questions that must be answered in order to understand how the lexicon develops.

Developing Effective Means for Perceiving Fluent Speech

There is considerable evidence documenting the abilities of infants for perceiving speech (for an overview see Aslin, Jusczyk, and Pisoni, in press).

I will review some of these findings in considerable detail later on. For the moment, note that many of the findings that demonstrate the detailed capacities that infants have for perceiving speech have typically been obtained under optimal testing conditions. Infants are usually tested in surroundings that are relatively free of any potential distractions, and the speech signals are presented "in the clear" (i.e., without any competing background noise). Moreover, infants are usually asked to discriminate only a single (already segmented) speech contrast at a time, and this contrast is often repeated many times. Finally, since many of these demonstrations are focused primarily on infants' abilities to discriminate certain speech contrasts, there are no demands made with respect to recovering meanings from the sound patterns that are presented. Data from such investigations are very valuable for determining the limits of infants' perceptual capacities. Indeed, such studies provide the background needed to begin to understand how speech processing develops during the course of language acquisition.

Nevertheless, understanding how well infants can perform under these ideal conditions will not necessarily provide an accurate indication of how they handle all of the demands associated with processing fluent speech in real time. The average adult listener is capable of processing speech at rates of 30 phonemes per second (Liberman et al. 1967). Furthermore, during conversational speech, listeners are not only accessing meanings from the sound patterns of words that they hear but they are also working out the syntactic and semantic organization of utterances. Moreover, they are capable of accomplishing this in the face of a wide variety of distractions (e.g., attending to competing conversations at a cocktail party, driving a car, viewing some interesting event, eating, understanding someone with a foreign accent, etc.)

Developing routines that are efficient and fast enough to handle the demands of understanding fluent speech requires taking advantage of any available cues for segmenting utterances and resolving ambiguities among potential lexical candidates. It is reasonable to expect that greater familiarity with the nature of possible sound patterns of words in the native language could facilitate on-line speech processing. Similarly, the size of one's vocabulary in a language might also affect the speed with which one is able to access the meanings of individual words in utterances. So, too, a fuller understanding of the syntactic organization of the language should affect the time required to understand the overall meanings of utterances.

Many of the structural regularities helpful in processing fluent speech are not features that all languages share but are those particular to the language that the infants are learning. Hence, their use in speech processing depends on the prior discovery of these properties of native-language sound patterns. As infants acquire information about the organization of their native language, their speech-processing routines are likely to be reorganized to reflect what they have learned about the language. One view of this developmental reorganization is that the learner is using "precompiled knowledge" to facilitate speech processing (Klatt 1979). According to a different theoretical perspective, what has changed with experience is that the infant has learned to detect the "higher order invariants" in the speech signal (Gibson 1969).

Mapping from the Speech Signal to Units at Other Levels of Linguistic Organization

Although it is clearly important that utterances be correctly segmented into words, it is also critical that listeners eventually arrive at the correct groupings of utterances into constituent clauses and phrases. Grouping the input in a way that lumped together bits of different phrases or clauses would make it impossible to discern the syntactic organization of utterances. The notion that the speech signal itself provides language learners with markers of important units of syntactic organization, such as clauses and phrases, has been widely discussed (Gleitman and Wanner 1982; Hirsh-Pasek et al. 1987; McNeill 1966; Morgan 1986; Peters 1983). Although the full extent of such marking is still a matter of some dispute (e.g., see Morgan and Demuth 1996), some units of syntactic organization do appear to receive acoustic marking in speech directed to infants (Fisher and Tokura 1996). Detecting the presence of any such marking obviously would be advantageous to language learners in determining the syntactic organization of utterances.

There may also be information in the speech signal that is relevant to other aspects of the syntactic organization of the language. Some have suggested that function words may be omitted from children's earliest word combinations because they are often unstressed in the input they hear (Gleitman et al. 1988). Indeed, Morgan and his colleagues (Morgan, Allopenna, and Shi 1996) report evidence that function and content words may have perceptibly different characteristics. To the extent that language learners detect these sorts of differences, it could provide them with a foothold toward distinguishing the grammatical categories of words.

Overview of the Remaining Chapters

In this chapter, I have tried to indicate the kinds of phenomena likely to be relevant to understanding the development of speech perception capacities and their possible role in language acquisition.

Chapter 2 provides a brief historical overview of some important issues in language-acquisition research. This chapter focuses on what is needed in order to acquire a native language. I begin with a consideration of how language acquisition was viewed prior to the onslaught of empirical investigations that began in the 1960s. The grounds that led some researchers to postulate specialized, innate linguistic capacities are reviewed. Developments in this theoretical position having to do with learnability theory and parameter-setting models are also considered. The discussion then shifts to alternative approaches that emphasize the role of multiple sources of information in acquiring a native language. In particular, I examine those approaches that have suggested that learners draw on the speech signal for clues to the organization of their native language.

Chapter 3 provides a review of some major issues in speech research with adults and infants. I discuss some of the important phenomena that have been studied and what these imply about speech perception capacities in infancy and adulthood. Similarities and differences in speech and nonspeech processing are also discussed, as well as comparative studies with nonhuman species.

Chapter 4 deals with how speech perception develops during the first year of life. Changes that have been noted in the way sensitivity develops to native and nonnative speech contrasts are discussed along with theories about why these changes take place. Recent investigations of when infants attend to regularly occurring features of native-language sound patterns are also documented in this chapter. In addition, information is presented about when and how infants begin to segment words from fluent speech.

Chapter 5 focuses on issues of attention, representation, and memory for speech information. In particular, I present some views about the nature of infants' representations of speech sounds, such as how detailed these representations are and whether they take the form of abstract prototypes or specific exemplars. Information about infants' memory and attentional capacities for speech is considered in relation to developing a lexicon for the native language.

Chapter 6 discusses the relation of speech perception to other levels of linguistic organization. Claims regarding the kind of information that is available in child-directed speech are considered. Findings from recent investigations of infants' sensitivity to potential markers of grammatical units are also presented. Possible links between prosodic bootstrapping and subsequent on-line sentence-comprehension strategies are explored. In particular, consideration is given to how information derived from the speech signal may interact with other sources of information (e.g., semantic and syntactic) that are available to the language learner.

Chapter 7 reviews some of the literature on the development of speech production. In particular, it focuses on the available information regarding native-language influences on babbling and other aspects of speech production. The relationship between babbling and the production of the first words is explored. Also, this chapter examines the extent to which changes in speech perception and production capacities are linked either from the outset or during the course of development.

Chapter 8 pulls together different themes from the earlier chapters. I discuss some implications of these and also present an updated and elaborated version of my Word Recognition and Phonetic Structure Acquisition (WRAPSA) Model. This model is intended to account for the way infant speech-perception capacities evolve to support word recognition in fluent speech. In addition to describing the model, I examine how it relates to earlier attempts to deal with the development of perceptual and linguistic capacities. I conclude with a brief discussion of some important problems and issues that require additional research.

I have added an appendix, which provides a detailed description of some of the procedures that have been used to study speech-perception capacities in infants. This section may be helpful to readers who are unfamiliar with the specifics of these procedures. I have tried to outline the way these procedures have been adapted to address different types of research questions. Readers who are not acquainted with the methodology used in testing infants may want to read this appendix before reading the rest of the book.

Chapter 2

A Brief Historical Perspective on Language Acquisition Research

A chief objective of this book is to provide a better perspective on the kinds of contributions that speech research may make to our overall understanding of language acquisition. For this reason, it is useful to consider what the critical issues are in explaining how one acquires a language. This chapter focuses on some important views that have shaped research on language acquisition. The past 35 years have coincided with a tremendous growth in language acquisition research. Although a great deal of useful information has been collected during this period, considerable disagreement still exists regarding the capacities involved in language acquisition—that is, are these capacities general ones or are they specific to the domain of language? In this chapter, I review some of the arguments for and against the proposition that specialized capacities underlie the acquisition of language. I also describe some of the models that have been proposed to account for the way a learner acquires a native language.

The Original Word Game

Before considering the pros and cons of arguments about specialized, innate linguistic capacities, I think that it is helpful to have a fresh perspective on what is entailed in language acquisition—one that is not necessarily strongly tied to a priori beliefs about general or language-specific mechanisms. This kind of perspective is hard to achieve for someone exposed to the debates of the last 35 years. Therefore, it is worthwhile to consider what the language acquisition problem looked like to someone before the last few decades of research on this topic.

Roger Brown and his students contributed enormously to the development of the field of language acquisition research. Their pioneering studies helped to document many important changes in language acquisition and did much to create excitement about this area of research. They also developed some new methods for eliciting information about the state of children's linguistic knowledge (Berko and Brown 1960). Their studies of three children—Adam, Eve, and Sarah—focused attention on the organization behind children's earliest word combinations and how these related to the adult grammar. Once Brown and his students began collecting data from these children, most of their observations focused on the acquisition of syntax (Brown 1964, 1973; Brown, Cazden, and Bellugi 1969; Brown and Fraser 1964). Thus, in these writings, they had little to say about how children acquired the sound structure of language or what, if any, role it played in the discovery of syntactic structure. However, prior to the time that his language acquisition studies were in full swing, Brown wrote a book, *Words and Things*, that contained a thoughtful assessment of some of the problems facing the language learner, including how to extract meaning from the speech signal. It is instructive to consider some of his intuitions about this process because his reflections occurred prior to the first studies of infant speech perception. Moreover, some of his characterizations of these issues are still right on the mark.

Many of his most pertinent observations are contained in a chapter entitled "The Original Word Game" (Brown 1958). Brown uses this game as an analogy of how the child learns words. A tutor, who already knows the names of objects, names them according to the customs of the linguistic community. The player (or learner) tries to discern the categories to which the names apply. The player tests hypotheses by applying the names to other objects. Hypotheses are revised in response to feedback from the tutor. Brown suggests that we all play this game as long as we continue to extend our vocabularies, but he points out that by adulthood, many aspects of the game have already been perfected. By comparison, the child is still struggling with many of the rudiments of the game. Brown notes (p. 195):

He must learn to categorize speech itself so that he can identify equivalent and distinctive utterances in what the tutor says. He must learn the motor skill of producing such utterances so that they are recognizable to the tutor. Finally, he, like the adult, must form the referent categories. These part processes are not only analytically separable. They are actually separated in much of the child's learning. In the first two years he is forming conceptions of space, time, causality, and of the enduring object.... At the same time, through babbling and attending to the speech of others, the infant is learning to produce and perceive speech, though as yet he may have no idea of linguistic reference.

Brown goes on to discuss the development of speech production and perception. In relation to speech production, he discusses the communicative role played by crying, and he also discusses babbling. Brown suggests that in *babbling*, infants from any culture may draw on a similar inventory of sounds. He also observes that babbling "drifts in the direction of the speech the infant hears" and cites work by Irwin and Chen (1947) as empirical support for this notion. This particular point of Brown's is one that attracted considerable debate over the years. However, recent studies (e.g., Boysson-Bardies and Vihman 1991) appear to bear out Brown's contention.

Although Brown raises the possibility that children may first respond to intonation as opposed to phonetic properties, he sees the child's central problem in speech perception as one of learning "to categorize speech in terms of phonemic attributes." Reviewing the claims of Jakobson (1941/1968) about the order in which phonemic oppositions emerge, he concludes that more empirical evidence is required to verify these. He considers the possibility that "perceptual phonemics might develop with the progressive differentiation of distinctive features" and then raises the question of what kinds of experience are required to bring about this differentiation. Noting the difficulties listeners face when presented with speech in another language, he suggests that whatever is going on must be specific to that language. "Nothing sounds at all familiar. The spoken language seems to have no more structure than 'white noise.'" Brown's observation that the strategies used to segment speech are very closely tied to one's own native language is one that has been upheld by recent crosslinguistic research (Cutler et al. 1983; Cutler et al. 1986; Otake et al. 1993).

Brown goes on to consider the role that sound properties may play in the formation of categories. Using an example of a student learning new terminology in a class, he suggests that "the words are handed out early in the term like empty containers to be filled with experience." The point here is that hearing the sound pattern of a new word can lead one to look for new conceptual distinctions. The advantages of linguistic labeling over nonlinguistic responding are illustrated in the following quotations.

Suppose, for a moment, that a child used the responses of his tutors as a guide to equivalence and difference in nonlinguistic reality. He could have a cue to what is edible and what is inedible by noting what is eaten and what is not eaten.... Using the nonlinguistic responses of others as a guide to the categories of reality we should have to learn a set of response equivalents very nearly as complex as the stimulus equivalents in the world. (p. 209)

With regard to linguistic responses the player is in a more favorable position.... Once the speech system has been grasped, then, there is no problem of category attainment so far as the utterances themselves are concerned. The player of the Original Word Game who hears /kæt/ knows that these three phonemes, in the sequence given, define the speech category. He only has to remember the response in these terms to recognize new instances.... The point is that his experience in forming the first speech categories can bring him great secondary benefits. Incidental learning of the structure of speech can teach him to perceive new utterances in proper categorial fashion. (p. 210)

Brown here is referring to at least one way the acquisition of the sound structure of one's native language may serve in other aspects of language acquisition. In particular, he argues that having a name helps the learner by reducing the number of hypotheses about the reference category to a relatively probable few. The fact that different objects receive the same speech label suggests to the learner that the objects share some "referent invariance." In this sense, it may help the learner to focus attention on the set of objects that receive the same name (and thereby to exclude others with different names) and to seek out the ways the members of this name set are related. It was in this sense that Brown saw that learning about the sound structure of one's native language could serve as a stepping-stone to further cognitive and linguistic development.

The remainder of the chapter focuses on how language acquisition is influenced by the innate capacities of the learner and the nature of the linguistic input. Although researchers acknowledge that both factors are involved in acquiring language, there are strong differences of opinion about the relative contributions of each of these factors. Moreover, with regard to the innate capacities involved in language acquisition, there is considerable disagreement as to whether a significant proportion of these capacities are specific to language, as opposed to more general cognitive and perceptual capacities. Arguments advanced in favor of a key role for innate linguistic capacities are reviewed first, beginning with views associated with early models of tranformational, generative grammars. Next, views about innate linguistic capacities that are associated with more-recent developments in theorizing about universal grammars are considered. Then the focus shifts to arguments for alternative views of language acquisition. In particular, the possibility is considered that language acquisition is driven by more general cognitive and perceptual strategies, and that the input provides a rich source of information about linguistic organization. The chapter concludes with a consideration of claims that sensitivity information in the speech signal may facilitate the acquisition of the grammatical organization of the native language.

Production of sentences

Universal Grammar and Language Acquisition

During most of the first half of this century, American psychologists tended to treat language acquisition as just another accomplishment of more general learning principles. This point was made most forcefully by B. F. Skinner (1957) in his book *Verbal Behavior*. Skinner argued that a behaviorist framework drawing on the principles of "stimulus," "response," and "reinforcer" provides the means for understanding the complexities of verbal behavior, including its acquisition. In Skinner's framework, environmental factors such as present stimulation and the history of reinforcement are predominant in the development of verbal behavior, whereas any contributions arising from innate capacities of the learner are minimal. In a very influential review of Skinner's book, Noam Chomsky (1959) attacked its main thesis. He noted that many of the key principles were so broadly defined as to make them untestable. Chomsky also pointed out that the child's mastery of language and productions of sentences go well beyond imitations of what is heard in adult speech: "A child will be able to construct and understand utterances which are quite new, and are, at the same time, acceptable in his language" (p. 563). Chomsky argued that the only way to account for this creative aspect of the production of such new utterances was to assume that the child was following some underlying system of grammatical rules.

The child who learns a language has in some sense constructed the grammar for himself on the basis of his observation of sentences and nonsentences (i.e., corrections by the verbal community). Study of the actual ability of a speaker to distinguish sentences from nonsentences, detect ambiguities, etc., apparently forces us to the conclusion that this grammar is of an extremely complex and abstract character, and that the young child has succeeded in carrying out what from the formal point of view, at least, seems to be a remarkable type of theory construction. (p. 577)

Consideration of how the child could induce the grammar from the input led Chomsky to claim that the child must be equipped with some very powerful learning devices that are specially designed for dealing with language.

The fact that all normal children acquired essentially comparable grammars of great complexity with remarkable rapidity suggests that human beings are somehow specially designed to do this, with data-handling or "hypothesis-formulating" ability of unknown character and complexity. (p. 577)

Thus, Chomsky views the language learner's task as finding the correct set of grammatical descriptions that correctly characterize the linguistic

input (what Chomsky (1965) calls "the primary linguistic data"). A critical issue in subsequent theorizing on language development concerned just how much assistance a learner needs from innate capacities to select the correct grammar on the basis of the input. Chomsky (1965) maintained that the primary linguistic data is fairly degenerate in quality. That is, it generally includes false starts and stops resulting in utterances that are interrupted, or ill formed in some other way (Fodor 1966). Attempts to deduce the correct grammatical organization from such degenerate input would be doomed to failure, since among other things it would allow for too many possible alternative descriptions of the data. Consequently, Chomsky assumed that there had to be some powerful innate constraints to restrict the sets of grammatical descriptions that a learner would try to apply to the linguistic data. His theory assumed that the child begins language learning with a tacit knowledge of linguistic universals.

It proposes, then, that the child approaches the data with the presumption that they are drawn from a language of a certain antecedently well-defined type, his problem being to determine which of the (humanly) possible languages is that of the community in which he is placed. Language learning would be impossible unless this were the case. (Chomsky 1965, p. 27)

Chomsky discussed two types of linguistic universals: formal and substantive. *Formal universals* refer primarily to constraints on the kinds of rules that can appear in natural languages, whereas *substantive universals* refer to the possible grammatical categories and their hierarchical arrangement. Note that both types of universals refer to properties that are specific to language rather than to some more general range of cognitive abilities. It is in this sense that innate knowledge of these universals constitutes a claim about specialized linguistic capacities. As Chomsky (1965) observed,

It is not often realized how strong a claim this is about the innate concept-forming abilities of the child and the system of linguistic universals that these abilities imply. Thus what is maintained, presumably, is that the child has an innate theory of potential descriptions that is sufficiently rich and developed so that he is able to determine, from a real situation in which a signal occurs, which structural descriptions may be appropriate to this signal, and also, that he is able to do this in part in advance of any assumption as to the linguistic structure of this signal. (p. 32)

To refer to the range of capacities that allow the learner to analyze the primary linguistic data and arrive at the correct set of grammatical descriptions, Chomsky (1961, 1965; see also Katz 1966) adopted the term Language Acquisition Device (LAD).

Applying the LAD to Child-Language Research

McNeill (1966) contributed the most extensive attempts to elaborate on the notion of a *Language Acquisition Device*. The content of the LAD was a set of formal and substantive linguistic universals. One of McNeill's aims was to determine how language learners could move from the types of grammatical categories that were apparent in their earliest forms of word combinations to the ones employed in the adult form of their native language. For example, the data provided by language researchers of that era (Bellugi and Brown 1964; Braine 1963; Brown and Fraser 1964; Ervin 1964) suggested that when they produced their first word combinations, children apparently had two broad grammatical classes: *pivot words* (a small class of words whose members were used relatively frequently, usually not alone, and in relatively fixed positions in utterances) and *open words* (a much larger class, whose members could occur in combination with each other). According to Braine's description, pivot words behaved much like function words in adult language, whereas open words resembled content words. McNeill claimed that there was little evidence that these particular form classes could be learned from distributional properties of the input and suggested instead that early utterances were organized around the basic grammatical classes contained in the LAD (i.e., they were part of the innate hierarchy of grammatical categories). He noted, "Although the rules of the child's grammar do not result in well-formed sentences, they do appear to generate major constituents of well-formed sentences" (p. 44).

In addition to claiming that LAD includes a description of the hierarchy of potential grammatical categories, McNeill argued that the basic grammatical relations (e.g., subject, predicate, object, modifier, etc.) are part of innate linguistic capacity. He cited Greenberg's (1966) finding that these basic relations were present in all the languages in his survey as an indication that these relations were linguistic universals. Thus, the LAD was hypothesized to simultaneously scan the linguistic input for information about both grammatical categories and grammatical relations. The role of the linguistic data in the acquisition process was to "help LAD choose among a narrow set of possibilities defined by linguistic universals" (p. 50). The optimal grammar to describe the input would be chosen from among a set of candidate grammars, each of which is compatible with the input. The selection of the correct grammar depends on applying an evaluation metric to the set of candidate grammars. The resulting choice of the grammar is said to be an instantaneous process.

McNeill argued that the "LAD must be equipped with knowledge of just those specific aspects of linguistic competence that cannot be extracted from overt speech, namely, appropriate generic grammatical classes and hierarchical structure" (p. 50). It is this last assertion that is particularly pertinent to issues raised in this book. To what extent is there information in the speech signal that the language learner could use to infer the appropriate grammatical categories and their hierarchical structure? McNeill's position was that the speech signal was of limited utility in providing information about the relevant grammatical categories and relations. In part, this was because he believed that the early word combinations directly reflected the underlying (or deep) structure of native language utterances rather than their surface-structure features. In McNeill's view, information in the speech signal might be expected to mark the surface structure of utterances but not their deep structures. He considered the proposition that the close relation between phonology and syntax would allow the learner to use the speech signal as the vehicle for arriving at the rudiments of syntax. He cited findings from Lieberman (1965) indicating that when linguists transcribed real speech, the actual and perceived contours differed sharply, suggesting that structure was an important source of information about perceived intonation but that the reverse was not true. McNeill concluded that the prelinguistic child using intonation to infer syntax would be in the same position as the linguists.

Infants could note only the physical contour in parental speech, not the perceived contour that is correlated with grammatical structure. It is difficult, therefore, to see how intonation could guide a child to syntax, for no matter how strong the tendency is for children to imitate speech from their parents, they will not imitate the appropriate feature unless the important parts of syntax have already been acquired. (p. 53)

McNeill's arguments on this point seem to have been effective in dissuading language researchers, for many years, from exploring whether children do use information in the speech signal as clues about other aspects of linguistic structure. In fact, because he subscribed to Lenneberg's (1967) view that the evolution of infants' vocalizations and babbling during the first year were "matters of maturation," he did not believe that much real language acquisition took place during this period.

The notion that a device such as the LAD might account for language development has been attacked on a number of different grounds. Pinker (1982) criticized the psychological implausibility of the model and argued that it failed to predict the developmental sequence for language acquisition. Other investigators (e.g., Brown 1977; Levelt 1975) claimed that the powerful innate linguistic capacities of the sort included in the LAD are unnecessary in view of findings demonstrating that the input data is less noisy than had been supposed. Morgan (1986) noted that the assumption that selection of the optimal grammar was instantaneous was problematic because unless the LAD could filter out ungrammatical input, it would make the wrong generalizations about grammatical structures.

Learnability Theory and Parameter Setting
Although the original LAD model has fallen into disfavor, there is still a need to characterize any constraints that enable learners to derive the appropriate set of generalizations about the grammatical organization of a language from the input. *Learnability theory* is an attempt to specify the nature of the constraints required (e.g., Gold 1967; Hamburger and Wexler 1975; Lightfoot 1989; Morgan 1986; Osherson, Stob, and Weinstein 1986; Pinker 1984; Wexler and Culicover 1980). Models based on this approach start with the strong assumption that learners have accurate perceptual descriptions of the linguistic input as well as the ability to form a semantic interpretation of the real-world context in which the utterance is made (Pinker 1984; Wexler and Culicover 1980). In addition, learners begin with some set of candidate grammars that could potentially map the linguistic input onto the contextually derived semantic interpretation. Incoming linguistic data are compared to the set of grammars that has provided the best description of the structure of the target language to that point. Whenever an inconsistency is found between the current internal grammar and the linguistic input, the grammar is modified. The modifications to the internal grammar conform to a set of cognitive and linguistic constraints that limit the kinds of grammatical hypotheses that are available to the learner. Eventually, by this process of modifying the internal grammar in response to new linguistic input, the learner converges on the one that is the most appropriate description of the target language.

In contrast to earlier theorizing within the Chomskian framework, universal grammar is no longer conceived of as a set of rules. The earlier conceptualization has given way to what Chomsky (1995) has called "the minimalist program." In this new approach, the variation that occurs across grammars of natural languages is described in terms of a set of *principles* and *parameters* (Chomsky 1981; Hyams 1986; Manzini and Wexler 1987; Williams 1987). For example, one such principle might specify the general format of a syntactic phrase. However, the internal structure of the phrase may vary across different languages. The parameter associated with this particular principle refers to the options that are available with respect to the internal structure of the phrase. In general, parameters specify the dimensions along which languages differ and indicate what options are available. During the initial phases of language learning, a parameter is set to some default value. However, the information in the linguistic input may cause the learner to reset this parameter to another value. Setting the direction of a parameter can cause a group of apparently unrelated grammatical properties to appear in the language. In this way, the learner can use the deductive consequences of the parameter to facilitate the acquisition of other elements in the language (Mazuka 1996). Chomsky (1986) has argued that knowledge of the principles and parameters that define the set of possible human languages is genetically transmitted and constitutes the initial state of the language faculty. Although the linguistic input may set the direction of a particular parameter, the principles and parameters are not themselves derivable from the input.

Key issues for any learnability model are how much and what kind of linguistic input are necessary for language to be acquired within the kind of time frame achieved by human learners. A learnability model with assumptions that failed to target the correct description within a human lifetime would not provide a psychologically plausible account of how infants acquire a language. Similarly, a model that depended on exposure to input sentences that have three or more levels of embedding would be implausible, given that language learners succeed in acquiring a language on the basis of much less complex input. The model that Wexler and Culicover (1980) proposed was a Degree 2 Learnability Theory (i.e., it required exposure to sentences with at least two levels of embedding in order to converge on the correct grammar of the target language). However, Morgan (1986) demonstrated that a Degree 1 Learnability Theory (i.e., exposure to sentences with a single level of embedding) is feasible as a model of language acquisition, provided that the input provides clues to the syntactic bracketing of utterances. The notion that the learner's task may be simplified by access to more structure in the input is interesting because it may indicate that any specialized innate capacities required to account for language acquisition are less powerful than previously was supposed. We will further examine how information in the speech signal may simplify the task of discovering the grammatical organization of language when we discuss bootstrapping in the final section of this chapter.

A critical feature shared by the approaches reviewed in this section is that they assume that specialized linguistic capacities play a significant role in acquiring language. Proponents of these approaches certainly recognize that some general cognitive constraints may influence the course of language acquisition. However, many of the constraints postulated to explain how the learner induces the appropriate grammatical organization from the input are ones that refer explicitly to structural features of language. Whether a plausible account of language acquisition can be forged without recourse to such specialized linguistic capacities remains to be seen.

Emphasis on the Role of Cognitive and Perceptual Resources in Language Acquisition

All students of language acquisition would acknowledge that the cognitive and perceptual resources of the learner affect the course of language acquisition. However, there is considerable disagreement as to whether nonlinguistic cognitive and perceptual resources play a leading or a supporting role. The approaches considered in the previous section claim that many of the critical constraints in language learning are not attributable to broader cognitive or perceptual constraints. Rather, a significant proportion of these constraints are held to be specific to language. Indeed, Chomsky (1980) has argued that the faculty underlying language is specialized enough to be considered to be a "mental organ." Similarly, Fodor (1983) postulates that there is a special module that is devoted to language processes. At the other extreme, some investigators have suggested that the abilities underlying language acquisition (and its subsequent use) are drawn from more general cognitive and perceptual capacities (e.g., Anderson 1983). Other investigators have acknowledged some role for specialized language capacities but have advocated that researchers consider most closely the possibility that cognitive and perceptual factors can explain a significant part of linguistic behavior and its acquisition (e.g., Bever 1970; Macnamara 1972). To the extent that more general cognitive and perceptual capacities suffice to account for aspects of language acquisition, there will be less need to appeal to the existence of highly specialized, innate linguistic capacities. In the remainder of this section, several approaches are considered that attempt to incorporate more general cognitive and perceptual capacities into models of language acquisition.

Operating Principles

Cross-linguistic studies of language acquisition have been an impetus for researchers to reflect on the cognitive and perceptual bases for acquiring a language. Consider the fact that infants with approximately equal perceptual and cognitive capacities are exposed to ranges of input data with very different structural properties (i.e., different languages). Yet, despite the differences that exist among natural languages, children manage to acquire any one of these languages within roughly the same time frame. Given that the kinds of generalizations required about the input often vary from language to language, language learners must be flexible enough to entertain a variety of different possibilities about language organization. At the same time, the range of possible generalizations that learners consider must be limited enough to converge quickly on the correct ones for their target language. What underlies language learners' abilities to make the appropriate generalizations so rapidly? Of course, one possible answer to this question is to assume that the learner possesses some innate set of specialized linguistic capacities that allow the learner to draw the right inferences from the input. However, another possibility is that a great deal of the learner's success in the language domain stems from more general operations of their cognitive and perceptual systems.

One suggestion as to how learners may draw on more general cognitive and perceptual abilities in acquiring language comes from an investigator who has been a keen student of cross-linguistic differences in language acquisition. Dan Slobin's research has provided much useful information about cross-linguistic differences in language acquisition (Slobin 1966, 1982, 1985b; Slobin and Bever 1982). The perspective that he developed from his investigations positioned him to note commonalties and differences in how different languages are acquired. Slobin's observations about which elements recur in the way that different languages are learned have led him to propose a set of operating principles that guide the course of language acquisition (Slobin 1973, 1985a). In formulating his operating principles, Slobin noted that children learning different languages sometimes differ as to when they begin to express the same linguistic intentions. Slobin (1973) argues that this difference in when children learning different languages express the same function is attributable to how the function is encoded in the language and the state of the child's own cognitive and perceptual capabilities.

Cognitive development and linguistic development do not run off in unison. The child must find linguistic means to express his intentions. The means can be easily accessible (as, for example, the Hungarian locative), or quite unaccessible (as, for example, the Finnish yes-no question or the Arabic noun plural). The problem is: What makes a given linguistic means of expression more or less accessible to the child? (pp. 182–183)

In fact, Slobin ascribed a leading role to cognition in setting the pace for the acquisition of linguistic forms—"many linguistic forms cannot appear in the child's speech until he is capable of grasping their meaning" (p. 187). With this assumption in mind, he then reconsiders why a child who is cognitively ready to express the same linguistic function may be slower to acquire the relevant linguistic forms in one language than in another. Noting that children learning Serbo-Croatian are slower to express the locative than are children learning Hungarian, he remarks that in the latter, the locative is expressed by noun suffixes. He then goes on to cite cross-linguistic evidence suggesting that for children, "the end of a word seems to be perceptually salient." The cross-linguistic evidence that he reviews also seems to indicate that locative markers in postverbal and post-nominal positions tend to be acquired before ones in preverbal and pre-nominal positions. But he argues that something is happening here that goes well beyond what happens with locatives. This observation leads to the formulation of the first of his proposed operating principles governing language acquisition.

In fact, it seems to reflect a general early tendency on the part of the child to attend to the ends of words when scanning linguistic input in a search for cues to meaning. This is a sort of general heuristic or operating principle that the child brings to bear on the task of organizing and storing language. Phrased roughly, one can say that the following is one of the basic self-instructions for language acquisition:

OPERATING PRINCIPLE A: Pay attention to the ends of words. (p. 191)

Slobin discussed another operating principle that relates specifically to the sound patterns of language: "OPERATING PRINCIPLE B: The phonological forms of words can be systematically modified". He also proposed a number of other operating principles, most of which refer to syntactic properties of the input. The important point about these principles in general is that they are intended to describe the foundation on which a language learner could construct a grammar on the basis of the linguistic input. As Slobin put it,

Such operating principles guide the child in developing strategies for the production and interpretation of speech and for the construction of linguistic rule systems. The operating principles function within a framework of constraints on linguistic performance. (p. 194)

In more recent work, Slobin (1985a) has distinguished between two major types of operating principles: *perceptual and storage filters*, that convert speech input into the stored information that the child uses in constructing the linguistic system, and *pattern makers*, that organize these stored data into linguistic systems. It is the principles of the first type that are most germane to the kinds of issues that we are considering here; they determine "which segments of the speech stream will be of sufficient perceptual salience to be noticed and stored, and they establish the basic 'filing systems' for such speech segments in storage." The purpose of these operating principles is to provide what Slobin refers to as the Language Making Capacity (LMC) with a body of preliminary data to analyze. "The child must extract, segment, and store input in ways that allow for language making." This conceptualization is similar to the one that is presented in chapter 6.

The newer principles that are associated with the perceptual and storage filters subsume the old Operating Principle A. One of these principles is an instruction to "store any perceptually salient strings of speech." Other principles of this type give some indication of what might count as perceptually salient. In particular, one of these says to attend to ends of units, another to attend to stressed syllables in extracted units, and a third to pay attention to the beginnings of units. In addition, there is an operating principle that dictates that the learner should "keep track of the frequency of occurrence of every unit and pattern that you store." Evidence indicates that infants do seem to register the frequency with which certain sound patterns appear in the input. Two further principles elaborate on the storage of patterns. One of these has the learner check to see if the input pattern is similar to one encountered before; if it is, it is stored with the other similar patterns. If it is a different pattern, it is stored separately. The other principle is an instruction to take account of cooccurrence relations between successive units. Findings from speech-perception studies suggest that infants also seem to be attuned to these kinds of features in the input.

Many of the operating principles that refer to the way speech input is stored and used have been more fully described by Peters (1977, 1983, 1985). Her experience in studying a child who used only relatively long units in production led Peters to suggest that there might be a more gestalt (or holistic) style of acquiring language in addition to the analytic style that most investigators assumed was the norm (Peters 1977, 1983). Her concerns about how a child with such a holistic approach ends up discovering the internal organization of such units prompted Peters to consider what information is available to facilitate the process of segmentation. She hypothesized that the salient chunks of information that the language learner pulls out of the speech stream could provide a means of bootstrapping the acquisition of language. Inspired by Slobin's (1973) early accounts of operating principles, she described an extended set of such principles that focused on the extraction of meaningful units from the linguistic input (Peters 1983, 1985).

Peters (1983) suggested that the simplest strategy used at the beginning stages of acquisition is to consider any utterance as a potential lexical entry. Consequently, learners should copy each utterance, and store it whole. This proposal has the advantage of simultaneously allowing her to account for both one-word and formulaic learning styles. Peters suggested that the child relies on suprasegmental properties in extracting whole utterances from surrounding ones in the signal. Thus, the child might use information about the occurrence of silence, intonation contour (both in terms of boundary cues and its overall melodic tune), and rhythmic properties to identify the occurrence of important chunks of speech in the input. Although Peters based these principles on observations about speech production, recent studies of speech perception offer additional empirical support for many of these (see the discussion in chapter 6).

Other principles in Peters's account are directed at the internal segmentation of these larger chunks of speech. Different means are postulated to accomplish this end. Some of the principles have to do with information at the boundaries of these units. For example, two of them suggest segmenting off the first and last syllables from the rest of the unit. Three other principles refer to prosodic features useful for achieving internal segmentation: (1) segmenting stressed syllables; (2) segmenting at rhythmically salient places; and (3) segmenting at intonationally salient places. As Peters (1985) noted, there is data from comparative studies of different languages that suggest that stress cues could be effective in signaling word boundaries. Specifically, Hyman (1977) reported that in his survey of 444 languages, 406 had fixed stress relative to word boundaries. Of these, 114 had word-initial stress, 97 had word-final stress, and 77 had penultimate stress. Although English does not have fixed stress per se, there are some indications that both English-speaking adults (Cutler 1990; Cutler and Butterfield 1992; Cutler and Norris 1988) and English-learning infants (Jusczyk, Cutler, and Redanz 1993; Newsome and Jusczyk 1995) can use the location of stressed syllables to help in identifying the onsets of words in fluent speech.

Another of Peters's principles for segmenting larger units draws on the use of a distributional property. This principle states that learners should segment subunits that are repeated within the same unit. In this regard, Peters (1983) provides some nice examples of dialogues in which the same key word is repeated in different sentence frames over a relatively short span of time. Peters's view that changes in the surrounding word context (i.e., across different sentence frames) is an important factor in extracting words from fluent speech fits well with the one adopted in chapter 4 (see also Brent, Cartwright, and Gafos in press).

The view that language learners may draw on a relatively small set of operating principles to segment the input into linguistically relevant units is appealing. However, the plausibility of such accounts rests on tying these principles more closely to general features of cognitive and perceptual processing that are exhibited by children. If such processes are reflective of general cognitive and perceptual functioning, then they should be observable as well in nonlinguistic domains. Attempting to tie these principles more closely to nonlinguistic aspects of perceptual and cognitive functioning may also curb the tendency to proliferate the number of principles that are hypothesized to exist. At present, there are few restrictions on adding new principles to fit any new unexplained pattern that is observed in language acquisition data. Similarly, it would be useful to have a more precise description of any organization that governs how and whether different principles interact.

The Competition Model
One approach to specifying how cognitive and perceptual constraints facilitate language acquisition is to attempt to build a coherent model that makes use of such constraints. One effort to devise such a model is based on what is known as a *functionalist* approach to language acquisition. "Functionalism claims that language acquisition is guided by form-function correlations" (Bates and MacWhinney 1989, p. 26). The func-

tional level is where all the meanings and intentions to be expressed in an utterance are represented. The formal level is the one in which all the surface forms or expressive devices used in the language are represented. Bates and MacWhinney (1982) note that the basic communicative function of language appears to be universal. In fact, it extends even to children deprived of most systematic communicative input as the work of Goldin-Meadow and her colleagues shows (e.g., Feldman, Goldin-Meadow, and Gleitman 1977; Goldin-Meadow and Feldman 1977; Goldin-Meadow and Mylander 1984). However, in contrast to the stability of the communicative functions, the particular forms or surface devices that are used to encode the functions vary greatly across languages. Bates and MacWhinney assume that "function plays a strong causal role in the way that particular forms have evolved and in the way those forms are used by adults and acquired by children" (1982, p. 175). They also claim that form-function correlations exist in the input and that children are able to take advantage of this fact. One example of a form-function correlation that they discuss is the one that relates to the "sentence subject."

In our view, "subject" is neither a single symbol nor a unitary category. Rather, it is a coalition of many-to-many mappings between the level of form (e.g., nominative case marking, preverbal position, agreement with the verb in person and number) and the level of function (e.g., agent of a transitive action, topic of an ongoing discourse, perspective of the speaker). (Bates and MacWhinney 1987, p. 166)

Bates and MacWhinney's observations about the way language learners map expressive functions to linguistic forms led them to develop a model of language acquisition called the Competition Model (Bates and Mac-Whinney 1987, 1989; MacWhinney 1987).

In the Competition Model, language acquisition is characterized as cue-driven distributional analysis. Primary among the various cues the child detects are those involving form-function correlations. Children take advantage of form-function correlations in the course of language learning, insofar as they are able to understand and formulate the relevant dimensions of meaning. In addition, however, they are also capable of detecting certain distributional facts in the sound stream even in the absence of an interpretation of those facts. They can treat sound as an object, just like any perceptual object, and pick up recurring patterns whether they understand them or not.... However, this process is greatly facilitated when meaning is available (1) to motivate the child's attention to the relevant facts and (2) to add critical patterned information of its own. (Bates and MacWhinney 1989, pp. 26–27)

Many of the findings that are reviewed in subsequent chapters provide support for their claims regarding learners' sensitivity to distributional facts, even in the absence of any specific meanings being attached to these. Although meaning is a critical factor in driving the kind of distributional analysis that they envision during language acquisition, Bates and MacWhinney do note that extracting patterns from the speech input plays a critical role in acquisition.

Language acquisition is a perceptual-motor problem. The child is trying to extract patterns, islands of regularity that can be isolated within a noisy sound stream. This is the perceptual side of the problem, and it is subject to all the vicissitudes of perceptual learning and pattern recognition in any domain.... Once the patterns have been isolated, the child will also try to reproduce them. This is the motor side of the problem, and it can only be understood within a much broader theory of motor learning. All of our claims about form-function mapping presuppose this perceptual motor framework. Forms exist, and they must be perceived before any mapping can occur at all. (Bates and MacWhinney 1989, p. 31)

Thus, Bates and MacWhinney posit that a critical starting point for the acquisition of language is to pull out the relevant forms from the input, which, of course, includes the speech signal itself. Once potential forms have been identified in the input, the learner attempts to map these to particular communicative functions. Bates and MacWhinney claim that learners adjust the weights of form-function mappings in response to linguistic input until they identify the mappings that provide an optimal fit to the processing environment.[1] They note that this is very similar to what Gibson (1969) referred to as "detection of invariance."

One way to explore the plausibility of Bates and MacWhinney's claims is by devising a reasonable computer simulation of the Competition Model and then determining whether it is able to arrive at the correct set of generalizations on the basis of linguistic input. Bates and MacWhinney (1987) have suggested the likeliest implementation of their model is one based on connectionist approaches. However, the Competition Model is incomplete in many respects, so at best one can only attempt to implement those elements of the model that are described in sufficient detail. One such aspect of language acquisition that has received a great deal of attention from connectionist modelers has to do with learning the appropriate inflectional morphology for past tense forms of verbs in English.

Rumelhart and McClelland (1986) proposed a connectionist model that they claimed could account for how past tense forms are acquired. Even though their model included no explicit statement of linguistic rules, it appeared to simulate the developmental course of English-learning children's acquisition of past tense forms, including even the kinds of overregularization errors that children make. However, Rumelhart and McClelland's model was attacked on the grounds that its success was the result of certain programming tricks (Lachter and Bever 1988; Pinker and Prince 1988). Nevertheless, subsequent connectionist models (based on more realistic assumptions about the input data) have also achieved results that, in certain respects, appear to parallel those of human learners (e.g., MacWhinney and Leinbach 1991; Plunkett and Marchman 1991, 1993). Still, certain objections have been raised regarding these more recent models (e.g., Marcus 1995; Marcus et al. 1992), so this matter has not been fully resolved yet (for a further discussion of these issues, see Plunkett 1995). In any case, these recent efforts to provide computational models in order to test functionalist accounts of language acquisition are clearly a step in the right direction. Ultimately, the success or failure of such modeling efforts will help determine the plausibility of these kinds of approaches.

Bootstrapping and Language Acquisition

The term *bootstrapping* has been applied to a wide range of different approaches in language acquisition. Consequently, bootstrapping models do not fit easily into a dichotomy between the approaches based primarily on specialized linguistic processes and those based more on general cognitive and perceptual processes. The best way to illustrate this point is to examine the various types of bootstrapping theories that have been proposed. In what follows, I will give a brief description of "syntactic," "semantic," and "prosodic" bootstrapping. The latter form of bootstrapping will be discussed more extensively than the others because it is more closely tied to the issues pursued in the rest of this book.

Syntactic Bootstrapping

The idea behind *syntactic bootstrapping* is that information about known nouns and the structural positions that they occupy with respect to some unknown verb can furnish the language learner with certain aspects of the meaning of the verb (Fisher et al. 1994; Gleitman 1990, 1994; Landau and Gleitman 1985). The information about nouns and their structural positions are deemed to be helpful to the learner because "the surface structural properties of sentences are well correlated with (in fact, are projections from) certain aspects of their semantics. To use such clues, the learning device must analyze the structure within which the novel verb is being heard" (Fisher et al. 1994, p. 337). As Gleitman and her colleagues have noted, their position is similar to earlier proposals in its assumption that previously learned information about nouns is involved in verb learning. In line with earlier suggestions, the syntactic bootstrapping account assumes that learners use sophisticated perceptual, conceptual, and pragmatic knowledge when viewing events to extract the meanings of verbs. In describing what sets this position apart from previous ones, Fisher et al. (1994) note:

> The innovation has to do with the way learners are posited to represent the *linguistic* input that is to be paired with the extralinguistic input: as a parse tree within which the novel verb occurs. The structured sentence representation can help in acquiring the novel verb just because it is revealing of the argument-taking aspects of the verb's interpretation. (p. 338)

With respect to the issues raised earlier in this chapter, syntactic bootstrapping accounts do assume that learners have some knowledge of certain grammatical principles and potential grammatical categories (although not the specific forms that these principles and categories take in a particular language). However, as noted above, proponents of this view do not discount the importance of perceptual, conceptual, and pragmatic knowledge in acquiring language.

The kind of evidence that Gleitman and her students have produced in support of the syntactic bootstrapping account comes from investigations that learners are much more successful at intuiting the meaning of unknown verbs when they have access to information about co-occuring nouns and their structural positions relative to these verbs (Fisher in press-b; Fisher et al. 1994; Gleitman 1990, 1994; Lederer, Gleitman, and Gleitman 1995). Moreover, there are some indications from recent studies with older infants that the same factors appear to affect what types of actions they associate with verbs (Naigles 1990; Naigles, Gleitman, and Gleitman 1993; Naigles and Kako 1993).

Pinker (1994) has raised questions about the plausibility of syntactic bootstrapping, at least with respect to getting the child started in acquiring verbs in the native language. Although he raises some valid points with respect to the issue of whether syntactic bootstrapping could be viable at the very beginning stage of language acquisition, his arguments do not appear to apply as forcefully to the acquisition of new verbs at other points in language acquisition.

Semantic Bootstrapping
Pinker has primarily been associated with the view of language acquisition known as *semantic bootstrapping* (Pinker 1982, 1984). This view
originated in the work of Wexler and Culicover (1980) on learnability
theory and was elaborated on subsequently by other investigators (e.g.,
Grimshaw 1981; Macnamara 1982; Pinker 1982, 1984). Simply stated,
this approach holds that language learners can use information from
events and objects in the real world to derive information about the
semantics of various words and structures. Once basic meanings have
been identified, these then serve as the basis for formulating hypotheses
about their linguistic classifications. For example, a word describing an
action is a good bet to be a verb, whereas one describing an object is more
likely to be a noun.

As Pinker (1987) notes, semantic bootstrapping depends on four key
background assumptions. These are:

1. the learner can acquire the meanings of content words independently
of learning grammatical rules;
2. the environmental context and the meanings of individual words in a
sentence are sufficient to allow the child to construct a semantic representation of an input sentence;
3. the child has access to substantive linguistic universals that express and
are correlated with certain semantic concepts and relations; and
4. sentences that embody such correlations are identifiable for learners by
some means such as special intonation, discourse context, amount of
"perceptually salient affixation," or by the exclusion of nonstandard uses
of the critical forms on the part of caregivers.[2]

Given these assumptions, it is clear that semantic bootstrapping accounts
clearly assume that learners have some innate knowledge of universal
grammar. At the same time, successfully mapping information from the
real world to parts of sentences depends on the learner to correctly identify and interpret objects and events in the environment. Consequently,
nonlinguistic cognitive and perceptual capacities also play a critical role
in semantic bootstrapping accounts.

Prosodic Bootstrapping or "Bootstrapping from the Signal"
Peters (1983) and Gleitman and Wanner (1982; Gleitman et al. 1988)
were instrumental in reviving the idea that learners could use information in the speech signal to gain valuable knowledge about the syntactic

organization of their native language. Recently, there has been a great deal of interest in the prospect that the speech signal may provide important cues to the underlying syntactic organization of utterances (e.g., see Morgan and Demuth 1996). This general viewpoint has been called *prosodic bootstrapping*. This label is really a misnomer because most proponents of this view assume that learners are drawing on a range of information available in the speech signal that extends beyond prosody. However, the term "prosodic bootstrapping" has gained wide currency in the field, so I continue to use it here. Finally, note that because much of the empirical research on bootstrapping from the signal will be considered extensively in chapter 6, this section will focus mostly on the background for this proposal. Of the various bootstrapping accounts, prosodic bootstrapping is the one that relies most obviously on the perceptual capacities of language learners. The plausibility of prosodic bootstrapping depends not only on the presence of cues to syntactic organization in the speech signal but also on the capacities of learners to pick up these cues. The issue of whether what is required for detecting cues to syntactic organization in the signal are innate linguistic capacities or more general perceptual capacities used in a language context is not settled (although the latter position is the one adopted in chapter 6).

In their proposal about prosodic bootstrapping, Gleitman and Wanner (1982) indicated some ways learners could use their speech perception capacities to infer information about the syntactic organization of their native language. They focused specifically on the recovery of information about phones, words, sequences, and phrases. With respect to the extraction of phones, Gleitman and Wanner (1982) interpreted the infant speech-perception findings of that time (e.g., Eimas et al. 1971) as proof that infants perceive speech as composed of phonetic segments. As findings that are reviewed in chapter 3 demonstrate, this was an overinterpretation of the data. However, this overinterpretation does not undermine other claims that they made about using the sound structure for clues to the grammatical organization of the language.

Gleitman and Wanner agreed with Slobin (1973) that children might be prepared to look for words in the input, but they wondered what the salient acoustic features of such items might be. They were skeptical about the utility of using information about phonetic sequences to identify words because of the potential for missegmentations.[3] Instead, their suggestion was that words were initially coextensive with stressed syllables. They pointed to evidence from children's speech production as an indication that learners are less successful in segmenting the speech wave into words on the basis of unstressed syllables. Their suggestion was that information encoded in unstressed syllables was learned over a lengthy developmental period—"But unlike adults, children become sensitive to the unstressed subcomponent of the language during the later phases of language acquisition" (1982, p. 24). In a subsequent paper, Gleitman and her colleagues (Gleitman et al. 1988) pointed to an interesting finding by Pye (1983) that children learning Quiché Mayan, a language in which inflections are stressed but verb roots are not, actually produce the stressed inflections before they produce the semantically more salient unstressed roots. However, Gleitman and her colleagues also noted other evidence that suggested that learners might detect information in unstressed syllables in speech, before they actually begin producing these regularly (Katz, Baker, and Macnamara 1974; Shipley et al. 1969). In the interim, there have been a number of investigations demonstrating that this is, in fact, the case (Gerken, Landau, and Remez 1990; Gerken and McIntosh 1993; Shady, Gerken, and Jusczyk 1995).

Another element present in the speech wave is information about sequences of sounds. Gleitman and Wanner's view is that language learners are sensitive to this and could use it to provide clues to syntactic organization. There is evidence that provides empirical confirmation of the fact that infants are not only sensitive to sequential order (Morgan 1994) but that they also encode such information from an early age (Mandel et al. 1996).

Gleitman and Wanner offered an interesting suggestion about the identification of units larger than words in the speech stream. In particular, they argued that prosodic cues might help the learner to isolate syntactic phrases in the speech stream. The empirical support that they cited in favor of this hypothesis came largely from studies with adults, plus an investigation with 7-year-olds by Read and Schreiber (1982). Their suggestion, that "an infant who is innately biased to treat intonationally circumscribed utterance segments as potential syntactic constituents would be at considerable advantage in learning the syntactic rules of his language" (p. 26), is the core of the prosodic bootstrapping hypothesis. As Gleitman et al. (1988) noted, the course of any learning procedure for acquiring the syntactic organization of the language is strongly affected by the kinds of units that are available in the speech stream. In general, the more information that can be recovered about relevant syntactic units in the input, the less powerful are the kinds of innate parameters that are required for a plausible learning procedure to discover the syntactic organization of the native language. In other words, the speech signal may be a less-impoverished source of information about syntactic organization than proponents of universal grammar have led us to believe.

Pinker (1984) considered the possibility that information in the speech signal, such as its prosody, could provide the learner with some useful information relevant to the syntactic organization of the native language. He noted, "I am pessimistic, however, about the possibility that some 'prosodic bootstrapping' model could do without the assumptions about semantics that I have made altogether" (p. 51). He pointed out that studies investigating prosodic cues to syntactic organization, such as the one by Cooper and Paccia-Cooper (1980), had used carefully designed stimulus sets of minimally contrasting sentences. These types of stimulus sets were required because changes in the prosodic correlates of syntactic units, such as lengthening and pausing, could be caused by a variety of other factors such as intrinsic word length, syllable structure, phonetic composition, word frequency, and so on. This posed a potential problem for prosodic bootstrapping accounts of syntactic acquisition.

Thus the child must have some way of mentally subtracting the effects of all of these factors in natural discourse before he or she can invert the syntax-to-speech encoding function and recover the syntactic analyses of sentences. I think that it is fairly unlikely that a universally valid subtraction-and-inversion procedure of this sort exists, let alone that it is available to the child who has not yet learned anything about his or her language. Finally, Cooper and Paccia-Cooper note that they failed to find any prosodic reflexes of syntactic categories, only of tree geometry. Thus the child would need some other sort of information to know whether a phrase is a noun phrase or a verb phrase. Thus some use of prosodic information can perhaps be made in language acquisition, but I doubt that it can replace the use of semantic information entirely. (Pinker 1984, 51–52)

Research suggests that Pinker's overall assessment of the situation was probably correct. Not all syntactic boundaries can be read off the prosody of utterances, and other information is required to label syntactic categories correctly. Morgan (1986) acknowledged this point in his proposals about how prosodic cues could simplify the learnability problem. However, as he and others (e.g., Hirsh-Pasek, Tucker, and Golinkoff 1996; Jusczyk and Kemler Nelson 1996) have noted, prosodic bootstrapping accounts were never intended to supplant all other accounts for the acquisition of syntax. Learners may use more than one source of information to learn about the syntactic organization of their language. There is no principled reason why bootstrapping from the speech signal could not work in concert with semantic bootstrapping during the acquisition process. It seems reasonable to assume that learners will use whatever means are at their disposal to arrive at the underlying organization of sounds and meanings in their native language.

In conclusion, bootstrapping accounts of language acquisition have suggested ways learners draw on one type of information in the linguist input (i.e., syntax, semantics, or prosody) to provide clues about other levels of linguistic organization. None of these approaches is itself sufficient to account for all of language acquisition. However, it is plausible that a more satisfactory account of acquisition can be framed in terms of a general model that embodies elements of all these bootstrapping approaches, such as the constraints satisfaction model suggested by Pinker (1987) or the dynamic systems model offered by Hirsh-Pasek et al. (1996). The overall form of such a model would not be all that different from the ones proposed for functionalist accounts, although proponents of these differing views might differ about the nature of the information incorporated into the initial states of the models.

Summary

This brief survey reviewed some of the perspectives that have influenced research on language acquisition. I have tried to indicate some of the problems that are facing the learner who has to induce the structure of a native language from the input. Researchers investigating language acquisition have differed about the kind and amount of information that is available in the initial state of language learning. Is it necessary to postulate the existence of special innate linguistic capacities to account for language acquisition? Is the input structured in ways that facilitate the detection of its underlying organization? These are issues that are still very much debated. However, one point that researchers do agree on is that any satisfying explanation of language acquisition must account for how the learner is able to extract the appropriate generalizations about the input in a relatively short span of time. In the remainder of this book, the main focus is on how learners arrive at the correct generalizations about the sound structure of their native language.

Chapter 3
Early Research on Speech Perception

Research on speech perception expanded greatly during the 1950s. Places such as Bell Labs investigated speech perception and production as a means of improving communications technologies. In the meantime, researchers at Haskins Laboratories, such as Frank Cooper and Al Liberman, were at work on a project to develop reading machines for the blind (for a very illuminating account of what speech research was like in this era, see Liberman 1996). Initially, the task of designing such a machine did not look particularly daunting. It was simply a matter of detecting the invariant acoustic properties that correspond to each phoneme in a language, and then putting out the correct strings of phonemes for each utterance. However, Cooper and Liberman soon realized that finding the correct set of acoustic invariants was a lot harder than they first thought. In the process, they began to experiment with synthetic speech sounds and to observe the perceptual consequences of manipulating certain portions of the speech wave (Liberman, Delattre, and Cooper 1952). These studies led to the discovery of a number of interesting phenomena, some of which we are still trying to explain today.

Acoustic Invariants for Phonemes

Working with acoustic representations of speech based on a sound spectrogram (i.e., a time-by-frequency-by-intensity analysis of speech), Delattre, Liberman, and Cooper (1955) explored possible invariants for different phoneme classes. They soon became aware of the consequences that coarticulation has for finding acoustic invariants for particular segments. Specifically, they used simple consonant-vowel (CV) syllables and attempted to separate a stop consonant such as [d] from its accompanying vowel. They proceeded by beginning in the middle of the syllable and

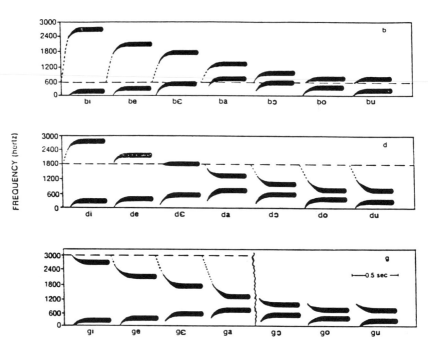

Figure 3.1
Schematized sound spectrograms corresponding to two-formant versions of synthesized syllables consisting of the voiced stop consonants [b] (top), [d] (middle), and [g] (bottom) before seven different English vowels. Note the great changes in shape and spectral frequencies in the second formant for each of the stops as they are paired with different vowels. Dashed lines indicate the "locus" frequency from which the second formants were hypothesized to have diverged.

trying to divide it so that one portion contained only the consonant, and the other portion only the vowel. They found that there was no place in which they could cut the syllable to yield a percept of the consonant without an accompanying vowel. Moreover, when they examined the acoustic realizations of the same consonant in the context of different vowels, they discovered that there were no obvious properties in common across all of these contexts. This is demonstrated in figure 3.1. The dark bars in the figure indicate where the main concentrations of acoustic energy (or formants) are during the production of the specified syllables. These concentrations of energy reflect the natural resonances of the vocal tract (formants) during production. The absence of invariant properties in the spectrographic displays of these sounds is most easily seen in the case

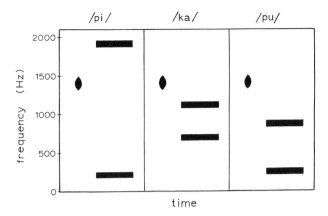

Figure 3.2
Schematic spectrograms of the syllables [pi], [ka], and [pu]. Notice that the football-shaped noise burst is identical in all three cases, yet it contributes to the distinctive consonants in the different vowel contexts. Removing this noise from the syllables would cause listeners to perceive the remaining portion of the signals as [i], [a], and [u], respectively.

of [d] (middle portion of the figure). The second formant (i.e., the top one) for [d] has an initial rising transition in some vowel contexts, but an initial falling transition in others. Moreover, because the first formant (i.e., the bottom one) is identical for the different consonants in a given vowel context, it is clear that, by itself, the first formant is not an invariant cue to the identity of the consonant.

Confidence in acoustic invariants for phonetic segments was further shaken by the results of another investigation (Liberman et al. 1952). This time, Liberman and his colleagues found that the same acoustic information could give rise to the perception of distinctly different phonemes, depending upon the vowel context in which it occurred. An identical noise burst was placed in front of synthetic versions of the vowels [i], [a], and [u] (see figure 3.2). When listeners were asked to label these noise plus vowel stimuli, they identified them as [pi], [ka], and [pu]. In other words, the same noise burst that contributed to the perception of [p] in some contexts led to the perception of [k] in a different context.

These early investigations by Liberman and his colleagues suggested that there would be no simple set of acoustic invariants that serve to identify particular phonetic segments across all contexts. Although there have been many attempts to capture some invariant acoustic descriptions of particular phonemes since that time (e.g., Blumstein, Isaacs, and Mertus 1982; Blumstein and Stevens 1978; Kewley-Port 1983; Sawusch 1992; Searle, Jacobson, and Rayment 1979; Stevens and Blumstein 1981; Sussman, McCaffrey, and Matthews 1991), investigators still have not successfully found a description that works across all contexts. Liberman and his colleagues have come to the conclusion that the invariants for a particular phoneme reside not in the acoustic signal, but rather in the way particular speech sounds are produced (Liberman et al. 1967). This view has been termed the *motor theory* of speech perception.

Categorical Perception

In the course of their investigations of possible acoustic invariants, Liberman and his colleagues also discovered another interesting phenomenon, which had to do with how adult listeners categorize certain speech sounds. In the case of many previously studied acoustic signals, listeners' ability to discriminate differences between stimuli far exceeds their ability to assign distinct labels to the different sounds. For example, Miller (1956) cited data from a study by Pollack (1952) that showed that average listeners can discriminate on the order of twelve hundred pitch differences between 100 Hertz and 8000 Hertz but that they can only consistently use about seven category labels within this range. In contrast, Liberman and his colleagues found that listeners' abilities to discriminate stop consonant contrasts were not much better than their abilities to assign the stimuli to different phoneme classes. In other words, their ability to discriminate two stimuli from within the same phoneme category tended to be poor. This is illustrated schematically in figure 3.3.

The phenomenon that Liberman and his coworkers observed has been designated *categorical perception*. Subsequent investigations by Liberman and his colleagues (Liberman et al. 1961) suggested that categorical perception might be a special feature of speech processing. In particular, there were indications that adult listeners responded differently to the same acoustic differences when they were embedded in speech contexts than when embedded in nonspeech. More specifically, differences that were perceived categorically in speech contexts were perceived more continuously in nonspeech contexts (i.e., discrimination of within-category differences was better in nonspeech). Over the years, a variety of different models were put forth to explain the occurrence of categorical perception for speech sounds. The most popular of these postulated that any acoustic

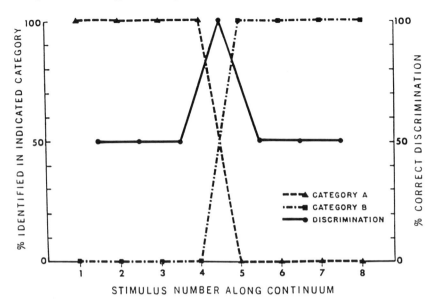

Figure 3.3
Idealized form of the pattern of identification and discrimination results expected
for categorical perception. The identification function (plotted along the left
ordinate) shows steep slopes at the category boundary and consistent labeling of
the items within a particular category. The discrimination function (plotted along
the right ordinate) indicates the probability of distinguishing adjacent points along
the continuum. Note that there is chance level responding within a given category
but a sharp increase in discriminability at the category boundary.

differences that might differentiate items from within the same category
are lost once the information is recoded into phonetic representations
(Fujisaki and Kawashimi 1969, 1970; Pisoni 1971, 1973).

At first glance, it appears that categorical perception is an impoverished
form of perception. After all, for many other types of acoustic stimuli,
listeners do a much better job of discriminating within category differences. However, it is worth considering how categorical perception might
help to improve the speed and efficiency of speech processing. As noted
earlier, speech is produced by vocal tracts of many different shapes and
sizes. Furthermore, the production of any given speech sound requires the
coordination of many different components. As with any other complex
motor skill, it is virtually impossible to produce the same speech sound in
the same way on two different occasions. Consequently, there are almost
always going to be differences between two speech tokens from the same

category. However, such differences are irrelevant to the identity of the phonetic segments in the utterances. Instead, what the listener needs to do is to focus on those kinds of differences that are relevant to distinguishing among words with different meanings (i.e., phonemic differences). Categorical perception recodes the acoustic signal in a way that preserves just those distinctions that are relevant to distinguishing among different words. That this recoding occurs so rapidly is useful for dealing with the rates at which conversational speech is typically produced.

Although it was subsequently demonstrated that categorical perception does occur for various kinds of nonspeech stimuli (e.g., Miller et al. 1976; Pastore et al. 1977; Pisoni 1977; Pisoni, Carrell, and Gans 1983), the view that categorical perception was specifically linked to speech processing influenced both the paradigms used and the questions addressed in speech research in the 1960s and 1970s. In fact, the kinds of problems that researchers initially set out to resolve (i.e., finding the invariant acoustic properties and understanding categorical perception) had a lot to do with focusing investigations of speech processing on studies directed at how listeners identify phones, as opposed to how they recognize words in fluent speech. The general assumption appeared to be that word recognition was dependent on a prior stage of phoneme identification. Hence, any progress in understanding word recognition first required an explanation for how phonemes were extracted and identified from the speech signal.

Early Studies of Infant Speech Perception

There was another source that shaped early investigations of infant speech-perception capacities. In particular, Roman Jakobson's influential view (Jakobson 1968) that children gradually acquire a system of phonemic contrasts contributed to the tendency to construe the infant's first task as one of learning to distinguish phonetic segments from one another. Hence, when speech researchers first presented infants with pairs of syllables differing by a single phoneme, they interpreted their findings in terms of whether the infants were able to distinguish one phoneme from another.

Prior to the first studies of infant speech perception, the most widely held view of how infants learned the phonemes characteristic of their native language was one that emphasized links between perception and production. In particular, because of the lack of success in finding acoustic invariants for phonemic segments, motor theorists proposed that speech sounds are perceived by reference to the way they are articulated (Liberman et al. 1967). It was assumed that the child first discovered these kinds of relations in babbling, essentially by experimenting with articulations and listening to the resulting sound patterns. Gradually, the infant would learn which articulatory maneuvers were associated with which acoustic patterns. Because the location of phoneme boundaries was known to differ from language to language (Abramson and Lisker 1967; Lisker and Abramson 1964, 1967), the phenomenon of categorical perception was explained in terms of learned equivalence and acquired distinctiveness. For instance, the infant would learn to ignore slight acoustic differences among productions of sounds from the same phonemic category, whereas differences that resulted in sounds from opposing phonemic categories would be magnified. Hence, categorical perception developed as a result of the infant's practice in producing and perceiving speech (Fry 1966).

The arguments of Chomsky and others (Chomsky 1965; Fodor 1966; Lenneberg 1967; McNeill 1966) that certain linguistic abilities had an innate, rather than experiential, basis raised questions regarding the origins of speech perception capacities. Might categorical perception be a part of a human's innate linguistic endowment? To explore this possibility, Eimas and his colleagues (Eimas et al. 1971) decided to investigate the speech discrimination abilities of prebabbling infants. They used a *high-amplitude sucking* (HAS) procedure (Jusczyk 1985a; Siqueland and DeLucia 1969), in which infants control the presentation of a speech syllable by sucking on a pacifier. The higher the sucking rate, the more often the speech sounds are played. During an initial "familiarization" period, infants hear repetitions of a particular syllable until their sucking rates decline to some predetermined criterion level; then the "test" phase begins. Infants in experimental conditions hear repetitions of a different syllable in response to sucking on the pacifier, whereas infants in control conditions continue to hear repetitions of the initial syllable. Discrimination of a particular stimulus pair is inferred from differences in the sucking behavior between the control and experimental conditions during the test phase. (For a more complete description of this procedure, see the discussion in the appendix).

Eimas et al. (1971) tested infants at two different ages, 1 and 4 months, for their ability to discriminate the English voicing contrast that is observed in the syllables [ba] and [pa]. In articulatory terms, the voicing distinction has to do with the timing of glottal adjustments relative to supraglottal articulation. As Lisker and Abramson (1967) have noted, "this relation is realized acoustically by what we call voice onset time (VOT), i.e., the interval between the release burst and the onset of laryngeal pulsing." Put another way, it is the interval between the release of the closure of the vocal tract and the vibration of the vocal folds. VOT, which underlies voicing distinctions in many languages, is perceived categorically by adult listeners (Lisker and Abramson 1967). Specifically, previous research with the stop consonants [b] and [p] had shown that when the release from closure precedes the onset of vocal fold vibration by intervals greater than 25 milliseconds, adult English-speaking listeners perceive the resulting utterance as beginning with [p] (i.e., as a voiceless stop). For intervals in which vocal fold vibration occurs within 25 milliseconds of the release from closure, the utterances are perceived as beginning with [b] (i.e., as a voiced stop).

Eimas and coworkers used this fact in constructing the stimulus pairs for testing their infants. Specifically, they chose some contrasts to span the voicing boundary between [ba] and [pa], and they chose other contrasts with a voicing difference of the same magnitude but that occurred within the same phonemic category (i.e., either two different [ba] sounds or two different [pa] sounds). In this way, they could compare infants' performance in discriminating both between- and within-category acoustic differences. A finding indicating that infants' discrimination of within-category pairs was inferior to that of between-category pairs would be an indication that categorical perception was in place prior to any experience with babbling. Alternatively, an indication that infants performed at the same level with both kinds of contrasts would be in line with the view that categorical perception is a learned phenomenon. In fact, the findings were in line with the first view: Infants at both ages only discriminated syllables from different phonemic categories.

Eimas and his colleagues demonstrated two things. First, infants as young as 1 month of age had some capacity to discriminate speech-sound contrasts. Second, like adults, infants' discrimination of these contrasts is categorical. Moreover, because these were prebabbling infants, it was clear that experience in producing and perceiving one's own speech sounds is not a prerequisite for categorical perception. Eimas and coworkers also took their conclusions a step further by claiming that categorical perception was part of infants' biological endowment for language. Of course, this claim was predicated on the belief that categorical perception was exclusively associated with the processing of speech, as opposed to other kinds of acoustic signals. As will be discussed shortly, the claim that categorical perception is part of one's biological endowment for language has proven to be problematic in a number of respects.

Regardless of whether Eimas and colleagues were correct in all their claims, their study engendered a whole new area of infant-language research. What immediately followed was a series of studies that aimed to document the extent of infants' speech-discrimination abilities. These studies helped to delineate the range of infants' capacities for perceiving speech distinctions. Investigations of this type continue to the present day. In addition, Eimas and coworkers' findings also inspired a great deal of research concerning the underlying mechanisms for infants' speech-discrimination capacities. Many of these studies compared the processing of speech and nonspeech materials or investigated similarities and differences in the way humans and nonhuman species perceive the same kinds of acoustic contrasts. Finally, other investigators looked beyond infants' capacities for discriminating speech sounds and explored other important elements of speech processing having to do with perceptual constancy. We consider each of these developments in the following sections.

Delineating the Extent of Infants' Speech-Discrimination Capacities

It was important to establish whether the ability that infants as young as 1 month of age had shown for discriminating voicing distinctions was indicative of a general ability to discriminate speech contrasts along a number of dimensions or simply an interesting, but isolated, curiosity. For this reason, speech researchers began to test infants on other kinds of phonetic contrasts, most of which related to consonantal differences.

Perception of place-of-articulation contrasts has been of great interest over the years because of the apparent lack of invariant acoustic cues to place distinctions across different contexts (Liberman 1970; Liberman et al. 1967; cf. Stevens and Blumstein 1978). The earliest studies with infants simply tested whether or not place-of-articulation contrasts were discriminable for infants. Moffit (1971) used a heart-rate dishabituation procedure and found that 5-month-olds were able to discriminate a place-of-articulation contrast between the syllables [ba] and [ga]. Morse (1972) used the HAS procedure to investigate the same contrast with 2-month-olds and found similar results. Interestingly enough, Morse found that when infants were tested with the same kinds of acoustic differences in nonspeech sounds, they did not discriminate these differences. This contrast in how the same kinds of acoustic differences were processed in speech and nonspeech contexts fit the pattern reported for adults listening to comparable stimuli (Mattingly, Liberman, Syrdal, and Halwes 1971).

A subsequent investigation by Eimas (1974) demonstrated that infants, like adults, discriminated the place of articulation distinction between [bæ] and [dæ] in a categorical manner. Moreover, a later investigation conducted by Bertoncini et al. (1987) with newborns demonstrated that the ability to discriminate place-of-articulation differences among stop consonants does not depend on exposure to speech information within the first few months of life. Rather, this capacity is apparently in place at birth. Furthermore, although the early investigations always tested the critical phonetic contrasts in the syllable-initial position, Jusczyk and his colleagues found that 2-month-olds were able to distinguish comparable place-of-articulation contrasts when these were located in syllable-final (Jusczyk 1977) and utterance-medial positions (Jusczyk and Thompson 1978). Therefore, there is ample evidence that place of articulation contrasts among stop consonants are discriminable for even very young infants.

Other kinds of distinctions involving stop consonants were also examined. Several studies focused on infants' discrimination of stop/glide distinctions (e.g., [ba] vs. [wa]). Hillenbrand, Minifie, and Edwards (1979) found that 6- to 8-month-olds are able to discriminate these syllables, and subsequent research by Eimas and Miller (1980a; Miller and Eimas 1983) demonstrated categorical discrimination of the same contrast by 2-month-olds. The oral/nasal distinction between syllables like [ba] and [ma] was tested by Eimas and Miller (1980b). Once again, 2- to 4-month-olds discriminated this contrast. However, unlike the earlier consonantal contrasts examined, the infants also showed some ability to discriminate within category distinctions for these stimuli. Hence, perception of this distinction is apparently not categorical for infants.

Phonemic distinctions involving classes of phonemes other than stop consonants have also been scrutinized. For instance, Eimas (1975a) tested 2- to 3-month-olds on a distinction between two liquids, [ra] and [la]. This contrast is one that children often master late in speech production (Strange and Broen 1981; Templin 1957) and also one that is notoriously difficult for certain nonnative speakers of English, such as Japanese listeners (Miyawaki et al. 1975). Eimas found that American infants reliably discriminated this contrast and, like native English-speaking adults, gave evidence of categorical discrimination along this speech continuum. Jusczyk, Copan, and Thompson (1978) tested 2-month-olds' ability to discriminate a place of articulation distinction involving the glides [wa] and [ja] and found that their subjects detected this contrast regardless of whether it occurred in utterance-initial or utterance-medial positions. Finally, Eimas and Miller (1980b) found that 2- to 3-month-olds also discriminated the place of articulation distinction between the nasal consonants [ma] and [na].

The consonantal contrasts that have generated the most controversy are those involving fricatives. This is one area in which there have been conflicting reports as to whether or not infants can discriminate a particular contrast. For example, Eilers (1977) reported that 3-month-olds were able to discriminate a voicing contrast between [s] and [z] in syllable-final position (i.e., [as] vs. [az]), but not in syllable-initial position ([sa] vs. [za]). However, the latter result has been criticized on methodological grounds (Aslin, Pisoni, and Jusczyk 1983). Place of articulation differences between fricatives have also been investigated. Once again, Eilers, Wilson, and Moore (1977) reported that 6- to 8-month-olds, and even 12- to 14-month-olds, did not successfully discriminate contrasts involving [f] and [θ]. However, Holmberg, Morgan, and Kuhl (1977) reported that 6-month-olds in their study were able to detect a contrast between [fa] and [θa]. Similarly, Levitt et al. (1988) investigated the same contrast with 2-month-olds and found evidence for categorical discrimination of place of articulation differences with both the voiceless fricative pair, [fa] vs. [θa], and the voiced fricative pair, [va] vs. [ða]. Consequently, it does appear that even young infants have some capacity to distinguish fricative contrasts, although it is possible their ability to detect such distinctions may not be as robust as their ability to detect phonetic contrasts involving other types of phonetic segments.

In addition to investigations of consonantal contrasts, there have been a number of studies examining young infants' capacities to discriminate vowel contrasts. The first investigation of vowel discrimination by infants was conducted by Trehub (1973). She used the HAS procedure to present natural speech tokens of two different vowel pairs (either [a] vs. [i] or [i] vs. [u]) to 1- to 4-month-old infants. The infants were able to discriminate both pairs of vowels. Swoboda, Morse, and Leavitt (1976) presented 2-month-olds with the more subtle contrast between [i] and [ɪ] in a study that also used the HAS procedure. They tested not only for discrimination of the contrast but also for whether perception was continuous or categorical. Their results indicated that infants discriminated both within-category and between-category pairs, suggesting that, like adults (Fry et al. 1962; Pisoni 1973; Stevens et al. 1969), their perception of vowel contrasts is continuous. Evidence for the discrimination of another subtle vowel distinction (between [a] and [ɔ]) has been reported in a study with 6-month-olds by Kuhl (1983).

In addition to examining infants' abilities to discriminate differences in phonetic contrasts, some research was also carried out on their ability to discriminate prosodic features that are present in the speech signal. Morse (1972) explored whether infants were capable of discriminating syllables that differed only in their intonational characteristics (i.e., whether they were produced with a rising or a falling pitch). He found that 2- to 3-month-olds had no difficulty discriminating these kinds of differences. Kuhl and Miller (1982) used isolated vowel stimuli such as [a] or [i] and replicated Morse's basic finding when the phonetic content of their stimuli was held constant (although not when the phonetic identity of the stimuli continuously varied between [i] and [a]). Other investigations examined the ability of infants to discriminate prosodic differences in multisyllabic stimuli (Jusczyk and Thompson 1978; Spring and Dale 1977). The results of these investigations indicated that infants at this age could discriminate multisyllabic stimuli that differed solely in their stress patterns (i.e., whether the first or second syllable received the primary stress). Thus, as was the case for phonetic contrasts, infants, from an early age, appeared to be well attuned to prosodic differences among speech sounds.

So far, I have only discussed studies that focused on the perception of contrasts that occurred in the native language spoken in the infant's immediate environment. However, because researchers were interested in the extent to which infants' discriminative capacities are innately determined or based on experience with a particular language, a number of studies examined whether infants might also perceive nonnative language contrasts. Streeter (1976) investigated Kikuyu infants' perception of English voicing contrasts. The contrast between [ba] and [pa] is not one found in Kikuyu, although the language does include contrasts between prevoiced consonants (sounds in which vocal fold vibration precedes the release from vocal tract closure) and voiced consonants. Despite their lack of familiarity with the contrast, Kikuyu 1- to 4-month-olds were able to discriminate the voiced/voiceless pair. A similar finding was reported by Lasky, Syrdal-Lasky, and Klein (1975), who tested $4\frac{1}{2}$- to 6-month-old Guatemalan infants on English and Spanish voicing contrasts between [ba] and [pa]. Although Spanish does have a voicing distinction, it is not the same one that occurs in English (Lisker and Abramson 1967; Williams 1977b). Despite the fact that Spanish was the language spoken at home for these infants, they discriminated the English voicing contrast, but not the Spanish one. We will consider the implications of the infants' nondiscrimination of the Spanish voicing distinction shortly. For the time being, we note that they did discriminate the nonnative voicing contrast.

A number of studies have also investigated how infants from English-speaking homes perceive foreign-language contrasts. One of the first attempts was reported by Eimas (1975b), who investigated whether American infants could discriminate the prevoiced/voiced distinction that occurs between stop consonants in languages like Thai (Lisker and Abramson 1967). Eimas found that only when a voicing difference between prevoiced and voiced stops was very large (on the order of 80 ms), did the American infants discriminate it. More convincing evidence that American infants can discriminate the prevoiced/voiced contrast comes from a study by Aslin et al. (1981), who used the operant headturn procedure to test 6-month-olds. They found that although the smallest difference to discriminate the prevoiced/voiced contrast was larger than that for the voiced/voiceless contrast, all of their subjects discriminated both contrasts.

Although many early studies investigated voicing contrasts, information is also available about how infants respond to other types of foreign language contrasts. Trehub (1976) examined 1- to 4-month-old English Canadian infants' responsiveness to an oral/nasal vowel contrast ([pa] vs. [pã]), found in languages like Polish and French, and a contrast between ([řa] vs. [za]), which occurs in Czech. Despite their lack of experience with these contrasts, infants discriminated each one. Moreover, studies evaluating possible changes in sensitivity to foreign contrasts also have shown that nonnative contrasts are discriminated by young infants. For example, 6-month-old English Canadian infants can discriminate a retroflex/dental place of articulation contrast from Hindi and a glottalized velar/uvular contrast from Nthlakapmx (Werker and Tees 1984a). Moreover, English-learning $4\frac{1}{2}$-month-olds are sensitive to the German vowel contrasts [ʊ] vs. [Y] and [u] vs. [y] (Polka and Werker 1994).

Taken together, these studies of the perception of foreign language contrasts suggest that young infants' capacities for discriminating speech contrasts extend beyond those sounds that they are likely to have encountered in their native environment. Thus, for at least some speech contrasts, infants do not require prior experience in order to discriminate them. However, it must be noted that this is not the same thing as saying that infants have an innate ability to perceive the phonemic contrasts of their native language. A comparison of the findings from Streeter (1976) and Lasky et al. (1975) is interesting with respect to this issue. In particular, the behavior of the Guatemalan infants contrasted with that of the Kikuyu infants. The Kikuyu infants discriminated the prevoiced/voiced contrast that does occur in their native language, whereas the Guatemalan infants did not discriminate the voicing contrast that occurs in Spanish. It is hard to explain this difference if one views infants as discriminating actual phonemic contrasts.

However, there is another way to describe what infants are doing at this age. Consider the possibility that infants' categorization of speech contrasts does not so much reflect the phonemic categories of any particular language but rather a language-general categorization of speech information. Hence, it is not so much the fact that Kikuyu and Guatemalan infants are somehow wired to perceive the English phonemic contrasts as it is that this particular English contrast happens to line up with the language-general voicing boundary. By this reasoning, the Kikuyu and English contrasts are better discriminated because they come closer to the infants' innate perceptual boundaries than does the Spanish contrast. Discriminating the Spanish voicing contrast may actually require some realignment of the infant's perceptual categories (Aslin and Pisoni 1980).

In any event, the findings from the studies reviewed in this section indicate that infants do possess some innate ability to discriminate many different kinds of speech contrasts. Indeed, these sorts of findings have led to the view that infants are born with the capacity to discriminate contrasts that could potentially appear in any of the world's languages (Eimas, Miller, and Jusczyk 1987; Werker and Pegg 1992). Nevertheless, the findings also suggest that experiential factors do contribute to where the perceptual boundaries are set for fluent speakers of a language.

Efforts to Specify the Nature of the Underlying Mechanisms

Eimas et al. (1971) believed that their findings provided evidence for innate linguistic capacities, that is, that the mechanisms underlying the infant's speech-perception capacities were linguistic rather than general auditory capacities. Early comparisons with nonspeech stimuli appeared to bear out this contention. Morse (1972) reported that infants who discriminated differences in formant transitions relating to place of articulation contrasts in speech did not discriminate the same kinds of changes when the formants were isolated and heard as nonspeech sounds. Eimas

(1974, 1975a) went a step further by demonstrating that the same sets formant transition changes that were discriminated categorically by infants in speech contexts were discriminated continuously when presented in nonspeech contexts. Hence, the earliest investigations supported the view that speech sounds were undergoing specialized processing, even at the earliest ages.

Shortly thereafter, the claims about specialized processing of speech sounds were shaken by two types of findings. First of all, Kuhl and Miller (1975) reported evidence that chinchillas appeared to perceive voicing differences in speech sounds in a categorical manner. This finding raised the possibility that categorical perception may have more to do with properties inherent in the mammalian auditory system than with any specific kind of adaptation for language processing. Second, the first reports of categorical perception for certain kinds of nonspeech stimuli began to appear (Cutting and Rosner 1974; Miller et al. 1976; Pisoni 1977). These findings raised the specter that categorical perception was not a special property of processing in the speech mode but rather a general feature of the way certain kinds of complex signals are processed. Let us consider some of the relevant findings in each domain and what implications we can draw from these about the nature of the underlying mechanisms for speech perception.

Perception of Speech Sounds by Nonhuman Species

I will first focus on what the nonhuman animal studies have to say about the possibility of specialized speech-processing mechanisms. Kuhl and Miller (1975, 1978; see also Kuhl 1981) demonstrated that chinchillas manifest some characteristics of the way humans discriminate and categorize voicing contrasts. For instance, Kuhl and Miller (1978) reported that the locus of the perceptual boundaries for voicing contrasts in chinchillas shift slightly with changes in place of articulation, as is true for human listeners (i.e., the voicing boundary for labial stops differed from that for alveolar stops, and both of these differ from that for velar stops). Subsequently, Kuhl and Padden (1982) demonstrated similar effects for voicing contrasts presented to macaque monkeys. Furthermore, another study by the same investigators (Kuhl and Padden 1983) indicated parallels in the way this species and humans processed place-of-articulation contrasts. More recently, Kluender and his colleagues reported that Japanese quail can be trained to categorize place of articulation contrasts in the same way as human listeners (Kluender, Diehl, and Killeen 1987).

However, as Eimas (1996) has noted with respect to the latter finding, the quail required thousands of training trials. By comparison, human infants, even newborns (e.g., Bertoncini et al. 1987), display good discrimination of these contrasts within the first few minutes of laboratory testing. This difference seems to indicate either that the two species may use different means to discriminate the contrasts or that human infants are biased to attend more readily to the critical information that signals these place-of-articulation differences.

Although the results of these investigations suggest that human and nonhuman species categorize and discriminate speech sounds in much the same way, there are some discrepancies that have been reported as well. For example, Waters and Wilson (1976) found that although the rhesus monkeys they tested gave evidence of perceiving voicing contrasts categorically, their boundaries (unlike those of humans) were influenced by the nature of the initial training stimuli. Similarly, although Sinnott and her colleagues (Sinnott et al. 1976) found evidence that macaques could discriminate place-of-articulation differences, the monkeys required much larger differences between stimuli than did human listeners. Morse and Snowden (1975) reported that, unlike humans, the rhesus monkeys that they tested on place of articulation contrasts discriminated both between-category and within-category differences.

Taken together, then, the overall picture provided by results of these comparative studies of human and nonhuman speech processing is a complex one. On the one hand, the correspondences that have been observed across species demonstrate that the kinds of perceptual phenomena, such as categorical perception, that are often observed with respect to human speech processing do not necessarily require an explanation in terms of specialized speech-processing mechanisms. Nature tends to be conservative and uses the same mechanisms over and over again to serve different but similar functions in different species. On the other hand, the fact that discrepancies do arise between the performance of humans and nonhumans raises the possibility that the different species could be using different means to categorize and discriminate the stimuli. Indeed, Osherson and Wasow (1976) made a similar point regarding possible parallels between human language learners and sign-language-learning chimpanzees. Hence, the mere fact that humans and nonhumans exhibit the same pattern of behavior does not rule out the possibility that species-specific mechanisms are involved in human speech perception (Jusczyk 1986a).

Speech and Nonspeech Processing by Human Infants

Now let us examine some of the relevant findings that bear on whether or not nonspeech sounds are processed like speech sounds by human infants. The first hints of parallels in infants' perception of speech and nonspeech stimuli came from an investigation by Jusczyk et al. (1977) with 2-month-old infants. Previous work with adults by Cutting and Rosner (1974) had suggested that rise-time cues were perceived categorically in both speech (e.g., as the cue underlying the distinction between [ba] and [wa]) and music (i.e., as to whether a musical note was played on a plucked or bowed string). Jusczyk and coworkers tested infants on a series of musical pairs that were chosen from either within or between the categories labeled "pluck" and "bow" by Cutting and Rosner's adult listeners. The infants gave evidence of distinguishing the between-category pairs but not the within-category pairs. Thus, Jusczyk and coworkers concluded that the infants' discrimination of these nonspeech stimuli was categorical. Unfortunately, as Rosen and Howell (1981) later determined, there was an artifact in the preparation of the Cutting and Rosner stimuli that led to their being perceived categorically. Because these were the same stimuli that Jusczyk and coworkers had used, no firm conclusions could be drawn from their experiment.

However, other demonstrations that infants showed categorical discrimination for nonspeech contrasts soon followed. Jusczyk et al. (1980) used stimuli from a tone-onset-time continuum that had been developed for perceptual studies with adults by Pisoni (1977). The stimuli consisted of two co-occurring tones (one at 500 Hz; the other at 1500 Hz). A stimulus continuum was generated by offsetting the onsets of the tones with respect to one another (i.e., the onset of the lower tone could lead the higher tone by some amount, the onset of the lower tone could lag behind that of the higher tone, or the two onsets could occur simultaneously. These tone-onset differences were meant to provide a nonspeech analogue to VOT differences in speech). When adult listeners were asked to label and discriminate the stimuli from this series, they displayed categorical perception and grouped the stimuli into three classes—lagging, leading, and simultaneous (ones that appeared to parallel the prevoiced, voiceless, and voiced categories in speech). Moreover, the locations for the perceptual boundaries along the continuum corresponded to those observed for speech stimuli along the voicing continuum for labial stops. This led Pisoni to conclude that general auditory mechanisms involved in the perception of temporal order differences lay at the heart of the perception of voicing differences in speech.

However, given that Pisoni's subjects already had a long history of perceiving voicing cues in speech contexts, one could claim that these adults simply transferred their experience with language to their processing of the tone-onset-time stimuli. To determine whether a long period of experience with speech stimuli was really required to perceive these non-speech sounds categorically, Jusczyk et al. (1980) presented stimulus pairs from the tone-onset-time continuum to 2-month-old infants. The results indicated that the infants' discrimination of these stimuli was categorical, although the perceptual boundary appeared to occur at a different location than what is typically observed for voicing differences (between 20 ms and 40 ms). Specifically, infants were shown to discriminate pairings of stimuli with onset differences of 40 milliseconds and 70 milliseconds, indicating a perceptual boundary somewhere in between. As Jusczyk and coworkers noted, one possible explanation for the difference in boundary locations is that temporal order cues are only one of several kinds of acoustic cues that contribute to the perception of voicing differences (Lisker 1975; Stevens and Klatt 1974).

A subsequent investigation conducted by Jusczyk et al. (1989) used nonspeech stimuli with a richer acoustic structure, as well as two different voicing contrasts, [ba]–[pa] and [du]–[tu]. Once again, infants gave evidence of discriminating temporal order differences in nonspeech sounds categorically. Moreover, this time the estimated perceptual boundaries for the speech and nonspeech boundaries occurred at the same points on the stimulus continua, namely, between 20 milliseconds and 40 milliseconds. Although Jusczyk and coworkers acknowledged that the infant testing methods do not have sufficient precision to determine how closely the speech and nonspeech boundaries correspond, their results are consistent with the possibility that a common auditory process underlies infants' perception of temporal order cues in both speech and nonspeech contexts.

Studies of Context Effects and Cue-Trading Relations
The increasing indications that certain nonspeech stimuli are perceived categorically by infants and adults alike led investigators to seek other dimensions that might help differentiate speech from nonspeech processing. One such dimension that was investigated had to do with the kinds of changes that occur in speech processing as listeners adjust to changes in speaking rates. That is, the phonetic significance of certain acoustic

properties depends on the context within which they occur. For example, in an elegant series of experiments, Miller and Liberman (1979) found that adult listeners' interpretation of the acoustic cues to the stop/glide distinction between [ba] and [wa] varied depending on speaking rates. That is, the same kinds of acoustic cues that would lead to the perception of [wa] in fast rates of speech were perceived as indicating [ba] at slower speaking rates. Eimas and Miller (1980a; Miller and Eimas 1983) subsequently demonstrated that 2- to 3-month-olds also appeared to make similar kinds of adjustments in their categorizations of speech sounds in relation to changes in speaking rates. A stimulus difference that infants responded to as a between-category pair at a rapid rate of speech was perceived as a within-category pair when presented at a slower rate of speech. Eimas and Miller argued that this kind of responsiveness to changes in speaking rates was evidence that infants possessed specialized speech-processing mechanisms.

However, Eimas and Miller's arguments were undercut by the demonstration that similar kinds of adjustments occur in the perception of certain nonspeech stimuli. Adult listeners were shown to adjust their categorization of rapid spectral changes in response to changes in the overall durations of the stimuli (Pisoni et al. 1983). Moreover, when infants were tested on the same kinds of nonspeech stimuli (Jusczyk et al. 1983), they showed exactly the same patterns of discrimination that Eimas and Miller (1980a) had reported for their speech stimuli when the speaking rate was varied. Therefore, Jusczyk and colleagues argued that general auditory mechanisms were sufficient to account for infants' behavior with both the speech and nonspeech stimuli.

More recently, the arguments for and against specialized speech-processing mechanisms have shifted to different battlegrounds. One issue concerns evidence for the way acoustic cues are integrated during the perception of speech. As noted earlier, the specific acoustic properties associated with a particular phoneme can vary greatly depending on their context. Consequently, the most effective acoustic indices of a particular phonetic distinction in one context may not be the same as in another context (Oden and Massaro 1978). At the same time, multiple sources of information are often available to signal the presence of a particular phonetic contrast in the same context (Lisker 1986). The availability of different acoustic correlates of phonetic contrasts suggests that listeners may integrate these different sources of information in identifying phonetic segments. Indeed, more robust information about one of these sources may allow listeners to compensate for weaker information about other sources. Alternatively, the different sources of information regarding the identity of a phonetic segment can conflict, resulting in an ambiguous percept. Indeed, evidence for such *trading relations* among multiple cues to phonetic distinctions has been observed for adults (Best, Morrongiello, and Robson 1981; Fitch et al. 1980; Harris et al. 1958; Liberman, Delattre, and Cooper 1958; Lisker et al. 1977; Repp 1982; Stevens and Klatt 1974). To the extent that the integration of or trading among the same acoustic cues differs in speech and nonspeech contexts (particularly if infants display such behavior), this would tend to point to the existence of specialized speech-processing mechanisms.

There are some indications that infants are sensitive to certain trading relations in speech. In particular, Eimas (1985) tested 2- to 4-month-olds on stimulus series ranging from "say" to "stay." For this series, spectral cues relating to formant transitions were traded with temporal cues relating to the duration of a silent gap. By comparing how infants responded to the stimuli when the spectral and temporal cues either conflicted or cooperated, he found evidence to support the view that infants treat these cues as perceptually equivalent. Specifically, only when the cues cooperated did infants discriminate the speech stimuli. Hence, infants appear to be sensitive to how these spectral and temporal properties enter into trading relations in speech contexts. A subsequent investigation by Eimas and Miller (1991) produced some further evidence for interactions of spectral and temporal cues in infants' discrimination of speech contrasts. In particular, formant transition differences indicative of a distinction between [t] and [k] were discriminated by 3- to 4-month-olds in the context of a preceding [s]-frication, but only when there was a sufficiently long silent gap (100 ms) to signal a closure duration appropriate for their occurrence.

Fowler, Best, and McRoberts (1990) investigated another aspect of the way context influences phonetic perception. In particular, they investigated whether 4- to 5-month-olds are sensitive to coarticulatory influences between liquids (i.e., [r] and [l]) on the production of following stop consonants (i.e., [d] and [g]). Previous research with adults (Mann 1980) had shown that when a [da]-[ga] continuum is preceded by either [al] or [ar], adults label more of the stimuli as [ga] when it is preceded by [al]. Fowler and coworkers found that, like the adults, 4- to 5-month-olds appear to take information about phonetic contexts into account (i.e., they compensate for coarticulatory effects) in discriminating place-of-articulation contrasts.

Another indication that infants are sensitive to the contexts in which acoustic cues are embedded comes from a study by Levitt et al. (1988). Previous work with adults had shown that listeners apparently interpret formant transition information relating to place-of-articulation distinctions in a contextually dependent manner (Carden et al. 1981). By varying the starting frequency of formant transitions at the onset of syllables, they constructed a stimulus continuum that ranged from [ba] to [da]. The addition of an identical frication noise to the onset of these syllables was sufficient to create a series that was perceived as ranging from [fa] to [θa]. When adults were tested on the two series, there was a discrepancy in the location of the perceptual boundary. Formant transition differences that were interpreted as place-of-articulation differences for the fricative consonants [fa] and [θa] were not discriminated without the context of an accompanying frication noise (both stimuli were perceived as [da]). Levitt and coworkers tested 2-month-olds on the same series of sounds. Their results suggested that infants' perception of the formant transition differences in the speech sounds also depended on the presence or absence of accompanying frication noises. Contrasts that were not discriminated without accompanying frication were discriminated when frication was present, and vice versa. These results paralleled the kinds of *context effects* that Carden and colleagues observed for adults' perception of the same contrasts. Levitt and coworkers concluded that the source of these effects does not depend on long experience in producing and perceiving but rather is a consequence of the inherent organization of the underlying perceptual mechanisms.

Studies of Duplex Perception

A different argument for specialized processing of speech sounds comes from studies of *duplex perception* (Liberman, Isenberg, and Rakerd 1981). In studies with adults, Liberman and colleagues showed that when speech information is manipulated so that information about the transition of the third formant is presented to one ear, and the remainder of the syllable is presented to the opposite ear, listeners report a "duplex" percept. That is, they report hearing both a complete speech syllable and a tone (that corresponds to the isolated third formant transition). Liberman and coworkers interpreted such results as proof that such signals are perceived simultaneously as both speech and nonspeech, and they view this as evidence for the operation of a special mode of perception for speech (Liberman and Mattingly 1985).

More recently, Eimas and Miller (1992) reported the results of an investigation of duplex perception in infants. They presented 3- to 4-month-olds with speech information dichotically, so that information about the third formant transition alone went to one ear, while information about the remainder of the syllable went to the other ear. The third formant contained the critical information for distinguishing the syllable [da] from [ga]. The infants not only discriminated the dichotic patterns in this situation but did so even when the third formant transitions were greatly attenuated. In the latter case, the infants' performance with the dichotic stimuli was significantly better than their capacity to discriminate the attenuated third formant transitions when they were presented in isolation. Eimas and Miller concluded that these young infants already possess the means to integrate disparate sources of information into coherent speech percepts.

Conclusions about Recent Attempts to Demonstrate Speech-Specific Processes

There is no doubt that these investigations of trading relations, context effects, and duplex perception demonstrate that infants are capable of a sophisticated integration of speech information. However, whether such investigations provide evidence for the operation of specialized speech-processing mechanisms during the first few months of life is another matter. To date, there have not been any attempts to determine whether infants exhibit comparable tendencies in their processing of nonspeech sounds. Nevertheless, there are indications that for at least some kinds of nonspeech stimuli, adults exhibit patterns of responding comparable to both cue trading (Sawusch and Gagnon 1995) and duplex perception (Nusbaum, Schwab, and Sawusch 1983). Hence, it is by no means certain that the demonstrations of such phenomena demand an explanation in terms of specialized speech-processing mechanisms.

At first glance, it may be discouraging that the kinds of investigations reviewed in this section have not resolved the issue of whether the underlying mechanisms are general to auditory processing or specific to speech processing. However, the fact remains that these studies have yielded a great deal of information concerning the full extent of infants' speech-perception capacities. Thus, they have contributed greatly to the description of speech perception capacities at the earliest stages of language acquisition.

Infant's Capacities for Coping with Variability in Speech

The acoustic characteristics of any particular word undergo considerable variation, owing to changes in speaking rate, speech register, and differences in the sizes and shapes of vocal tracts of individual talkers. Some of the potential problems posed by the variability in productions of speech sounds are apparent in Peterson and Barney's (1952) classic illustration of the vowel space of different American English talkers, which is shown in figure 3.4. As is apparent here, tokens of a particular vowel type produced by some talkers actually overlap with tokens of a different vowel type produced by other talkers. There are perceptual data to indicate that this kind of variability in production can cause listeners, under some circumstances, to perceive the same formant pattern as different vowels depending on the vocal characteristics of the talker who produced the preceding words (Ladefoged and Broadbent 1957). Still, listeners typically have little difficulty with variability attributable to differences among talkers (Creelman 1957; Verbrugge et al. 1976), although there are some indications that adjusting to such differences may have consequences for processing time (Nusbaum and Morin 1992; Summerfield and Haggard 1973) and in subsequent memory for speech information (Mullennix, Pisoni, and Martin 1989).

The mechanisms by which listeners perceptually compensate, or "normalize," for talker differences are not well understood at present. Consequently, data about any capacities that infants may have to cope with talker variability might provide further insights about the nature of the mechanisms underlying this process. At some point, all language learners must be able to adjust to talker differences. Without some minimal ability to recognize the same word produced by different talkers, it is hard to see how the infant could ever learn which acoustic differences are pertinent to distinguishing among the meanings of words.

Kuhl (1976, 1979; Kuhl and Miller 1982) conducted the first investigations of infants' ability to handle variability, both within and among different talkers. In one investigation using the HAS procedure with 1- to 4-month-olds (Kuhl 1976; Kuhl and Miller 1982), she showed that infants were able to discriminate a vowel contrast between [a] and [i], even when the pitch of the talker's voice was varied irrelevantly. In a subsequent

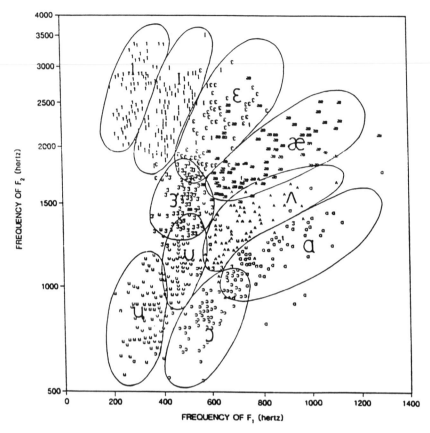

Figure 3.4
The vowel space plotted from observations of frequency values for the first and
second formants of various English vowels produced by 76 talkers. The data
points are indicated by the phonetic symbols, and the loops enclose about 90 percent of the tokens for each vowel category. Note the overlap that occurs between
adjacent categories (from Peterson and Barney 1952).

study with 6-month-olds, she explored whether changes in pitch and talker's voice would interfere with infants' abilities to detect certain vowel contrasts (Kuhl 1979). Infants were trained using the operant headturn procedure to discriminate a contrast between [a] and [i] when both talker's voice and pitch contour were held constant. In this procedure, an infant hears a repeating background stimulus (e.g., [a], [a], [a], . . . , [a]). At certain points, the stimulus is changed to several repetitions of a different stimulus (e.g., [i], [i], [i]). If the infant makes a headturn in the direction of a display box during the presentation of the change stimuli, the box lights up and a mechanical toy inside the box is activated. Discrimination of the stimuli is indexed by comparing the number of headturns during these change trials to spontaneous headturns made during no-change control trials (for further details about this procedure, see the appendix).

Once Kuhl's infants demonstrated discrimination of the [a]–[i] contrast, they were tested for their ability to maintain the discrimination in the face of variability in pitch and talker's voice. Variability was increased gradually over a series of training stages. In the final stage, there were tokens of each vowel produced by three different talkers using two different pitch contours. Even with this degree of variability, the infants continued to successfully detect the vowel contrast. Thus, Kuhl concluded that because the infants were able to ignore the irrelevant changes in pitch and talkers' voices, they had demonstrated some capacity for perceptual normalization.

In another study (Kuhl 1983), 6-month-olds were tested on a more difficult vowel contrast, [a] vs [ɔ]. This contrast is particularly hard because productions of these vowels by different talkers often have considerable acoustic overlap. What counts as an [ɔ] for one talker may be an [a] for another talker. There were indications that infants had more difficulty with variability for this vowel contrast than the [a]–[i] contrast. In one of the reported experiments, only four of eight infants exhibited high levels of discrimination; the other four performed at near chance levels. Nevertheless, at least half of the infants were able to reliably detect the [a]–[ɔ] contrast even with the maximum degree of variability present. Thus, by 6 months of age, infants clearly do possess some ability to deal with the kind of variability attributable to different talkers.

More recently, Jusczyk, Pisoni, and Mullennix (1992b) found that infants as young as 2 months old display some capacity for handling variability. In one experiment with the HAS procedure, Jusczyk and his coworkers presented infants with twelve different tokens of each of the words "bug" and "dug" produced by the same talker. Infants heard all twelve tokens of one of these words during the preshift period. During the postshift period, infants in the experimental condition were switched to the tokens of the other word, whereas infants in the control condition continued to hear the same tokens as in the preshift period. The findings indicated that, relative to the control subjects, infants in the experimental condition did detect the phonetic change. Thus, these infants were able to cope with the variation among the tokens produced by the same talker. More impressively, the results of another experiment in this investigation demonstrated that the 2-month-olds are also able to deal with variability among different talkers. This time, Jusczyk and colleagues used recordings of "bug" and "dug" produced by six male and six female talkers. During the preshift phase, one group heard all 12 tokens of one of the two words, and in the postshift phase they heard the tokens of the other word. Infants in this group significantly increased their postshift sucking, indicating that they detected the change from one word to the other despite talker variability. In fact, the postshift performance of this group did not differ significantly from one who had been exposed to only a single token of each word produced by the same talker. These results, showing that 2-month-olds can detect a stop consonant difference in the face of talker variability, parallel Kuhl's findings for 6-month-olds' capacities with respect to vowel differences. Thus, at the very least, the rudiments of perceptual normalization seem to be present at a very early point in infancy.

Nevertheless, as noted above, talker differences are not the only source of variability that infants must cope with in processing speech. Changes in speaking rate can also affect the acoustic characteristics of speech sounds. Phonetic differences that rely on temporal cues might be expected to be most affected by changes in speaking rate. An example of this, mentioned earlier, is the distinction between [ba] and [wa] that appears to depend on the rate of change of the formant transitions (Hillenbrand et al. 1979). At a given speaking rate, the formant transitions will be longer for [w] than for [b]. However, the absolute durations of these formant transitions will change with changes in speaking rate, and therefore whether a particular duration of formant transition will cue the perception of either [b] or [w] will vary, as Miller and Liberman (1979) demonstrated. Eimas and Miller (1980a; Miller and Eimas 1983) demonstrated that 2- to 3-month-olds do perceptually compensate for such changes in speaking rate.

Less is known about infants' abilities to adjust to differences in speech register. Studies demonstrating that infants prefer listening to infant-directed over adult-directed speech (Cooper and Aslin 1990, 1994; Fernald 1985; Fernald and Kuhl 1987; Werker and McLeod 1989) certainly provide evidence that infants are sensitive to changes in speech register. However, to the present time, there have been no investigations of whether changes in speech register might affect infants' recognition of particular sound patterns.

Drawing Conclusions about Infants' Early Capacities

What do the findings reviewed here tell us about the nature of speech perception capacities during the first six months of life? First of all, they indicate that young infants have the capacity to discriminate speech-sound contrasts along a number of different phonetic dimensions, such as voicing, place of articulation, and manner of articulation. Although the bulk of the investigations have focused on speech-sound contrasts involving consonants, there is also evidence that infants discriminate various kinds of vowel contrasts. As noted in our review of these findings, there are very few reports of infants' failures to discriminate contrasts (e.g., Eilers, Wilson, and Moore 1979), and in almost all instances, there is evidence from other sources suggesting that infants can discriminate the contrasts in question (Holmberg et al. 1977; Levitt et al. 1988). Thus, one implication that may be drawn from previous research is that infants already possess the underlying perceptual capacities to discriminate phonetic contrasts from any natural language.

However, there are two caveats regarding this conclusion. The first is that although investigators have endeavored to test a range of different types of phonetic contrasts, the contrasts that they have sampled to date represent only a relatively small portion of the total number of contrasts that exist. The second caveat has to do with the fact that the vast majority of studies have tested infants from English-speaking homes in North America. Thus, it is conceivable (although, in my opinion, unlikely) that a greater sampling of phonetic contrasts, or of infants from different language backgrounds, may uncover some evidence of contrasts that infants are unable to discriminate.

Beyond their capacities for discriminating phonetic contrasts, infants display some other useful speech perception capabilities. For example, they appear to be able to tolerate the kind of acoustic variability that accompanies changes in speaking rate or differences in talkers' voices. In this regard, as in other domains such as the perception of the size or shape of visual objects (Spelke 1994; Spelke et al. 1992), infants appear to demonstrate perceptual constancy for speech sounds. Moreover, the type of constancy that they exhibit is precisely what is required in order to relate speech sound differences to changes in meaning. In other words, infants are able to generalize across the kinds of acoustic variability that is irrelevant for making meaningful distinctions among words.

Can we then assume that these findings, implying that infants exhibit perceptual constancy for speech sounds, demonstrate the existence of specialized linguistic mechanisms? Recall the earlier discussion of attempts to resolve the issue of whether or not the underlying mechanisms are specific to speech processing. Data from studies with nonspeech sounds often reveal parallels to phenomena observed in speech processing. Similarly, parallels tend to arise in the way human and nonhuman species discriminate speech sounds. The situation with respect to perceptual constancy in speech also has parallels in nonspeech processing and also in the way that nonhumans respond to speech. The nonspeech-processing examples come from studies of music perception with infants. These studies show that infants are able to recognize familiar melodies despite changes in key (Demany 1982; Trehub, Bull, and Thorpe 1984; Trehub, Thorpe, and Morrongiello 1985) or in musical tempo (Trehub and Thorpe 1989). Thus, just as infants are able to compensate for changes in talker voice and speaking-rate characteristics, so too are they able to recognize the same melody in a different key or at a different tempo. Finally, there are some indications that nonhuman species, such as dogs (Baru 1975), are able to ignore talker differences in their discriminations of speech contrasts. Again, such findings, by themselves, cannot prove that general auditory capacities, rather than language-specific ones, underlie infants' capacities to compensate for talker differences and speaking-rate changes. But they certainly raise the possibility, contra modularity (Fodor 1983; Liberman and Mattingly 1985), that what we are observing in speech perception at this age is the operation of general auditory capacities in a particular task domain.

What other conclusions might be drawn from the findings reviewed in this chapter? In most of the investigations, the stimuli were designed to contrast with respect to a single phonetic segment. Therefore, there is an inclination to view the infant who successfully discriminates "bug" from "dug" as detecting a difference between the initial phonetic segments [b] and [d]. Although this is an accurate enough description of how the experimenter views the contrast, it may not be a valid description of what infants are doing. In order for infants to discriminate a syllable like "bug" from one like "dug," all they need to do is perceive that the first utterance differs as a whole from the second. In this respect, what is required is no more than what is needed to distinguish Bob's utterance of "bug" from Sally's utterance of "bug." In other words, there is no requirement that the infant attribute the difference between "bug" and "dug" specifically to something that is different about the first phonetic segment in each syllable. We will examine this issue further in chapter 5. For the time being, I note only that the findings indicating that infants discriminate syllables that differ by a single phonetic segment do not necessarily imply that they are perceiving speech in terms of these segments.

category. Broadening leads to a more widely tuned category (e.g., the tendency for English listeners to include prevoiced stops in their voiced category). *Realignment* describes the situation in which the perceptual boundary between two phonetic categories undergoes a shift, as in the differences in the voiced-voiceless boundaries of English and Spanish speakers (Elman, Diehl, and Buchwald 1977; Lisker and Abramson 1967; Williams 1977b). In addition to considering how experience might modify existing perceptual categories, Aslin and Pisoni also speculated that new perceptual contrasts could sometimes be induced from the input. However, the data collected since they originally published their account (1980) do not offer much evidence of induction processes in speech perception.[1]

Although Aslin and Pisoni's framework could account for many of the results that had been reported in infant and adult speech perception at that time, their views were subsequently criticized by MacKain (1982). She pointed out the lack of detailed evidence regarding the nature of the speech input directed to the infant (a situation that is, unfortunately, still true today). She argued that in order for phonetic distinctions to be lost, infants would have to have no exposure to the critical properties in the input and that this was unlikely. However, even in languages without a particular phonetic category (e.g., one for prevoiced stops in English), the infant might occasionally hear tokens produced with these characteristics. Although MacKain's point about the need for better indices of speech input is certainly correct, her view about how much exposure is required for contrasts to be maintained or lost implied that experience with a few instances of a phonetic category might suffice for the category's preservation. However, relatively infrequent encounters with instances of phonetic categories may not actually be sufficient to ensure that phonetic distinctions involving these categories will be maintained during development. Evidence that will be reviewed later in this chapter demonstrates that infants are very attuned to the frequency with which certain sound patterns appear in the input.

Innately Guided Learning

How might infants' initial capacities process speech and promote learning a language? For one thing, these capacities may provide infants with a rough categorization of the information that is available in the input. The capacities allow for some generalization across utterances by different talkers and at different speaking rates. Grouping utterances according to salient acoustic and/or general phonetic dimensions may permit infants to observe the frequencies with which certain kinds of speech sounds appear in the input. Eventually, discrepancies noted among the categories could be a factor that leads to some scrutiny of particular utterance types, resulting in some reorganization of the categories themselves. The point is that any innate or early capacities that infants possess should allow them to begin to make sense of sound patterns in the input and help them to detect any inherent regularities that are present.

In this sense, the initial categorization skills of infants provide a foundation for what might be described as *innately guided learning* (Gould and Marler 1987; Jusczyk 1993a; Jusczyk and Bertoncini 1988; Marler 1991). The basic notion behind innately guided learning is that many organisms are preprogrammed to learn particular things and to learn them in a particular way. One of the classic examples of this process is song learning in birds (Marler and Peters 1981). As Marler (1990) has noted,

> The invocation of innate influences in no way implies a commitment to completely stereotyped, inflexible patterns of development. Birds are innately responsive to certain features of conspecific song, but these abilities are used, not to generate stereotyped and immutable behavior in adulthood, but rather to guide the direction of processes of learning. (p. 565)

An interesting aspect of innately guided learning is the speed at which relatively complex patterns of behavior unfold in the presence of appropriate input during a sensitive period in development. With respect to the matters being considered here, the argument is that infants' initial perceptual capacities put them in a position to pick up the kind of information that is needed to further develop these capacities. In the case of speech perception, this means adapting the categorization of speech sounds to reflect the underlying structural regularities of the input. This need not involve specialized perceptual processing mechanisms for the initial categorization of the speech signal. Rather, what may be central to the process is a bias, or interest, to selectively attend to signals of a certain form. These particular signals would be more likely to undergo further processing and to be encoded into memory. Yet sounds that fall outside this range of salient signals might still be processed by the same set of underlying perceptual mechanisms. Note that even some recent connectionist accounts of developmental change have included the assumption that "initial weights in the learning network ... may themselves have been selected so as to facilitate the acquisition of knowledge in a given domain" (A. Clark 1993, 181).

Is there any indication that infants respond differently to speech sounds than to other kinds of acoustic signals, as might be expected if innately guided learning underlies the development of speech perception? In fact, there are some reports that speech sounds are more likely than nonspeech to elicit interest and sustained attention from infants (Colombo and Bundy 1981; Friedlander and Wisdom 1971; Glenn, Cunningham, and Joyce 1981). For instance, Colombo and Bundy (1981) showed that 4-month-olds display a preference for listening to a female voice over white noise or silence. Glenn et al. (1981) matched a speech and a nonspeech stimulus on dimensions such as pitch, rhythm, and amplitude and found that 9-month-olds preferred listening to a melody sung by an unaccompanied female voice than to a solo musical instrument playing the same piece.

How might a bias to attend to speech originate? One possibility is that prenatal experience plays some role in establishing the bias. It is known that the auditory system in the human fetus begins functioning during the last trimester of gestation (Birnholz and Benacerraf 1983; Krumholz et al. 1985; Lecanuet and Granier-Deferre 1993; Pasman, Näätman, and Alho 1991; Pujol and Uziel 1986; Rubel 1985; Starr et al. 1977). Moreover, because the uterine wall acts to attenuate and to low-pass filter acoustic signals (Armitage, Baldwin, and Vince 1980), the sounds that are best transmitted in utero tend to be ones generated by the infant's own mother. Thus the mother's speech occurs at considerably greater intensity than do sounds in the external environment (Lecanuet and Granier-Deferre 1993). Consequently, the mother's speech patterns, and particularly their prosodic characteristics, are the kinds of acoustic signals that infants are apt to have considerable prenatal experience with. These experiences could very well prime infants to attend preferentially to acoustic signals with the pitch characteristics and rhythmic patterning of human voices.

Of course, it is the case that the dynamic range of speech heard in utero is truncated and attenuated relative to speech outside of the uterus, that is, it is effectively low-pass filtered. However, indications are that newborn infants are able to recognize their own mother's voice regardless of whether or not it is low-pass filtered (DeCasper and Fifer 1980; Spence and DeCasper 1987). Still, the question of what properties an acoustic signal must have in order to be perceived as speech is an interesting one. Why apparently disparate acoustic characteristics cohere and are perceived as speech is not well understood. Human listeners can tolerate conditions that involve considerable distortions and noise masking, and still extract coherent messages from speech (Dirks and Wilson 1969;

Duquesnoy 1983; Gelfand, Piper, and Silman 1986; Liberman and Studdert-Kennedy 1978; Plomp and Mimpen 1979).

One of the more convincing demonstrations of the robustness of the speech processing capacities of adults comes from studies examining the perception of "sinewave speech signals." These signals are produced by synthesizing speech and substituting time-varying sinusoids in place of the first three formants. Such signals lack many of the traditional speech cues, including aperiodic noise and fundamental frequency. Yet, as the insightful studies by Remez and his colleagues have shown, the resulting sounds are still intelligible as speech under certain conditions (Remez et al. 1994; Remez et al. 1987; Remez et al. 1981). Indeed, a recent investigation suggests that even the necessary information for identifying a talker's voice is available in these sinewave analogues of speech (Remez, Fellowes, and Rubin, in press). By manipulating which speech features are required to preserve speech intelligibility, studies such as these may eventually delineate what the essential properties are that listeners, infants and adults alike, use in identifying an acoustic signal as speech. An initial bias to give greater attention to signals with just such properties could be a factor in why infants' capacities for processing speech develop so rapidly during the first year.

The point that I wish to emphasize is that explaining the many changes that occur in speech perception during the course of the first year does not necessarily depend on the existence of dedicated, hard-wired, specialized speech-processing mechanisms. In some domains, innately guided learning may draw on such specialized mechanisms (e.g., the echo-location system of bats). However, in other domains, innately guided learning might be a consequence of general perceptual mechanisms plus some basic biases to attend closely to some kinds of stimuli and to process them more fully than other stimuli. Such biases may be akin to what Edelman (1987; see also Thelen and Smith 1994) refers to as "values." With respect to acoustic signals, the infant may initially be drawn to attending more closely to sounds bearing certain characteristics (perhaps enhanced, in part, because of greater prenatal experience to sounds with these properties). Moreover, because of the contexts in which these sounds are likely to appear (i.e., most typically in social interactions), their processing may be additionally heightened relative to other kinds of acoustic signals.

The developmental data that I will review suggest that infants acquire much information about the structural organization of sound patterns in their native language within a relatively short period of time. Moreover, it appears that the first year of life marks a particularly fertile period for learning about these features of the native language. One reason that infants may be particularly focused on sounds, as opposed to other aspects of language, during this period is because the sound patterns constitute the most perceptibly transparent information in the signal. Furthermore, during this period, there is less information available to infants about other levels of native linguistic organization (e.g., syntax). Consequently, there is less competition for the infant's attention from other levels of linguistic organization. For this reason, the sounds of language and their organization may command a good portion of the infant's attention (although, to be sure, infants are also learning about concepts, hence meanings, during this period). As the infant becomes more skilled in apprehending information about native-language sound patterns, this may, in turn, free up processing resources to attend to other levels of linguistic information conveyed by the speech signal. We will consider these issues further at the end of this chapter, but first let us review the developmental changes that occur in infants' perception of speech in the first year.

Evidence of Changes in Infants' Perception of Nonnative Contrasts

Speech researchers have had a long-standing interest in the way that contrasts from nonnative languages are perceived by infants. The early investigations (e.g., Lasky et al. 1975; Streeter 1976; Trehub 1976) demonstrated that infants have the capacity to discriminate phonetic contrasts that they have never heard before. Yet, data with adults indicated that not only did speakers of different languages differ in where their perceptual boundaries were located (Lisker and Abramson 1967), but they also often experienced difficulty in perceiving nonnative phonetic contrasts (Flege 1989; Logan, Lively, and Pisoni 1989; Miyawaki et al. 1975; Strange and Jenkins 1978). This raised questions about when native language input begins to affect capacities for perceiving phonetic contrasts. In part, because of a widespread belief that a critical period for language learning closes off with the onset of adolescence (Lenneberg 1967), the first studies on loss of sensitivity to nonnative contrasts focused on the period between early childhood and adulthood. Werker and Tees (1983) sought to determine the age at which sensitivity to nonnative contrasts begins to decline by testing groups of English-speaking subjects between 4 years of age and adulthood on two nonnative contrasts from Hindi: a voicing distinction ([tʰ]–[dʰ]) and a place of articulation distinction ([ṭa]–[ta]). A prior investigation by Werker et al. (1981) had tested Hindi-speaking adults, and adults and 7-month-olds from English-speaking homes on these same contrasts. The results of that study indicated that the contrasts were readily discriminated by the Hindi adults and English-learning 7-month-olds. However, English-speaking adults performed significantly worse on the contrasts. Subsequently, when Werker and Tees (1983) conducted their investigation, they found that loss of sensitivity to nonnative contrasts was apparent even in their group of 4-year-olds.

Having narrowed down the possible time interval for developmental change in the perception of the nonnative contrasts to somewhere between 7 months and 4 years of age, Werker and Tees (1984a) next began to test infants of different ages on nonnative contrasts. Infants from English-speaking homes were tested on English ([ba]–[da]), Hindi ([ṭa]–[ta]), and Nthlakapmx[2] ([k'i]–[q'i]) contrasts at three ages: 6 to 8 months, 8 to 10 months, and 10 to 12 months. At 6 to 8 months, the infants discriminated all the contrasts. However, by 8 to 10 months, only some of the infants discriminated the non-English contrasts, and by 10 to 12 months, hardly any gave evidence of discriminating the non-English contrasts. The same pattern of results was also obtained when Werker and Tees tested infants in a longitudinal study. Furthermore, in a subsequent experiment, several Hindi- and Nthlakapmx-learning infants were tested on the contrasts appropriate to their native language. Even at 11 to 12 months, these infants had no difficulty discriminating their native-language contrasts. Thus, the failure of English-learning infants to discriminate these same contrasts is not simply attributable to general decline by all infants at this age to respond to these particular contrasts. Rather, it is the language-learning background of the infants that seems to determine whether they discriminate these contrasts. In particular, what Werker and Tees found could be described as a decline in sensitivity to certain nonnative speech contrasts.

Subsequent research by Werker and Lalonde (1988) with a different, synthetically produced, Hindi contrast ([ɖa]–[da]) also yielded evidence of a decline in sensitivity by English-learning infants between 6 and 12 months of age. In addition, Werker and Tees's (1984a) finding for the decline in sensitivity to the Nthlakapmx contrast was later replicated by Best and McRoberts (1989) using a different test procedure.

Consequently, the results from these studies appear to indicate a systematic decline in sensitivity to nonnative contrasts between 6 and 12 months of age. Werker's initial explanations for why the decline occurred suggested that the English-learning infants were moving from a phonetic classification of speech sounds to a phonemic classification that reflected the organization of the native language they were acquiring (Werker and Lalonde 1988). By this line of reasoning, one might have expected a similar pattern of declining sensitivity (or attenuation in Aslin and Pisoni's terminology) for other distinctions that were not phonemic in the native language. Of course, the decline might occur earlier for some contrasts than for others, depending on which phonemic contrasts were in place. In effect, sensitivity to contrasts that were not meaningful in the language would decline—an example of what developmentalists sometimes refer to as the "use it or lose it" principle (i.e., capacities that do not receive sufficient environmental stimulation deteriorate). However, unlike the case of kittens raised in environments in which they are deprived of some critical aspects of visual stimulation (Blake and Hirsch 1975; Blakemore 1976; Hubel and Wiesel 1970; Mitchell 1981; Packwood and Gordon 1975; Stryker et al. 1978), it was clear that no permanent loss of discriminative capacity was involved. Thus, there is evidence that, with proper training, adults can regain the ability to distinguish nonnative contrasts (Flege 1989; Flege, Takagi, and Mann 1995; Logan et al. 1989). Consequently, the decline more likely has to do with attentional factors than with the atrophy of a sensory substrate (Jusczyk 1985b, 1992; Werker 1991).

New findings from other investigators have indicated that the situation regarding developmental changes in speech perception capacities was more complicated than it first appeared. As a study by Best, McRoberts, and Sithole (1988) first demonstrated, declines in sensitivity do not necessarily occur for all nonnative contrasts. Specifically, Best and colleagues tested English-learning infants on their ability to discriminate a lateral vs. medial click contrast that occurs in Zulu but not in English. They found that infants at all four ages tested (6 to 8, 8 to 10, 10 to 12, and 12 to 14 months) were able to discriminate this contrast. Furthermore, even English-speaking adults had no difficulty in discriminating this contrast. Thus, unlike the contrasts that Werker and her colleagues had investigated, English-listeners show no decline in sensitivity to this nonnative Zulu click contrast.

In a subsequent investigation, Best (1991) reported evidence of both kinds of outcomes in the discrimination of nonnative contrasts. Specifically, she investigated two additional contrasts, an Ethiopian ejective place of articulation distinction and a Zulu lateral fricative voicing distinction. English-learning infants discriminated the place-of-articulation distinction for the Ethiopian ejectives. Moreover, their performance on this contrast did not decline between 8 and 12 months of age. This pattern of results matches those of Best and coworkers for the Zulu click contrasts. However, results for the Zulu lateral fricative voicing distinction were more in line with what had been observed for Hindi and Nthlakapmx contrasts. Namely, discrimination scores of 10- to 12-month-olds for the Zulu lateral fricative voicing distinction were significantly lower than those of 6- to 8-month-olds. English-learning infants between 6 and 12 months did not show any loss of sensitivity to an Ethiopian ejective place of articulation distinction, but they did display a decline in sensitivity to a Zulu lateral fricative distinction.

A more recent investigation has explored Japanese infants' perception of the [r] vs. [l] contrast. Ever since Eimas's original report that 2- to 3-month-old American infants discriminate this distinction, speech researchers have speculated that Japanese infants should also be able to perceive this distinction. Tsushima et al. (1994) finally provided the empirical data to support this contention. They tested infants at 6 to 8 months and 10 to 12 months on a contrast that does occur in Japanese, [wa] vs. [ya], and on a contrast not found in Japanese, [ra] vs. [la]. At the younger age, the infants were able to discriminate both kinds of contrasts, but at the older age, they were unable to discriminate the [ra]-[la] pair. Therefore, their pattern of responding to the nonnative contrasts is the kind showing a decline in sensitivity toward the end of the first year. Best (1995) has also reported that English-learning infants' sensitivity to a number of Zulu contrasts (e.g., plosive vs. implosive; lateral fricative distinctions; velar voiceless aspirated vs. velar ejective) undergoes a similar decline between 6 to 8 months and 10 to 12 months. However, in some instances (i.e., the lateral fricative distinction and the velar voiceless aspirated vs. velar ejective contrast), English-speaking adults' abilities to discriminate these pairs remained high.

Developmental Changes in the Perception of Vowels
Evidence has recently been reported that changes in sensitivity to nonnative distinctions also occur for contrasts between vowels. One indication of changes in vowel perception comes from the investigations of Kuhl and her coworkers (Grieser and Kuhl 1989; Kuhl 1991; Kuhl et al. 1992). Kuhl has suggested that native language input may have an impact on the nature of infants' vowel categories by 6 months of age. In partic-

ular, she has claimed that vowel categories are organized around proto-typical instances from native language input by 6 months. Grieser and Kuhl (1989) exposed groups of American infants to either a prototypical instance or an atypical instance of the English vowel [i] (as judged by adults). The particular instance served as a background stimulus. Novel instances from the category were used as test stimuli. Kuhl measured infants' discrimination of the novel instances from the familiar background stimulus. In effect, the procedure measures infants' ability to generalize from the background stimulus to novel stimuli. When a prototypical instance served as the background stimulus, infants generalized to a significantly larger number of novel instances (i.e., they were less likely to detect a change to one of these). Kuhl (1991) interpreted these findings as an indication that prototypical instances are "perceptual magnets" that shorten perceptual distances between the center and edges of the vowel category (but see Lively and Pisoni 1993; Sussman and Lauckner-Morano 1995). More recently, Kuhl et al. (1992) implicated the perceptual magnet effect as a factor in the decline in sensitivity that infants show for nonnative vowel contrasts (also see Kuhl 1993 for further discussion of this point). In particular, Kuhl and her colleagues tested American and Swedish infants on two vowel prototypes—the English [i] and the Swedish [y]. Infants showed the "perceptual magnet" effect only for their own native language vowel. Swedish infants demonstrated a magnet effect for [y], but not for [i], whereas American infants showed the reverse pattern. The suggestion is that experience with a range of native-language tokens helps to organize infants' vowel space to reflect the categories that are used in that language.

Polka and Werker (1994) have also investigated English-learning infants' perception of two German vowel contrasts: [ʏ]–[ʊ] (a lax high front-rounded vs. a lax high back-rounded vowel) and [y]–[u] (a tense high front-rounded vs. a tense high back-rounded vowel). Previous work by Polka (1991) had shown that such contrasts are difficult for native English speakers to discriminate. When English-learning 10 to 12-month-olds were tested on these contrasts, they gave no evidence of discriminating them. This is consistent with what had been reported for those nonnative consonants that have been shown to undergo a decline. However, unlike the results reported for consonantal contrasts, 6- to 8-month-olds tested on these vowel contrasts failed to discriminate them. Nevertheless, a younger group of infants, 4 to 6 months old, did discriminate these same contrasts.

The overall pattern of results—that is, sensitivity to a nonnative contrast followed by a decline in sensitivity—is preserved for vowel contrasts, but the studies to date suggest that any changes in sensitivity to nonnative language vowels apparently happen at a younger age than for consonants. One possible reason that changes in sensitivity to vowels may occur earlier has to do with their relative prominence in the speech stream. Vowels tend to be longer and louder than consonants, and they carry prosodic as well as phonetic information. For these reasons, they may be more likely than consonants to initially attract infants' attention.

Accounting for Changes in Sensitivity to Phonetic Contrasts
In reviewing the findings considered to this point, several things are apparent. First, there is evidence of a decline in sensitivity to nonnative speech contrasts during the first year. Second, sensitivity does not decline uniformly to all nonnative contrasts. Some contrasts that do not appear in native language input continue to be perceived, and some types of contrasts, notably those having to do with vowels, appear to undergo an earlier decline in sensitivity. How can we account for these facts? Clearly, an explanation that attributes the loss simply to a changeover from phonetic to phonemic perception will not suffice because it provides no rationale for why some nonnative contrasts are preserved when others disappear. The current alternative to this position is that whether or not a nonnative contrast undergoes a decline has to do with the specific way the nonnative contrast maps onto the kinds of phonemic distinctions made in the native language (Best 1995; Eimas 1991; Flege 1995; Werker 1991).[3] The most detailed account offered to explain developmental changes in sensitivity to nonnative phonetic contrasts is the Perceptual Assimilation Model (Best 1993, 1995). The basic premise behind the model is that nonnative contrasts that map onto two different native-language categories or to no native-language categories will be easy to discriminate, whereas those distinctions that map to a single phonemic category will be most apt to undergo a decline in discriminability. Although the model can account for many of the results that have been previously reported, there are some findings from Best's own investigations (Best 1995) that do not fit the predictions of the model. This suggests that there may be other factors at work beyond how the nonnative sounds map onto the categories used by in the native language. Just what these factors might be has yet to be determined.

Although we do not yet have a fully satisfactory explanation for why declines in sensitivity occur, the results of studies in this area have provided much evidence that developmental changes in infants' speech-processing capacities do occur during the first year. Hence, in line with what might be expected of innately guided learning, infants appear to be adapting rapidly to the characteristics of the input to which they are exposed. So far, we have discussed this notion in terms of a decline in sensitivity to information that does not appear often in the input. In the next section, I consider evidence that infants are learning about the structural organization that does appear in native-language utterances.

Learning about the Sound Patterns of the Native Language

As we have seen, young infants have the perceptual capacity to discriminate many sorts of differences in the utterances that they hear. This provides them with a way of distinguishing one utterance from another. However, acquiring a language requires learning which kinds of distinctions among different utterances are important for communicating successfully and which ones are not. The evidence reviewed in the previous section indicates that infants are learning something about which distinctions are not important for communication in their native language. This seems to imply that they might also be simultaneously learning something about those distinctions that *are* important in the language. Such information would help the learner to know when one utterance type really differs in a meaningful way from another. Yet, this information is still only a part of what a fluent speaker-hearer of a language needs to know in order to communicate successfully.

Words are not isolated from one another in fluent speech. Consequently, part of what must be acquired has to do with learning how word boundaries are marked in the language. Learning what features mark word boundaries in utterances from a particular language seems to involve discovering something about the way sounds can be ordered—phonetically and prosodically—within words in the language. Words from other languages will frequently differ with respect to these properties. Hence, one of the things that would be useful for infants to learn is what sound properties are characteristic of utterances in their native language.

Distinguishing Native from Nonnative Language Utterances

There are indications that from a very early age, infants have at least some ability to recognize global characteristics of utterances in their native language—that is, prosodic features relating to the intonational and rhythmic properties of sentences and longer strings of speech. In particular, they appear to distinguish utterances in their native language from those in a foreign language—a useful ability for someone growing up in a multilingual environment. Mehler et al. (1988) first explored this issue in a set of investigations that involved testing newborn infants in France and 2-month-olds in the United States. Specifically, they examined infants' responses to utterances in two different languages that were produced by bilingual talkers. In one experiment, the sucking rates of French newborns were recorded while they heard a set of utterances in either French or Russian produced by a single bilingual talker. Half of the infants then heard a new set of utterances by the same talker in either the same language or the other language. The French newborns showed an interesting effect: they sucked at higher rates when listening to French utterances than to Russian utterances, an indication that they discriminated speech from the two languages. In another experiment, Mehler and coworkers low-pass filtered their stimuli at 400 Hertz. Low-pass filtering at this frequency level prevents the recognition of phonetic, but not prosodic, characteristics of speech. French newborns listening to these stimuli showed comparable results to the infants who had heard the unfiltered utterances. Hence, Mehler and colleagues concluded that the information in the prosody of the utterances provided a sufficient basis for the infants to distinguish those of one language from the other. Indeed, one possibility here is that infants favor utterances in their mother's native language because of their prenatal experience in hearing such utterances.

Some empirical support for this notion came from the results of other experiments that Mehler and coworkers carried out. For instance, in contrast to French newborns, a group of newborns from parents whose native language was something other than French gave no evidence of distinguishing the French utterances from the Russian ones. Similarly, when French newborns were tested on utterances in English and Italian from a bilingual talker, they did not discriminate them. By comparison, a group of American 2-month-olds did discriminate the English and Italian utterances, but not the French and Russian utterances. Moreover, the American 2-month-olds also discriminated low-pass-filtered versions of the English and Italian utterances, suggesting once again that prosodic cues provided a sufficient basis for distinguishing the utterances in the two languages.

Mehler and colleagues concluded that within a few days of their birth, infants have an ability to distinguish utterances in their mother's native language from those of another language. Subsequent investigations have confirmed their findings. For example, Bahrick and Pickens (1988) used an audiovisual procedure with 5-month-old Spanish and American infants and found that they discriminated utterances in Spanish from ones in English. More recently, Moon, Cooper, and Fifer (1993) demonstrated a preference for native-language utterances in 2-day-olds listening to English and Spanish utterances. Therefore, as the results of these investigations show, even newborn infants have some ability to recognize the global characteristics of native-language utterances.

One way infants may distinguish utterances in the native language from those in a nonnative language is by relying on information about prosodic features. The fact that the same pattern of results occurs for low-pass-filtered speech supports this contention. Because the uterine wall acts as a low-pass filter, the information about speech that is apt to be best transmitted prenatally is that having to do with prosodic features. Moreover, there is other information that suggests that newborns may be particularly sensitive to prosodic features of language such as its rhythmic structure. Mehler and his colleagues (Bertoncini 1993; Mehler et al. 1996) have studied how infants respond to possible units of rhythmic organization in languages. They have reported evidence that French 4-day-olds are unable to distinguish changes in Japanese stimuli based on the mora—the rhythmic unit around which Japanese utterances are organized. More specifically, the infants did not discriminate a change from 2 morae to 3 morae, even though infants at this age were able to distinguish similar changes involving syllables—the elementary units of rhythmic organization in French utterances (Bijeljac-Babic, Bertoncini, and Mehler 1993). These findings suggest that infants identify the key properties of the rhythmic organization of their native language either prenatally or in the first few days of life. It bears mention that although infants may be more biased to listen more attentively to native-language utterances at a very early point, the bias is likely to be a relatively weak one that can be reset depending on the infant's experience. Hence, infants who are orphaned and raised in another language environment do not appear to have any difficulty in acquiring that language, even though it differs from their mother's native language.

Developing Sensitivity to Phonetic and Phonotactic Characteristics of the Native Language
Given that infants may respond to the global properties of native-language utterances soon after birth, when do they begin to pick up more

specific properties about how sound patterns are structured within the language? Jusczyk (1993a) wondered when infants might have some ability to detect whether a particular word had the appropriate sound properties to mark it as belonging to the native, rather than to a nonnative, language. There are at least three sources of information that could help in making a decision of this sort. First, the word must only include phonetic segments that the native language uses in forming words. For instance, the appearance of an implosive stop in an utterance should be a sufficient indication that this could not be a native English word. Second, the sequential ordering of segments in the word must reflect the phonotactics of the native language. Hence, beginning a word with two stop consonants in a row, such as in the Polish word "kto," is also an indication that the item is not a native English word. Third, the prosodic characteristics of the word must be consistent with what is permitted in the native language. The kind of alternating stress pattern of strong and weak syllables that is characteristic of English words is not a permissible feature of French words.

To determine when infants exhibit sensitivity to these features of native-language words, Jusczyk and his coworkers conducted a cross-linguistic investigation with American and Dutch infants. They presented infants with lists of unfamiliar, low-frequency words produced by a bilingual talker. Half of the lists contained words from the language spoken in the infant's home; the other half contained words from another language. In one set of experiments, the test words came from either English or Dutch. Jusczyk and colleagues chose these two languages because they have very similar prosodic characteristics (Crystal and House 1988; Ladefoged 1975; Reitveld 1988; Reitveld and Koopmans-van Beinum 1987). Consequently, this allowed the investigations to focus on whether infants could use phonetic and phonotactic information to identify native from nonnative words. The lists from each language contained items that were impermissible in the other language according to its phonetic and phonotactic structure. For example, the [r] in English words is very different from the [r] found in Dutch words. Whereas English allows [d] to occur in syllable-final position, Dutch does not. Similarly, Dutch allows phonetic sequences like [kn] or [zw] to begin syllables, English does not.

American 9-month-olds tested on these lists of words listened significantly longer to the English than to the Dutch words. By comparison, American 6-month-olds showed no preference for lists of either type. In another experiment, both American and Dutch 9-month-olds were tested on new lists of Dutch and English words. This time, Jusczyk and co-workers chose their words to include only phonetic segments that were permissible in words in both languages. The only differences among the words were phonotactic ones. Some sequences of phonetic segments in the English words were not permitted in Dutch, and vice versa. When the lists were presented to the infants, the American infants listened significantly longer to the English words and the Dutch infants listened longer to the Dutch words. That infants were distinguishing the words primarily on the basis of phonetic and phonotactic features (and not some remaining pro-sodic differences) is indicated by the fact that when the materials were low-pass filtered, no preference was observed for the native-language words. Hence, at some time between 6 and 9 months of age, infants have learned sufficient information about the phonetic and phonotactic prop-erties of the native language to distinguish words in that language from words in another language.

One interesting aspect of these results with native- and foreign-language words is the fact that infants appear to be developing sensitivity to the structural regularities of sound patterns in their native language, at a point well before there are any indications of significant vocabulary develop-ment in the native language. For example, previous investigations of the growth of word-comprehension skills generally cite the period between 8 and 10 months of age as the point when infants show evidence of com-prehending their first words (Benedict 1979; Huttenlocher 1974). Con-sequently, it does not appear that infants' knowledge of native-language phonetic and phonotactic patterns arises from extracting this information from large numbers of known words. Of course, it is possible that sensi-tivity to phonotactic and phonetic properties arise because infants are attentive to the way that sounds pattern at the beginnings and ends of longer utterance units (see Brent et al., in press, for a suggestion along these lines). Whatever the reason, infants appear to be developing sen-sitivity to regularly occurring phonotactic patterns that extends well beyond what is needed to distinguish between native and nonnative lan-guage items.

Friederici and Wessels (1993) found that Dutch 9-month-olds show sensitivity to phonotactically legal onset and offset clusters in Dutch words. Not only did the infants listen significantly longer to phonotacti-cally legal Dutch sequences for words occurring in isolation, but they also, under some circumstances, listened longer to sequences of syllables con-taining phonotactically legal clusters than to ones with phonotactically illegal clusters. The latter finding suggests that they might eventually be able to draw on information about phonotactic sequences to help in segmenting words from the speech stream. For example, in fluent speech, when phonetic strings occur that violate the phonotactics of the language, it might be an indication that these strings include a word boundary (which would break the string at a point to yield phonotactically legal sequences on either side of the word boundary).

Another recent investigation suggests that infants not only distinguish legal and illegal sequences in the native language, but they also are attuned to the frequency with which legal phonotactic sequences occur in words in the language. Jusczyk, Luce, and Charles-Luce (1994) presented American infants with different lists of monosyllables that contained phonetic sequences that were all phonotactically permissible in English words. However, half of the lists contained monosyllables with sequences of phonetic segments that occur frequently in English words. The other half of the lists were composed of monosyllables with sequences of phonetic segments that occur less frequently inside English words. For example, the sequence of phonetic segments in a syllable like [čʌn] (or "chun") occurs at a much higher frequency than the one in a syllable like [čɚg] (or "cherg"). Nine-month-olds, but not 6-month-olds, listened significantly longer to the lists with high-frequency phonotactic sequences. This finding that 9-month-olds are attentive to the frequency with which certain phonotactic sequences occur within native-language utterances was recently replicated in an experiment that employed bisyllabic items (Jusczyk, Gerken, and Turk, in preparation). In particular, Jusczyk and coworkers found that when word stress is held constant, infants exhibit preferences for items with more frequently occurring phonotactic sequences. Taken together, the results of these last two investigations suggest that not only are infants between 6 and 9 months of age learning about the phonotactic structure of native-language sound patterns, but that they are remarkably sensitive to how these patterns are distributed in the input. Moreover, they appear to acquire this information about the characteristics of native-language sound patterns within a relatively short period of time. This is certainly consistent with the innately guided learning view that infants are biased to learn particular things about language and to learn these things in particular ways.

Learning about the Prosodic Organization of the Native Language
To this point, we have largely focused on the information that infants pick up about the phonetic and phonotactic properties of their native

language. However, infants at this age also are beginning to learn about the prosodic organization of utterances in their native language. For instance, in their investigation, Jusczyk et al. (1993) also examined whether infants have learned to identify native language words on the basis of their prosodic characteristics. For this purpose, they used lists of English and Norwegian words produced by a bilingual talker. In contrast to English, pitch often rises on the final syllable of Norwegian words (Haugen and Joos 1972). Also, unlike English words, pitch is higher in Norwegian for unstressed than for stressed syllables (Peters, in press). Norwegian and English also differ in terms of their phonetic and phonotactic characteristics. For example, Norwegian contains vowels such as [y] and [ø] that do not appear in English words, and English has segments such as [θ] and [w] that are not found in Norwegian. However, the main focus of these particular studies had to do with the prosodic differences that exist between English and Norwegian words. This time, the results indicated that even at 6 months of age, the American infants were able to distinguish the English from the Norwegian words (i.e., they listened significantly longer to the English words). Furthermore, the preference for the English word lists was maintained when the phonetic and phonotactic cues were disrupted through low-pass filtering. Therefore, the results of these experiments indicate that, by 6 months of age, English-learning infants have learned something about the prosodic characteristics of words in their native language.

Jusczyk, Cutler, and Redanz (1993) went a step further by investigating infants' sensitivity to differences in the kinds of prosodic patterns that appear in native-language words. In particular, they found that English-learning infants listen longer to words that observe the predominant stress patterns of native-language words. The inspiration for this study was a finding reported by Cutler and Carter (1987). In analyzing a large corpus of spoken English utterances, Cutler and Carter determined that most strong syllables (i.e., syllables with a nonreduced vowel sound) begin new words. In fact, a very high proportion of words are either stressed monosyllables (i.e., they are strong syllables) or else begin with a stressed syllable. Moreover, English-speaking adults appear to distinguish strong from weak syllables (ones that contain a reduced vowel) in segmenting utterances: they assume that word boundaries occur before strong but not before weak syllables. On this basis, Cutler and her colleagues (Cutler and Butterfield 1992; Cutler and Norris 1988) have argued that the predominant stress pattern of English words as strong/weak (or trochaic).

Jusczyk, Cutler, and Redanz (1993) investigated whether English-learning infants display sensitivity to this property of their native-language words. They presented American infants with lists of bisyllabic English words that either followed (i.e., strong/weak) or did not follow (i.e., weak/strong) the predominant stress patterns in the language. Half of the lists were composed of bisyllables with strong/weak patterns (e.g., "loony," "pliant," etc.) and the other half consisted of bisyllables with weak/strong patterns (e.g., "abloom," "comply," etc.). Although 6-month-olds showed no difference in listening times to either type of list, 9-month-olds listened significantly longer to the lists with strong/weak stress patterns. Moreover, even when the lists were low-pass filtered, 9-month-olds listened significantly longer to the strong/weak patterns, suggesting that they were not simply responding to phonetic or phonotactic properties. Instead, it appears that American infants are also developing sensitivity to the predominant stress patterns of English words at some time between 6 and 9 months of age.

These findings of English-learning 9-month-olds' preferences for predominant word-stress patterns were recently replicated and extended. Turk, Jusczyk, and Gerken (1995) investigated the possible bases for infants' perception of syllable stress in English words. Specifically, they examined whether infants' perception of syllable stress depends on the presence of so-called *heavy syllables*. A syllable is considered heavy if it is closed (i.e., CVC) or if it is open (i.e., CV) but contains a tense vowel. In some languages, only heavy syllables can receive stress. Although in most cases, stress in English is associated with heavy syllables, it can also occur on light syllables such as the first one in "beckon." Turk and colleagues found that when 9-month-old English-learning infants were presented with lists of items of the latter type, they still demonstrated the preference for strong/weak patterns over weak/strong ones. Hence, the findings indicate that when they show preferences for words with strong/weak patterns, English-learning infants are not simply relying on syllable weight to indicate stress placement in these words.

Hence, at some point during the latter half of the first year, infants begin to display sensitivity to native-language sound patterns. It is probably significant that they begin to display sensitivity to such patterns around the time when sensitivity to certain nonnative speech contrasts begins to decline. Indeed, it appears that the two processes may be two sides of the same coin. So, as infants begin to attend more closely to, and perhaps even seek out, recurring patterns in native-language input, they may give less attention to the kinds of acoustic properties (and distinctions among these) that appear much less frequently. Thus, the decline in sensitivity to nonnative contrasts could be, in part, a result of trying to discover the regularities that hold among native-language utterances. Just why sensitivity to certain nonnative contrasts declines, but is preserved for others, is still not clear. However, which ones are spared and which are lost may be tied in some way to one of the purposes of developing sensitivity to native-language sound patterns—namely, the segmentation and recognition of words in fluent speech. Findings considered in the next section indicate that word segmentation skills develop considerably during the latter half of the first year.

Beginning to Segment and Recognize Words in Fluent Speech

The discovery that during their first year infants begin to learn about the segmental and suprasegmental organization of their native language has some interesting implications for understanding the development of speech segmentation skills. This is because both segmental and suprasegmental properties have been hypothesized to play a role in segmenting words in fluent speech. For example, knowledge of where certain types of phonotactic sequences are likely to appear in utterances could be a cue to word boundaries. Consider how this might work for English. If a listener is looking to segment a sequence like [bɪgdɔg] ("big dog"), then the phonotactics of English dictate that there can be a word boundary between [g] and [d], but not between [ɪ] and [g] (because this would leave [gd] as the onset of a syllable). Note that this is the point raised earlier in conjunction with the results of Friederici and Wessels (1993).

Another potential cue to word boundaries is one that has to do with the typical contexts in which variants (or allophones) of the same phoneme appear (Bolinger and Gerstman 1957; Lehiste 1960). Church (1987) has pointed out that the variant of [t] that begins words in English such as "tap," (i.e., [tʰ]), is not the same as the ones found in other positions of English words, such as the [t]s in "stop" and "pat." Therefore, a listener sensitive to this property of English words could conceivably use this information in deciding whether a word boundary has occurred or not. That is, if a listener hears a sequence such as [naistʰap], the presence of [tʰ] indicates that there must be a boundary before it (and therefore the sequence is "nice top" rather than "nice stop").

Finally, suprasegmental properties have also been hypothesized to facilitate word segmentation in some languages. Recall Cutler and Carter's (1987) finding that a high proportion of words in English conversational speech begin with strong syllables. Cutler and her colleagues (Cutler 1990; Cutler 1994; Cutler and Butterfield 1992; Cutler and Norris 1988) have suggested that English listeners can make a first pass at segmenting fluent speech into words by assuming that each strong syllable initiates a new word onset. Hereafter, I will refer to this view as the *metrical segmentation strategy*. Note that a language need not have word-initial stress in order to make use of some form of a prosodically based word segmentation strategy. Listeners might also be able to take advantage of regular stress marking of words, even if primary stress typically falls on another syllable such as the antepenultimate syllable (as in Polish) or the final syllable (as in Quiché Mayan). Discovering what sort of prosodic marking of word boundaries that ones's native language does or does not provide would certainly be useful in developing effective word segmentation strategies.

What abilities must infants possess to use any of these potential cues to word boundaries in fluent speech? First, they would have to be sensitive to the distinctions that mark the presence and absence of word boundaries. Thus, in the case of the allophonic variants of [t], they have to be able to discriminate [tʰ] from [t]. Second, they would have to know something about how these cues are distributed in the input (i.e., the contexts in which they can and cannot appear). Third, they would have to be able to detect and use these cues on line when processing fluent speech.

Investigations of Infants' Sensitivity to Potential Word-Boundary Cues

There are findings that are relevant to the issue of whether infants are sensitive to the kinds of distinctions that mark the presence or absence of word boundaries. With respect to possible prosodic markers of word boundaries, Christophe et al. (1994) found that French newborns discriminate pairs of disyllabic stimuli that either contain or do not contain a word boundary. The pairs of stimuli contained the same phonetic elements (e.g., [mati] from "panora<u>ma ty</u>pique" vs. [mati] from "mathe<u>mati</u>cian") but were distinguished primarily in terms of prosodic differences (i.e., stress and accent). Recall, as well, that Jusczyk, Cutler, and Redanz (1993; see also Turk et al. 1995) demonstrated that by 9 months, American infants listen longer to words with the types of patterns (i.e., strong/weak) that would favor a metrical segmentation strategy. Similarly, I have already reviewed findings showing that infants are sensitive to the kinds of phonotactic differences that potentially signal word boundaries. Recall that Friederici and Wessels (1993) found that Dutch 9-month-olds distinguish between phonotactically legal and illegal clusters at the beginnings of words. Finally, there are even some indications that infants are able to distinguish between the kinds of allophonic variants that could serve to mark word boundaries. Hohne and Jusczyk (1994) presented 2-month-olds with pairs such as "nitrate" and "night rate." The allophones of [t] and [r] for these items differ in ways that are consistent with the presence (for "night rate") or absence (for "nitrate") of a word boundary. Specifically, in "nitrate," the [t] is retroflexed and the [r] is devoiced—an indication that these are word-internal segments. The infants were able to distinguish the items on the basis of these allophonic differences, even when prosodic differences between the words were controlled via cross-splicing techniques.

The studies just mentioned indicate that infants in their first year have the prerequisite capacities to detect the kinds of distinctions that could be used in marking word boundaries. Whether they do use these kinds of distinctions to segment words in the context of fluent speech is another matter. It is only recently that speech researchers have begun to investigate word segmentation processes in infants. Still, even with the limited data that are available, it is apparent that infants begin to segment words from fluent speech at some point during the second half of their first year.

Evidence that Prosody and Distributional Cues affect Infants' Grouping of Syllable Sequences

Goodsitt, Morgan, and Kuhl (1993) investigated factors that might help to separate and cluster elements within an utterance. Their method built upon previous research with the conditioned headturn procedure that showed that $6\frac{1}{2}$-month-old infants can discriminate a speech contrast embedded in a three-syllable string (Goodsitt et al. 1984). Goodsitt et al. (1993) first trained 7-month-olds to discriminate the isolated syllables [ti] and [de]. When training was completed, the target syllables were combined with two other syllables to create a three-syllable string. These three-syllable strings were of three types. In invariant order strings, the ordering of the two nontarget syllables [ko] and [ga] was a fixed sequence (e.g., [koga]), although the ordering of the target syllable relative to them varied (sometimes before [tikoga], sometimes after [kogati]). In variable order strings, the two nontarget syllables could occur in either order (e.g., [kogati] and [gakoti] were both permitted). Finally, in redundant strings only one of the non-target syllables was used, and it was repeated twice in a row (e.g., [kokoti]). The general finding was that performance was best with the invariant order strings—that is, the infants were more apt to detect a change from [ti] to [de] with these strings than they were with either the variable-order or redundant-order strings. This finding held regardless whether the syllables were produced with varying intonation or as monotones.

Goodsitt and coworkers attributed the superior performance with their invariant order strings to the fact that it was easier to group the nontarget stimuli into a single cluster and, thus, to separate them from the target syllable. Their argument was that the two nontarget syllables cohered as a unit because they always occurred in the same order, whereas the ordering of the target syllable relative to them varied (sometimes before, sometimes after). Hence, the distributional properties of the input strings favored segmenting them as a two-syllable unit and a monosyllabic unit. In principle, the redundant strings should have behaved in the same fashion, but they did not. Goodsitt and colleagues suggested that the fact that the two redundant syllables were acoustically identical and lacked coarticulatory cues may have made infants less likely to group them as a unit.

Morgan (1994) extended this line of investigation by examining whether prosodic features (in this case, rhythmic properties) might also facilitate grouping and segmenting information in the input. In one experiment, he used a conditioned headturn procedure with 8-month-olds and found that rhythmic cues were effective in facilitating the grouping of the nontarget syllables into a unit. The most effective situation for grouping the nontarget syllables proved to be one that combined a trochaic rhythmic pattern with the distributional cues afforded by an invariant syllable order. However, even when the syllables occurred in a variable order (i.e., without accompanying distributional cues), the presence of a trochaic pattern appeared to induce some clustering (in one of the two test sessions). Converging evidence for the effectiveness of rhythmic properties in grouping the syllables was obtained with a second measure that involved the detection of noises superimposed on the stimulus sequences. Specifically, 8-month-olds were less likely to detect the noise when it occurred between the syllables that were rhythmically clustered and invariantly ordered than they were to detect it between syllables that were not clustered together. In line with adult studies involving click detection (Abrams and Bever 1969; Ladefoged and Broadbent 1960), the interpretation of this result is that the noises are harder to perceive in syllables that are clustered together because perceptual units resist interruption. Hence, one implication is that rhythmic and distributional properties of the input influence how infants segment speech.

Morgan and his colleagues have conducted additional investigations of the possible influences of rhythmic properties on infants' grouping of information in the input. In a series of studies with 9-month-olds, Morgan and Saffran (1995) extended the range of rhythmic properties investigated by using both iambic (weak/strong) and trochaic (strong/weak) patterns. A consistent pattern of results emerged with both the conditioned-headturn and click-detection paradigms. Performance on these tasks by 9-month-olds was best for sequences with consistent rhythmic patterns and a fixed syllable order. This finding suggests that infants at this age integrate information about both rhythmic and distributional properties. By comparison, 6-month-old infants appeared to respond primarily to consistent rhythmic orders, regardless of whether the syllables occurred in a fixed sequence or not. Hence, the behavior of the younger infants depended primarily on the presence or absence of rhythmic cues to grouping.

Interestingly enough, there was no indication that these English-learning infants, at either age, performed differently with strong/weak versus weak/strong patterns. Morgan and Saffran suggested that the nature of their test procedure may have worked to neutralize any potential processing advantages that there are for strong/weak patterns. Specifically, their procedures repeatedly present the same small set of strings to infants. Any advantage for trochaic patterns might be more evident for relatively unexpected or unfamiliarized strings.

Some empirical support for their view comes from another study that Morgan (in press) conducted with 6- and 9-month-old infants. Although both age groups perceived familiar bisyllables in a similar fashion (i.e., with no differences for iambic versus trochaic rhythmic patterns), 9-month-olds perceived novel bisyllables as cohesive only when they manifested a trochaic rhythmic pattern. As Morgan noted, these findings for the 9-month-olds are consistent with the use and development of a metrical segmentation strategy for parsing words from fluent speech.

Echols and her colleagues (Echols, Crowhurst, and Childers, in press) have also explored whether English-learning infants are better able to extract trochaic sequences than iambic ones in connected speech. They used a version of the headturn preference paradigm to present infants with sequences of three syllables. In one experiment, 7- and 9-month-olds were trained on two different weak-strong-weak sequences (e.g., [bəgúdi] and [dəbígə]). During the test phase, they were presented with two different variants of each string. One variant included a pause prior to the stressed syllable, yielding a trochaic pattern (after the pause) as a coherent unit (e.g., [bə gúdi]). The other variant included a pause after the stress syllable, resulting in an iambic pattern (before the pause) as a coherent unit (e.g., [dəbí gə]). The 9-month-olds, but not the 7-month-olds, had significantly higher listening times for the trochaic patterns. Echols and coworkers interpreted this finding as an indication that the older infants may have recognized that trochaic sequences tend to cohere in English (consistent with the results of Morgan, in press). They also conducted a follow-up study to explore whether 9-month-olds can more easily segment trochaic sequences than iambic ones from longer speech sequences. This time infants were familiarized with four-syllable sequences that included embedded trochaic and iambic sequences (e.g., [mústər pótnəd] and [pəméɪ dər son]. During the test phase, the infants were presented with the extracted trochaic and iambic sequences (e.g., [mústər] and [pəméɪ]) along with novel trochaic and iambic distracters (e.g., [lúkə] and [nədwót]). The infants displayed a significant preference for the trochaic distracters over the iambic ones. Echols and coworkers viewed this finding as an indication that 9-month-olds are more likely to extract trochaic sequences than iambic ones from longer strings of speech.[4]

In summary, the findings from these investigations indicate that not only do English-learning infants show some ability to group syllable sequences and extract them from longer strings of speech, but they also do so more readily for trochaic than for iambic sequences (i.e., ones that are consistent with the predominant stress pattern of English words).

Investigations of Infants' Abilities to Detect Words in Fluent Speech

The investigations just discussed provide some indications of how rhythmic and distributional properties can lead infants to group speech input into different clusters. Still, the infants tested in these studies did not have to deal with all the complexities that are presented by a continually changing stream of fluent speech. If an infant has learned to recognize the sound patterns of some words (e.g., "juice," "baby," "daddy") when they are produced as isolated utterances, will the infant still be able to recognize these words when they are embedded in a sentential context?

Jusczyk and Aslin (1995) attempted to answer this question. They used the headturn preference paradigm to familiarize infants with a pair of words, and then they tested whether infants listened longer to passages with sentences that included these familiarized words than to passages without these words. Four different monosyllabic words were used— "feet," "cup," "dog," and "bike." At the start of each experimental session, $7\frac{1}{2}$-month-olds were familiarized with two of the words on alternating trials until they accumulated 30 seconds of listening time to each word. Half of the infants were familiarized with "cup" and "dog" and the other half with "feet" and "bike." During the test phase, four different passages, each consisting of six sentences, were played for the infants. For a given passage, the same test word appeared in all six sentences (although in different positions within each sentence). Two of the passages contained the words heard in the familiarization period, and the other two contained the other (i.e., not previously heard) test words. Infants listened significantly longer to the passages containing the familiar test words.

Moreover, the results of a questionnaire in which parents rated the likelihood that their infants already "knew" any of the test words provided no indication that prior knowledge of the words had any significant bearing on the results. Rather, it appears that the exposure to the target words in isolation made it more likely that infants would attend to the sentences including these words. Finally, information from acoustical analyses and from judgments by adult raters indicated that in only about 12 percent of the cases was the target word the most-stressed word in a given sentence. In fact, for a number of the sentences, the target word was judged to be only the fourth or fifth most prominent word in the sentence. Hence, $7\frac{1}{2}$-month-olds' success in finding the target did not appear to depend on its prominence in the sentence. Interestingly enough, when 6-month-olds were tested in the same task, they showed no evidence of detecting the familiar words in the sentential contexts. This suggests that word-segmentation skills that are used in fluent speech perception may begin some time between 6 and $7\frac{1}{2}$ months of age.

It is impressive that infants as young as $7\frac{1}{2}$ months old can detect a word, first heard or learned in isolation, when it later occurs in a sentential context. However, there is good reason to believe that language learners only acquire a relatively small proportion of words in this way. Woodward and Aslin (1990) found that even when mothers were explicitly instructed to teach their children new words, only about 20 percent of the new words were ever presented in isolation. Hence, many words that infants learn are likely to be heard only in sentential contexts. Given the tendency of fluent speakers to coarticulate words (i.e., run one word into another), learning to recognize new words from sentential contexts would appear to be more difficult than learning the same words presented in isolation.

To examine the extent to which infants can extract new words from sentential contexts, Jusczyk and Aslin conducted another experiment in which $7\frac{1}{2}$-month-olds were first exposed to fluent speech passages containing two target words and then tested on repetitions of isolated words. The results were similar to their first experiment; namely, infants listened longer to isolated words that had previously been heard embedded in passages. This suggests that during the familiarization period, the infants were able to extract the target words, which were repeated in the different sentences, from their surrounding sentential contexts. Thus, they could learn to recognize the sound patterns of these new words, even when these words were presented only in complete sentences. Consequently, the results of Jusczyk and Aslin's investigation suggest that by $7\frac{1}{2}$ months, infants have at least some rudimentary ability to detect particular words when they occur in fluent speech contexts.

In Jusczyk and Aslin's investigation, the target words used were all monosyllabic items. This leaves open the possibility that the infants were really just extracting strong syllables from fluent speech as opposed to wordlike units. One way of disambiguating the results would be to use targets that consist of more than one syllable. In turn, the use of multisyllabic targets makes it possible to explore whether prosodic factors influence the ease with which infants are able to detect these targets in fluent speech contexts. One recent investigation (Jusczyk, Newsome, and Houston, in preparation; Newsome and Jusczyk 1995) has examined whether English-learning $7\frac{1}{2}$-month-olds are able to detect bisyllabic targets in fluent speech. In one experiment, $7\frac{1}{2}$-month-olds were familiarized with pairs of words with strong/weak stress patterns like "doctor" and "candle" (or "kingdom" and "hamlet"). Then, as in the Jusczyk and Aslin (1995) study, the infants were tested on four six-sentence passages: two passages contained the familiarized words (e.g., "doctor" and "candle") and two passages contained other novel words (e.g., "kingdom" and "hamlet"). As was the case for the monosyllabic targets in the Jusczyk and Aslin study, the infants listened significantly longer to the passages containing the bisyllabic target words. Moreover, the results of a second experiment indicated that the preference for the familiar words held even when the infants were first familiarized with the words embedded in the passages, and then tested on isolated words.

One interpretation of these findings is that $7\frac{1}{2}$-month-old English-learning infants are able to segment words with strong/weak stress patterns from fluent speech. However, another possibility is that the infants were still not actually responding to the whole strong/weak words but just to the strong syllables of these words (i.e., not to "candle," but to "can"). To explore the latter possibility, Jusczyk and his colleagues ran another experiment in which they familiarized infants with just the isolated strong syllable of the words (i.e., "dock" and "can" or "king" and "ham"), and then presented the infants with the passages containing the original strong/weak words. The infants did not show any significant tendency to listen longer to the passages with the strong/weak words (e.g., "hamlet" and "kingdom") that corresponded to the strong syllables heard during the familiarization period (e.g., "ham" and "king"). Nor, as another experiment revealed, did infants who were familiarized with isolated strong/weak words like "hamlet" or "kingdom" show any significant tendency to listen longer to fluent speech passages containing the words "ham" and "king." Consequently, the results suggest that the infants in the original experiment were matching a whole strong/weak pattern, as opposed to just the strong syllable, from the familiarization phase to the corresponding item in the test phase. Therefore, in at least some cases, it appears that the infants are extracting word-like units from fluent speech, not just single syllables.

The pattern of results obtained for the strong/weak words appears to fit well with Cutler and Norris's (1988) metrical segmentation strategy—namely, that English listeners make a first pass at segmenting fluent speech by assuming word boundaries at the onsets of each strong syllable. Of course, one consequence of exclusively relying on the metrical segmentation strategy for English fluent speech is that any words that begin with a weak syllable would be missegmented. Hence, were English-learning infants relying on such a strategy, they might have certain difficulties detecting weak/strong words in fluent speech.

To examine this possibility, Jusczyk and his colleagues also conducted a series of studies using words with weak/strong stress patterns like "guitar" and "surprise" (or "beret" and "device"). In contrast to the earlier findings with strong/weak words, $7\frac{1}{2}$-month-olds, familiarized with weak/strong words, gave no evidence of subsequently recognizing these words in sentential contexts (i.e., they did not listen longer to passages containing the words "guitar" and "surprise," after familiarization with isolated versions of these words). But when infants were familiarized with just the strong syllables of these words (i.e., "tar" and "prize") they *did* listen significantly longer to the passages containing the whole weak/strong words (i.e., "guitar" and "surprise"). It was as if the infants perceived the "tar" from "guitar" as initiating a new word when it occurred in a fluent speech context.

Before embracing the conclusion that English-learning infants begin segmenting words from fluent speech by using something like a metrical segmentation strategy, there is an apparent discrepancy in the findings with the strong/weak and weak/strong words that must be resolved. The discrepancy concerns the fact that the $7\frac{1}{2}$-month-olds did not match the strong syllables of strong/weak words to the whole words, although under comparable circumstances, they did match the strong syllables of weak/strong words to the whole words.

Jusczyk and his colleagues hypothesized that the distributional properties of the sentential contexts may have been a key factor. In particular, whenever a strong/weak word appears in a sentential context, the strong syllable for the word is always followed by the same weak syllable (namely, the one that belongs to the word). However, this is not necessarily true for the strong syllable of a weak/strong word. Thus, the "tar" of "guitar" might be followed by "is" on one occasion, by "has" on another, by a sentence boundary on another, and so on. These differences across the various contexts in which the word appears may help to signal a word boundary at end of "guitar" (just as the computational model of Brent et al., in press, predicts). Since the metrical segmentation strategy would generate a word boundary at the beginning of the strong syllable "tar," these two factors would combine to make "tar" pop out of the context as a word.

To explore the possibility that distributional properties are a factor in why $7\frac{1}{2}$-month-olds responded to the strong syllables of the weak/strong words, Jusczyk and his colleagues conducted some further experiments. In one of these, they rewrote their sentential materials to use a constant word following a particular target word. For example, "guitar" was always followed by "is" and "surprise" was always followed by "in." This time, when $7\frac{1}{2}$-month-olds were familiarized with the new passages containing "guitar is" and "surprise in," they did not listen signifiantly longer to the isolated syllables "tar" and "prize" during the test phase. Jusczyk and his colleagues suggested that this was because the context may have led them to find the pseudowords "taris" and "prizin." This interpretation was verified in another experiment in which infants who were familiarized with the same passages were found to listen longer to the isolated pseudowords "taris" and "prizin" during the test phase. In other words, when the distributional properties are appropriate, the use of a metrical segmentation strategy may cause infants to perceive strong/weak words in places where there are not any.

Taken as a whole, then, the pattern of findings across this set of investigations suggests that English-learning infants may begin to segment words from fluent speech by using the occurrence of strong syllables as an indication of the onsets of new words (i.e., a metrical segmentation strategy). The use of a strategy of this sort could help the infant to make a start at recovering words from fluent speech.

Using Nonprosodic Cues to Find Word Boundaries

As noted earlier, although the metrical segmentation strategy is useful for discovering words that begin with strong syllables, it could present problems for detecting words that begin with, or consist solely of, weak syllables. In order to recover these kinds of items from the speech stream, the listener has to either use an entirely different segmentation strategy or else supplement the metrical segmentation strategy with procedures that rely on other sources of information about possible word boundaries.

There are some indications that although younger English-learning infants may rely mostly on prosodic cues, such as the locus of strong syllables, to determine word boundaries, older infants may also draw on other sources of information. First, note that Jusczyk, Newsome, and Houston (in preparation) also tested $10\frac{1}{2}$-month-olds with the same weak/strong materials that they used in their studies with $7\frac{1}{2}$-month-olds. Unlike the younger infants, the $10\frac{1}{2}$-month-olds did detect the presence of words like "guitar" and "surprise" when they occurred in fluent speech contexts. Moreover, in contrast to the younger infants, when these older infants were familiarized with just the strong syllables of weak/strong words (i.e., "tar" and "prize"), they did not listen significantly longer to the passages containing the whole weak/strong words (i.e., "guitar" and "surprise"). Furthermore, even when the distributional context was manipulated to follow the weak/strong targets by a constant word (e.g., "guitar is" and "surprise in"), these older infants still were able to detect the weak/strong targets (i.e., "guitar" and "surprise"). In other words, the $10\frac{1}{2}$-month-olds appeared to not be misled by the context into looking for "taris" or "prizin." Therefore, by $10\frac{1}{2}$ months, the infants had much more success in segmenting weak/strong words from fluent speech than did their counterparts at $7\frac{1}{2}$ months of age.

Converging evidence regarding $10\frac{1}{2}$-month-olds' capacities for detecting weak/strong words in fluent speech was obtained by Myers et al. (1996) using a different paradigm. In a series of experiments, they presented infants with passages that contained a number of 1-second pauses that occurred either at boundaries between two words or between two syllables within a word. When listening to unfiltered versions of these passages, the infants listened significantly longer to the ones in which the pauses occurred between the words. However, when listening to low-pass-filtered versions of the same passages, infants displayed no differences in listening times for passages of either type. This suggests that infants' longer listening times for the passages with the pauses between the words was based on more than how the pauses interacted with prosodic cues to word boundaries. Furthermore, in other experiments comparing performance with strong/weak to performance with weak/strong words, Myers and coworkers found that infants were just as likely to perceive interruptions in weak/strong words as they were in strong/weak words. Analyses of these stimulus materials revealed the presence of good phonotactic cues in the weak/strong words. Myers and colleagues speculated that these phonotactic cues may have helped infants to detect interruptions in these words. Consequently, by $10\frac{1}{2}$ months, English-learning infants appear to use more than just the location of strong syllables to identify the onsets of words.

The results of another recent investigation by Jusczyk, Hohne, and Bauman (in preparation) are consistent with the possibility that older infants are using multiple sources of information in segmenting words from fluent speech. The study followed up on an earlier finding by Hohne and Jusczyk (1994) that 2-month-old infants have the capacity to discriminate the kinds of allophonic differences that can signal the occurrence of word boundaries. Jusczyk and coworkers tested to see whether older infants gave evidence of actually using this kind of information in segmenting fluent speech. They were specifically interested in the kinds of allophonic differences that serve to distinguish utterances such as "night rate" (where there is a word boundary present between syllables) from "nitrate" (where there is no word boundary between syllables). For this purpose, they used the same procedure as Jusczyk and Aslin (1995) and familiarized 9-month-olds with items such as "nitrates" or "night rates" (and "doctor" or "hamlet" as controls). All the infants were then tested on passages that either contained or did not contain the familiarized words. There was an interesting asymmetry in the results. The infants did listen significantly longer to the passage containing the familiar item when the items "doctor" or "hamlet" (the control words) were involved. However, with respect to the passages containing the critical items "night rates" and "nitrates," listening times to the passage containing the familiar item were not significantly longer than to the one without the item. This suggests that in the fluent speech contexts, the infants did not distinguish "nitrates" from "night rates." To explore this further, Jusczyk and colleagues conducted an experiment to see whether familiarizing the infants with the word "night" by itself, might lead infants to listen longer to the passage containing "night rates." If so, then this would be an indication that 9-month-olds could use allophonic cues to word boundaries under some circumstances. This time all the infants were familiarized with the words "night" and "dock" and were tested on passages that contained the critical words "night rates" or "nitrates" and the control words "dock" or "doctor." The infants in this experiment displayed the same pattern of behavior as infants in the previous experiment. They successfully distinguished "dock" from "doctor," but they did not distinguish "night rates" from "nitrates."

One apparently troubling aspect of these results is that the failure of the infants to detect the occurrence of "night" in the correct passage appears to contradict the earlier findings of Jusczyk and Aslin (1995), which showed that infants could detect monosyllabic words in fluent speech. However, it turns out that the same factors concerning distributional properties of surrounding word contexts are operating here as in the study by Jusczyk, Newsome, and Houston (in preparation). Thus, one reason the infants did not detect "night" in the "night rate" passage may have to do with the fact that the target word was always followed by "rate" when it occurred in the passage.

To test this, Jusczyk and his coworkers devised a new passage in which a variety of different compounds involving the word "night" were used (e.g., "night caps," night games," "night gowns," etc). This time, after familiarization with "night," the infants did listen significantly longer to the new passage than to the "nitrates" passage. Hence, when the distributional properties were favorable, the 9-month-olds could detect "night" in fluent speech contexts. What infants at this age do not appear to be able to do is to rely exclusively on allophonic information to find this word in sentences.

However, in the same study, there was also evidence that this picture changes by the time English-learning infants reach $10\frac{1}{2}$ months of age. Specifically, when Jusczyk and coworkers tested $10\frac{1}{2}$-month-olds on the same conditions as in their first experiment (i.e., familiarization with "nitrates" and "doctor" or with "night rates" and "hamlet"), the infants did have significantly longer listening times for the matching passage, regardless of whether "night rate" or "nitrate" was the target from the familiarization period.

Therefore, although the earliest attempts at word segmentation by English-learning infants may rely exclusively on the use of prosodic cues to signal word boundaries, this does not seem to be an accurate characterization of what $10\frac{1}{2}$-month-olds do. Rather, at this age, English-learning infants appear to be using multiple sources of information (prosodic, phonotactic, allophonic, etc.) to locate the boundaries of words in fluent speech (much as Morgan and Saffran 1995 have suggested). Drawing on multiple sources of information to word boundaries would give them a better chance at correctly segmenting weak/strong words as well as strong/weak words. In this sense, they might have something that approaches true word segmentation abilities. Thus, one possible scenario of how word segmentation skills develop in English-learning infants is that they begin with an approximation to locating word boundaries, such as identifying word onsets with strong syllables. This allows them to break up utterances into smaller processing units. The existence of these smaller units may, in turn, enable infants to detect the kinds of regularities (phonotactic, allophonic, etc.) within these units that may also be predictive of the presence of word boundaries. For instance, the infant may be in a better position to observe which types of sounds occur frequently at both edges of these smaller-sized units (see also Elman 1993; Gerken 1996; Newport 1990, 1991, for a discussion of how working with smaller units may facilitate certain aspects of language acquisition).

Some Reflections on Developmental Changes during the First Year

What should be apparent after this summary of recent findings is that during the first year there are rather dramatic changes in how infants process speech sounds. Moreover, the kinds of changes that occur appear to be specifically related to the kinds of input that infants are exposed to.

Sensitivity declines for many distinctions that are not frequently found in the input. At the same time, infants appear to be absorbing information about regularly occurring features of native-language sound patterns. Furthermore, sensitivity is developing to precisely those features that appear to be helpful in segmenting words from the input. Perhaps, then, it is not surprising that infants' skills at word segmentation are developing along with their knowledge of the way sound patterns are structured in their native language.

It is worth noting that the kinds of changes that occur throughout the first year reflect an interaction between the input and infants' underlying perceptual capacities. Infants' capacities provide them with some means of grouping and sorting the range of utterances to which they are exposed. However, because languages vary greatly in the ways they pattern sounds, infants' categorization skills must necessarily be tuned to deal with the way patterns are structured in the language that they are acquiring.

One issue not addressed in the discussion of word segmentation abilities above is how English-learning infants come to these abilities. Strategies for recognizing words in fluent speech, such as the metrical segmentation strategy, may be efficient for English utterances, but they will not necessarily work for all languages. For example, using such a strategy in Polish (where stress occurs regularly on the penultimate syllable of words) would ensure that most words in fluent speech would be improperly segmented. Indeed, work by Cutler, Mehler, and their colleagues (e.g., Cutler et al. 1983; Cutler et al. 1986; Mehler et al. 1981; Otake et al. 1993) suggests that mature listeners in different native languages take very different routes to extracting information about words in fluent speech.

So, how do infants develop routines that are useful for segmenting words in fluent speech? More to the point, what kind of information drives their initial attempts at segmentation? For example, how might infants learn about the predominant stress pattern of words in their native language before they have begun to segment words from fluent speech? Much of the prior discussion has suggested that the metrical segmentation strategy is language-specific in that it depends on facts about the typical prosodic patterns of words in a language. However, it is certainly possible that at some point in acquiring language, all infants might exhibit a general trochaic bias, regardless of the nature of the language that they are exposed to. This possibility cannot be dismissed in the absence of studies with infants learning languages other than English.

Alternatively, there is a possibility that English-learning infants may actually derive their word segmentation strategy from the input. In particular, there is evidence that by $4\frac{1}{2}$ months, English-learning infants display some recognition of the sound patterns of their own names (Mandel, Jusczyk, and Pisoni 1995). When trying to attract an infant's attention, parents commonly speak the infant's name in isolation. For a high proportion (22 of 24) of the infants tested in the Mandel et al. study, the names that parents most often used with their infants (including nicknames) had strong/weak stress patterns. Moreover, this seems to be a general pattern with English first names (Cutler, McQueen, and Robinson 1990). Also, consider the fact that many diminutive forms in English that are used in addressing infants have strong/weak patterns, including items that are likely to be spoken in isolation (e.g., "daddy," "mommy," "doggie," "cookie," "kitty," etc.) Consequently, it is not implausible that infants in English-speaking environments might develop a bias for trochaic patterns by hearing repetitions of names and diminutives that are presented in isolation. In general, isolated words in English are most apt to have stress on the first syllable. Thus, attention to those words that are most likely to occur in isolation may explain why, at least initially, English-learning infants appear to segment fluent speech at strong-syllable onsets.

Ultimately, adapting one's perceptual capacities to take advantage of the regularities that occur in a particular language should improve both the speed and accuracy of on-line word recognition. However, because the same set of regularities will not work for all languages, learners must discover the right ones on the basis of the input they receive. Based on the available data, infants seem to discover, in a very short period of time, what the critical features are that hold for their native language. The rapidity with which they discover these features is just what might be expected of a developmental process that is the result of innately guided learning. The behavior patterns that are developing in this case—word segmentation skills—are pivotal ones for the rest of language acquisition. Hence, they are exactly the kinds of abilities that one might expect to see driven by innately guided learning processes.

Finally, in presenting the findings discussed in this chapter, I have strongly emphasized the relation that many of them bear to the development of word segmentation and recognition skills. This is what I believe speech perception capacities are ultimately intended for. To be sure, these capacities do allow us to perceive similarities involving phonetic segments and to discriminate subtle distinctions among different syllables. In this way, these capacities provide the foundation for discriminating one word from another and for correctly classifying different tokens of the same word type. However, if we focus too closely on merely cataloguing what perceptual distinctions infants make at different ages, we can lose sight of what the primary purpose of these capacities is—namely, their use in segmenting and recognizing words in fluent speech. Hence, although at times we may talk of how infants come to learn phonemic distinctions and acquire phonemic categories, it is unlikely that filling in a phonetic inventory is the primary force that drives infants' acquisition of the sound structure of their native language. Rather, the acquisition of phonemic categories and phonemic distinctions falls out of learning to segment and recognize words in the fluent speech of one's native language.

Chapter 5

The Role of Memory and Attentional Processes in the Development of Speech Perception

In order to fully grasp the role that infants' speech-processing capacities play in their acquisition of a native language, we have to understand how memory and attentional processes affect what infants extract from the speech signal. For instance, although it would certainly be helpful to have more detailed accounts of the type of input that language learners receive, it would be even more useful to know which portions of the input infants actually attend to and store information about. Given the necessity of delineating the basic capacities of infants for perceiving speech, it is not surprising that most previous studies have been conducted under conditions that tend to minimize memory and attentional demands. Yet, to borrow an old distinction from the early psycholinguistics literature, whereas such investigations have told us much about infants' underlying *competence* for processing speech sounds, they have not necessarily been revealing about infants' *performance* in everyday listening situations. This picture is slowly beginning to change. Indeed, the recent studies on word segmentation skills mark one attempt to bring us closer to understanding infants' speech-processing capacities under real-world conditions. In addition, there have been other investigations that have tried to examine precisely what information infants represent about speech sounds, how well they handle competing distractions while processing speech, and what kind of detail they remember about what they have heard. Moreover, because these issues are not entirely independent of each other, several of them have sometimes been addressed in the same investigation. For the present purposes, I have roughly grouped the investigations discussed in this chapter according to whether their main focus was on the nature of the information in infants' representations, the kind of information that appears to be most salient to infants under different listening conditions, or the information that infants encode and remember about speech.

What Infants Represent about Speech Sounds

Because many speech perception studies have focused on infants' capacities to detect minimal distinctions among phonetic segments, there is a temptation to treat positive results as an indication that infants are representing the utterances in terms of a detailed phonetic description. However, because the task used in these studies is usually some variant of a same/different task, the assumption that infants must be representing speech as a string of phonetic segments is not necessary to explain why the infants discriminated the contrast in question. For example, consider what happens in a typical experiment involving the HAS procedure. The infant's sucking usually produces repetitions of a single syllable until the criterion for habituation, and hence shifting to a new stimulus, is met. The new stimulus is presented without any specific delay so that the infant merely has to compare two successive stimuli to notice that some change has occurred. There is no need for any elaborate encoding of the stimulus beyond what is necessary to detect that this stimulus is different from the preceding one. It is not necessary to analyze how the two stimuli are different. Much the same can be said for many of the results obtained with the conditioned headturn procedure.

My comments about the data gathered with these procedures are not intended as criticism of them. Rather, my intention is only to point out that when used as they typically are, these procedures do not provide us with much information about what goes into infants' representations of speech sounds. Consequently, the investigator who is interested in the nature of infants' representations is forced to either come up with new procedures or to adapt the existing ones to address this issue.

One means of requiring more than simple yes/no discriminations in speech perception tasks with infants is to increase the number of stimuli that are presented. If infants are habituated to a set of stimuli such that each successive stimulus differs from the preceding one in some way, then simply monitoring whether two successive stimuli differ in any way will not suffice to detect when some novel change in stimulation has occurred. This is because what is relevant is not simply whether two successive stimuli differ; the important point is whether a particular type of change that has occurred is critical to recognizing a novel element in the series.

One of the first efforts to investigate the nature of young infants' representations of speech sounds presented infants with an alternating pair of stimuli using the HAS procedure. Miller and Eimas (1979; Eimas and Miller 1981) investigated the degree to which featural information is associated within 3- to 4-month-olds' representations of syllables. More specifically, do infants at this age perceive the acoustic features within a syllable as being related and ordered in some way, or is their perception that these acoustic features are unrelated to each other? If the latter were true, then an infant who was habituated to a particular set of acoustic features in some syllables might not respond to a reordering of the same set of acoustic features. In fact, Miller and Eimas found that infants detect syllable contrasts that involve rearrangements of the same set of phonetic features (e.g., after being habituated to an alternating sequence of [ba]–[ta], the infants detected a change to [pa]–[da]). Thus, infants appear to be sensitive not only to the features that are present in syllables but also to the order and combination of such features.

A number of investigations have tried to establish whether young infants' representations of utterances are structured in terms of phonetic segments or larger units, such as syllables. For example, some investigators have claimed that syllables are the natural units of processing and representation for young infants. Bertoncini and Mehler (1981) found that 2-month-olds were better able to discriminate pairs of stimuli that conform to a syllabic ([tæp] vs. [pæt]), as opposed to nonsyllabic ([tsp] vs. [pst]), pattern in a language. They interpreted these results as an indication that the syllable is a natural processing unit for infants. Other investigations have tried to address more directly whether infants' perceptual representations are structured in terms of sequences of phonetic segments.

For instance, Jusczyk and Derrah (1987) used a version of the HAS procedure in which they familiarized infants with a series of four syllables, all of which shared the same initial consonant [b] (e.g., [bi], [ba], [bo], [bɚ]). Then they examined how infants responded during the postshift period to the addition of a new syllable that either did or did not share the same initial consonant. Based on findings from the visual categorization literature (Bomba and Siqueland 1983; Bornstein, Kessen, and Weiskopf 1976; Cohen and Strauss 1979), they expected that if infants perceived the presence of the common phonetic segment [b] in the syllables during the habituation phase, they might habituate to the phonetic category. If so, they would be apt to respond more to a new syllable containing a novel phonetic segment (e.g., [du]) than to a new instance with the familiar segment (e.g., [bu]).

Two interesting findings emerged. First, infants detected the addition of a new syllable to the familiarized set, suggesting that they were able to represent the different syllables heard during the habituation phase. Second, there was no indication that the addition of new syllables that shared the same initial consonant ([bu]) were treated any differently than ones that included a new consonant ([du]). Jusczyk and Derrah interpreted these results as an indication that the syllables were not represented as sequences of phonetic segments, but as whole units.[1]

Subsequent research by Bertoncini et al. (1988) replicated and extended Jusczyk and Derrah's findings. Bertoncini and colleagues tested both newborns and 2-month-olds. They investigated not only relations among syllables that shared a common consonant, [b], but also relations among syllables that shared a common vowel, [i]. Their results demonstrated that even newborns possess some capacity for representing differences in speech sounds, although representations in this age group appeared to be less detailed than those of 2-month-olds. However, once again there was no indication that infants of either age responded differently when the syllable added during the postshift period included a common phonetic segment than when it did not. Instead of focusing on common shared properties among the syllables, the infants appeared to be responding to differences at the level of whole syllabic units.

Another indication that young infants are attentive to the syllabic organization of speech comes from a recent study by Bijeljac-Babic, Bertoncini, and Mehler (1993). They examined whether newborns are sensitive to the number of syllables present in an utterance. For example, infants were familiarized with a series of different stimuli whose common property had to do with the number of syllables present (i.e., they were either bisyllables or trisyllables). For infants in the experimental groups, the number of syllables in the utterances was changed (e.g., from trisyllables to bisyllables). Bijeljac-Babic and coworkers found that newborns detected changes in the number of syllables in utterances. However, in another experiment, they found that the infants did not respond to comparable changes in the number of phonetic segments. Specifically, infants were exposed to a series of 75 different bisyllables, all of which were composed of the same number of phonetic segments (e.g., four) in the preshift phase of the experiment. During the postshift phase, they were presented with another set of 75 different bisyllables, all of which were composed of six phonetic segments. In contrast to what happened when the number of syllables was changed, the infants did not detect changes in the numbers of phonetic segments present in the bisyllables. Bijeljac-Babic and coworkers interpreted this as another indication that infants' representations are structured in terms of syllables rather than phonetic segments.

Thus, the findings from these studies provide evidence for syllabic representations in young infants. At present, there is no indication that infants under 6 months of age represent utterances as strings of phonetic segments. Whether or when infants actually do represent speech in terms of phonetic segments is less clear. Strictly speaking, even data demonstrating that sensitivity declines to certain nonnative phonetic contrasts do not necessarily require that speech be represented as strings of phonetic segments. For example, the losses in sensitivity could involve certain syllable types rather than phonetic segments per se. Nevertheless, there are some data that suggest that infants' representations become more fine-grained during the latter half of the first year. For instance, Hillenbrand (1983) used the operant headturn paradigm and first trained 6-month-olds on a contrast between the oral stop [ba] and the nasal [ma]. During subsequent stages of training, he added new syllables to each category (e.g., [da] and [na]) and showed that infants could generalize to different oral stops and nasals. Similarly, Hillenbrand (1984) reported that 6-month-olds found it generally easier to learn a rule based on a place of articulation distinction among nasals (i.e., [m] vs. [n]) rather than an arbitrary grouping of the same syllables. One possible implication of these results is that 6-month-olds are beginning to perceive some segmental and/or featural organization within syllables. But another possible interpretation is that 6-month-olds are becoming more sensitive to articulatory similarities and differences between whole syllables.

The studies reviewed in this section are ones that have focused on infants' immediate representations of speech sounds (i.e., perceptual representations that infants have available during on-line processing). Of course, one can also ask about more permanent forms of representations of speech sounds, such as those that might be stored in long-term memory. Indeed, it would seem that it is the more permanent types of representation that are likely to be critical in developing a lexicon for the native language. Many of the same issues considered in this section regarding representational units also arise in considering the nature of infants' more permanent forms of representations of speech. Thus, we will continue our discussion of representations when we consider the relationship between memory processes and speech perception in infants.

The Role of Attention in Infant Speech Perception

There are a number of ways attentional processes might bear on speech perception in infants. For example, it is reasonable to suppose that some aspects of the signal are simply more salient than others. Presumably, these salient features are the ones that are most likely to influence any further processing of the signal. However, in addition to information in the signal itself, other factors may influence which elements in speech are likely to draw infants' attention at a given moment. Developmental shifts in attention to information in speech are also a possibility. Thus one can ask whether the features most salient at one age are those most likely to draw the infant's attention at a later age. Finally, questions can be raised about the degree to which infants can actively deploy their attentional resources and select certain information to be processed. Although there is not a great deal of research on how attention affects speech processing in infants, each of the issues just raised has received some consideration in recent research.

A long-standing issue in speech research is whether stressed syllables are processed more easily and thoroughly than unstressed syllables. Indeed, there are many suggestions in the language acquisition literature that infants simply attend better to stressed than to unstressed syllables in the input. Lack of attention to information in unstressed syllables is a reason offered to explain why children may omit weak syllables in their early productions (Brown and Fraser 1964; Echols 1993; Echols and Newport 1992; but see Gerken and McIntosh 1993; Gleitman and Wanner 1982). Infants are sensitive to the contrast between stressed and unstressed syllables from an early age (Jusczyk and Thompson 1978; Spring and Dale 1977). However, the data with respect to whether infants are more attentive to information in stressed than to unstressed syllables is mixed. On the one hand, some studies that have used bisyllabic stimuli indicate that 2-month-olds are able to perceive phonetic contrasts in unstressed, as well as stressed, syllables (Jusczyk et al. 1978; Jusczyk and Thompson 1978). On the other hand, Karzon (1985) reported that when the number of syllables was increased to three ([malana] vs. [marana]), infants only discriminated a contrast if it occurred in syllables that received stress characteristic of child-directed speech. Perhaps, then, when the processing load becomes sufficiently great, exaggerating the syllable stress may help in directing infants' attention to the contrast.

Another factor that could influence which elements of the speech signal are easiest to attend to has to do with the position of the information within the utterance. All other things being equal, contrasts located medially in utterances might be expected to be more difficult for the infant than those located syllable-initially or syllable-finally. However, studies examining this issue have reported that discriminability of phonetic contrasts does not appear to vary with their location within utterances (Goodsitt et al. 1984; Jusczyk et al. 1978; Jusczyk and Thompson 1978; Williams 1977a). Still, the possibility remains that additional increases in processing load could reveal some differences in the discriminability of phonetic contrasts depending on their utterance position.

A different means of manipulating infants' attentional focus was adopted by Jusczyk et al. (1990) who tested 4-day-olds and 2-month-olds using a modified version of the HAS procedure. Jusczyk and his coworkers manipulated the attentional focus of the infants by systematically varying the perceptual similarity of items in the stimulus set. For example, in one experiment, four different consonants were used in preparing the stimuli. Three of these, [p], [t], [k], were chosen because of their close proximity in perceptual spacing according to psychological scaling data (Shepard 1972). The fourth consonant, [m], is located at considerable distance from the other consonants in perceptual space. The syllables used in testing were composed by pairing these consonants with the following vowel [a]. One group of infants was familiarized with a set of syllables that included highly similar consonants (i.e., [pa], [ta], [ka]) during the preshift phase. During the test phase, the more dissimilar syllable, [ma], was added to the set. Another group of infants was familiarized with [pa], [ka], [ma], and then heard the added syllable [ta] during the test period. Although both familiarization sets included at least a pair of highly similar consonants, the syllable added during the test phase was potentially harder to discriminate for the second group ([ta]), owing to its closer perceptual similarity to some of the familiarized syllables (i.e., [pa] and [ka]). In fact, just the inclusion of a pair of highly similar items in the familiarization set was sufficient to focus the infants' attention on fine-grained distinctions among the syllables, as both test groups at each age level detected the addition of the new syllable during the postshift period.

In a second experiment, Jusczyk and coworkers used a set of stimuli that were designed to induce a coarser-grained encoding of the stimuli.

This time, four different vowels were chosen for the stimuli, three of which are perceptually highly dissimilar: [i], [a], and [u]. The fourth vowel, [ʌ], is highly similar to [a]. To construct the test syllables, these four vowels were combined with an initial [b]. One group of infants was familiarized with a set of syllables that included the three perceptually dissimilar vowels [bi], [ba], [bu]. During the test phase, the new syllable added was [bʌ], which is highly similar to one of the familiarized syllables, [ba]. Another group of infants was familiarized with a different syllable set that did include a finer-grained distinction among the syllables. This group heard [bi], [ba], [bʌ] during familiarization, and in the test phase, a syllable highly dissimilar to the others, [bu], was added to the set.

Jusczyk and coworkers predicted that the infants in the first group would tend to focus on coarser kinds of distinctions among the syllables and thus have more difficulty discriminating a new item that was highly similar to one of the familiarized syllables. By comparison, because the second group was familiarized with a set that included a finer-grained distinction among syllables, they should have little difficulty in detecting the added syllable during the test phase. These predictions were borne out in the behavior of 4-day-olds. When the infants were exposed to the coarse distinction set (i.e., [bi], [ba], [bu]), they did not detect the addition of a new syllable [bʌ], which was perceptually very similar to one of the original set members, [ba].[2] However, when exposed to the other set (i.e., [bi], [ba], [bʌ]), they did detect the addition of [bu] during the test phase.

By two months of age, infants proved to be more resistant to this type of attentional manipulation. They detected the new syllable regardless of being focused on fine- or coarse-grained distinctions during the preshift period. One possible explanation for this change in susceptibility to the attentional manipulation is that the older groups are better able to cope with the processing demands of the task. They have greater facility in shifting their attention from coarser- to finer-grained distinctions among speech sounds. Alternatively, their memorial capacities for the fine-grained details of the stimuli in the familiarization period may be better than those of the 4-day-olds.

Another potential factor may have played a role in the differences displayed by newborns and 2-month-olds on this task. This factor involves the impact that the frequency of occurrence of certain syllable types has on what infants attend to in speech. The infants who were most affected by the manipulations of the input during the preshift period were those who had had the least prior experience with speech sounds—namely, newborns. The greater range of experience that 2-month-olds have had with native language input (including many fine-grained phonetic contrasts) may have already exerted some influence on which features they attend to when perceiving speech. Hence, considerably more exposure to input biased toward coarser distinctions might be required to shift the 2-month-olds' attention away from the fine-grained distinctions that they have already become adept at picking up. This is an interesting possibility because it suggests a way the relative frequency of certain properties in the input may interact with the infant's underlying perceptual capacities. This interaction may eventually influence the kinds of information that they extract from the speech signal.

Bauman, Goodman, and Jusczyk (1995) focused on a different sort of issue regarding what commonalties infants attend to when listening to speech. They examined the extent to which 9-month-olds attend to similarities in the sounds of different syllables. They used the headturn preference procedure to present infants with lists of monosyllabic (CVC) items. For half of the test trials, the items in a particular list shared some common feature, whereas for the other half of the trials, the items within a particular list were unrelated. Four different kinds of similarity relations were investigated across a series of four experiments. Bauman and co-workers found that when the items on the list either shared their initial consonant (e.g., "foat," "feev," "fas," etc.) or their initial consonant plus vowel (e.g.,"bife," "bime," "bige," etc.), the infants listened significantly longer to these than to the ones in the unrelated lists. However, when the items on the lists merely shared the same vowel (e.g., "med," "jek," "pesh," etc.) or the same vowel plus final consonant (e.g., " bod," "yod," "lod," etc.), the infants showed no preferences for these items over the ones from the unrelated lists. What these results indicate is that English-learning infants appear to be attending more closely to some types of similarities among syllables than to others. In particular, they appear to be more sensitive to similarities involving the onsets of syllables than they are to those involving syllable rhymes.

What prompted infants to listen longer to the lists with common onsets? One possibility is that the infants were displaying some recognition of the fact that some of the lists began with a common phonetic segment. Alternatively, the infants may have been responding to some more global property having to do with commonalties in the manner of onsets of the syllables in a list. To explore this issue, the same investigators conducted an additional study. This time, they constructed six lists in which the items did not all begin with the same phonetic segment but rather shared a common manner of articulation at onset (e.g., all the items in one list began with either [b], [d], or [g]). Once again, the infants listened significantly longer to these lists than they did to the lists with unrelated items. Hence, it appears that 9-month-olds are attending to more general properties of the onset characteristics of the items rather than extracting information about common phonetic segments in these items. Regardless, these indications that 9-month-olds are more apt to focus on onsets than the ends of items presented in lists is interesting in light of Slobin's (1973) well-known language-acquisition operating principle that learners should "Pay attention to the ends of words." Of course, the focus of Slobin's principle was on the acquisition of morphology. It is still possible that attention to onsets at an earlier phase of language acquisition may give way to greater attention to offsets at a later phase.

There are several possible explanations why the 9-month-olds may have shown this asymmetry with respect to the kinds of similarities that they attended to. One possibility is that this sequence is particular to learning English. For example, English does not make widespread use of similarities in the ends of words to mark the way words are grouped within an utterance. Languages with well-developed marking systems for gender, number, and case, such as Spanish, may be more likely to have words within a particular syntactic grouping agree in terms of their endings. Another possibility is that the asymmetry that Jusczyk and colleagues observed is actually a language-universal rather than language-specific one. An account along these lines is that the attention to onsets of words may go hand in hand with the development of a lexicon, wherein distinctions and similarities among the onsets of words may be, at least initially, more important for infants to encode in order to avoid confusions among lexical items.

Regardless of its source, the tendency for infants to detect similarities among the onsets of different syllables could be an indication that they are beginning to develop subsyllabic representations of speech. Thus, we note that a potential developmental change may occur with respect to the kind of features that draw infants' attention. Whereas younger infants may attend more to similarities and differences involving entire syllables, older infants may begin to attend to relations among parts of syllables.

Other indications of developmental changes in what information infants attend to in speech come from some of the studies that were reviewed in chapter 4. In particular, the investigations demonstrating developmental changes between 6 and 9 months of age in infants' sensitivity to phonotactic sequences (Jusczyk, Friederici, et al. 1993) and word prosody (Jusczyk, Cutler, and Redanz 1993) in the native language are an indication of attentional shifts in what infants are detecting in the input. As Gibson (1969) might put it, the same information is available in the signal to perceivers at both ages, but the older infants have developed better means of picking it up.

How Well Do Infants Process Speech in the Presence of Distracting Stimuli?

To this point, we have focused mostly on how stimulus properties and various exposure conditions affect what infants attend to in the speech signal. To what extent are infants able to selectively attend to speech information when other potential distractions are also present? Studies considered in chapter 3 indicate that infants are able to ignore at least some of the potentially distracting variability that occurs in speech due to talker differences and changes in speaking rates (e.g., Eimas and Miller 1980a; Kuhl 1979). In a recent unpublished investigation, we explored the consequences of showing a distracting, continually changing visual pattern (a computer screen saver) while 2-month-olds were performing a speech perception task. Just as in the study by Jusczyk et al. (1990), the infants were familiarized with a set of syllables with three different vowels ([bi], [ba], [bʌ]), and during the postshift period a new syllable [bu] was added to the set. Despite the presence of the distracting visual pattern, the 2-month-olds had no difficulty detecting the addition of the new syllable to the set. Hence, these results indicate that infants at this age can at least tolerate a certain amount of visual distraction and still detect a relatively subtle speech contrast.

Along with the visual distractions that are present while speech occurs, infants also have to ignore competing sounds. The developmental literature indicates that infants have a higher auditory threshold than adults (as much as 15 to 25 dB) for both pure tones (Nozza and Wilson 1984; Ruben 1992; Sinnott, Pisoni, and Aslin 1983) and speech (Nozza et al. 1990; Nozza, Wagner, and Crandell 1988). Some research has suggested that 6- to 8-month-old infants also need a higher *signal-to-noise ratio* (S/N) than do adults in order to detect speech (Nozza et al. 1988; Trehub, Bull, and Schneider 1981) and to make phonetic distinctions (Nozza et al. 1991; Nozza et al. 1990). For example, Nozza et al. (1990) found that 7- to 11-month-old infants, who were tested on a [ba]–[ga] distinction, needed S/N ratios as high as 8 decibels in order to reach 85 percent correct. It is worth noting that most of these studies with infants (e.g., Nozza et al. 1990; Nozza et al. 1988; Trehub et al. 1981) have used random or broad-band noise as a masker. There is some reason to believe that infants' processing of a particular speech stream would be even more disrupted if the competition came from a simultaneously occurring speech signal (Young, Parker, and Carhart 1975). Speech input to infants in a typical home, especially one that includes other children, is likely to occur against a background of competing speech and other noises. This situation raises some interesting questions about just what kinds of information infants are able to extract under such conditions.

Of course, even adults are familiar with the difficulties of trying to follow a conversation in a noisy room. This is an example of what has been called the "cocktail party problem" (Broadbent 1952; Cherry 1953). In order to accurately judge how the input affects the acquisition of a native language, it is crucial to determine whether infants have the attentional resources to contend with the cocktail party problem. But how can one determine whether infants are following a stream of speech that is directed to them, rather than following some simultaneously occurring speech signal?

As a first pass at addressing this issue, Newman and Jusczyk (in press) devised a series of experiments that relied on a version of the word-detection paradigm used by Jusczyk and Aslin (1995). They familiarized $7\frac{1}{2}$-month-olds with pairs of repeated, isolated words such as "cup" and "dog" that were produced in a lively voice by a female talker. However, the familiarization words occurred against background speech produced by a male talker reading a rather dull passage from the methods section of an infant research paper. After the familiarization phase was concluded, the infants were tested on passages that were presented without any competing background signal. As in the earlier study by Jusczyk and Aslin, two of the four test passages included the familiarization words. If during the familiarization period, the infants were able to follow the female voice producing the isolated words, then they were expected to listen longer to the fluent speech passages containing these words. Newman and Jusczyk found that this was the case when the S/N ratio for the female voice versus the male voice during the familiarization period was either 10 decibels or 5 decibels. However, when the S/N ratio was reduced to 0 decibels (so that the female and male voices were played at equal loudness levels), the infants did not listen longer to the passages with the target words during the test phase.

The results of these experiments from Newman and Jusczyk indicate that infants have at least some ability to attend selectively to one of two competing speech signals. However, the case that they examined was one that pitted a repeated, isolated word against a continuous speech background. One could argue that a more realistic situation for infants to contend with is one in which two competing continuous streams of speech occur simultaneously. To get some indication of how infants do under these circumstances, Newman and Jusczyk ran an additional experiment. This time the familiarization consisted of the female talker producing two fluent speech passages containing the target words. Once again these were presented against the background of the male talker who was reading the same dull methods section. The test phase consisted of trials on which four different repeated, isolated words (two of which occurred in the familiarization passages) were presented in the clear to infants. Newman and Jusczyk found that with a 10 decibel S/N ratio during the familiarization period, the infants did listen longer to the corresponding target words in the test phase. However, the data suggested that this S/N ratio was at the very limit of what $7\frac{1}{2}$-month-olds can do. In fact, about half of the infants at this age did not perform the task successfully.

Newman and Jusczyk's results are interesting in light of questions about the impact of hearing loss on language acquisition. One implication of their findings is that even a relatively minor reduction of S/N ratio could impair infants' abilities to extract information from speech in noisy environments. Actually, the situation in the real world is probably a bit better for infants, because in Newman and Jusczyk's test situation there were no localization cues present to help in separating the two voices. In any case, their results show that infants at this age have some ability to selectively attend to speech that is addressed to them, even when it occurs against a background of another competing speech signal.

In summary, although research on infants' attentional capacities in the context of speech perception has been limited, there are indications that infants have at least some capacity to cope with the variability present in the signal and to selectively attend to speech in noisy environments. The existing data on the development of speech perception capacities also offers some reason to believe that the information that infants attend to in the speech signal changes during the course of the first year. Clearly, a deal remains to be learned about how attentional capacities develop what their impact is on speech processing in infants.

What Infants Remember about Speech

Although experience with the input could help to modify infants' speech-processing capacities, if they are to progress in acquiring a language, it is also critical that infants retain information about specific lexical items over relatively long periods. Memory processes are clearly necessary for building up a lexicon, but they also play other important roles in language acquisition. For instance, knowing that a particular lexical item usually occurs in a certain utterance position could provide clues about the syntactic role of that word in the language. Similarly, the ability to remember the order of information in utterances, and to track how often certain constituents move around, could be helpful to working out the syntactic organization of the language. I will have more to say about these kinds of relations in the next chapter. For the moment, I will focus on what is known about how infants' memory for speech information develops, what this says about the resources they have available, and what this implies about the beginnings of the lexicon.

Young Infants' Memory for Speech over Brief Delay Periods
Even though the role of memory in infants' detection of speech perception contrasts has been acknowledged in previous studies (e.g., Bertoncini et al. 1988; Kuhl and Miller 1982; Swoboda et al. 1978; Swoboda, Morse, and Leavitt 1976), until relatively recently there were very few attempts to investigate memory processes directly. In order to study memory processes, investigators need to systematically vary factors related to capacity and decay, for example memory load and the length of delay periods. Because many of the standard infant-testing procedures rely so heavily on habituation to index infants' responses to changes in stimulation, they are not ideally suited for studying memory processes. This is because such techniques usually rely on comparisons of experimental groups with no-change control groups. Generally speaking, after habituation, the longer the delay period before stimulation starts up again, the more likely that control groups are to show release from habituation, thereby swamping any performance differences between them and experimental groups. Consequently, speech researchers have to work hard to devise techniques

that use some form of delayed testing but do not result in spontaneous recovery of performance by control subjects.

Some early indications that performance on infant speech perception tasks may be affected by delays in testing come from Swoboda et al. (1976). These investigators did not directly manipulate delay periods. However, they presented indirect evidence about the effects of delays in testing by relating the discrimination of vowel contrasts to the length of time that passed between the the last stimulus presented in the preshift period and the first stimulus presented in the postshift period. In noting the failure of some of their subjects to detect certain vowel contrasts, they remarked that failures to discriminate appeared to be inversely related to the length of the time interval between the two stimuli.

More recently, several studies have directly examined infants' retention of information over brief delay periods. P. Jusczyk, Kennedy, and A. M. Jusczyk (1995) tested 2-month-olds with a modified version of the HAS procedure, which included a delay period between the preshift and post-shift phases of the experiment. During the delay, a series of slides was shown without any accompanying auditory stimulation. Jusczyk and his colleagues found that 2-month-olds retained enough information about a set of three different syllables to detect changes involving a single phonetic feature, even after a 2-minute delay interval. Moreover, infants did not appear to gain any advantage in retaining information about the syllables even when all three-syllables in the familiarization set shared the same initial consonant. Thus, infants who were exposed to a three syllable familiarization set with no common phonetic segments (e.g., [si], [ba], [tu]) were as likely to detect changes after the delay interval (e.g., changing [ba] to [da]) as were infants who were exposed to the familiarization sets with a common phonetic segment (e.g., [bi], [ba], [bu]). Jusczyk et al.'s inter-pretation of these findings was that no difference occurred in memory for the two types of sets because the infants were encoding the sounds as syllabic units. Hence, in each instance, the infants had to remember the same number of items—three. In any event, this study demonstrated that infants are able to retain a considerable amount of detail about different syllables over brief delay periods.

If Jusczyk et al.'s interpretation is correct, and syllable-sized chunks really function for young infants as units in their retention of information about speech, then one might expect to find a difference between sets with and without common elements only when the commonality among the familiarization set members involves whole syllables. So, if syllables play a role in speech processing at this age, infants might show better retention for a set of bisyllables that shares a common syllable than for an equivalent sized set of bisyllables without any syllable in common. Jusczyk et al. (1995) investigated this possibility by exploring infants' retention of information about bisyllabic utterances. During the preshift phase, 2-month-olds were exposed to a set of bisyllabic utterances that either shared (i.e., [ba' mɨt], [ba' zi], [ba' lo], [ba' dɛ́s]) or did not share (i.e., [nɛ' lo], [pæ' zi], [ču' dɛs], [ko' mɨt]) a common syllable. The presence of a common syllable during the preshift phase did lead to a significant improvement in the infants' ability to detect the addition of a new item to the set during the postshift phase. Only infants who had heard the set with the common syllable detected the addition of a new bisyllable [pa' mʌl] to the postshift set. Interestingly enough, another group of infants exposed to the common syllable set did not detect the addition of a new item [ba' nʌl], which shared the same initial syllable as the other bisyllables. This seems to be an indication that infants treated it as another instance of a now-familiar category (i.e., bisyllables beginning with [ba]).

In an additional experiment, Jusczyk and coworkers examined the possibility that infants were simply benefiting from the presence of two common phonetic segments, regardless of whether or not they occurred in the same syllable. Hence, this time the infants were familiarized with the bisyllables [ma' bɨt], [za' bi], [la' bo], [da' bɛs]. In contrast to the common-syllable condition in the experiment described above, the infants in this experiment did not detect the addition of a new bisyllable to this set after the delay period. Jusczyk and colleagues took this as a further indication that it was the presence of the common syllable that had enhanced the encoding of the bisyllables in the first experiment and allowed them to be better remembered after the delay.

In the investigation of bisyllabic stimuli just described, the common syllables that Jusczyk and coworkers manipulated in their stimulus sets were always stressed syllables. This raises an interesting issue. Would infants display the same sensitivity to the presence of common syllables in bisyllabic utterances, even if these syllables were unstressed? Or, is syllable stress needed to draw infants' attention to this common feature of bisyllabic utterances? Houston, P. Jusczyk, and A. Jusczyk (in preparation) addressed this issue in a recent investigation. They used a familiarization set consisting of four bisyllables beginning with a common unstressed syllable (i.e., [bə mɨt'], [bə zi'], [bə lo'], [bə dɛs']). During the test phase after the 2-minute delay period, a new bisyllable was added to the familiarization set. The new bisyllable either shared ([bə nʌl']) or did not share ([sə nʌl']) the same initial unstressed syllable as the ones from the famil-iarization set. The 2-month-olds in this study behaved exactly like their counterparts in the earlier investigation. Namely, they responded to the addition of [sə nʌl'], but not to the addition of [bə nʌl']. Hence, the pres-ence of even a common *unstressed* syllable in the familiarization set led to a significant improvement in the infants' ability to detect the addition of a new item to the set during the postshift phase. Further work is under way to determine whether this finding for unstressed syllables occurs regardless of their position in an utterance or only for those in utterance-initial positions.

In general, then, the findings from these studies of young infants' memory for speech information are in line with those from the earlier investigations of infants' immediate representations of speech sounds. The data from both types of investigation suggest that syllables are important units for young infants' encoding of speech information. At present, there is little indication that young infants represent speech sounds, either immediately or in memory, as strings of phonetic segments. Although we cannot totally preclude the possibility that young infants' representations are also structured in terms of phonetic segments, whether other measures will be more revealing of such representation remains to be seen.

How Stimulus Variability Affects Young Infants' Memory for Speech

The information that infants remember about speech is not limited solely to phonetic or prosodic features. In their examination of how variability affects infants' memory for speech sounds, Jusczyk, Pisoni, and Mullennix (1992) presented 2-month-olds during the preshift period with a series of different voices of the same gender all producing the same word (e.g., "bug"). During the postshift period, and after a 2-minute delay, they presented a new set of talkers from the opposite gender producing the same word. The infants evidently encoded sufficient information to detect gender changes in voice quality. However, in other experiments, Jusczyk and coworkers also found evidence that talker variability, and even vari-ability among tokens produced by a single talker, can affect infants' encoding and memory of speech sounds. For example, even though infants were able to discriminate tokens of "bug" produced by 12 differ-ent talkers from ones of "dug" produced by the same set of talkers when tested without a delay period, the infants did not detect the same contrast when tested after a 2-minute delay. A similar pattern of results occurred when infants were presented with 12 different tokens of each syllable that were all produced by a single talker. In contrast, infants who were presented with a single token of "bug" during the preshift period were able to discriminate it from "dug" even after a 2-minute delay.

In explaining their results, Jusczyk and colleagues suggested that the variability among the tokens might have interfered with infants' encoding of the syllables. They pointed to similar findings in studies with adults. For instance, Martin et al. (1989) found that memory processes in recall tasks were adversely affected when listeners had to cope with talker variability. In particular, their results suggested that both encoding processes and the efficiency of rehearsal processes used to transfer items into long-term memory were disrupted by talker variability. Similarly, Goldinger, Pisoni, and Logan (1991) found that talker variability can either help or hinder recall performance—the outcome is dependent on rate of presentation. At fast presentation rates, talker variability interferes with rehearsal and encoding, preventing subjects from using elaboration techniques. At slow presentation rates, subjects have more time to encode the stimulus items and elaborate on them in rehearsal. The suggestion is that the elaboration process provides additional talker-specific cues in long-term memory that can be used at the time of retrieval to improve recall performance.

Are Memory Representations Abstract or Talker-Specific?
These findings concerning the effects of stimulus variability raise another interesting issue with respect to infants' representations of speech information, namely, how abstract are these representations? For instance, do infants have a representation that is detailed with respect to information about talker's voice, speaking rate, speech register, and so forth, or is their representation one that simply specifies abstract phonetic properties? Kuhl has argued that her "perceptual magnet" effects in infants' categorization of vowel stimuli suggest that infants are encoding prototypes of native-language vowel categories (Grieser and Kuhl 1989; Kuhl 1991; Kuhl et al. 1992). However, because the stimuli used in these studies are synthetically produced, it is not possible to determine the extent to which magnet effects are influenced by talker differences, speaking rate, and so on. More recently, Kuhl (1993; Kuhl and Iverson 1995) has raised the possibility that the magnet effect may be based on storage of specific instances of items infants have actually encountered. Still, it is not clear exactly how this would work because the vast majority of instances of any

vowel category that infants encounter will come in the contexts of words, rather than from the productions of isolated vowels. Just how perceptual magnets for individual vowel categories are derived from all the different phonetic contexts in which a vowel might appear is not apparent at this point.

Nevertheless, the view that the sound patterns of lexical items are stored in terms of some prototypical form (or as an abstract phonological representation) is the starting assumption of most models of adult word-recognition processes (e.g., Lahiri and Marslen-Wilson 1991; Luce, Pisoni, and Goldinger 1990; Marslen-Wilson and Welsh 1978; Morton 1969). Such prototypes are usually held to be normalized across a range of different utterance variables such as talker's voice, loudness, speaking rate, speech register, and so on. The alternative view that listeners might actually store individual traces of instances of individual words is often considered to be unrealistic and computationally inefficient. However, findings from implicit memory tasks suggest that listeners do seem to retain information about specific instances of previously experienced items (e.g., Craik and Kirsner 1974; Goldinger 1992; Martin et al. 1989), and these findings have raised anew the prospect that the representations of the sound patterns of lexical items may correspond to specific instances, as opposed to abstract prototypes (Goldinger 1992; Jusczyk 1992, 1993a). In chapter 8, we will discuss further just how such an account fits with what is known about word recognition processes. For the present, let us note that findings that indicate that language learners and fluent speakers preserve very detailed information about the acoustic characteristics of previously encountered speech tokens would be in line with accounts of word recognition that are based on the storage of specific exemplars.

Long-term Retention of Speech Information by Infants
To this point, our survey of infants' memory for speech information has focused on what happens over delay intervals of only a few minutes. One can ask whether infants engage in any longer-term storage of information about specific items. Certainly, it is long-term storage that is required to begin to build up a lexicon. As mentioned above, owing to limitations in current methodology, it is difficult to study long-term memory for speech information in younger infants. One notable exception has been the research that has involved studying newborn infants' reactions to information that was presented to them prenatally. For example, DeCasper

and Spence (1986) had pregnant mothers read a particular story aloud twice a day during their last 6 weeks of pregnancy. Shortly after birth, their infants were given a choice between listening to the familiar passage or a novel one. The infants exhibited a significant preference for the familiar passage. In contrast, a control group showed no significant preference for either of the two passages. Thus, prenatal exposure to the passage subsequently affected the infants' choice of which passage to listen to. The infants clearly retained at least some information about these passages. Although it is difficult to know exactly what information from the stories may have triggered the newborn's subsequent recognition of these, it seems likely that what they were able to retain had to do with some general rhythmic properties of the particular passages.

Prospects of carrying out investigations of long-term memory for speech are considerably brighter with older infants. Still, such investigations of memory for speech information by older infants are really only in the beginning stages. Certainly, there is ample reason to believe that during their first year, infants have some capacity to remember information about specific words that they have heard. Studies of the development of word comprehension suggest that infants first begin to show recognition of words around 8 to 10 months (Benedict 1979; Huttenlocher 1974). Moreover, a recent investigation with French-learning 10-month-olds by Hallé and Boysson-Bardies (1994b) compared listening times to lists of words that were either likely or unlikely to be familiar to infants at this age. Even when the types of lists were closely matched for their phonetic properties, the infants displayed significantly longer listening times to the lists of familiar words. Hence, findings from these studies provide some indication that infants are retaining information about the sound structures of some words to which they have been exposed.

The results from another recent investigation suggest that the process of learning about some specific lexical items may actually begin fairly early during the first year. Mandel, Jusczyk, and Pisoni (1995) found that $4\frac{1}{2}$-month-olds show signs of recognizing the sound patterns of their own names. In particular, they found that infants listened significantly longer to repetitions of their own names than to other infants' names. This preference for the infant's own name occurred even when one of the other names had the same stress pattern as that name. Thus, it was not simply the prosodic features of their names that infants were responding to. Instead, infants seem to have stored sufficient detail about the sound patterns of their names to distinguish them from other names with similar prosodic characteristics.

Certainly, the infant's own name is an item that he or she is likely to have heard frequently in the input, particularly when the individual uttering the name is making eye contact with the infant. Thus, it is probably not surprising that this is an early sound pattern that is stored on a long-term basis. One can ask whether the name is only one of many frequently occurring sound patterns of words that $4\frac{1}{2}$-month-olds retain. Results of a follow-up study that we have conducted bear on this issue. We have explored the possibility that infants might display some recognition of items apt to appear frequently within their hearing. In particular, we have compared infants' listening times for items such as "mommy" and "baby" to their listening times for relatively unfamiliar items, like "hamlet" and "kingdom." In contrast to the situation with their own names, the listening times in this experiment were not significantly longer for "mommy" and "baby." Hence, there was no evidence that infants recognized the sound patterns of these particular items. An analogous experiment with 6-month-olds yielded some recognition of "baby," but no recognition of "mommy." Of course, this follow-up study with $4\frac{1}{2}$- and 6-month-olds does not rule out the possibility that infants might display recognition of other kinds of sound patterns (such as siblings' names or the names of family pets). Regardless, for the present purposes, it is interesting that $4\frac{1}{2}$-month-olds retain some information about at least one frequently occurring sound pattern, and that this one happens to be one associated with their own names.

Studies that investigate which words an infant at a particular age recognizes give us some indication of the kinds of sound patterns that the infant encodes into long-term memory. However, such studies cannot provide information about how much experience with a word is necessary for infants to recognize it on another occasion. For this purpose, what is required is to systematically control the amount of exposure that infants have to particular items, and then to test recognition of these same items. We have made an initial step in this direction in a recent study (Hohne, A. M. Jusczyk, and Redanz 1994; Jusczyk, Hohne, et al. 1993). We arranged to visit 8-month-olds in their homes for 10 days during a 2-week period. Each day, the infants heard a series of tape-recorded stories produced by the same talker (half the infants heard one talker, half heard another). The talker was not one of the individuals who actually visited the infants' homes. Approximately, two weeks after the last home visit, the infants were tested in the laboratory to see what they remembered about what they had heard. Infants were presented with lists of words that had actually been used in the stories. The words were produced by either the familiar talker or another talker. The infants listened significantly longer to the words produced by the familiar talker, suggesting that they retained information about her voice quality, despite the fact that they had never directly interacted with this individual.

In a related investigation (Hohne et al. 1994), infants heard a subset of the same stories for a 10-day period. However, this time the focus was on whether or not the infants remembered specific words from the stories. Five different talkers recorded the three stories, and two different story orders were used, so that on each day an infant heard a different talker/ story order combination. Once again, the talkers were not the same individuals who visited the infants in their homes. After a two-week delay, the infants came to the lab for testing. This time they heard lists of words from the stories and lists of novel foil words that were matched to the story words in their frequency of occurrence. Care was also taken to match the overall phonetic characteristics of the lists of foils as closely as possible to the lists of story words. For a given infant, the lists used in the experiment were produced by a single talker (who was one of the five who had recorded the stories). The infants who had participated in the home visits listened significantly longer to the words that came from the stories. Therefore, there was some indication that the infants had extracted and remembered the sound patterns of some of the frequently occurring words in the stories. To verify this, a control group (who had not heard the stories) was tested on the same lists of words. This group showed no preference for either type of list.

Thus, the last two studies provide some indication that 8-month-old infants do engage in some long-term storage of information about voices and words that they have heard. In light of the fact that word comprehension skills appear to begin around this time, it is interesting that infants are storing information about the sound patterns of words, even in the absence of any clear referents to tie them to. Traditionally, studies of early word learning have tended to concentrate on the cognitive underpinnings needed to learn words. That is, these studies typically examine the state of the child's conceptual structures and their abilities to pick up the relevant attributes of the objects to which the words refer (Clark 1973, 1983; Markman 1991; Mervis 1989; Nelson 1988; Waxman 1991). With the exception of the work of some child phonologists (Vihman 1993b; see also Plunkett 1993), it is hard to find much mention of how the sound properties of a word affect which words appear in a child's vocabulary.

However, in the end, knowing a word requires that one attach a meaning consistently to a particular sound pattern. One has to be capable of identifying this sound pattern in the speech stream. It is this part of the sound/meaning equation that seems to get left out of many accounts of how the child learns words. The findings from these studies on infants' memory for sound patterns seem to show that word learning may occur in two different ways. Sometimes infants may have a meaning in mind that they attempt to find the right sound pattern for. On other occasions, they may store a sound pattern first and then look to link it to the appropriate meaning.

Some Implications for Language Development

Much remains to be discovered about the way that memory and attention processes interact with infants' speech-perception capacities in the context of acquiring a native language. The studies to date show that infants are attentive to a range of information in the speech signal. They seem to be especially sensitive to the distributional frequencies of certain patterns in the input. This is particularly evident in the findings showing that sensitivity declines to nonnative contrasts and that infants begin to respond to the phonotactic and prosodic organization of their native language. However, infants are also able to exercise enough control over their attentional resources to perceive speech under less-than-ideal conditions.

That infants' attentiveness to speech information is something that extends beyond the bounds of the laboratory is shown by their retention of information about speech that they have previously heard. Thus, we reviewed evidence that suggests that not only do young infants retain details about speech sounds over brief delay intervals, but older infants also seem able to retain information about frequently occurring speech sounds for periods as long as two weeks. Nevertheless, considerably more research is needed to determine the level of detail present in any long-term storage of speech information by older infants. It will be especially useful to see whether these representations are structured with respect to syllabic units, as those of younger infants appear to be, and also to determine whether infants store individual instances of utterances or more abstract representations of their sound patterns.

There are a number of other issues concerning attention and memory that deserve further investigation. One such issue concerns what the attentional capacities of infants are at a given age and the extent to which these change with development. Studies that vary the information load on infants at a given age may be one way to obtain the necessary information. Some of the studies focusing on how infants handle stimulus variability may be a reasonable starting point. Indeed, there are already some suggestions that variability can affect infants' encoding and retention of speech information. The next step is to systematically manipulate load and task demands. Exploring how these factors affect processing at various ages will provide an indication of how processing resources develop during the course of the first year. Similar sorts of investigations evaluating infants' memory for speech information would help to fill out the picture of how memory capacities develop.

At an even more basic level, it would be interesting to know how memory and attentional limitations might affect the kinds of relations that infants are able to pick up from the speech signal. Do infants only associate bits of information that occur within close succession to each other in the speech wave, or are they also able to detect and encode relationships among elements that occur more remotely from each other? How, if at all, does this span for relating different bits of information change in the course of development? An answer to these last two questions is particularly important for understanding the extent to which infants can use information in the speech signal to provide clues to certain syntactic dependencies that occur in the language (e.g., the relation between verbs and particles in English, or the components of negation in French).

One interesting suggestion that has been offered about the course of language acquisition (Newport 1990, 1991; see also Elman 1993 for a similar suggestion) is the "less-is-more hypothesis." This is the notion that having a restricted range of capacities and a smaller processing window might actually make it easier to pick up certain kinds of information in the input than would be the case at a later point when processing capacities have increased. One reason the first year may be such a productive time for learning about the nature and organization of the sound properties of the native language is that infants' processing capacities are ideally suited to pulling out the kinds of dependencies that hold within the structure of a word. The tendency of English-learners to begin segmenting fluent speech into chunks involving stressed syllables could be an illustration of how having a processing window of a certain size then allows the infant to more easily discover relations that hold within such units (such as allophonic and phonotactic properties). By the time that infants have successfully extracted these kinds of relations from the speech signal, their processing resources may have expanded, allowing them to notice new kinds of relations that are present in the input. Indeed, in seeking out such new relations, they may not attend as closely to the relations they were most sensitive to at an earlier point in development. Some of the newer kinds of relations that are discovered may supersede the earlier ones in terms of their utility in on-line speech comprehension. We shall return to this issue in the next chapter when we discuss the way information in the speech signal may help infants to discover relations that hold at other levels of linguistic organization.

Chapter 6

How Attention to Sound Properties May Facilitate Learning Other Elements of Linguistic Organization

It seems pretty clear that the basic speech perception capacities that infants possess should prove useful in learning how the sound structure of the native language is organized. What is less obvious is that these same perceptual capacities could play a role in acquiring information about other levels of language structure. Languages vary in terms of their sounds and their meanings, and the way that sound patterns are organized does not bear an obvious relation to how patterns of meanings are organized in the language. The simple notion that similarities in sound patterns predict similarities in word meanings is easily disproved by considering a few examples in any language. Thus, in English, the sound patterns of the words "rat" and "cat" are more similar to each other than either is to the word "mouse," yet a consideration of the referents of each of these items would clearly find "rat" and "mouse" are more closely grouped together than either is to "cat." Similarly, "mushrooms" and "mush" are less semantically related than "mush" and "cereal," and so on. Consequently, any approach that looks for a very direct mapping between similarities at the level of sounds and the level of meanings is doomed to failure.

However, there are other ways the sound structure of native-language utterances could bear a relation to other levels of linguistic organization. One possibility, often discussed, is that elements of the syntactic organization are marked in the acoustic structure of utterances. As was noted in discussing McNeill's work, this possibility was considered and rejected about thirty years ago on the grounds that units derived from the acoustic signal do not necessarily correspond to the critical units in the linguistic analysis of the utterances. For example, pauses in speech can be the result of hesitations that have to do with finding the correct word as well as for syntactic reasons. In fact, McNeill believed that correctly interpreting many of the kinds of acoustic changes that occur in fluent speech could only come about if one already was in possession of a grammar. Without a grammar, learners could only track the physical changes in the signal, not the perceived contour that is correlated with the syntactic organization. Hence, the idea that the child could learn the syntax from what happens to the speech signal seemed unlikely to him.

Actually, McNeill's arguments were directed at whether there was sufficient information in the speech signal to pull out the syntactic structure. He was reacting to a very strong version of what is now usually called prosodic bootstrapping. More specifically, he was evaluating the possibility that one could recover the entire syntactic description of an utterance from the speech signal. Thus, his arguments were directed at this strong view. He never did claim that there was no useful information about syntactic organization to be derived from the acoustic signal.

It was not until the 1980s that researchers in language acquisition seriously considered how information in the signal could facilitate the acquisition of syntax. Until then, researchers more or less sidestepped the issue of how the child ends up with the right pieces of the speech signal to use for syntactic analysis. For most accounts, the starting point was that the child was already dealing with clauses and simply had to discover their internal syntactic organization. How the child succeeded in isolating the right units, and not fragments from different units, was not seriously considered until investigators such as Gleitman and Wanner (1982; Gleitman et al. 1988) and Peters (1983, 1985) began to suggest that information in the speech signal itself could be used for this purpose. The basic notion was that prosodic (and other) markers in the speech signal provide clues to syntactic units such as clauses and phrases. In addition, there was speculation that such marking could even be helpful in working out the syntactic tree (i.e., the hierarchical arrangement of grammatical units) underlying the utterance (Gleitman et al. 1988).

One reason for the renewed interest in the information available in the speech signal had to do with a reaction to proposals based on learnability accounts of language acquisition, such as those offered by Wexler and Culicover (1980). In particular, these accounts appeared to demand exposure to a range of very complex sentence structures in order to select the grammar that correctly characterizes utterances in the native language that the learner is acquiring and to rule out possible alternative grammars. Morgan (1986) demonstrated that access to information in the speech signal that helps to bracket syntactic units appropriately could effectively reduce the degree of complexity required for learners to select the grammar that corresponds to the native language that they are acquiring.

It is important to note that information available in the signal was seen as a means of complementing, but not supplanting, other sources of information that learners draw upon to discover the syntactic organization of their language. For example, although there might be information in the signal to help in correctly bracketing the input, the learner still needed some means of labeling the brackets appropriately (i.e., assigning each such unit to the correct grammatical category) and of working out the relations among the items clustered within a particular bracket. Hence, prosodic bootstrapping accounts were intended to show how information in the speech signal could interact with innate linguistic capacities or with other cues to sentence structure and lead to the acquisition of a native language (Morgan 1990).

The notion that learners may rely on information in the speech signal to help in the discovery of syntactic organization has come to be known as "prosodic bootstrapping." Still, the speech signal contains other potentially valuable sources of cues that are not necessarily prosodic in nature. For example, some languages use *concord morphology*, wherein words that appear with certain syntactic units share similar affixes. Also, the recurrence of function words in certain sentential positions could be helpful in signaling certain types of syntactic units. One indication that all of these kinds of cues are potentially helpful in learning the syntactic organization of a language comes from a study of adults learning artificial grammars (Morgan, Meier, and Newport 1987). In separate experiments, Morgan and colleagues found that the presence of prosodic markers, concord morphology, or function words resulted in faster and more accurate learning of artificial grammars. It is conceivable that some of the success that the adults had with these cues is attributable to their knowing a first language and how comparable cues operate in it. Nevertheless, the results of this study offer an important demonstration that the presence of these kinds of cues can facilitate the learning of syntactic relations.

What conditions must hold to seriously entertain the proposition that prosodic bootstrapping occurs in first-language acquisition? First, there must be some indication that there are acoustic correlates of syntactic organization present in speech. Second, the potential prosodic correlates must be ones that infants are able to detect in speech. Third, there must be some indication that infants actually rely on these correlates in organizing the input. Let us first consider the evidence for these conditions. Then, we will consider how other possible sources of information in the signal that are not prosodic in nature could also bear on the acquisition of the syntax of a native language.

Evidence for Prosodic Marking of Grammatical Units

There are a number of cues associated with prosody, such as fundamental-frequency changes (i.e., intonation contours), stress patterns, pausing, and durational differences that could serve as potential markers of units in the speech stream. It has been noted that clause boundaries in English are often marked by pauses, increases in the duration of syllables preceding the boundary, and changes in fundamental frequency (e.g., Klatt 1975; Luce and Charles-Luce 1983; Nakatani and Dukes 1977). For example, Cooper and Paccia-Cooper (1980; see also Martin 1970) reported evidence of longer pauses at clause boundaries. Similarly, a number of investigators have found evidence of segmental lengthening in the syllable immediately preceding syntactic boundaries (Cooper and Paccia-Cooper 1980; Klatt 1975, 1976; Price et al. 1991; Wightman et al. 1992). Price et al. (1991) also found evidence of pitch changes in the vicinity of syntactic boundaries. In addition, linguistic analyses of different languages point to a tendency for intonation groups to correspond to major syntactic units such as clauses or their important components (Bolinger 1978; Cruttenden 1986; Selkirk 1984).

There are also indications that some of these potential cues to syntactic boundaries do play a role in how listeners perceive these fluent utterances. A number of relevant demonstrations have used sentences with potentially ambiguous phrasal boundaries (Collier and t'Hart 1975; Lehiste, Olive, and Streeter 1976; Scott 1982; Scott and Cutler 1984). In one such study, Streeter (1978) independently manipulated intensity, duration, and intonation cues. She found that each of these cues could affect the way that ambiguous sentences were interpreted. More recently, Price et al. (1991) conducted an extensive investigation using a systematic set of materials that were produced by radio announcers on different occasions. In addition to analyzing these materials for acoustic cues to boundaries, investigators collected perceptual data from adult listeners that confirmed that changes in syllable durations, fundamental frequency, and pausing were used as indices of syntactic units. Finally, the results of several investigations suggest that listeners are sensitive to speech cues that are correlated with phrasal units in unfamiliar foreign languages (Pilon 1981; Wakefield, Doughtie, and Yom 1974).

Nevertheless, it must be noted that many of the same acoustic changes that frequently coincide with important syntactic units in speech also occur in utterances for nonsyntactic reasons (Beckman and Edwards 1990; Grosjean and Gee 1987; Nespor and Vogel 1986; Vassiere 1981). For example, lengthening may occur to distinguish a voiced stop consonant from a voiceless one (Klatt 1976). Intonation may convey stylistic and affective attributes of the talker (Fairbanks and Pronovost 1939; Lieberman 1961; Williams and Stevens 1972). Consequently, if listeners were to rely on any one of these cues for information about grammatical units, they still would need some other mechanism to let them know when the cues were actually relevant to syntactic matters. Hence, we cannot assume that listeners can read the entire syntactic organization of a sentence from an analysis of the speech signal.

The upshot of all this is that although syntax is an important factor, it is not the sole determinant of the organization of suprasegmental information in a sentence. At the same time, the fact that a particular prosodic cue can serve other functions does not mean that it is useless for signaling important grammatical units. First, as the data reviewed above indicate, these cues have been shown to affect the interpretation of sentences. Second, prosodic cues to phrasal boundaries commonly act in combination with one another. For example, pitch changes at the ends of clauses in English tend to occur in combination with increased final syllable durations and pausing (Price et al. 1991). As with other cases involving multiple cues, the contribution of any one cue may not be as important as the summed tendency or possible interaction of several different cues. Thus, it is the constellation of cues from the speech signal, rather than any single cue, that is likely to provide information helpful to the grammatical organization of utterances.

So far, the evidence considered only relates to the prospect that there are potential prosodic markers of syntactic units in fluent speech between adults. The acoustic characteristics of child-directed speech are known to differ from adult-directed speech in several ways (Ferguson 1977; Garnica 1977; Grewel 1959). Many prosodic features have been shown to be exaggerated in speech that is addressed to children. Among other things, the average pitch of child-directed speech is known to be higher, the pitch range more exaggerated, and the durations of content words longer than for adult-directed speech (Garnica 1977). Moreover, these kinds of prosodic differences between child- and adult-directed speech have been observed across a range of different languages (Fernald and Simon 1984; Fernald, Taeschner, Dunn, Papousek, Boysson-Bardies, and Fukui 1989; Grieser and Kuhl 1988; Papousek, Papousek, and Haekel 1987; Stern, Spieker, Barnett, and MacKain 1983). In addition, more consistent use of pitch changes at clause boundaries has been observed for child-directed than for adult-directed speech (Garnica 1977; Stern et al. 1983). Similarly, Broen (1972) reported that pauses were used more often at clause boundaries, and Bernstein Ratner (1986) found more pronounced segmental lengthening in the vicinity of these boundaries.

Other recent investigations have provided strong evidence for the prosodic marking of clause boundaries in child-directed speech, although the picture with respect to the marking of sub-clausal units (such as syntactic phrases) is more mixed (Fisher and Tokura 1996; Jusczyk et al. 1992; Lederer and Kelly 1991). For instance, Fisher and Tokura (1996) found no consistent prosodic marking for units smaller than clauses in the sample that they analyzed, whereas Jusczyk et al. (1992a) found correlations of pitch and duration cues with subject/predicate phrase boundaries in their samples. Lederer and Kelly (1991) reported that even minor differences in syntactic structure (e.g., prepositional phrases) were marked in the samples that they analyzed. We will return to this issue when we consider results pertaining to infant's sensitivity to phrasal boundaries.

There are indications that prosodic changes frequently coincide with syntactic boundaries in speech between adults. Changes in pitch, syllable duration, and pausing have been shown, both individually and in combination, to affect the perception of syntactic boundaries. In addition, many of these same prosodic cues appear in an exaggerated form in speech directed to children.

Sensitivity to Prosodic Markers in the Input

Although it is interesting that some prosodic marking of syntactic units is present in the input received, we need to know whether infants are actually sensitive to its occurrence. For example, there is information to be perceived in the ultraviolet region of the spectrum but, unlike bees, humans are not capable of seeing it. Likewise, in order for prosodic cues to play any explanatory role in how the syntactic organization of language is acquired, we must show that infants are capable of responding to this information. Thus, the first order of business is to devise a means to find this out.

Hirsh-Pasek et al. (1987) reasoned that if infants respond to prosodic markers in the input, then they should prefer to hear speech that is segmented in accordance with these markers as opposed to speech that is segmented inappropriately. Hence, they collected samples of speech from a young woman who was talking to a 19-month-old. They excised a set of passages that were five to seven sentences in length, and they inserted a series of 1-second pauses in each of them. Two versions of each passage were produced. In one case, all the pauses were inserted at the boundaries between two clauses (we will refer to these as the *coincident versions*); in the other case, an equal number of pauses was inserted but between two words in the middle of a clause (we will call these the *noncoincident versions*). It is important to note that the location of the pauses in the coincident versions coincided with other markers of the clause boundary such as syllable lengthening and pitch declination. Hence, for the coincident versions, the pause locations cooperated with whatever other prosodic markers of clause boundaries were present, whereas for the noncoincident versions, the pause locations competed with other potential markers of clause boundaries.

Hirsh-Pasek and colleagues hypothesized that if infants are sensitive to the prosodic marking of clauses in the input, they would prefer to listen to the coincident versions of their samples than to the noncoincident versions.[1] In their first experiment, they used the headturn preference procedure to present samples of both types to 10-month-olds. The infants listened significantly longer to the coincident than to the noncoincident versions of the samples. In a second experiment, they demonstrated that 7-month-olds also displayed the same listening preferences for the coincident versions. Hirsh-Pasek and coworkers interpreted these findings as an indication that infants as young as 7 months old are sensitive to the presence of prosodic markers to clausal units. A subsequent investigation by these same researchers examined whether the exaggerated prosody of child-directed speech may have enhanced the infants' ability to detect markers to clausal units (Kemler Nelson et al. 1989). The same woman who had recorded the child-directed speech in the previous experiment produced adult-directed speech samples for the new study. Once again, passages between five and seven clauses in length were chosen, and two versions of each one were prepared by inserting 1-second pauses either at clause boundaries (coincident versions) or in the middle of clauses (noncoincident versions). As in the previous study, the $8\frac{1}{2}$-month-olds who heard the child-directed speech displayed a significant preference for the coincident versions. However, the infants tested on the adult-directed speech samples showed no such preference, prompting Kemler Nelson and colleagues to conclude that the exaggerated prosody of the child-directed speech samples may have facilitated the detection of markers of clausal units in these samples.

A subsequent investigation by Morgan, Swingley, and Miritai (1993) provided converging evidence that English-learning infants are sensitive to the prosodic marking of clause boundaries in the input. In particular, they used a paradigm in which infants had to respond by turning their heads whenever a noise stimulus occurred. The infants were better able to detect the noise when it occurred between words from different clauses than between words within the same clause. The suggestion here, as in click-detection experiments with adults (Abrams and Bever 1969), is that the noises are more easily detected when they do not interrupt perceptual processing units (in this case, clauses).

How can we be certain that infants in these studies were actually responding to the prosodic markers rather than to some other information available in the utterances? One demonstration that prosodic cues are important is to show that they are sufficient to produce the longer listening times to the kinds of coincident samples that Hirsh-Pasek et al. (1987) used in their study. To explore this possibility, Jusczyk (1989) low-pass filtered Hirsh-Pasek et al.'s coincident and noncoincident samples at 400 Hz to eliminate most of the available phonetic information in the samples. Six-month-olds tested on these low-pass-filtered samples displayed the same listening preferences for the coincident versions. Hence, even when most of the phonetic information was removed from the signal, infants still responded to the way the pauses were related to the prosodic information in the utterances. Therefore, these findings are consistent with the view that infants are sensitive to the type of prosodic marking that could ultimately provide cues about clause boundaries in utterances.

What is the basis of infants' sensitivity to prosodic marking of clausal units? Is this sensitivity specific to native-language patterns that the infants have experienced, or is there a more general basis for the way the infants respond? There are indications that the kinds of prosodic changes that occur at clause boundaries in English also occur in many other languages (Cruttenden 1986). Hence, one possibility is that infants are responding preferentially to the coincident versions of the samples for reasons other than the fact that they have picked up something specific to English prosodic structure. Rather, their responsiveness to these types of changes may reflect a more general bias for processing auditory input. What kind of evidence might lead to such a conclusion? A demonstration that infants are sensitive to the marking of clause boundaries in a language, regardless of any experience with it, might be an indication of a more general bias. Also, evidence that the cues that are important in signaling clause boundaries are the same as those used to signal other kinds of event boundaries in auditory perception would seem to favor a more general mechanism, rather than one that is specific to language.

There have been several investigations of how infants respond to clause boundaries in other dialects of their own language and in unfamiliar languages. In one study that is reported in Polka, Jusczyk, and Rvachew (1995), American 9-month-olds were presented with samples produced by a female talker of British English. As in the Hirsh-Pasek et al. (1987) study, the samples included pauses either at clause boundaries or between words in the middle of clauses. Even though the speech patterns of British English were unfamiliar to them, the infants still listened significantly longer to the coincident versions of the samples. In another investigation, Jusczyk (1989) reported that American $4\frac{1}{2}$-month-olds not only listened significantly longer to coincident versions of samples in English, but they also showed the same pattern of responding for utterances in an unfamiliar language, Polish. Interestingly enough, by 6 months of age, the American infants no longer showed a preference for coincident over noncoincident versions of the Polish samples, even when these were low-pass filtered to remove potentially distracting phonetic information. One possible interpretation of these results is that a language-general ability to perceive prosodic marking of clausal units by the $4\frac{1}{2}$-month-olds has given way to more language-specific processing of the utterances, and that by 6 months, the rhythmic patterns of Polish mark it as nonnative input.

To this point, the findings are consistent with the notion that, at least initially, there is a general, rather than language-specific, basis for sensitivity to prosodic marking of clausal units in utterances. However, this picture is complicated by the results of a study that investigated American $4\frac{1}{2}$-month-olds' perception of Japanese utterances. Mandel, Jusczyk, and Mazuka (1992) presented American infants with child-directed speech samples produced by a Japanese mother. They found no evidence that infants at this age listened significantly longer to coincident versions of these samples than they did to noncoincident versions. Another investigation using new samples produced by a different Japanese mother yielded the same pattern of results, that is, American $4\frac{1}{2}$-month-olds did not show a significant listening preference for coincident versions (Jusczyk, Mazuka, et al. 1993).

While it is always difficult to interpret null results, the behavior of American $4\frac{1}{2}$-month-olds toward the Japanese samples certainly seems to contrast with how they responded to the Polish samples. Two possible explanations for the discrepancy come to mind. The first is that the basis for the detection of prosodic markers to clause boundaries is basically language-specific. By this line of reasoning, at least initially, Polish patterns (but not Japanese ones) are simply close enough to the English ones to have engaged the processing routines that American $4\frac{1}{2}$-month-olds use for their native-language utterances. The second possible reason is that the use of such prosodic markers is somehow tied to the rhythmic properties of languages. Japanese is organized around the mora as a rhythmic unit, Polish and English are not. Perhaps this basic feature of rhythmic organization is one that even $4\frac{1}{2}$-month-olds pick up. There are indications that although French newborns are sensitive to changes in numbers of syllables, they do not react to changes in the numbers of morae present in utterances (Bertoncini 1993; Mehler et al. 1995). Thus, it may be that the fact that rhythmic patterns of Japanese are perceived to be nonnative by American infants earlier than the rhythmic patterns in Polish. If so, then this may cause the American infants not to process prosodic cues in the same way as they would for utterances with a rhythmic basis similar to that of English. Of these two possible explanations, the first seems less complicated and hence more plausible. However, further research with other languages is needed to decide between them or among other possible alternatives.

At the same time, there are hints of possible nonspeech parallels to the sensitivity that infants show to the prosodic marking of clausal units in utterances. Specifically, studies with musical stimuli (Mozart minuets) indicate that $4\frac{1}{2}$-month-olds listen significantly longer to samples with pauses inserted at musical phrase boundaries than they do to samples with pauses inserted in the middle of musical phrases (Jusczyk and Krumhansl 1993; Krumhansl and Jusczyk 1990). Interestingly enough, the cues that appear to signal musical phrase boundaries for infants are a decline in pitch and a lengthening of the final note at the musical phrase boundary. These cues parallel ones associated with clause boundaries (i.e., decline in pitch and clause-final syllable lengthening). These parallels observed between the perception of phrase boundaries in music and clause boundaries in speech are tantalizing. They indicate that we cannot totally preclude the possibility that common mechanisms underlie the perception of event boundaries for both speech and music.

Although it is certainly valuable for language learners to have some means of locating clausal units in the input, it would be even more valuable for them to have some way of further segmenting the input into subclausal units, such as phrases. Indeed, as Pinker (1984) has commented, the ability to track the distribution of phrases and of constituents within phrases would take the child a long way toward constructing a grammar. Obviously, prosodic marking of phrasal units is more likely for languages in which word order is more constrained (and hence, likely to keep words within the same constituent together) than for ones in which word order is free. For this reason, the means by which languages mark subclausal units in the input could vary considerably. Concord morphology and other such devices may be a more useful means than prosodic marking to identify elements of the same phrasal constituent in languages with relatively unrestricted word order. Consequently, not unlike the situation of learning about the phonetics and phonotactics of sound patterns in one's native language, learners may have to discover the specific means by which phrasal units are marked in their native language.

In a language like English, which relies on word order to signal syntactic relations, it is not unreasonable to expect that some prosodic marking of phrasal units could occur. Indeed, as noted earlier, there are indications that English-speaking adults are sensitive to potential acoustic correlates of phrase boundaries (e.g., Lehiste et al. 1976; Price et al. 1991; Scott 1982). Among the various kinds of phrasal units in English, subject phrases and predicate phrases are ones that might receive significant marking in the linguistic input. For example, sentence subjects in English function in a number of important ways: (1) they carry nominative case marking; (2) they control agreement in person and number with the verb; (3) they are usually identified as the agent of a transitive verb; and (4) they function as the topic of the sentence (Givón 1979). Similarly, predicate-verb phrases define the architecture of the sentence. The verb phrase, particularly the verb, is responsible for assigning thematic roles in the sentence. In fact, the learning of verbs and verb-phrase structure is seen as pivotal to the induction of grammar in some current theories of language acquisition (e.g., Fisher et al. 1994; Gleitman 1990, 1994; Golinkoff et al.

1987; Naigles and Kako 1993; Pinker 1989). Finally, there is evidence that, at least under some circumstances, intonation groups do align with the subject–predicate division in sentences (Beckman and Edwards 1990; Cruttenden 1986).

For the reasons just described, Jusczyk et al. (1992a) decided to investigate English-learning infants' detection of prosodic marking of subject and predicate phrasal units in utterances. In a series of experiments, using materials drawn from either child-directed spontaneous speech or from stories read to a child, they inserted pauses either at boundaries between subject and predicate phrases (coincident versions) or at locations in the middle of phrases (noncoincident versions). Several interesting findings emerged from this investigation. First, 9-month-olds, but not 6-month-olds, proved to be sensitive to the location of the pauses. That is, only at 9 months of age did infants listen significantly longer to coincident versions than they did to the noncoincident versions. This was confirmed both in cross-sectional comparisons involving different infants at the two ages and in longitudinal comparisons at 6 and 9 months of age with the same infants. The finding that 6-month-olds do not respond to marking of phrasal units is interesting in light of the findings reviewed above that indicate English-learning infants as young as $4\frac{1}{2}$-months of age are sensitive to the marking of clausal units. This may be an indication that infants require more extensive experience with their native language before they detect prosodic markers of phrasal units in the input.

The case that infants in Jusczyk and coworkers' studies were responding to prosodic markers in the passages is strengthened by the results of additional experiments with low-pass-filtered versions of the stimuli. Once again, the 9-month-olds listened significantly longer to coincident than to noncoincident versions of the samples, even when they were low-pass filtered. Furthermore, acoustic analyses of the passages indicated that relative to the noncoincident versions, the coincident versions were more apt to have syllable-final lengthening and pitch drops just prior to where the pauses were inserted (i.e., at the phrasal boundaries in the coincident versions).

At first glance, Jusczyk and his colleagues' findings seem to offer some hope for proponents of the view that, at least for languages like English, infants may be able to discover the syntactic organization of utterances (including the hierarchical ordering of different phrases) directly from prosodic features (e.g., see Lederer and Kelly 1991 for a suggestion along these lines). However, as mentioned above, the likelihood is that prosodic marking of phrasal units would not be equally effective for all languages. Moreover, even for a language like English, the situation is much less straightforward than it first appears. As has been observed in many contemporary accounts of prosodic phonology, prosodic boundaries do not always map directly onto syntactic ones (Hayes 1989; Nespor and Vogel 1986; Selkirk 1981). Indeed, mismatches in the prosodic and syntactic organization may occur even in the simple sentences that are directed to infants acquiring language. Consider the following two sentences.

(1) Mary ate the cake.

(2) She ate the cake.

In (1), the talker is likely to produce prosodic boundary cues after the subject NP, "Mary." However, in (2), even two-year-old talkers (Gerken 1991; Gerken 1994b) either produce no prosodic boundary cues or produce them between the verb and the object NP, "the cake." This is because of the prosodic structure of English. The elementary unit of rhythmic organization is the "foot." In English a foot consists of a strong syllable followed by either zero or one weak syllable (Gerken 1994a, in press; Hayes 1982; Selkirk 1980). Because a weakly stressed pronoun subject cannot begin a foot in (2), it is said to be unfooted (Gerken 1994a, in press). However, at the level of a phonological phrase, it will be joined into the same unit as the following stressed verb–that is, the subject and verb form a prosodic unit. Hence, there is no prosodic marking of the syntactic boundary between the subject and the predicate phrases in (2). By comparison, Mary has a strong first syllable in (1), and therefore is in a foot separate from the following verb. Hence, in this case, a prosodic break is possible between the subject and the verb.

The point here is that in cases with a pronoun subject, like (2), the learner who is looking for prosodic clues about the internal syntactic constituents of the utterance either would receive no information or, maybe worse, would get misleading information about what the major constituents are. It turns out that only a small percentage of the spontaneous speech samples (about 15 percent) used by Jusczyk et al. (1992a) contained potential mismatches of the sort found in (2). Hence, most of the utterances that they used were ones in which prosodic phrase boundaries coincided with syntactic ones. (This fact may be responsible for some of the discrepancies between the results of Jusczyk and coworkers' acoustic analyses and those of Fisher and Tokura (1996) that were mentioned in the previous section.)

Gerken, Jusczyk, and Mandel (1994) explored how English-learning infants respond to utterances in which prosodic and syntactic boundaries mismatch. For this purpose, they created new materials to compare infants' responses to sentences with lexical NP subjects, as in (1), to sentences with pronoun subjects, as in (2). An example of a lexical NP type of sample is:

(3) This is a story about a little boy named Sammy. Sammy is a baseball player. Sammy can run fast. And Sammy never misses a ball. Every Saturday, Sammy plays baseball in the park.

A comparable example of a sample with pronoun NPs (after the lead-in sentence) is:

(4) This is a story about a little boy named Sammy. He is a baseball player. He can run fast. And he never misses a ball. Every Saturday, he plays baseball in the park.

Coincident versions of both types of passages were prepared by inserting a 1-second pause in all sentences (after the lead-in sentence) between the subject and predicate phrases. Noncoincident versions had the same number of pauses but these were inserted between the verb and its complement. Nine-month-olds exposed to the sentences with lexical NP subjects behaved exactly like the 9-month-olds in the Jusczyk et al. study— namely, they listened significantly longer to samples in which pauses were inserted between the subject and verb phrases than to ones in which pauses were inserted between the verb and object NP phrases. In contrast, infants who heard the sentences with pronoun subjects did not show a significant preference for either type of segmentation. This is one indication that it is prosodic phrase boundaries, and not necessarily syntactic phrase boundaries, that infants are responding to.

Of course, the English-learning child eventually has to be able to extract information about the internal organization of sentences with pronoun subjects. How could they begin to do this, given the apparent absence of prosodic marking of the subject-predicate boundary in such sentences? One possibility is that they use other (nonprosodic) cues to work out the syntactic relations of such sentences. Another possibility is that learners may benefit by contrasting cases in which pronouns and verbs belong to the same prosodic group with those in which they belong to different groups. In other words, they make cross-sentential comparisons of different utterances. Morgan, Meier, and Newport (1989) found that such cross-sentential comparisons benefited adult learners of arti-ficial grammars. Conceivably, this might hold as well for first-language learners. Resolving the conflict in prosodic organization across cases in which a prosodic boundary sometimes occurs before a particular lexical item and sometimes after it could actually lead the learner toward the discovery of the syntactic organization. Naturally, such a solution assumes that the learner has access to such contrasting cases in the input and is able to recognize the similarities that exist across these (e.g., the presence of familiar words or word sequences).

In fact, there are indications that the needed contrasting cases are readily available in the input that the learner receives. In sentences that involve yes–no questions, there is a tendency for the pronoun and auxil-iary to form a prosodic group that may be separate from the verb. For example, a talker tends to impose a prosodic boundary just before the verb in an utterance like "Did she / throw the ball?" In these cases, the prosodic input favors a marking of the boundary between the pronoun and the main verb. But are infants sensitive to these markers? In the study that we have been considering, Gerken and colleagues conducted an additional experiment to test this possibility. They constructed passages with sentences involving inversions between a pronoun and an auxiliary, that is, yes–no questions. Pauses were inserted either before or after the main verb in these sentences to create the coincident and noncoincident versions. Nine-month-olds listened significantly longer to versions in which the pauses occurred between the subject and verb phrases (i.e., the coincident versions). The implication of these findings is that 9-month-olds are sensitive to the prosodic break between the pronoun and main verb in such sentences. So, in some situations, they may be able to assign a phrase with a pronoun subject to a separate prosodic group than the one that includes the predicate phrase. This suggests that infants at this age are, at least, positioned to notice contrasting cases in which pronouns and verbs belong sometimes to the same prosodic groups and other times to different ones.

Evidence that Prosodic Organization Is Actually Used in Infant's Speech Processing

Given that infants demonstrate some sensitivity to potential prosodic markers of syntactic units, we can ask whether they use this information in organizing their representations of speech. With respect to the way prosodic bootstrapping unfolds, it could be that sensitivity to prosodic markers actually develops long before prosodic groupings play any role in organizing the information provided in fluent speech. Alternatively, it may be that infants are able to make immediate use of their sensitivity to prosodic markers as a means for organizing the input that they receive.

How can we determine when the organization that is potentially available in the prosody begins to play a significant role in speech processing? That is, how can we know whether or not infants are truly organizing the incoming speech signal into units such as clauses or phrases? The problem here is not far removed from one that early psycholinguistic researchers faced when trying to convince skeptical behaviorists that certain units of linguistic analysis corresponded to psychologically real processing units for listeners. The means by which the early psycholinguists were finally able to make their case was to show that linguistic units tend to be natural units for encoding and remembering information conveyed in speech.

A method used successfully with adults to demonstrate that linguistic units are actually used in on-line speech processing was to show that the organization provided by the linguistic structures had an impact on what information was remembered. Specifically, it was found that adults could better remember information from stimuli with a linguistic organization than with an arbitrary one (Marks and Miller 1964; Miller and Isard 1963; Suci 1967). Analogously, one can ask whether for the language learner, a sensitivity to prosodic information also affords an organizational structure for encoding and remembering speech information.

Mandel, Jusczyk, and Kemler Nelson (1994) followed this research strategy in an investigation of whether infants are able to use prosodic organization to encode and remember speech information. Two-month-olds were tested using the version of the HAS procedure with the 2-minute delay between the preshift and postshift periods. To determine whether sentential prosody plays some role in organizing infants' memory for speech, Mandel and colleagues contrasted conditions in which such prosodic information was present to conditions in which it was not. In particular, they examined whether the phonetic properties of words that are prosodically linked within a single clause are better remembered by infants than the same words produced as individual items from a list. Mandel and coworkers reasoned that if prosody really helps in perceptual organization during on-line speech processing, memory for words should be better in the sentential context. Alternatively, there are certain perceptual grounds for actually predicting the opposite pattern of results (i.e., better performance in the list conditions than in the sentence conditions). This is because in some respects, the words in the list condition might be expected to include clearer phonetic cues. In particular, the words in the lists were produced one at a time and in citation form. By comparison, the phonetic characteristics of the individual words in sentential contexts are more apt to be influenced by the phonetic characteristics of surrounding words. It is well known that words produced in fluent speech contexts are often less clearly articulated and more difficult to perceive when excised from context than the same words produced in citation form (Lieberman 1963; Pollack and Pickett 1964).

In their first experiment, Mandel and colleagues used three spoken sentences that had been recorded and selected from a larger group of unrelated sentences. The words in citation form were similarly selected from a longer spoken list of unrelated words. The words from the list were excised and rearranged to form three different word sequences that were otherwise identical to the three sentences. The overall durations of the list sequences were equated to the comparable sentences. Half of the infants in the study heard the sentences; the other half heard the lists. Thus, both groups of infants heard the same words in exactly the same order. The only difference was the prosodic envelope in which the words had been spoken.

During the preshift phase of the experiment, each criterion sucking response resulted in the presentation of either a single sentence or list sequence (e.g., "The rat chased white mice"). For a given infant, the same sentence or list sequence was played throughout the preshift phase. When the infant's sucking response habituated to this stimulus, the preshift phase ended and was followed by a 2-minute silent interval in which a series of colorful slides was presented. Then the postshift phase began. The infants heard either the same stimulus as in the preshift phase (control), one that differed by a single segment in one word (one phonetic change—e.g., "The cat chased white mice"), or one that differed by one segment in each of two words (two phonetic changes—e.g., "The cat raced white mice"). The results indicated that performance was significantly better for the sentential materials than for the lists. In particular, the infants responded with significant increases in sucking to both kinds of phonetic changes with the sentential materials, but not to either type of change with the list materials. Mandel and coworkers concluded that even 2-month-olds derive some benefit from the organization offered by sentential prosody in remembering speech information.

A follow-up experiment in the same study replicated and extended the findings by showing that 2-month-olds' memories for information within a sentence is better than for the same information in fragments of two adjoining sentences. Thus, infants were more likely to notice a change in "Cats like park benches" when this had been spoken as a single sentence than when the same words were excised from the sentences, "I know what cats like. Park benches are their favorite things to play on." Taken together, the results of the two experiments in this study suggest that the prosodic organization afforded by well-formed sentences facilitates infants' processing and memory for speech information.

More recently, the same investigators (Mandel, Kemler Nelson, and Jusczyk 1996) explored how prosodic structure may affect infants' abilities to better encode sequential order information. The ability to encode serial order is important for many different aspects of language acquisition. For example, serial order is important for the recognition of multisyllabic morphemes and words. The toddler learning English will find it valuable to distinguish between [ti' pat] and [pat' ti] ("teapot" and "potty"). An ability to encode serial order is also important for learning how word forms are formed and related to other words in the native language. For instance, derivational morphemes occur closer to word stems than do inflections (Kiparsky 1982; Mohanon 1986). In languages with highly developed morphological systems, such as Turkish, there are strict constraints on the ordering of sequences of morphemes within a word (Kenstowicz 1994). Finally, an ability to encode and remember serial order information may also be important for learning about syntactic relations within sentences and within phrases. For instance, changes in the ordering of words in English sentences often result in changes of meaning (compare "The dog bites the man" vs. "The man bites the dog"). In the long run, an inability to encode the order of lexical items would make it impossible for a learner to acquire a language like English, in which word order is used to encode many syntactic functions.

To determine whether prosodic organization helps infants in their encoding of the sequential ordering of speech sounds, Mandel, Kemler Nelson, and Jusczyk (1996) presented the same information either within a single well-formed prosodic unit or as fragments of two adjoining prosodic units. The sentence materials were created by having a naive female talker read the test sentences as part of a list of 15 unrelated sentences. The test sentences were "Cats would jump benches" and "Cats jump wood benches." The two sentences contained the same phonetic materials; only the ordering of the second and third words in each sentence changed. The creation of the comparable sentence fragment sequences was accomplished by having the same talker read a series of questions, followed by well-formed, but abbreviated two-word answers that might occur in the course of conversational speech. The answers used as stimuli were actually embedded in a larger set of questions and answers. The question "Do cats jump or run?" was followed by "Cats jump," whereas the question, "Are those metal benches or wood benches?," was followed by "Wood benches." Subsequently, these sentence fragments were concatenated using a waveform editor to form the sequence "Cats jump. Wood benches." A different series of questions and two-word answers were used to prepare the sequence. "Cats would. Jump benches." Note that each two-word answer was a well-formed prosodic unit. However, when these two-word sequences were combined to form the four-word test sequences, they did not conform to sentential prosody, making them less prosodically coherent than the comparable sentential materials. Half of the infants were tested on the sentential materials and the other half were tested on the fragment sequences. During the preshift phase of the experiment, the 2-month-olds heard a stimulus such as "Cats would jump benches." After a 2-minute delay, the infants heard either the original stimulus or one in which a different ordering of the words occurred (e.g., "Cats jump wood benches"). Once again, infants performed significantly better when the information was presented within the same prosodic unit than when it occurred as parts of two different prosodic fragments. That is, only infants who heard the sentential materials reacted with significant increases in sucking to the word order changes. Therefore, these results provide another indication that the prosodic organization afforded in sentences does play some role in infants' processing and memory for speech information.

What these studies show, then, is that the prosodic packaging of clausal units seems to facilitate even very young infants' memory for speech information. What is not currently known is the extent to which the prosodic organization of units smaller than the clause might also influence language learners' encoding of and memory for speech. Given the likelihood that prosodic cues to subclausal units may be language-specific, and the data that suggest that infants do not show sensitivity to such units before 9 months of age, it does not seem promising to investigate whether 2-month-olds show similar memory benefits for information within prosodic phrases. Rather, it is important to develop procedures that could tap memory processes of older infants. One possibility is to adapt the methodology that Jusczyk and Aslin (1995) used to look at the detection of words in fluent speech. For instance, if infants were familiarized with information that occurred within a particular clause or phrase, as opposed to information that occurred in fragments of clauses or fragments of phrases, would they be more apt to recognize this material when it appeared later in a longer passage? Kemler Nelson, Mandel, and I have tried this for clausal units with 6-month-olds and find that they do perform better when they have been familiarized with material that occurred as a well-formed clausal unit, as opposed to fragments of two different units. Thus, we were able to replicate the findings that we had obtained with 2-month-olds in this older age group and with a new procedure. The next step is to test 9-month-olds with material within phrasal units, which we hope to do in the future.

Reassessing Prosodic Bootstrapping

Considering the evidence reviewed in the preceding three sections, how far can prosodic bootstrapping take the language learner? What the findings show is that clausal units are well marked in the prosody of utterances, that infants are sensitive to this marking, and that it appears to play some role in their encoding and retention of speech information. There is some evidence as well that subclausal units such as major phrases receive prosodic marking and that infants are sensitive to this when it occurs in the input. However, the marking appears to be primarily directed toward prosodic phrase boundaries rather than syntactic ones per se (see Gerken 1996 for a similar view). Moreover, when prosodic and syntactic phrase boundaries do not correspond to each other, it appears to be the prosodic phrase boundaries that young language learners respond to.

One interpretation of this pattern of findings is that prosodic bootstrapping accounts help to explain how infants correctly locate clausal units in the input, but nothing beyond that. This view is based largely on the assumption that if the marking of syntactic phrase boundaries by prosodic cues is less than perfect, then prosodic bootstrapping accounts must fail. Moreover, the fact that on any given occasion, a putative prosodic marker of syntactic boundaries (e.g., syllable lengthening) can also be used for some other communicative function or purpose is seen as problematic. How is the infant to know whether, on a given occasion, the prosodic cue is marking a syntactic boundary or something else?

The position just outlined is probably overly pessimistic for a number of reasons. Consider the last sort of objection, that any particular cue has various uses on different occasions. In fact, the different prosodic indices of phrasal boundaries often work in combination with one another rather than singly. Because these cues are multiple and tend to covary, ambiguity is less troublesome than it would be if the cues were single. Moreover, prosodic bootstrapping is not equivalent to reading the syntactic organization directly from the prosody. Rather, prosodic bootstrapping provides the learner with a kind of rough grouping of elements in the input that then positions the learner to pull out the underlying syntactic organization. Hence, it may be equivalent to the kind of rough categorization of speech sounds that very young infants have before their perceptual categories are modified by language-specific input. Consequently, the prosodic groups do not have to correspond to the syntactic groups on every occasion to be helpful in discovering the underlying syntactic organization of native-language utterances. Just the mere grouping of the input into smaller processing units may prove helpful in itself. The process may facilitate further analyses in much the same way as the $7\frac{1}{2}$-month-old English-learner's use of a metrical segmentation strategy for word segmentation does (i.e., as when the latter strategy provides smaller units of analysis that then allow for a distributional analysis of phonotactic and allophonic cues to word boundaries). The analogous situation in the present case is that prosodic phrase groupings, combined with infants' developing word segmentation abilities, provide the means to work out the distributional patterns of words within such prosodic units.

Finally, as Fisher (in press-a) has noted, language learners typically receive sentence fragments in addition to whole sentences in the input. Most of these are well-formed phrasal units, which the learner could use in cross-sentential comparisons to derive information about syntactic constituents in utterances. For example, the child who hears "the chocolate cake" in response to a question may subsequently be able to use this information in figuring out the constituents of the sentence "She dropped the chocolate cake." Furthermore, it is worth noting that the kinds of fragments that are *not* well-formed phrasal units (viz., errors, hesitations, interruptions, etc.) are precisely those kinds of utterances that are likely to be marked with prosody that suggests that these are not complete units. The prosodic features of such utterances are likely to be similar to what occurs in the noncoincident samples in the studies of perception of phrasal units by infants, namely, they have pauses in places not predicted by the other prosodic correlates to phrasal boundaries.

Before turning to a discussion of other kinds of information in the speech signal that may prove useful for learning about syntactic organization, there is another point that should be considered. Specifically, what is the relationship between sensitivity to prosodic groupings and the capacity for segmenting words from utterances? At one point, Kemler Nelson, Hirsh-Pasek, and I (Kemler Nelson et al. 1989) suggested that sensitivity to units in the input might follow some sort of differentiation process from larger to smaller. That is, sensitivity would develop first for clausal units, then for phrasal units, and ultimately for word units in the input. Indeed, such a developmental sequence is suggested by the pattern of results in our studies (e.g., Hirsh-Pasek et al. 1987; Jusczyk et al. 1992a; Myers et al. 1996) that measure preferences for speech in which pauses have been inserted at or within unit boundaries.

However, the development of new test procedures has produced new evidence that has caused us to reconsider our account. In particular, there is now ample reason to believe that infants begin some sort of rough word segmentation process before they exhibit sensitivity to prosodic markers of phrasal groupings in utterances. Thus, what seems to be happening is that two sorts of processes are going on at the same time with respect to how the infant analyzes the speech signal. On the one hand, the infant is discovering important ways information is grouped or clustered in utterances (i.e., into clauses, and subsequently, into phrases). On the other hand, the infant is also discovering the elementary units (i.e., words) that function inside such larger groupings of information. This latter process that may yield some wordlike units (based on metrical stress properties) at $7\frac{1}{2}$ months and more precise word segmentation (perhaps based on phonotactic and allophonic properties, among other things) over the course of the next three months or so. Ultimately, both kinds of processes can have some bearing on the discovery of the syntactic organization of the native language. To this point, we have focused on the first of these processes— prosodic cues to the way that information is grouped within utterances. Let us now explore how other information in the speech signal may provide clues to syntactic organization.

Other Information in the Signal that May Facilitate the Acquisition of Syntax

We have been considering the way prosody could help to mark breaks in utterances that could reflect their underlying syntactic organization.

However, information about specific sound patterns and where these occur could also provide hints about the nature of syntactic constituents. For example, correlations between certain types of sound patterns of words and their grammatical categories could be potentially helpful in acquiring syntax. Kelly (1992) has noted a number of ways information in the speech signal may be correlated with grammatical category assignment (see also Sereno and Jongman 1995). For example, in bisyllabic English nouns, stress typically occurs on the first syllable, whereas in bisyllabic English verbs, stress is often on the second syllable. In fact, in a survey of over 3,000 nouns and 1,000 verbs in English, Kelly and Bock (1988) found that 94 percent of the nouns had first-syllable stress and 69 percent of the verbs had second-syllable stress.

These distributional properties have some real consequence for fluent English-speakers' behavior: Subjects were more likely to pronounce pseudowords with stress on the first syllable if they thought that these were nouns and on the second syllable if they thought these were verbs. In addition, Cassidy and Kelly (1991) have observed evidence for a significant relationship between syllable number and grammatical class in parental speech to 15-month-old infants. Nouns generally had more syllables than did verbs. In fact, the likelihood that a given word was a noun was 38 percent for one-syllable words, 76 percent for two-syllable words, 92 percent for three-syllable words, and 100 percent for four-syllable words in the input corpora that they analyzed. Obviously, in order to use these kinds of phonological properties to differentiate among nouns and verbs in the input, the learner must have already stored some exemplars of each type of category, along with the frequency with which certain sound patterns are associated with them. One way this may happen is that when words begin to be acquired, learners track the sound properties of words that refer to objects separately from those that refer to actions. This strategy would allow them to note any differences in the frequency with which certain sound patterns are associated with these categories. As the investigations of the perception of phonotactic patterns demonstrate (e.g., Jusczyk et al. 1994), infants are very sensitive to the frequency with which certain patterns appear in the input. Once these kinds of relationships are detected with respect to the first few nouns and verbs in the lexicon, they could be applied to routines that are used to analyze new input strings.

In addition to potential differences in the sound patterns of nouns and verbs, many investigators have focused on similar sorts of distinctions among content and function words. For example, Jakobson and Waugh

(1987) observed that function morphemes from the same language usually share certain phonological properties. Function words are also usually shorter than content words, and they often have different phonemes, such as [ð] in English (Gerken 1996). Moreover, content words are more likely to be stressed than are function words (Gleitman et al. 1988; Kelly 1992). Thus, infants could potentially use such differences as a means of distinguishing function and content words. Morgan and his colleagues have explored a whole range of acoustic properties that could serve to differentiate function words from content words across a range of different languages (Morgan et al. 1996). They did not find evidence that any one property was strongly correlated with either class of words. Nevertheless, they found that function and content words did differ significantly in their distributions of such cues, such that the combination of several such cues was predictive of which class a particular item was likely to belong to. Moreover, in analyzing input to English-learning children, they found that the words with the highest frequencies of occurrence tended to be function words.

In considering these findings on the relation between phonology and grammatical categories, it is important to keep in mind that what the sound properties can provide is a rough categorization of the input. Counterexamples will inevitably arise. Sound properties are surely not perfect predictors of a word's grammatical category. But once again, they may help in a first-pass analysis; they may enable the learner to correctly categorize the information on a number of occasions and then to use other sources of information (semantic, syntactic, pragmatic) to eventually correct those erroneous categorizations that do occur. Moreover, some of these other sources of information may, in the long run, turn out to be more reliable than the information regarding the sound properties of words. If so, we should expect to see a greater reliance on these other kinds of properties as the infant's grasp of the different levels of organization of the native language increases during the course of development.

Thus, the use of these kinds of sound relations may be an interim strategy until the infant's skills are better developed and more established. This, after all, is what bootstrapping is all about. It is a means to get the system started in the right direction. The routes that were used early on need not be involved in how the system functions in adults (Bever 1975) other than to show up occasionally in some psycholinguistic task, such as judging whether a particular pseudoword is more likely to be a noun or a verb in the absence of any semantic information. This may be another example of Newport's "less is more" principle at work. As processing resources come on line and new skills are developed, the infant has more possibilities to choose from. The kinds of information that were relied on heavily when resources were scarce are used less often as other alternatives increase. Thus, infants could at times be more sensitive to the presence of certain kinds of acoustic information than are adults because the greater processing resources of the latter group have led them to rely on other kinds of information.

We have been considering the way the presence of certain kinds of sound patterns could play a role in facilitating the assignment of grammatical categories to words. However, there are other ways simply learning to recognize the sound pattern of certain words could help in discovering the syntactic organization of utterances. By identifying and storing information about certain sound patterns, and by being able to recognize these when they occur in fluent speech, the infant is in a position to observe how these are distributed within the groupings that they extract from utterances. In English, frequently occurring articles such as "the" or "a" rarely occur at the ends of such units, but they commonly occur at the beginnings of these. Moreover, they occur prior to nouns and adjectives, but not immediately before verbs. Thus, by restricting distributional analyses to co-occurrences involving the phonologically defined set of grammatical morphemes and the content words with which they co-occur, learners could potentially distinguish among syntactic phrase types.

One possible problem with the picture that was just presented is the widespread belief that language learners have difficulty perceiving function words because they are unstressed (Echols and Newport 1992; Gleitman et al. 1988). If such words are difficult for language learners to detect in fluent speech, then it is hard to see how they could play much of a role in facilitating a distributional analysis of the input. However, several recent investigations suggest that infants are sensitive to the occurrence of function words in fluent speech. Initial support for such a view comes from a study demonstrating that by 11 months, infants appear to be sensitive to the phonological contribution that grammatical morphemes make to the overall "sound" of their language (Shafer et al. 1992). In particular, Shafer and coworkers found that infants could distinguish a normal English passage from one in which nonsense syllables that were phonologically unlike English grammatical morphemes replaced a subset of actual morphemes.

In another study, Shady, Gerken, and Jusczyk (1995) investigated whether $10\frac{1}{2}$-month-olds show any recognition of the correct ordering of function and content words in their native language. They modified a series of speech passages by interchanging the order of one function-content word pair in each sentence (e.g., "She her felt mother's soft, warm fur," where "her" and "felt" were reversed). The original and modified passages were synthesized using a DECTalk speech synthesizer to ensure that the prosody was not unnatural in the case of the modified samples. When the infants were tested on both versions of these synthesized passages with the headturn preference procedure, they listened significantly longer to the original than to the modified passages. Inspection of the individual passages that were used in testing indicated several kinds of cues that infants may have used to detect the word order reversals. For example, in a number of the modified passages, reversing the order of function and content words led to a sequence of two function morphemes in a row (a sequence that is relatively infrequent in English sentences). Further research is necessary to determine precisely just which sources of information Shady and colleagues' infants were responding to. In any case, English-learning $10\frac{1}{2}$-month-olds seem to have discovered some source of information about how function and content words are typically ordered in utterances in their native language.

The findings reviewed in this section point to other ways information that is available in the acoustic signal could be involved in discovering the syntactic organization of one's native language. The sensitivity that infants display to the recurrence of certain sound patterns in the input, plus their apparent ability to detect the occurrence of words in fluent-speech contexts, are two factors that may position them for a distributional analysis of the input. What is needed at this point is more detailed information about when particular words (especially function words) are recognized by infants. Also, it would be interesting to know whether infants display sensitivity to the kinds of differences that are potentially correlated with grammatical classes of words. A better understanding of these matters would help delineate how much the acquisition of syntax is facilitated by information in the speech signal. Finally, since our focus is on acquisition of the sound structure of the language, we have concentrated on the kind of bootstrapping that could be derived from information in the signal. This does not preclude the possibility that bootstrapping of other sorts also occurs during language acquisition. In fact, it seems very likely that the language learner draws on information from many other sources in order to determine the organization of utterances in the native language.

Exploring Relations between Sounds and Meanings

At some point, in order to fully understand and explain language acquisition, it is necessary to determine how processes at various levels of linguistic organization interact during the course of development. For example, although it is reasonable to suppose that the most important factors influencing whether or not a child will learn a new word meaning have to do with semantic organization (and the child's current cognitive state), other levels of language organization could also affect the process. Thus, the achievement of an optimal way of processing information at some level of linguistic organization (e.g., phonological, syntactic, semantic) may well constrain the possible forms of organization at other levels. That is, the language learner has to find the path that simultaneously satisfies best the task demands at all levels of linguistic organization.

One area in which influences from different levels of organization might be expected is in the development of a lexicon for the native language. Current views are that lexical entries contain information from a number of different levels of organization (e.g., see the papers in Gleitman and Landau 1994). In addition to some description of the sound properties of a lexical item and its associated meanings, an entry may include information about the word's syntactic category and the kinds of syntactic structures that it can participate in. The assumption that lexical entries are potentially rich in information raises some interesting questions about how the lexicon in general and lexical entries in particular develop. For example, do lexical entries all begin in the same way, perhaps as meanings that then get associated to sound patterns, with syntactic information only added at some subsequent point? Are the only limitations on the addition of new lexical entries ones that have to do with whether or not some particular meaning already has a sound label attached to it—that is, something along the lines of Markman's (1989; 1991) mutual exclusivity principle? Does the nature of the sound pattern of a particular word ever affect the likelihood of its being added to the lexicon?

Some Influences of Naming on Categorization Behavior
For the moment, let us consider how the sound structure of words could potentially impact on lexical growth. One possibility is that the presence

of a verbal label influences the learner's categorization of objects and events. By now there are many demonstrations that the nature of verbal labels influences the categorization behavior of older infants. For example, 2- to 3-year-olds have been shown to interpret novel count nouns as referring to basic level and superordinate level categories of objects (D'Entremont and Dunham 1992; Markman and Hutchinson 1984; Soja, Carey, and Spelke 1991; Waxman and Kosowski 1990). However, when novel adjectives are used, children appear to interpret them as referring to object properties or to subordinate level distinctions (e.g., Gelman and Markman 1985; Hall, Waxman, and Hurwitz 1993; Katz, Baker, and Macnamara 1974; Smith, Jones, and Landau 1992; Taylor and Gelman 1988). Moreover, just the mere fact that a name is used in a situation has been shown to influence children's categorizations of objects (Gelman and Taylor 1984; Golinkoff et al. 1992; Markman and Hutchinson 1984; Waxman and Gelman 1986). For example, in their investigation, Markman and Hutchinson (1984) found that 2- and 3-year-olds who heard an object labeled with a term like "dax" were much more likely to respond to a request to "Find another dax" by choosing an object with similar properties (i.e., a taxonomic choice) than one that bore a thematic relation to the first named object (i.e., a thematic choice). By comparison, when the label was not used in the request (i.e., "Find another one"), the same children were more likely to make a thematic choice. More recently, Landau and Shipley (1995) reported results of an investigation that demonstrated that the number of different labels used (one vs. two) influences whether children as young as 2 years are likely to group objects into a single category or not.

Furthermore, the impact that naming an object has on categorization performance has been reported for 1-year-olds and even younger infants. In a series of studies, Waxman and Markow (1995) found that 12-month-olds responded differently on a categorization task depending on the availability of a verbal label. Half of the infants heard an experimenter label an object using a novel noun phrase (e.g., "Look, an animal"); the other half a heard a more general phrase (e.g., "Look, what's here"). During a subject test period, the infants who heard the noun phrase were significantly more likely to distinguish between a new instance from the familiar category and an instance from a novel category. Waxman and Markow interpreted this finding as an indication that the availability of the same label "invites infants to search for coherence among the different objects and to form object categories."

Balaban and Waxman (1995) extended these findings in several interesting directions. First, they demonstrated that infants as young as 9 months of age are affected by the availability of a verbal label on a categorization task. Second, they demonstrated that the changes in categorization behavior by the presence of a verbal label involve more than a general alerting effect provided by auditory stimulation. In particular, they found differential patterns of responding when a verbal label (even a low-pass-filtered one) was used during a familiarization period with an object as compared to when a nonspeech auditory stimulus (a sinewave tone matched to the label in loudness and duration) was used. Novelty preferences during the test period were greater when infants had heard the words rather than the tones during familiarization. Thus, there are some indications that the presence of verbal labels are beginning to influence categorization behavior in language learners around the time when they begin to show the first signs of comprehension of words (e.g., Benedict 1979; Huttenlocher 1974). Infants at this age appear to be primed to begin to link verbal labels to their categorizations of objects and events in their immediate environment.

Sound Patterns and Representations in the Lexicon

Investigations by child phonologists (e.g., Ferguson and Farwell 1975; Schwartz 1988; Vihman et al. 1985) suggest another way the sound structure of words can affect the pattern of lexical growth—namely, infants may avoid words that contain sounds that are difficult for them to produce. However, as Schwartz has noted, although this tendency would be expected to affect the nature of the lexicon underlying the child's production of words, there is no necessity that it should affect the words in the child's receptive lexicon. Another possibility is that the infant might at least initially avoid adding to the lexicon words that are difficult to discriminate from existing items in the lexicon. For example, models such as WRAPSA (Jusczyk 1993a) and CHIPHO (Suomi 1993) assume the representations of sound patterns of early lexical items are not fully detailed descriptions. Consequently, if many words with very similar sound patterns are added at an early stage, then the lack of sufficient detail in the representations might lead the infant to recognition errors. In fact, studies based on estimates of the vocabularies of children 5 to 7 years old suggest that children's lexicons have many fewer lexical neighbors than the same words in adults' lexicons (Charles-Luce and Luce 1990, 1995; Walley 1993; but see Dollaghan 1994). This finding is consistent with the view

that children may have less-detailed representations of the sound structures of lexical items.

However, there is also evidence from studies of vocabulary growth that
even young children do not avoid learning homonyms and do not seem to
be confused by them (E. V. Clark 1993; Landau and Shipley 1995; also
see the arguments in Gerken, Murphy, and Aslin 1995). Homonyms seem
to lie at the most extreme end of confusability of sound patterns of words
(i.e., they are identical). Nevertheless, there may be a difference between
having two items with the same sound pattern, and two items that are
only minimally different in their sound patterns. Ultimately, this issue will
only be resolved through studies that systematically chart the growth and
organization of the lexicon.

We will return to the issue of lexical organization in the next two
chapters. The aim here was only to point out some possible arenas in
which we might expect to see constraints pertaining to sound properties
interact with those pertaining to meaning.

Chapter 7

Relating Perception to Production

Acquiring a spoken language requires becoming not only a fluent perceiver but also a fluent producer of speech. At the same time that infants are listening to and learning about speech sounds produced by others around them, they are beginning to produce speech sounds of their own. Their productions of speech must eventually conform to the sounds that they hear in the native-language input. Yet, to this point, we have been considering developments in speech perception without regard to what is happening in speech production during the same time frame. Whether it truly makes sense to study the development of speech perception independently from the development of speech production is debatable. On the one hand, there are theories that argue that speech production is intimately involved in the process of speech perception, either because decoding the signal requires reference to the movements used to produce it, as in *motor theory* (Liberman et al. 1967), or because articulatory gestures are directly perceived in the speech signal, as in *ecological theories* (Best 1995; Fowler 1986; Studdert-Kennedy 1991b).

If one adheres to either of these views, the core of perception and production is the same—motor plans in one case, gestures in the other—in which case it makes the most sense to study the development of the two systems together. On the other hand, there is the fact that different peripheral physiological devices are involved in these activities—the articulatory system, for production, and the auditory system, for perception. Thus, although the speech signal provides a common ground as the output of production and the input to perception, differences in the organizations of the articulatory and auditory systems raise the possibility that the systems may develop more or less independently of each other. Of course, the degree to which the two systems are inextricably linked or independent in their development is a question that can only be answered by empirical research.

This chapter reviews some of the important findings regarding the development of speech production. As with the earlier discussion of speech perception capacities, I focus on changes in speech production that relate to the acquisition of a native language. Much as my review of speech perception capacities began by focusing on their relation to phonetic distinctions and then moving on to a consideration of how these develop to support word recognition in fluent speech, I follow a similar course with respect to the development of speech production. Hence, after a brief description of Roman Jakobson's influential views on phonological development, I discuss babbling and how it develops in accordance with speech input, and then move toward the production of words and larger utterances. Along the way, wherever possible, parallels between significant changes in production and perception are noted. Some discussion of the development of the lexicon as it relates to speech production is also included. The chapter concludes with an examination of the means by which production and perception are related in the course of acquiring a native language.

Jakobson's Views on Phonological Development

Jakobson (1941) was responsible for the first, and best-known, theory of phonological development. He proposed a structuralist account of the way children acquire the sound structure of their native language. He distinguished between two periods of phonological development: babbling (which he believed to be prelinguistic) and the true acquisition of language sound structures. Jakobson did not actually collect any data regarding children' s speech productions. Rather, he based his arguments on observations reported by Gregoire (1933), who had claimed that babbling behavior is "prelinguistic" and not "the first genuine stage of language." Jakobson also endorsed the view that during the prelinguistic stages, the child would produce a large variety of different sounds that were not found together in a single language or even a group of languages.

A child during his babbling period can accumulate articulations which are never found within a single language or even a group of languages—consonants of any place of articulation, palatalized and rounded consonants, sibilants, affricates, clicks, diphthongs, etc. According to the findings of Gregoire (1937), the child at the height of his babbling period "is capable of producing all conceivable sounds." (Jakobson 1941, 21)

This claim bears certain parallels to the more recent claims in the speech perception literature (see chapter 3) that infants begin speech perception with the capacity to discriminate contrasts in any of the world's languages. However, unlike Jakobson, most contemporary speech perception accounts see a continuity between these early perceptual capacities and subsequent language-specific perception. By comparison, Jakobson believed that following the babbling period in which infants were producing this large variety of sounds, there was a discontinuity that occurred between babbling and speech.

As all observers acknowledge with great surprise, the child then loses nearly all of his ability to produce sounds in passing over from the pre-language stage to the first acquisition of words, i.e., to the first genuine stage of language. (Jakobson 1941, 21–22)

Jakobson sometimes referred to an intervening silent period between these two phases of development (see also Velten 1943). However, at other times, he seemed to suggest that the silent period was not a necessary step in the developmental sequence.

As Meumann has already stated (1903, p. 23), a short period may sometimes intervene between the stage of spontaneous babbling and that of true language development in which children are completely mute. For the most part, however, one stage merges unobtrusively into the other so that the acquisition of vocabulary and the disappearance of the prelanguage inventory occur concurrently. (Jakobson 1941, 29)

In any case, the true beginnings of language acquisition were hypothesized to commence only at the end of the babbling period. Thus, babbling came to be seen as at best a preparatory stage for language production, but something short of true linguistic behavior (e.g., Fry 1966).

Jakobson believed that linguistic universals, principles that hold across all languages, were the major determinants of how infants learned language. Although there might be individual differences in the rate of acquistion, each child was hypothesized to go through an orderly series of stages in mastering the full range of phonemic contrasts that appeared in the native language. The sequence of these stages was determined by what he called "laws of irreversible solidarity," which were basically an inherent universal hierarchy of structural laws. A phonological system for a given language was stratified, or layered, and this ordering of layers was taken to be universal across languages, and therefore invariable. Ferguson and Garnica (1975) offer a concrete example of this sort of relationship:

"No language has nasal vowels unless it also has one or more nasal consonants." This universal property of language structures would then translate into a prediction about acquisition of nasal consonants and nasal vowels, namely, children should acquire nasal consonants before they acquire nasal vowels. More generally, because of this stratified arrangement, the discovery of a certain type of phonemic contrast within the phonological system might depend on first discovering some other type of phonemic contrast, depending on how the two types are ordered. Another way to put this is that, if the phonological system has a contrast of type Y (e.g., nasal vowels in the example above), this would necessarily imply that the system also has a contrast of type X (e.g., nasal consonants). That is, the occurrence of Y is dependent on the occurrence of X in the system.

One interesting aspect of Jakobson's views was that he expected these kinds of universal principles to apply to all aspects of linguistic behavior. Thus, when language abilities degenerate because of aphasia or some other language disorder, the layers that are added last in development should be the first to disappear, whereas the ones that were developed first should be the last to go. Moreover, whenever reacquisition is necessary, such as after a stroke that results in language loss, then the course of reacquisition must follow the original developmental sequence. Because the universal order of phonemic development that Jakobson proposed was derived from his inspection of different languages, he also assumed that phonemic contrasts that were relatively rare across languages would be ones that were most likely to be acquired late in development (and consequently, the first lost by aphasics).

The sequence of stages was hypothesized to proceed from a simple undifferentiated state toward an end state that was stratified and highly differentiated. He proposed that children begin with the optimal vowel (i.e., a wide vowel such as [a]) and the optimal consonant (i.e., a labial stop, such as [p]). The pairing of these two elements in succession in a single syllable, serves to define the basic syllable structure as CV. From this point, differentiation occurs with the production of other syllables with this same basic form (e.g., from "papa" to "mama" or "tata"). The component segments of these new syllables differ with respect to certain distinctive features from those in the first CV syllable. These distinctive features pertained primarily to the manner in which sounds are articulated (e.g., whether they are voiced or voiceless, whether they are produced with nasal resonance or not, whether there is complete or incomplete closure of the vocal tract, whether there is a secondary source of noise present or not) and with the resonance characteristics of the oral cavity (e.g., whether the closure or narrowing of the vocal tract during production occurs in the front, middle, or back of the oral cavity). With respect to the sequence in which phonemic oppositions are acquired, after the initial oral-labial stop, the child was usually expected to acquire a nasal consonant next—an observation that subsequently led Jakobson (1971) to suggest this as the reason why parental names in various languages are likely to begin with these kinds of consonants.

Jakobson's theory had a great impact on views about how children acquire the sound patterns of their native language. His views served as a reference point for many other investigators who gathered data about speech production and phonological development.

Babbling as the Beginning of Speech Production

A factor that has worked to divorce research on the development of perception from that on production is that most data relating to these two domains were collected with infants at different ages. Many speech perception studies focused on infants 6 months of age or younger, whereas most of the data collected on speech production was with infants well beyond their first year. This picture has changed during the past decade or so, in part because many more studies of speech production have more carefully documented the development of babbling and its relation to early word productions. Certainly, improvements in the technology available for recording and analyzing babbling have helped to encourage such studies.

Aside from the sheer technical problems, another factor tended to hold back research on babbling behavior during the first year. This had to do with the legacy, derived from Jakobson's writings, that babbling has little to do with phonological development as it relates to word production. The view that there was a discontinuity between babbling and true language acquisition was reinforced by reports about the behavior of deaf infants. Lenneberg (1967) noted that the onset of babbling in deaf infants appeared to occur at about the same age as in their normally hearing counterparts. Consequently, babbling was deemed to arise independently of any experience in hearing language input. By comparison, there was no indication that deaf infants actually began to produce words at the age when normally hearing infants did. Thus, this pattern of results was seen as another indication that babbling is prelinguistic.

The explosion of studies on phonological development from the late 1970s onward has yielded much information about the relationship between early babbling and productions of the first words. The evidence from these investigations challenges Jakobson's claims regarding the discontinuity between babbling and word production and casts doubt on the existence of an intervening silent period (for extensive reviews see Locke 1983; Vihman 1996; Vihman and Elbert 1987). Contrary to the notion of a silent period, a survey of many previous investigations reveals that many of the children studied continued to babble even after they began producing their first words (Blount 1969; Elbers 1982; Ferguson and Farwell 1975; Labov and Labov 1978; Leopold 1947; Olmsted 1971).

Moreover, the phonetic characteristics of early words often are continuous with patterns prevalent in the child's babbling. Elbers and Ton (1985) have commented on the fact that "words and babble are formed from the same pool of productive sound patterns." Similarly, other investigators (Stoel-Gammon and Cooper 1984; Vihman et al. 1985; Vihman and Miller 1988) have reported that the repertoire of sounds and sound combinations used by any given child in late babbling and in early word production are closely related. Thus, not only is there no evidence of a silent period, but there is also little support for the notion of a discontinuity in the sounds that appear in babbling and those that occur in the production of the first words. Therefore, rather than accept Jakobson's claims that babbling is prelinguistic, it is more reasonable to treat babbling behavior as a genuine stage of language development.

Similarly, the assumption that deaf infants babble normally has been further scrutinized and found wanting. Gilbert (1982) criticized the nature of the evidence on which Lenneberg had based his claims. Furthermore, several recent investigations with deaf infants who were more carefully screened with regard to the nature and extent of their hearing losses have yielded findings that are inconsistent with Lenneberg's claims. For example, in their study with hearing-impaired and normal infants, Stoel-Gammon and Otomo (1986) found that hearing-impaired infants produced utterances with fewer different consonant types per session. Moreover, in contrast to normally hearing infants, the hearing-impaired infants showed a clear decrease in the production of different consonant types over sessions.

A longitudinal investigation with hearing-impaired infants by Oller and Eilers (1988) produced evidence even more damaging to Lenneberg's claims. Oller and Eilers obtained extensive auditory screening measures for their subjects. They noted that by comparison to normally hearing infants who begin canonical babbling (i.e., producing strings of alternating consonants and vowels) at between 6 and 10 months of age, the hearing-impaired infants did not enter this stage until much later, 11 to 25 months of age. Furthermore, several months after the onset of this stage of babbling, only a third of the hearing-impaired infants produced vocalizations that were judged to be in the range of ones that normally hearing infants produced. Consequently, these findings suggest that babbling does not develop normally in the absence of auditory input.

Similarly, the available evidence suggests that Jakobson's claim about the diversity of sounds present in babbling is also in error. Locke (1983) points out that data collected with 12-month-olds in studies by Irwin (1947) and by Pierce and Hanna (1974) indicate that the 12 most frequent consonants that occur in babbling account for 95 percent of all the consonants heard in the infants' productions. By comparison, the 12 least frequent consonants in babbling, which were largely fricatives, affricates, and liquids, appeared in only about 5 percent of the infants' utterances. In addition, Cruttenden (1970) reported that two children whom he studied showed a number of important omissions with respect to the sounds included in their babbling repertoire. He concluded that contrary to Jakobson's claims, the subjects that he followed did not babble all the sounds of English. In fact, as data from more recent investigations based on acoustic analyses of babbling show, children's productions of particular speech-sound categories only roughly approximate those in any adult language (Boysson-Bardies 1993; Boysson-Bardies et al. 1989).

Thus, although infants are certainly gaining more control over their vocalizations during the babbling period, there is no reason to treat this phase of development as separate from what happens when infants actually begin to attempt to produce their first words. In fact, as the data from speech perception suggest, infants at the ages when babbling is prevalent (from 4 to 12 months and beyond), are very attentive to the sounds of language. Although the infants clearly are not speakers of any language, they are certainly no less involved in the process of acquiring a language than they are at a later age when producing their first words.

There is also evidence of a different kind that supports the notion that babbling is a natural and, likely, a necessary part of language acquisition. In view of the earlier discussion above, it is ironic that some of these data were obtained with deaf infants. Work by Petitto and her colleagues (Petitto 1993; Petitto and Marentette 1991) on the acquisition of sign language suggests that learners of such languages also go through a period of babbling. Thus, in addition to the usual range of nonlinguistic gestures that infants produce, infants who are exposed to sign language begin to produce a range of gestures that are signlike. Moreover, these productions are not limited to infants who have been deprived of spoken language input. Hearing infants who have been exposed to sign language because their parents are deaf begin to produce such "manual babbling" more or less simultaneously with vocal babbling. Thus, as with learners of spoken languages, learners of sign languages appear to go through a period in which they experiment in producing the kinds of elements that potentially could be combined to form words in their native language. Hence, these parallels in how production develops for units in sign languages and in spoken languages provide an additional reason for considering babbling behavior to be a true part of the development of speech production.

Developmental Changes in Babbling

Having made the case for babbling as a part of language development, let us consider what is known about the development of babbling. Vocalizations prior to 6 months of age are often confined to isolated vowellike sounds that are sometimes accompanied by nasalization or glottal consonants and velar/uvular fricatives (Roug, Landberg, and Lundberg 1989). An important development occurs at around 6 months of age, when the infant begins to engage in so-called reduplicated (or canonical) babbling (Oller 1980; Roug et al. 1989; Stark 1980; Vihman 1993a). *Reduplicated babbling* is said to occur when the child begins to produce sequences of syllables, usually consisting of a stop consonant combined with an open, central vowel (e.g., "bababa"). There is little variation in either intonation or constituent consonant and vowel segments. Similar tendencies have been noted for such languages as English (Oller 1980; Stark 1980), Dutch (Koopmans van Beinum and van der Stelt 1986) and Swedish (Roug et al. 1989). Oller (1980) has argued that this period is the first point at which the child produces syllables that could potentially serve as building blocks of words.

Following this period in which reduplication of syllables is prevalent in infants' vocalizations, babbling becomes more complex in ways that approximate utterances from the native language. This period has been referred to as *variegated babbling*. Vocalizations are now characterized by an alternation of consonantal segments rather than a reduplication of a consonant (Roug et al 1989). The production of variegated babbling overlaps with reduplicated babbling. However, the proportion of variegated babbling seems to increase considerably around 12 to 14 months when the child begins to produce a variety of consonants overlaid on a sentencelike intonation pattern. It is during this time that word production is beginning and a marked increase occurs in the number of word patterns that the infant attempts to imitate (Vihman and Miller 1988).

A number of general trends in the way that babbling behavior develops among infants from different language backgrounds have been ascribed to anatomical and physiological changes that occur throughout the first year. The infant's vocal apparatus undergoes many changes during this period of time. For example, the newborns' vocal tracts are considerably shorter, their tongue shapes are different, and their larynges are in a much higher position than those of adults (Lieberman 1984). Kent and Miolo (1995) suggest that until about 3 months of age, infants' vocal-tract configurations are more similar to those of nonhuman primates than to those of adult humans, and only at 4 months of age do infants' vocal tracts begin to resemble those of human adults. However, development of the vocal tract continues well after this point. Crelin (1987) has observed that the descent of the larynx to its eventual adult locus only begins during the third year. Because of the immature configuration of their vocal tracts, it is difficult for young infants to produce sounds corresponding to the vowels [i] and [u] (Buhr 1980; Lieberman 1977; Lieberman, Crelin, and Klatt 1972). A general tendency that has been noted in babbling behavior is an evolution from a rather centralized vowel space to one that is considerably more spread out at the end of the first year (Buhr 1980; Kent and Murray 1982). In addition, there is evidence that early on in development there is a predominance of front vowels relative to back vowels (Lieberman 1984).

Other regularities in babbling that have been observed appear to be related to infants' ability to gain control and coordination over jaw movements. For example, tendencies for particular consonants and vowels to occur together with greater frequency in babbling than in the adult target language led MacNeilage and Davis (1990) to suggest that these kinds of co-occurrence patterns might have a common frame that was produced by the oscillation of the jaw. Thus, the frequent association of labial consonants and central vowels was explained as the result of lip closure produced by the oscillation of the jaw combined with the tongue remaining in its resting position. Similarly, they found evidence for the association of front consonants with front vowels, which they attributed to the absence of active changes of tongue position during oscillation. Indeed, MacNeilage and Davis (1991) have even offered an explanation for variegated babbling that is based on variation in the amplitude of jaw movements during successive oscillations.

Davis and MacNeilage (1994) also reported evidence for the interaction of segmental and suprasegmental properties in the productions of an English-learning infant whom they studied between 7 and 12 months of age. In particular, one unexpected finding was that when stress increased from one syllable to the next, the vowel tended to shift from central to front (and in the opposite direction—from front to central—when stress decreased). This pattern is counter to the usual relationship found for vowel quality and stress. Davis and MacNeilage suggest that one possible reason for the association that their infant displayed is that the production of front vowels (which involve moving the tongue forward) may be easier to combine with the increased amplitude of jaw opening (which is itself related to the production of stress). Davis and MacNeilage suggested that this kind of association between stress and vowel type in early productions may not be a universal tendency because many languages make little or no use of stress. For this reason, it would be instructive to know just how widespread this kind of relation is in the babbling behavior of infants. Information about the behavior of infants exposed to languages that differ in their predominant word-stress patterns would help resolve the question of the association that Davis and MacNeilage observed is universal or not.

In any event, the studies reviewed in this section indicate that, not surprisingly, certain characteristics of infants' babbling patterns stem from the nature of their articulatory apparatus and the degree of control that they have over its movements. We now turn to a consideration of the effects that exposure to sound patterns of a specific language have on infants' vocalizations.

Effects of Linguistic Experience on Babbling

Given that reduplicated babbling is observed cross-linguistically, one can ask about the impact of the native language on babbling. Recall that Brown (1958) had suggested that babbling drifts in the direction of the target language. Subsequently, Weir (1966) reported that analyses of her data pointed to considerable differences in the babbling behavior of American, Russian, and Chinese infants from 6 months onward. However, other researchers found little empirical support for babbling drift toward the sound patterns of the native language. For example, Atkinson, MacWhinney, and Stoel (1968) reported that adult listeners could not reliably judge the language background of infants based on their babbling. Similarly, Olney and Scholnick (1974) found no evidence that their subjects could reliably distinguish samples from English and Chinese infants ranging from 6 to 18 months. In contrast, Boysson-Bardies, Sagart, and Durand (1984) reported that French adults distinguished the babbling of a French infant from an Arab infant but not from a Chinese infant.

However, using adult judgments of native and nonnative babbling patterns is not the only way to evaluate claims that native-language input affects babbling patterns. Collecting cross-linguistic data on infant vocalizations and subjecting these to acoustic analyses can provide a means of assessing the effects of linguistic experience. In a survey of existing reports of babbling from a variety of different languages, Locke (1983) found little evidence of differences in phonetic repertoires related to language background. He also remarked that there was considerable variation in the phonetic repertoires of infants from the same language background. Hence, there were large individual differences in the pattern of phonetic acquisition among infants exposed to the same language input. On the basis of these findings, Locke argued that there was little support for the view that babbling drifts toward the native language at this phase of development.

Much of the data that Locke reviewed relied exclusively on investigators' phonetic transcriptions of infants' babbling patterns. Better audio recording techniques and acoustic analysis tools have helped to improve the quality and reliability of judgments regarding the phonetic patterns found in infants' babbling. Investigations using these new techniques combined with larger cross-linguistic sample sizes have provided empirical support for the claim that babbling drifts toward native-language sound patterns. For example, Boysson-Bardies et al. (1989) noted that vowel production in 10-month-olds from four different language backgrounds (Parisian French, Algerian Arabic, British English, and Hong Kong Cantonese) tends to parallel differences found in adult productions of vowels in these languages. In particular, the formant structure of vowellike patterns produced by infants from different language backgrounds differ from each other in ways that resemble productions of these vowels by adult speakers of these languages. Moreover, similarities have also been noted between infants' babbling and adults' productions of consonants. An extensive longitudinal study (Boysson-Bardies, Vihman, Roug-Hellichius, Durand, Landberg, and Arao 1992) with infants from French, Swedish, English, and Japanese backgrounds plotted the drift toward native-language consonantal categories. The infants were seen from 9 months of age until they achieved vocabularies of 25 words or more. The distributions of consonants in infants' babbling and in their early word productions were compared to the sample of adult words that served as targets in the language that the infants were acquiring.[1] Even at 10 months, there were differences in the distribution of manner and place categories in the vocalizations of infants from the different language backgrounds. For example, analyses of the distribution of stop consonants in adult production indicated that these were most prevalent in Swedish followed by English, then Japanese and, lastly, French. The production of stops by the infants showed exactly the same pattern. Thus, there are indications that the phonetic segments that appear in babbling from 10 months of age onward are influenced by the target language.

Native-language influences on babbling occur not only for phonetic properties but also for other aspects of sound pattern organization. For instance, there is evidence for early language-specific prosodic influences (Levitt 1993). In a study of five French- and five English-learning infants between 5 and 13 months, Whalen, Levitt, and Wang (1991) found intonational differences in babbling that were consistent with those in the adult target languages. Also, rhythmic properties relating to the timing of syllables in the native language may emerge even earlier than any influences on segmental properties of babbling (Levitt, Utman, and Aydelott 1992).

Just as studies in the perceptual realm indicate that 9-month-olds are attentive to the way that segments are typically ordered and combined in their native language (e.g., Friederici and Wessels 1993; Jusczyk, Friederici, et al. 1993), investigations of syllable structure in babbling also reveal effects of language-specific influences toward the end of the first year. Levitt et al. (1992) found that between 11 and 13 months, their French-learning infant was less likely to produce closed syllables than was their English-learning infant. This difference is in line with the distribution of open and closed syllables in the two target languages.

Vihman (1992) also found evidence for differences in syllable structures among infants from four different language backgrounds (Swedish, Japanese, English, and French). In particular, although all the children she studied had certain phonetic tendencies in common (producing syllables such as [da], [ha], and [hə]), there were also cross-linguistic differences that were in line with tendencies found in the input language. For instance, Japanese infants were much more likely to produce velars in association with back vowels (e.g., [ko], [go]). In addition, Swedish infants produced syllables in which [t] and [d] were associated with a full range of vowels, rather than just front vowels, as infants from the other language backgrounds tended to do.

Therefore, in addition to the constraints that are imposed on infants' speech sound repertoires by the nature and maturation of their articulatory apparatus, the distribution and variety of sounds that they babble are affected to some degree by the characteristics of their target language.

Relating Babbling to Word Production

Until fairly recently, much of the research on phonological development focused on the production of words by language learners. Such studies generally examined the numbers and kinds of words that children have in their productive vocabularies (e.g., Ferguson and Farwell 1975; Menn 1978; Moskowitz 1970; Smith 1973). In noting the growth and development of the child's productive vocabulary, many of these approaches have emphasized the progress that language learners make toward producing the full range of phonemic oppositions in their native language (Ferguson and Garnica 1975; Ingram 1974a, 1978; Macken 1980a; Menn 1978; Stampe 1969). The descriptions provided in many of these early studies are stated in terms of the acquisition of particular phonemic contrasts and phonological rules (Garnica 1973; Ingram et al. 1980; Menn 1980; Moskowitz 1970; Smith 1973). Hence, one can come away with the impression that the child's focus at this stage is on learning new phonemic contrasts, rather than new words (although see Ferguson 1986; Ferguson and Farwell 1975; Waterson 1981 for views that whole words may constitute the initial representations).

From the point of view of a linguist interested in when a child might give evidence of having a particular contrast, these kinds of descriptions were certainly appropriate. However, it is important not to assume that the linguist's description of what oppositions are appearing at a given age is equivalent to what actually drives the child's behavior during acquisition. The child's goal at a given moment may not be so much to acquire a certain phonemic contrast as it is to successfully produce particular words (recall the parallel point that was made about speech perception in the discussion at the end of chapter 4). Indeed, changing the focus from the production of phonemic segments to the production of words may even help account for some of the puzzles in phonological development (such as the variability in the production of particular segments on different occasions or in different contexts) that Ferguson and Garnica (1975) noted in their review. In what follows, rather than addressing particular theories of phonological development, I confine the discussion to some important phenomena that have been noted in children's productions of words in their native language.

One important issue concerns the relation between the sounds that appear in babbling and those that occur in the first words that learners produce. For example, Vihman and her colleagues (Vihman et al. 1985) found that the phonetic characteristics of English-learning infants' early words are highly similar to those of their contemporaneous babbling. Similarly, in their investigation of the babbling monologues of a Dutch child during the period of the production of first words, Elbers and Ton (1985) reported mutual influences between babbling and word production. Babbling seemed to give rise to phonological preferences in the selection of word targets from the adult language, whereas word production also led to changes in the kinds of phonetic segments that appeared most frequently in babbling patterns. In a cross-linguistic investigation that involved infants from English-, French-, Swedish-, and Japanese-learning environments, Boysson-Bardies and Vihman (1991) also found some evidence for continuity between the characteristics of babbling and early word production. Language-specific patterns with respect to the production of consonants in babbling (i.e., asymmetries in terms of the frequencies with which certain manner or place classes occurred across the languages), also tended to show up in the early productions of words by these same infants. At the same time, Boysson-Bardies and Vihman noted that there were some interesting differences that occurred in the productions of some types of consonantal classes. For example, across all the languages, the percentage of stops was higher in word production than it was in babbling, whereas for fricatives the reverse trend occurred. Following Kent's (1992) hypothesis regarding avoidance of or substitutions for phonetic segments, they attributed these changes to production constraints. Specifically, they cited constraints that arise from the control required to produce fricative segments intentionally, which may have led to the substitution of stops for fricatives.

Findings such as these do point to continuities in babbling and in early word production. At the same time, they give an indication that things change when the infant moves from simply producing strings of sounds, or as Ferguson and Macken (1983) put it, "playing with sounds," to intentionally trying to produce words. Although the same articulators are involved in each instance, the task demands associated with trying to use sounds to convey a particular meaning appear to cause the child to fall back on articulatory routines that may be simpler to control. Perhaps these sorts of task demands are also a contributing factor to the use of vowel or consonant harmony in children's early attempts at producing certain words in the adult language (e.g., [gʌk] when attempting to produce "duck").

Another frequently cited phenomenon in children's early productions has to do with the variability that arises in the production of the same word by the same child on different occasions. Perhaps the best-known case comes from Ferguson and Farwell (1975), who reported that the word "pen" received a number of phonetically different pronunciations by the same child in the course of a single observation period. This type of variability in pronunciation has been widely reported (Leonard et al. 1982; Menn 1976; Priestly 1976; Schwartz and Folger 1977; Waterson 1978). In addition, Locke (1983) has noted that many of the simplifications that appear in children's early words have been observed cross-linguistically (e.g., stopping, fronting, initial stop voicing, final obstruent devoicing, gliding, consonant harmony, cluster reduction, etc.). This suggests that variations in the input that the child receives are not likely to be a major factor in accounting for variability in production. For example, although it is conceivable that variations in input account for some small proportion of variability across children, this would not explain why the productions of a single child (like the one that Ferguson and Farwell observed) should be so variable. It seems far more plausible to attribute the variability to factors having to do with the infant's ability to control fine movements of the articulators. Indeed, studies have shown that infants are variable with respect to timing of motor movements (Kent and Murray 1982; Macken and Barton 1980). The pressures of having to produce an utterance whose meaning is correctly conveyed to the listener could further reduce the capacity of the infant to control the timing of the relevant articulatory movements.

The suggestion that variability in production is not so much an inability to produce the required articulatory gestures as difficulty in producing them while trying to convey meaning is further supported by the prevalence of several other phenomena that have been noted. For example, there is the phenomenon that Gerken (1994a) has referred to as *chain shifts*. In such a shift, a child substitutes a different sound for one in an adult word (e.g., refers to "duck" as "guck"). This might lead one to conclude that the child has difficulty in producing [d] in word-initial positions. However, the same child might at the same time produce [d] in word initial position as a substitute sound in a different word, such as saying "duck" to refer to "truck" (Macken 1980b; Menn 1978; Smith 1973; Stemberger 1992). Another situation that demonstrates that the child's problem does not have to do with a general inability to make the required articulatory gestures is the case that Leopold (1939) first described with respect to his daughter Hildegard's early word productions. Her correct pronunciation of the word "pretty" as [priti] was well in advance of her ability to produce consonant clusters in other words, which she routinely reduced to single segments. In other instances, a child's favored, but inaccurate, pronunciation of some adult word might remain in the child's vocabulary long after he or she is producing other words with the same target sounds correctly.

These findings suggest that when a child consistently produces an item in the same way, it may be because he or she has articulatory (motor) routines that are, more or less, rotely associated with that particular word. By comparison, other words in the child's vocabulary may not have specific, stored articulatory routines associated with them. Instead, the child may have to generate and sequence the correct articulatory routines on-line from a stored representation of the word's sound pattern. If this view is correct, then variability in production of the same word stems from difficulty in handling the processing demands of generating the appropriate articulatory routines from a stored representation of the sound pattern while trying simultaneously to convey a specific message.

In addition to having particular articulatory routines that are associated with specific lexical items, learners may also have some general kinds of routines that they apply to many different kinds of items. For instance, the child may follow some general routine that allows only certain types of sounds to be produced in particular word positions, such as producing only voiced consonants in word-initial positions or producing fricatives only in word-final positions (Ingram 1974b; Kiparsky and Menn 1977; Menn 1980). Moreover, these general routines that the child employs can be quite idiosyncratic. Thus, Ferguson (1979) commented on the fact that a child may have a favorite sound that he or she uses repeatedly in the production of different lexical items. Vihman (1986) has suggested that the child may accidentally stumble across the correct production of a particular kind of sound, such as a liquid, in the course of articulatory exploration and then end up producing this sound in word productions more frequently, relative to other children at the same age. In fact, in her study of 10 English-learning children who were observed at weekly intervals between 9 and 16 months of age, Vihman (1986) noted a number of individual differences among her subjects in the diversity of segments used, the range of adult consonants that were targeted, the extent to which children continued to babble after they were producing 15 words, and the consistency and integrity of word shapes. However, when these same children were later seen at 36 months of age, many of these differences had receded. Vihman pointed to this fact as an indication of the unifying influences that native-language input has on the course of phonological development—a point that was further reinforced in the cross-linguistic data that she and Boysson-Bardies subsequently collected (Boysson-Bardies and Vihman 1991).

A number of investigators have pointed out that at least two distinct kinds of learning styles appear in the acquisition of phonology. Ferguson (1979) discussed one type of learner as a "cautious system builder" who constructs a tight phonological system. He characterized the other type of learner as a bolder child who shows a loose and variable phonological organization. Many others have found evidence that concurs with Ferguson's observation (Bretherton, McNew, Snyder, and Bates 1983; Klein 1978; Menn 1978, 1983; Peters 1977). A recent paper by Peters and Menn (1993), which contrasts the ways two different children, Seth and Daniel, acquired grammatical morphemes in English, provides a further elaboration of the differences in these styles. Specifically, they note:

At least two strategies have been identified in the language acquisition literature: (1) The formulaic strategy (also called gestalt, expressive, or pronominal) where the focus is on multisyllabic chunks of speech and (2) the word-oriented strategy (also called analytic, referential, or nominal) where the focus is on shorter stretches (Peters 1977, 1983). From a prosodic point of view, it looks as though formulaic children, like Seth, pay initial attention to 'horizontal' information such as the number of syllables, stress, intonation patterns (with only secondary attention to particular consonants and vowels); word-oriented children, like Daniel, pay more attention to the vertical segmental information contained in single (usually, stressed) syllables focusing on the details of consonants and vowels. (p. 745)

As Peters and Menn go on to suggest, the adoption of one of these two styles does not prevent children from learning the kind of information that is the focus of the alternative style. Eventually, children who follow either one of these two strategies end up learning the full range of facts concerning the organization of sound patterns in their native language. However, these children appear to take very different routes to acquire the same phonological ends.

Note that the categorization of children as being either formulaic or word oriented should not blind us to the fact that these are broad characterizations of learning styles and that there are many individual differences among those who might be assigned to either group. As Gerken (1994a) has remarked, the reasons for the appearance of these individual differences in acquisition strategies are not clear. Differences in the input to which the child is exposed may have something to do with these differences, but so far there is little empirical evidence to support this hypothesis (Leonard, Newhoff, and Mesalam 1980; Vihman 1993b). Another possibility is that these differences in style simply reflect temperamental differences among learners. Thus, it has often been suggested that some children may avoid attempting to produce words with sounds that they have not fully mastered in their phonetic repertoire (Ferguson and Farwell 1975; Macken 1978; Schwartz and Leonard 1982). These children may be conservative about making mistakes and thus end up as the kind of cautious system builders that Ferguson described.

Another possibility that has been mentioned is that differences in the perception and production systems of different children could influence the kinds of sounds that are most salient to them in the input and therefore most likely to be attempted by a given child (Studdert-Kennedy 1986). Along these lines, Vihman (1993b) has put forth the idea of an *articulatory filter* that is defined as "a phonetic template (unique to each child) which renders similar patterns in adult speech unusually salient or memorable." Her suggestion is that language learners' choices of which words to imitate are influenced by their knowledge of their own vocal motor schemes, so that patterns in the input that match those schemes are the ones most likely to be attended to and imitated. That is, sounds that learners hear frequently and that they know they can produce are more likely to capture their attention.

Whatever the reason for the individual differences in learning styles, there are still some generalizations that we can make about children's first word productions relative to targets in the adult language. For the most part, when differences occur between targets and actual productions, the latter are apt to be simplifications of the adult words in terms of the numbers and kinds of phonetic segments that are produced (Ingram 1974b, 1978; Macken 1979; Menn 1978; Smith 1973). Gerken (1994a) describes several of the more commonly observed types of changes that children make. Substitutions occur whenever the child replaces a sound in an adult word with another one. Usually, the substituted sound is one with similar phonetic properties to the one replaced. In deletion, the child simply leaves out some of the phonetic material from the adult word. For example, the child may pronounce "banana" as [nænə]. Metathesis occurs when the child reorders some of the phonetic material in the adult word such as in pronouncing "spaghetti" as [pʌzgɛti]. Another simplification, cluster reduction, is one that we have already referred to. The child will often reduce consonant clusters by deleting one or more of the component consonants. Finally, assimilation is a process by which the child alters the pronunciation of one part of the word with a feature or phoneme from another part of the word. We considered an instance of this sort in describing the behavior of a child who pronounces the word "duck" as [gʌk].

Prosodic Characteristics of Children's Early Productions

In addition to the phonetic composition, target words in the adult language have particular prosodic characteristics that also must be reproduced properly in order to ensure their correct recognition. Most investigations of phonological development, until relatively recently, have focused more on the phonetics than the prosody of children's word productions. Still, some tendencies were noted in the prosody of children's early productions. For example, Macken (1979) reported that when her Spanish-learning subject noticed that two words had the same rhythmic structure, she began to produce them both with an identical initial consonant. Elbers (1985) commented that whenever her subject had difficulty recalling an adult word, he substituted one with the same number of syllables and a similar stress pattern as the target word.

One prosodic characteristic of children's early word productions that has been frequently noted over the years is their tendency to omit unstressed syllables from adult target words (Blasdell and Jensen 1970; Ingram 1974b; Smith 1973). This tendency is usually attributed to unstressed syllables being less perceptible than stressed ones in speech directed to the language learner (Brown and Fraser 1964; Chiat 1979; Echols and Newport 1992; Gleitman and Wanner 1982). However, as we noted then, the data from studies of speech perception abilities of infants suggest that they are capable, from a young age, of detecting phonetic differences between unstressed syllables of speech sounds (Jusczyk et al. 1978; Jusczyk and Thompson 1978; Williams 1977a).

Recent investigations by Gerken (1991, 1994b, 1996; Gerken et al. 1990; Gerken and McIntosh 1993) have suggested another explanation for the child's omission of unstressed syllables in early productions of both words and phrases. In particular, Gerken has argued that these omissions are attributable to constraints on production rather than perception. For example, she (Gerken 1994b) and others (Wijnen, Krikhaar, and den Os 1994) have pointed to the fact that children are more likely to omit unstressed syllables from some word positions as opposed to others as evidence against a perceptually based explanation for these omissions. In fact, these kinds of omissions are more likely to occur in unstressed word-initial syllables than in unstressed word-final syllables (Echols and Newport 1992; Gerken 1994b; Ingram 1974b; Vihman 1980). Thus, children are much more likely to omit the unstressed first syllable of "giraffe," than they are to leave out the unstressed second syllable of "monkey."

Gerken (1991) has argued that this pattern of unstressed syllable omission reflects the use of a particular type of production strategy on the part of early learners. In particular, she hypothesizes that the utterances that children produce at this early stage of word production are governed by a metrical production template that follows a trochaic pattern (i.e., an initial stressed syllable, followed by an unstressed one). Moreover, Gerken has shown that this kind of template can not only account for unstressed syllables in individual words, but it also accounts for which syllables the children are likely to leave out when they produce their first word combinations (Gerken 1994b; in press). For example, the use of a trochaic template for production helps to explain why children are prone to leave function words out of utterances, despite the fact that they apparently perceive them (Gerken and McIntosh 1993). However, another recent investigation by Boyle and Gerken (in press) showed that multiple factors are responsible for the omission of function words. In particular, the presence of unfamiliar lexical items in an utterance may itself be a sufficient reason for children to omit function words from sentences. Thus, across a series of three experiments in which 2-year-olds were asked to repeat sentences, they more frequently omitted function words in sentences that contained either novel nouns or novel verbs than they did for sentences with familiar nouns and verbs. This familiarity effect did not interact with whether the critical function word fit into a trochaic template. Thus, lexical familiarity and metrical properties appear to independently influence children's productions of function words.

Still, it is interesting that, just as the beginning stages of word segmentation in speech perception are characterized by the use of a strong/weak (i.e., trochaic) template, a similar tendency to impose a trochaic template also shows up in the child's early productions of meaningful words. We will return to this point shortly.

How Are Perceptual Representations Related to the Child's Productions of Words?

Another kind of behavior that appears in children's early productions has been termed the "fis" phenomenon (Berko and Brown 1960; Dodd 1975; Gerken 1994a; Smith 1973). A child may systematically mispronounce a particular word in a certain way (e.g., "fish" is pronounced as [fɪs]). One possible interpretation of this is that the child has somehow misperceived the adult word. Consequently, it is the perceptual representation on which the pronunciation of the word is based that is the source of the error. However, this explanation of the child's behavior is undercut by the fact that the child who makes these sorts of errors will often object if adults use the child's own pronunciation of the word. In fact, it has been argued that children not only perceive contrasts that they do not appear to produce, but they may even make distinctions in their productions of such contrasting words, albeit not the ones adults are expecting to hear (Braine 1976; Macken and Barton 1980).

At first glance, another reason it seems implausible that language learners' perceptual representations of words are the cause of mispronunciations is all the research on the speech discrimination capacities of young infants. Given that young infants are so adept at detecting fine distinctions between speech sounds, why should they not have sufficiently detailed representations of their first words? Still, there are indications that some of the phonemic contrasts that were easily discriminated at a younger age in speech perception tasks may present problems for older infants when the contrasts occur between words. An early study by Shvachkin (1973) with Russian-learning infants suggested that they might only gradually perceive the full range of Russian phonemic contrasts in words. In a longitudinal study with infants between the ages of 10 and 24 months, Shvachkin attempted to teach children minimal word pairs. Each child was taught to associate a nonsense word with a particular toy. The sound patterns of these items differed by a single phonetic feature. The child's task was to produce the appropriate toy from an array of different toys upon hearing the word. By the end of the study, about half of the children were responding correctly to the whole range of contrasts. However, initially the children could only respond to a few discriminations. Moreover, some discriminations appeared to be easier than others, and the children were reported to follow the same developmental sequence with respect to the kinds of contrasts that were discriminated at various ages. (In this respect, Shvachkin's data appear to bear out Jakobson's claims about a developmental progression in phonemic acquisition.)

Subsequently, several American researchers carried out investigations along the same lines as Shvachkin (Edwards 1974; Garnica 1973). In Edwards's study, the infants tested were considerably older (20–47 months), but there was still evidence for differences in order of acquisition of certain contrasts. In particular, the children had more difficulty with contrasts involving fricatives than with other types of distinctions. More recently, Werker (1994) has reported on an investigation using a version of the word-learning paradigm with infants. Infants at 15 months of age were shown videos of two different nonsense objects, each of which was paired with a different nonsense syllable. During the test phase, infants heard one of the original nonsense syllables paired with both of the test objects (correctly in one case, but wrongly in the other). Although Werker found that infants at this age did react to incorrect pairings when the original test words differed in several phonemes, she did not find evidence that infants at this age learned a minimal pair distinction.

How can we explain why older infants appear to have so much difficulty discriminating the kinds of contrasts that were easily discriminated by them at 2 months of age? One possible explanation focuses on the obvious differences between the tasks that the infants are expected to perform at the two ages (Jusczyk 1977, 1985b; Locke 1988). The 2-month-old simply has to pick up an acoustic contrast between a pair of syllables, but the task for the older infant is considerably more complex because it involves associating a particular sound pattern with a particular referent. Moreover, success on this task requires representing, encoding, and recalling a particular sound pattern in sufficient detail to discriminate it from sound patterns that could be similar to it in many unforeseen respects. Much as task-demand differences between babbling sounds and producing particular sounds to convey a meaningful word may affect children's control over their articulatory routines, so too might discrimination processes be affected by having to encode and access the right meanings in conjunction with particular sound patterns.

The child's attentional focus is at the very least split between the visual properties of the object and its similarities and differences to other objects in the task, and the acoustic and/or phonetic properties of the speech sounds used to label the objects. It is not even inconceivable that infants at this age might attend more closely to the visual stimulation in such tasks than to the auditory stimulation. This may be true of word learning in the real world, as well as in these experimental settings. This brings up another point to bear in mind. Although, on the surface, word-learning tasks reproduce certain aspects of learning the names of objects in the real world, they may lack a critical component, namely, the child's intrinsic motivation to learn the name of a particular object. It is possible that the latter factor does affect the encoding of words in these experimental tasks. Indeed, children tend to perform better on these types of discrimination tasks when they are tested on words that they already know, as opposed to ones that they have learned during training (e.g., Barton 1976).

In addition to the possibility that more complicated task demands affect infants' discriminative capacities on word learning tasks, it must be noted that we know very little about the kind of information that goes into infants' early representations of words. It has been suggested by many investigators that the early representations may only include global descriptions of a word's sound pattern such as its prosodic structure and gross acoustic shape (Ferguson and Farwell 1975; Jusczyk 1985b, 1992; Menyuk and Menn 1979; Studdert-Kennedy 1986; Walley 1993; Waterson 1971). Although such representations are likely to include information about some salient acoustic features (e.g., manner of onset, presence of aperiodic noise, nasal resonance, etc.), this information is likely to be incomplete and not organized into phonetic segments. Because younger infants' lexicons have fewer acoustically similar items (lexical neighbors) than do adults, they could rely on less-detailed acoustic information to recognize words (Charles-Luce and Luce 1990, 1995; Jusczyk 1992; Walley 1993).

Thus, the fact of the matter is that there is still a great deal of uncertainty about the nature of infants' perceptual representations of words, including those that show up early in production. Nevertheless, the belief that infants' perceptual representations of speech are reasonably close approximations to phonetic descriptions led to proposals of *two-lexicon* models (Ingram 1976; Menn 1983; Spencer 1986; Vihman 1982). The basic premise of these models is that an input lexicon is used in recognizing words, and a separate output lexicon, containing information derived from the input, is used for word production. Among the arguments advanced in support of these models is the fact that children can perceive many more sound distinctions than they produce (Matthei 1989). Critics of two-lexicon models have pointed to the redundancy involved in storing information relevant to a word's use, such as its syntactic, semantic, and morphological information in two different places (Wheeler and Iverson 1976).

However, a reasonable alternative to the two-lexicon model is what has been termed a *two-entry* approach (Matthei 1989; Wheeler and Iverson 1976; cf. Menn and Matthei 1992). Such a model has only a single lexicon containing relevant syntactic, semantic, and morphological information. However, two-entry models have separate access routes to the information contained in the central store for perception and production. Thus, one means of accounting for some of the differences noted in the development of phonological categories in perception and production is to view them in terms of a two-entry approach to the lexicon. Each type of access route might develop independently, at least initially. Furthermore, given the differences in the sensory and motor systems underlying perception and production, respectively, it would not be unreasonable to expect some sort of developmental décalage in terms of when the learner gains command of a word in perception and production. The fact that the vocal tract undergoes large changes in shape and dimensions, plus the amount of coordination required to sequence the articulators properly, might well cause productive capacities to lag behind perceptual ones.

Assessing the Relation between Changes in Perception and Production

One implication of a two-entry approach to the lexicon is that perception and production develop relatively independently of each other. Their main point of contact comes through links to a common meaning in the lexicon. This means that perceptual and productive processes are more likely to influence each other after links to common meanings have been established. However, does this imply that there are no links between perception and production prior to this point? Ruling out any mutual influences at younger ages appears to be too strong a claim in view of findings indicating that 5-month-olds show some ability to match vowel sounds to the sight of appropriate mouth movements (Kuhl and Meltzoff 1982, 1984; MacKain et al. 1983). Furthermore, infants' own productions are also an available source of perceptual input. Certainly, one would expect that some play in producing sounds in babbling involves exploring the acoustic consequences of various articulatory gestures. The point here is that as "meaning" and the desire to be understood become the child's primary preoccupations, there is greater pressure to bring productive representations of words more closely in line with perceptual representations.

Maybe we should step back for a moment and ask when the lexicon actually begins to develop. Some of the evidence suggests that infants may begin storing information about sound patterns at some point during the second trimester of their first year (Hallé and Boysson-Bardies 1994b; Hohne et al. 1994; Mandel et al. 1995). Moreover, there is evidence indicating that infants begin to comprehend a few words at some point between 8 and 10 months of age (Benedict 1979; Huttenlocher 1974). Thus, there is some reason to believe that the formation of the lexicon occurs during the latter half of the first year. Consequently, one might expect to see the perception and production systems beginning to interact during this period. Let us consider what kinds of changes are taking place in perception and production at this time and the degree to which they may be related.

With respect to perception, the latter half of the first year is characterized by a marked increase in sensitivity to the structure of native-language sound patterns. This shows up with respect to phonetic, phonotactic, and prosodic features. The infant displays a sensitivity to the frequency with which these kinds of patterns appear in the input. Moreover, infants advance in their abilities to segment words from fluent speech and to detect the natural groupings of words that the language imposes on utterances (i.e., clauses and phrases). With respect to production during this same period, most of the infants' vocalizations still consist of babbling. However, it is at this point that native-language input begins to influence the kinds of strings that are produced in babbling. As the work of Boysson-Bardies and her colleagues shows, the kinds of vocalic and consonantal elements that appear in babbling are influenced by the distribution of such elements in the input that the infant is receiving. Similar changes are evident in the prosodic structure of babbling, as the work of Levitt and her colleagues also indicates. Moreover, there are even cross-linguistic differences in the frequency with which certain kinds of syllable structures appear in babbling that begin to show up late in the first year (Vihman 1993b). What these findings demonstrate, then, is that linguistic input affects infants' productions, just as it also affects their perceptual capacities. However, since the input comes through the perceptual system, these examples are largely demonstrations of how perception affects changes in production that occur during this time.

The influences of production on perception are not as obvious. However, Vihman has mentioned several interesting possibilities. One of these is her notion of an articulatory filter that affects what learners attend to in speech input. More specifically, children's abilities to produce some kinds of sounds better than others could affect their attention and memory for words by favoring words that include sounds that they have mastered. Although Vihman herself sees the articulatory filter as primarily affecting word production rather than comprehension, it would be interesting to explore the extent to which infants' recognition of words might show these same influences. For example, if an articulatory filter serves to focus attention on certain patterns in the input, then this might increase the chances that words embodying such patterns are the most likely to be added to the lexicon. Hence, one might find that the proportion of such items in the lexicon is greater than otherwise might be expected.

A second way the child's productive schemes could influence perceptual processes is in the decline of sensitivity to nonnative contrasts. Specifically, Vihman (1991; see also Studdert-Kennedy 1991a) indicates that when these declines appear, infants have already begun to favor in their productions the kinds of articulatory gestures that are used in the native language. She points out that because infants are in the process of matching patterns that they hear to their developing vocal motor schemes, this may mean that nonnative sounds are not "meaningfully processed at this point." She suggests further that perhaps the same thing occurs for native-language sounds that are not within the child's articulatory repertoire at this stage. This last point is intriguing, in light of the difficulties that infants have in word-learning experiments—although it is by no means clear that their difficulties are confined to words that include segments that they do not yet produce.

In considering how changes in perception might affect production and vice versa, we should not lose sight of the fact that some determinants of developmental change in each of these systems will have little to do with what happens in the other system. Thus, there are changes in production that will have to do with maturation and a greater ability to coordinate one's own motor patterns. Similarly, there are changes in speech perception that are more likely to reflect changes in memory and attentional capacities than any influences from speech production. Each system brings with it a particular set of constraints that affects performance. For example, from the point of view of ease of operation, there are pressures on the developing articulatory system to produce all sounds in much the same way. However, in this case the resulting sounds would be difficult to discriminate. From the point of view of perception, it is ideal to have the sounds that one uses be as distinct as possible so that they will be less confusable. However, this would increase the range of different kinds of articulatory gestures that have to be mastered and coordinated. What happens in the sound systems of natural languages is some sort of compromise between these two extremes (although there are very likely other factors that also affect how the sound system of any given language is structured, as Anderson 1981 has suggested). Each language has its own solution to this problem.

Lindblom and his colleagues (e.g., Lindblom 1986, 1992; Lindblom, MacNeilage, and Studdert-Kennedy 1983) have proposed a model of how the interaction between perceptual and articulatory constraints may lead the language learner to develop a phonological system from more-global lexical representations. They identify discriminability and pronounce-ability (a tendency to reduce articulatory complexity) as important constraints on listening and speaking. They also propose that a combination of production and perception constraints, which they call *sufficient contrast*, helps to shape phonetic inventories in languages. Their assumption that phonological units and rules emerge as a consequence of lexical development is similar to the assumption that underlies the view presented below.

There is another way interactions between the developing perception and production systems may affect the growth and character of language learners' knowledge of native-language sound patterns. Pressures to co-ordinate the way that these systems function and to relate the perceptual representations of words to the articulatory representations used to produce these words may force learners to derive a more abstract description that captures relevant generalizations that apply to both systems. The abstract description in this case is phonology. Thus, one suggestion is that it is the coordination of perceptual and productive representations that may lead the language learner from a more global representation of sound patterns of words to one that is structured with respect to phonetic segments.

The notion that phonological descriptions emerge from efforts to coordinate the outputs of perception and production systems during development is not new. Bever (1975, 1981) proposed something along these lines in his reflections about the purpose of a grammar during development. Speaking more generally about grammar than about phonology per se, he noted that

the reason that a psychogrammar exists is because of the vital role it plays during language acquisition, much of which occurs during the first five years of life. The psychogrammar is needed during that period to mediate between the systems of speech production and perception. It is the internal translator that regulates conflicting capacities which arise as each of the two systems of speech develop separately: if one system gets ahead of the other the psychogrammar can equilibrate their capacities. (Bever 1975, 65)

Thus, according to Bever, the whole reason for the existence of a grammar is that it helps to coordinate the systems of perception and production during development. He also argued that once this coordination was achieved, the grammar need not play any direct role in on-line processing (i.e., grammatical rules are not necessarily executed as steps during processing, nor does processing require computing the kinds of successive representations that are associated with derivations of sentences). Also, he speculated that the successful completion of the coordination process was what effectively shut down the critical period for language learning. In his view, this occurs earlier for the phonological system than it does for either syntax or semantics.

The phonological structure of a grammar as a mediating system becomes unused earlier than the semantic or syntactic structures. This is not to say that the phonological system is easier to learn—only that sufficient data for its complete acquisition are available to the child at an early age: once the speaking and identifying capacities are equilibrated, further phonological learning stops, and the constructed mapping lies fallow.... The critical age for phonological learning will be younger than for syntax and semantics. (Bever 1981, 195)

The framework within which Bever proposed his explanation was the Language Acquisition Device, which was part of the innate endowment of the language learner. Among other things, the LAD was expected to include information about formal and substantive linguistic universals (see chapter 2). Thus, with respect to the phonological component of the LAD, the infant would use knowledge of formal and substantive universals to find a successful way of resolving the outputs of both the perception and production systems.

I am a bit more agnostic regarding the amount of innate knowledge that language learners have regarding linguistic universals. Thus, I would like to suggest that some generalizations about phonological universals may actually arise from the process of coordinating the outputs of the perception and production systems. What may be innate about the whole thing is not so much a set of categories or constraints on formal rules but rather the drive to find a more general abstract system and a means of representation that coordinates the outputs from the perception and production systems. Thus, the coordination between the perception and production systems need not depend on the existence of a hardwired device such as the LAD.

Finally, the notion that production and perception may become coordinated and more integrated during the course of development seems to fit with what Gathercole and Baddeley (1993) have noted about the component of working memory that they call the *phonological loop*. In their view, the phonological loop is a system that is specialized for the storage of verbal material. It has two subcomponents: (1) the phonological store, which represents material in a phonological code that decays over time; and (2) an articulatory rehearsal process, which refreshes and maintains the decaying items in the phonological store. Spoken information gains direct access to the phonological store without articulatory rehearsal. Consequently, it is possible that this store is active in perception even during the first year. Although Gathercole and Baddeley indicate that the phonological loop is present and functioning from the preschool years onwards, they also note that there is little evidence that the articulatory rehearsal process is fully operative at this stage. For example, articulatory suppression, which prevents the rehearsal process, does not have the same disruptive effects on recall of auditory lists by 5-year-olds, as it has with older children and adults (Henry 1991). One possibility here is that a functioning articulatory rehearsal process depends on close coordination and integration of the perception and production systems. It may take several years to achieve the kind of coordination that is required, and until this point the phonological loop may be quite limited in how it operates.

Chapter 8
Wrapping Things Up

The field of infant speech-perception research has come a long way over the past quarter century. Not only do we now know that even newborn infants have some capacity to discriminate differences in speech sounds, but it is increasingly apparent that real language learning does begin during the first few months of life. Thus, contrary to the view that the babbling period is prelinguistic and discontinuous with the rest of language acquisition, it is clear that infants embark on the route to discovering the organization of their native language soon after birth. Indeed, infants are learning about the nature of sound patterns in their native language long before they begin to produce their first words. The picture of development that we now have is one in which the production and comprehension of the first words is continuous with infants' babbling and listening habits. More importantly, there is reason to believe that what transpires during the first year lays the foundation for subsequent achievements in language acquisition.

In our survey of spoken language capacities during the first year, there have been a number of themes that have recurred. These themes capture some essential features of the way that speech perception capacities develop and relate to other aspects of language acquisition. Therefore, they are relevant to an overall account of how infant speech perception capacities develop to support native-language word recognition and comprehension processes. With a clearer understanding of the changes that occur during the early stages of language acquisition, it is time to reexamine some of these themes and to explore how they fit with the view that has been developed in this book. This will be followed by an updated version of a model of how infant speech-perception capacities evolve in the course of language acquisition. Finally, the chapter concludes with a brief discussion of some problem areas that have not been well studied and are thus deserving of future research.

Innately Guided Learning

In chapter 4, I offered the suggestion that the development of speech-perception capacities is perhaps best described as an instance of innately guided learning. The idea behind this notion is that development is neither fixed and hardwired nor totally unrestricted. Rather, learning the sound system of one's native language is a constrained process. Out of all the possible ways in which learners could conceivably categorize the speech signal, some dimensions are favored, and others are not. For example, although learners are clearly capable of discriminating male voices from female voices (Miller, Younger, and Morse 1982), there is no indication that they attempt to make meaningful distinctions between words on this basis. Nor do they appear to use loudness differences as a basis for distinguishing among meanings of words, even though they certainly have the auditory sensitivity to do so. Instead, the information that they do use as an indication of meaningful distinctions among lexical items is what we refer to as phonetic distinctions and, under some input conditions, tonal distinctions. Still, the range of acoustic differences subsumed under phonetic distinctions constitutes a pretty broad range of possibilities—everything from vowels to clicks. Yet, within this range, infants appear to track, in fairly short order, the set that works best for the language that they are trying to acquire. In other words, they are counting the right sorts of properties in any distributional analysis that they perform on the input. Recall that the definition of innately guided learning that Gould and Marler provide is that *organisms are preprogrammed to learn particular kinds of things and to learn them in particular ways.*

Moreover, it is not only with respect to learning meaningful distinctions in the native language that we see rapid development during infancy. Other key developments in the acquisition of native-language sound structure seem to be achieved with the same rapidity. Consider the progress made during the first year on segmenting words from fluent speech. The data gathered to this point suggest that infants are not proceeding randomly with respect to cues for word boundaries. Rather, they appear to be attentive to the right kinds of cues, and they are evidently tracking the distribution of these in the input, long before they put together their own strings of words. Similarly, when it comes to the way that information is grouped together in the input, infants are able to home in on the appropriate sets of markers in the speech signal.

In the kinds of cases that we have been considering, there is often a complex relation among different kinds of acoustic properties that are involved in signaling the particular linguistic distinction or grouping. When multiple acoustic cues are present, the learner needs to discern which ones are relevant and how the cues are related. As Gibson (1969) has put it, they must find the higher-order invariants (relations that remain constant over change). In the case of finding the boundaries of words, there are indications that infants are able to do this by $10\frac{1}{2}$ months of age. Considering that infants only show the first signs of segmenting words at $7\frac{1}{2}$ months, this is another process that does not appear to require a long period of trial-and-error learning. Clearly, some learning is involved because the cues that work best for finding word boundaries in English are not necessarily the ones that work best for another language. In fact, learning to pick up the right set of cues that works best for one's own native language, as opposed to another, is a classic case of perceptual learning. The combination of cues that one uses is specific, in much the same way that the cues that wine connoisseurs use to identify different wines would not necessarily transfer to tasting different teas or beers.

There are a number of points of contact between the approach that I have tried to develop here and some of Gibson's (1969) views about perceptual learning. In her classic book on perceptual learning, she characterized what is involved in this process as learning "to attend to distinctive features of things, to invariants that lead to perceptual constancy and permanence, and to higher order structures and rules" (p. 445). It may be useful to point out some of the similarities and differences between my views on innately guided learning and Gibson's position. For instance, Gibson's view on the general developmental course of perceptual learning—"it is one of seeking stimulus information in a directed, systematic fashion" (p. 448)—appears to fit well with the description that I have offered about the way that infants in their first year approach language learning. Moreover, I am also sympathetic to her views on how perceptual learning improves in some domain of knowledge. Thus, Gibson claims that the pickup of structure is "a perceptual economy that develops with age and experience. The abstracting of common features or dimensions over time also increases developmentally" (p. 470).

Gibson's characterization of a trend in perceptual development toward what she calls "the optimization of attention" is also consonant with the views expressed here. For Gibson, this particular developmental trend is evident in

first, a tendency for attention to become more exploratory and less captive; second, the tendency for the exploratory search to become more systematic and less random; third, the te
ndency for attention to become more selective; and fourth, the inverse tendency for attention to become more exclusive. (p. 456)

Gibson's description of how attention is optimized in the course of perceptual learning accords with my observations on the way speech perception capacities become tuned and more closely focused on those properties in the signal that are most relevant to communication in a specific language.

One difference between innately guided learning and Gibson's (1969) view of perceptual learning is that the former view presupposes that the problem space is constrained so that only a limited set of cues is tried out in a particular situation. Moreover, with respect to this set there may even be some biases that determine the order in which various possibilities are checked. These kinds of innate biases do not have a prominent role in Gibson's theorizing.

Another difference between innately guided learning and Gibson's characterization of perceptual learning has to do with the speed with which learning occurs in certain domains. Humans appear to be primed to learn languages in a way that differs from becoming experts in other domains of perceptual knowledge. Becoming a wine connoisseur, an oboist, or a jet pilot, or for that matter a brain surgeon, involves the kind of explicit training and feedback that is not necessary for language acquisition, even though some of the same principles may be involved in learning across all of these different domains.

What is the nature of the constraints that apply in an innately guided learning process for acquiring the sound structure of a native language? Naturally, some of these constraints arise because, for most of us, language is a spoken medium. We perceive it primarily with our ears, rather than with our eyes (even though visual information can influence the process). Hence, some constraints on learning language through speech are ones that come from the way our auditory systems are structured and from the fact that speech unfolds over time.[1] Still other limitations have to do with general constraints on how much information we can process at one time and how much of the available information actually makes its way into memory.

It is also likely that some of the constraints involved in innately guided learning of a native language are ones similar to the kinds of operating principles that Slobin (1973, 1985a) and Peters (1983, 1985) have proposed. Biases to attend to certain portions of the speech signal, to encode and remember chunks of information, to keep track of the frequency with which certain patterns occur, and to note relations between ones that occur together could be the kinds of biases that work to constrain the possible search space in learning the sound structure of language. A bias to assume that a perceptual chunk is a possible candidate for a unit at the level of syntactic organization (as suggested by Gleitman and Wanner 1982) would also shape the course of learning. Just how many of the operating principles that have been proposed are actually involved in innately guided learning remains to be determined. My own assessment is that the set is likely to be limited to a relatively small number and that some, but not all, of these will generalize to other domains of learning.

At this point, it might be helpful to consider a potential sort of constraint that does not appear to be one that language learners use. For example, just as there is a bias to treat perceptually isolable chunks as candidates for important grammatical units, there could be a bias to treat sound patterns that are similar in their acoustic structure as being similar in their meanings. However, this does not appear to be a bias that is widely, if ever, applied to language learning, even though it might be sensible to apply it to perceptual signals in some other domains (e.g., such as treating different growls as warning signals). In fact, if anything, there are suggestions from the language-learning literature that children may be slow to recognize relations between different forms (e.g., past and present tenses of verbs) of the same words (Bowerman 1982).

In summary, the rapidity with which infants pick up information that is germane to the specific organization of sound patterns in their native language argues for the operation of an innately guided learning process that governs acquisition in this domain.

The Less-Is-More Principle

Newport (1990, 1991) first advanced the idea that "less is more" in her discussions of critical periods in language acquisition. In considering why learning some kinds of information about language (e.g., learning the morphology of verbs in American Sign Language) is more effective before a certain age, she suggested that limitations on information-processing capacities at a younger age could actually be beneficial to picking up the relevant cues. In particular, Newport noted that late learners' lack of facility with the morphology of verbs in ASL had less to do with their length of experience with sign language than it did with the age at which they began to acquire it. She argued that the very limitations of the child's information-processing capacities provide the basis for successful language acquisition (Newport 1988). She noted that a different pattern of errors occurs during the learning of morphological information for early and late learners. Early learners make componential errors, in which structures are produced in part, with whole morphemes omitted. By comparison, at the same stage of learning, late learners produce "frozen" structures in which whole-word unanalyzed signs are produced.

These differences in approach appear to derive from how linguistic input is perceived and stored by these two groups. The reduced storage capacities of the younger groups may mean that they are only able to perceive and store component parts of complex linguistic stimuli as opposed to the whole complex stimulus. Hence, for those aspects of learning that require componential analysis, their attention to such features in the input may facilitate working out of the mapping relations more effectively for early learners than for late learners. In part, limitations on how much information that they can store at once means that they have fewer possible components of form to match to meanings in a given situation. By comparison, a larger memory capacity results in a large increase in the number of alternative mappings from forms to meanings that must be considered. Newport further suggests that using a smaller window for processing information may help in perceptually highlighting relevant units in the input.

Elman (1993) has made a similar point about the way that constraints on processing at an early stage of acquisition could actually facilitate the pickup of certain structural properties of the input language. He developed a connectionist model based on a simple recurrent architecture to learn the key features of a simple grammar. Elman found that at first the model failed to successfully generalize from the cases used in the training set to new cases (not given during training). However, he discovered that by restricting the short-term memory resources of the model during the early training trials, and then gradually increasing these resources as training progressed, the model was able to learn the key features of the grammar and generalize these to new instances. He concluded that the early memory limitations block access to the full range of complexities in the input data and restrict learning to those regularities that are available within the smaller memory span. Thus, a combination of early memory limitations and subsequent maturational growth could play a critical role in enabling an individual to learn about a complex domain such as language.

According to Newport, less is more will be helpful for those aspects of language acquisition that require componential analysis. In contrast, the limitations of a smaller window for processing and remembering information may hinder the acquisition of language features that require integration. Newport's focus was on the morphology of words. Her findings in this domain led her to claim that adults might have an advantage over children in situations in which whole-word learning was required (as compared to the learning about component parts of words). However, given the recent findings that $10\frac{1}{2}$-month-olds show some ability to use multiple sources of information to word boundaries, the picture may be a little more complicated than this. There are some elements of whole-word learning that might also draw on componential analysis, such as segmenting words from fluent speech. Thus, because of their smaller processing windows, infants might actually be in a better position to detect the kinds of phonotactic and allophonic cues to word boundaries than are adults. Indeed, this may also account for their apparent sensitivity to the distributional properties of phonotactic patterns in the input, as recent investigations have reported (Friederici and Wessels 1993; Jusczyk, Friederici, et al. 1993; Jusczyk et al. 1994).

The developing memory and attentional capacities of older infants bring with them not only the ability to consider more of the same type of information simultaneously, but they also provide the opportunity to consider more different kinds of information (i.e., information from different sources). This could be another way "less is more" is a factor in infants' sensitivity to information in the sound stream of language. Early on, infants may be limited to focusing on one source of information about language at a time (e.g., sounds, meanings, or some other properties). Sound properties of language appear to be especially attractive for infants during the first year. Limiting one's focus to such properties in a given situation (as opposed to immediately trying to relate sounds to other aspects of language) may permit infants to more effectively pick up regularities relating to the organization of native-language sound patterns. However, as the ability to integrate information from different sources develops, these sources not only compete for infants' attention, but they also proliferate the kinds of different regularities that can be extracted from the input. Consequently, the relative salience and importance of information about the sound properties of the input may decline from what it once was. This may be a reason that infants in word-learning tasks have difficulties distinguishing minimal contrasts, despite earlier successes in discriminating the same kinds of contrasts on speech perception tasks. It could also explain why infants might rely more heavily on prosodic marking of units in fluent speech than do adults, since there are many more sources of information available to adults regarding the marking of syntactic units in utterances.

In summary, although at first glance it seems counterintuitive, learners could actually benefit from having fewer resources available for analyzing information in the speech signal. A smaller processing window might actually increase the chances of finding the kind of information needed to tailor speech perception capacities to respond to the critical features of native-language sound patterns.

Phonology as a Mediator between Perception and Production

In describing how speech perception capacities develop during language acquisition, I have focused on their role in speech segmentation and word recognition. This is the essential function of these capacities in speech perception. To be sure, the capacities that underlie speech perception can be, and often are, put to other uses, including word games, poetry, and linguistic analyses. However, the function they perform that no fluent speaker-hearer can do without is to find and identify words in continuous speech. Moreover, as Liberman and his colleagues pointed out many years ago (Liberman et al. 1967), the rate of information transmission in speech is quite rapid as compared to other types of signals. Thus, it stands to reason that speech perception capacities adapt to take advantage of how the signal is structured in a particular language. Much of this structure has to do with the types of sound patterns that are available for conveying different meanings. It is in this sense that the development of speech perception is basically about learning to identify words, rather than strings of phonemes.

There is no denying that most of us eventually develop some capacity to represent words in terms of some more-elementary sound units corresponding to phonetic segments. It is a fair assumption that it would not be possible to read this text in English without first accessing a phonetic representation. However, the extent to which recovering a phonetic representation is essential to the process of spoken-word recognition is another matter (Klatt 1989). Certainly, there are situations in which it is handy to have access to a phonetic representation, such as when one encounters some speech pattern that does not match any words already in one's lexicon. Access to a phonetic representation under such a circumstance could help in the encoding of the sound pattern. The use of speech production abilities to accurately reproduce the pattern would allow one to seek out information about the meaning that is attached to it. In fact, a force that may drive the development of phonology in general, and of phonetic representations in particular, is the need to coordinate the systems of speech perception and speech production.

From the standpoint of word recognition, there is no need of an ability to detect the similarity in the initial portions of the words "big," "beet," "bop," and "bun." Nor is there any particular need for the speech perception system to extract any similarity between the way that the word "park" begins and the way that "tip" ends (although this ability is critical for learning to read English). However, in order to produce, and reproduce, any of these items correctly on another occasion, it may be helpful to take note of any similarities in the articulatory gestures that are required to produce these. Moreover, successfully coordinating the timing of gestures to cut down on variability in productions of the same word on different occasions could well lead one in the direction of an elementary unit of organization on the order of a phonetic segment.

It would be foolish to suggest that representations from perception and production are completely independent until they are tied together in reference to particular meanings. In the demonstrations that babbling does indeed drift toward the kinds of sound patterns that infants hear spoken around them, there is clear evidence that perception exerts some influence on infants' productions. Moreover, because most infants perceive what they themselves produce (and those who do not end up producing aberrant patterns according to Oller and Eilers 1988), both kinds of activities are associated with some of the same task settings. As Fry (1966) observed, one purpose of babbling may be to help forge links between perception and production so that one can hit the right perceptual targets with one's articulatory gestures and so that one can find the right sequencing of gestures to reproduce a sound pattern that someone else has produced. Nevertheless, tying the representation of a particular set of gestures and the perceptual representation of a particular sound pattern to the same representation of word meaning could encourage the further development of a level of description that is applicable to both production and perception. The desire to have one's intentions understood is likely to be an additional impetus to achieve a closer coordination of the two systems. Access to some common level of representation may allow the learner to capture a range of generalizations that apply to both systems. It is in this way that phonology may emerge from the efforts to coordinate the outputs of perception and production.

The Impact of a Developing Lexicon

Given the present view that speech perception capacities develop to support word recognition in fluent speech, it follows that the development of a lexicon containing information about native-language words is likely to have an important impact on these capacities. There are some indications that lexical development gets under way during the second trimester of the first year. Thus, infants begin to respond to some patterns that have potential significance for them, such as their own names (Mandel et al. 1995). They also show some signs of comprehending a few words (Benedict 1979; Huttenlocher 1974), and they seem to store and retain information about the sound patterns of words heard frequently in the input (Hallé and Boysson-Bardies 1994b; Hohne et al. 1994). However, because their abilities to segment words from fluent speech are still in the beginning stages of development, one might ask how the first words are acquired. One possibility is that they store information about short sound patterns that may be produced in isolation from time to time. Words like "baby," "mommy," "daddy," siblings' names, and pets' names are logical candidates for such treatment. As noted earlier, in English, these items tend to embody the predominant word-stress pattern (i.e., they begin with strong syllables), which may foster a bias to segment longer strings of fluent speech at the onsets of strong syllables.

Once sound patterns are encoded and stored in the lexicon, they are available for further processing. Attending to the onsets and offsets of such stored items could also be a first step in learning the distributional properties that the beginnings and endings of words are likely to have. Even if the strings of speech that infants store initially are sometimes longer than a single word, infants could potentially derive information about how words are likely to begin and end in the language by analyzing these items. Performance on tasks in which infants are presented with lists of words that are either consistent or inconsistent with native-language phonotactic or prosodic patterns (Friederici and Wessels 1993; Jusczyk, Friederici et al. 1993; Jusczyk et al. 1994) could follow from a bias to attend more closely to patterns that match ones in the developing lexicon. This might be helpful for discovering the properties that characterize the most frequently occurring kinds of word patterns in the language. Of course, once the infant has become more adept at picking up such information, a bias to attend to familiar patterns would have to recede, or else infants would never acquire information about items with less frequently occurring properties.

Because meanings of spoken words are accessed through the representations of their sound patterns, the nature of the stored representations is critical to the process of word recognition. Representations of the sound patterns of words that are incomplete in important respects could lead to misses and false alarms in word recognition. However, a number of investigators have also pointed out that even if infants' representations are more global and less precise than adults', this might not unduly detract from their word-recognition abilities (Charles-Luce and Luce 1990, 1995; Jusczyk 1986b, 1993a; Logan 1992; Walley 1993; but also see the arguments in Gerken et al. 1995). The reason for this is that there are some indications that young children's lexicons may be less densely populated than are adult lexicons. Consequently, a given word in the lexicon may have no or few highly similar competitors ("neighbors") relative to the comparable items in the adult lexicon (Charles-Luce and Luce 1990, 1995; Logan 1992). For example, Logan used the CHILDES database (MacWhinney 1991) to perform a longitudinal survey of the vocabulary growth of five children. He found that something less than a complete phonetic encoding of a word's sound pattern (such as a coarse coding that includes manner features and lexical stress) would be enough to keep most words in these children's lexicons distinct from other similar items. However, as Logan noted, both his survey and previous ones in this area (Charles-Luce and Luce 1990, 1995; Dollaghan 1994) have estimated neighborhood size based on children's productive vocabularies. The story with respect to their receptive vocabularies could well be different. Unfortunately, there are no available data plotting the growth of and full range of children's receptive vocabularies during the first few years of language acquisition.

Nor do we have sufficient data, at present, to assess just how precise infants' representations of the sound patterns of words are. The limited data that are currently available provide no clear indication of the detail present. For example, a recent investigation by Hallé and Boysson-Bardies (1994a) indicated that 11-month-old French-learning infants listened longer to nonsense words that differed from known words by only one or two phonetic features than they did to other nonsense words (i.e., ones based on unfamiliar words). This could be an indication that they accept the former as tokens of the known word types. However, in another investigation that looked at whether infants would generalize from a nonword that they were familiarized with (e.g., "tup") to a very similar sounding real word in sentential contexts (e.g., "cup"), Jusczyk and Aslin (1995) found no evidence that $7\frac{1}{2}$-month-olds generalized from one to the other. There were a number of differences between the two tasks that were used (e.g., Hallé and Boysson-Bardies used one familiar and one unfamiliar list across a series of trials, whereas Jusczyk and Aslin used their word-detection paradigm.) It is also possible that whether or not an item is previously known to the child may make a difference. In any event, considerably more research is needed to determine what kind of detail is included in infants' early representations of words.

Information about what infants remember about the sound patterns of words that they have heard, and the circumstances under which they are likely to encode them, is crucial for understanding many different facets of the development of speech perception. The most obvious area has to do with changes that occur as speech perception capacities become better adapted to recognizing words. However, understanding the way that perceptual and productive capacities relate to each other depends on a clear picture of the representations that infants are working from. Traditionally, most speech researchers have assumed that any stored representations of the sound patterns of words are abstract (Forster and Bednall 1976; Marslen-Wilson and Welsh 1978; Morton 1969). They are abstract in the sense that they are normalized with respect to variables such as talker's voice, speaking rate, loudness, and so on. The assumption is that information relating to the specific characteristics of a given utterance are somehow removed during speech processing, leaving a representation that is basically a phonetic description of the information in the utterance. This normalized description is then in the same form as the descriptions of the sound patterns of words in the lexicon and hence can be matched to the correct lexical entry.

The alternative to the view just presented is that listeners store representations of specific instances of tokens previously heard and match new instances to these. Until recently, this alternative had been considered implausible because of the memory-storage capacities it appears to require—enough to store everything that one hears. However, several developments in recent years have led some researchers to seriously consider the possibility that listeners encode specific instances, rather than abstract representations of the sound patterns of words (Goldinger 1992; Jusczyk 1992, 1993a). The first set of developments has to do with evidence regarding listeners' memories for specific information about instances of words they have heard, whereas the second set concerns the successful performance of computer simulation models of memory that store specific instances.

With regard to the kinds of information that listeners store about speech, there are demonstrations of listeners' abilities to recognize familiar voices (Bricker and Pruzansky 1966; Clifford 1983; Ladefoged and Ladefoged 1980; Remez et al. in press), famous voices (Van Lancker, Kreiman, and Emmorey 1985; Van Lancker, Kreiman, and Wickens 1985), and even unfamiliar voices (Carterette and Barneby 1975; Papcun, Kreiman, and Davis 1989; Remez et al. in press). Of course, the fact that one can recognize a particular voice does not mandate that one actually stores individual instances of words. There could be other routes to voice recognition that are used, such as a set of adjustments that one might make to normalize the speech produced by a particular individual.

Nevertheless, there are other kinds of findings, involving particular instances of words, that are hard to explain in this fashion. For example, several investigations have provided evidence that subjects can, under some circumstances, recognize changes in speaking voices used to present particular words during familiarization and test periods (Hintzman, Block, and Inskeep 1972; Light et al. 1973). There are other indications that subjects retain information about voices even under incidental learning conditions. For example, Geiselman and Bellezza (1976) presented subjects with 20 sentences to remember; half were produced by a male talker and half were produced by a female talker. On a surprise memory test that quizzed the ability to recall voices as well as the sentences, subjects did retain information about which voice produced which sentence. Even more interesting are the results of an investigation by Craik and Kirsner (1974), which suggested that subjects' abilities to remember the identity of words that they had previously heard were directly affected by whether these words were produced by the same voice across familiarization and testing. Craik and Kirsner found that during testing, subjects were better able to judge whether a given word was "old" or "new" when it was repeated in the original, as opposed to a different, voice. More recently, Palmeri, Goldinger, and Pisoni (1993) replicated and extended this finding, using as many as 20 different voices and longer retention intervals. Increasing the number of talkers from 2 to 20 had no appreciable effect: recognition of words in the original voice was always better than when they were presented in a different voice, regardless of how many different voices were used or how long the testing lag was.

If listeners do store specific instances of words that they have heard, why have researchers been so slow to recognize this? The plausibility argument regarding limitations on storage capacity certainly has been a factor. However, another reason may have to do with the fact that our ability to recall information relating to the specific characteristic of a particular word token appears to decline over longer retention intervals (McGhee 1937). However, recent evidence suggests that this may have to do more with the use of measures that tap explicit, rather than implicit, memory (Goldinger 1992; Schacter, Church, and Treadwell 1994; Schacter and Church 1992). *Explicit measures* of memory involve having subjects consciously recall some piece of information, whereas *implicit measures* investigate whether prior experience with some particular stimulus facilitates performance, without any attempt at conscious recollection (Johnson and Hasher 1987; Schacter 1987). As an example of the latter, perceptual identification of words has been shown to improve when the words were previously read, even when subjects did not recall reading them before (Jacoby and Dallas 1981). With respect to spoken materials, Schacter and Church (1992) observed performance differences between repetitions of words in the same voice and in a different voice on measures that tapped implicit memory (e.g., a stem-completion task), but not on ones that tapped explicit memory (e.g., cued-recall tasks). By comparison, Goldinger (1992), who used a wider range of tasks and delay conditions, found evidence of greater facilitation for same-voice repetitions with explicit, as well as implicit, memory measures. However, he also found that the magnitude of same-voice effects decreased over longer delays for explicit measures but not for implicit ones. Similarly, the magnitude of same-voice effects decreased with deeper levels of processing for measures of explicit memory, but remained constant for measures of implicit memory.

Finally, there is some suggestion that infants may store information about the sound pattern of words that includes details relating to specific instances. First, Jusczyk et al. (1992b) found 2-month-olds' retention of information about sound patterns of particular words was disrupted when a range of tokens from different talkers, or even from the same talker, was used. These findings suggest that the infants were registering the differences among the tokens and that their capacities for encoding information may have been overloaded by all of the different instances to be represented. Second, Jusczyk, Hohne et al. (1993) found that infants retained information for a two-week interval about a previously unfamiliar voice that they had heard reading stories.

In summary, the results of investigations regarding adults' and infants' retention of specific details of particular items suggest that this information is not discarded but is encoded into long-term memory. Information about particular instances does appear to facilitate performance in tasks involving memory and perceptual identification, even when these details are not directly accessible on measures that involve conscious recollection. The fact that information about particular instances is retained suggests that listeners do not simply encode abstract phonetic representations of words, which leave out details of speaker's voice and other situation-specific information. Rather these kinds of details appear to be encoded along with other information about sound properties of the word. Regardless of whether they account for such findings by storing specific exemplars of experienced word tokens or use some alternative solution, models of word recognition ultimately need to account for why these kinds of facilitation effects occur.

How could a model that stores specific instances, or exemplars, ever work as a plausible explanation of word recognition? Some hints as to how this might occur come from the other set of developments that have piqued interest in models of exemplar storage. In particular, there are indications that models based on the storage of exemplars can account for the same range of facts as models based on the storage of prototypes (Estes 1994; Hintzman 1986, 1988; Medin and Schaffer 1978; Nosofsky 1986, 1988, 1991; Nosofsky, Clark, and Shinn 1989). Hintzman's MINERVA 2 is a prime example of such a model. The model stores memories of specific events as collections of primitive properties that include perceptual details, context, affect, semantic connotation, and so on. Although each individual instance is stored independently in memory, through the activation of individual traces at the time of retrieval, the model can reproduce effects that are typically associated with prototype models, even though the model does not explicitly store prototypes.

Recognition in a *multiple-trace system* like MINERVA 2 occurs when the processed input, or probe, is broadcast simultaneously to all traces in secondary (i.e., long-term) memory. Each memory trace becomes activated in proportion to its similarity to the probe. Traces with structural features that overlap most closely with ones in the probe are activated most strongly. Other traces with little similarity to the probe may only be activated weakly, or not at all. The reply received in response to a probe to secondary memory is described by Hintzman (1986) as an "echo" that is sent to consciousness. Although all of the traces contribute to the echo, the contribution of ones most similar to the probe is greater because they produce a more intense response. The more specific the probe (i.e., the more detailed the information in the representation), then the smaller the set of highly activated traces. Whenever several traces are very strongly activated, then the content of the echo primarily reflects their common properties. This has the consequence of emphasizing their shared characteristics while downplaying their discrepancies in the echo. Thus, in effect, the echo takes on many of the characteristics of a prototype, even though no such abstract representation is actually stored in memory. The echo can also act to enhance the probe's representation through the comparison process by filling in details that are missing. This enhancement helps to associate the new probe with past information in memory.

The echo that is returned to consciousness can vary with respect to both its intensity and its content. The intensity, which reflects the familiarity of the stimulus being perceived, is a function of the similarity of the traces to the probe, and the number of traces that contribute to the echo. The content of the echo relates to the distinctiveness of the probe as compared to what is already in memory. The more similar a new instance is to previously stored traces, the more the echo reflects their common properties (i.e., the more prototypical the instance seems). However, if the probe resembles only a few of the previously stored traces, the echo that is returned is likely to reflect more idiosyncratic properties of those traces that are activated.

Multiple-trace models have a number of attractive features for explaining certain observations made about word recognition. Not only are such models able to account for important findings associated with prototype models (e.g., differential forgetting of prototypes and old instances, typicality effects, and category-size effects), but they can also provide explanations for phenomena that are not accounted for by such models. Chief among these phenomena are the kinds of context-dependent effects discussed above, as well as others reported in the memory and concept-learning literature (Jacoby 1983; Osgood and Hoosain 1974; Potter and Faulconer 1979; Roth and Schoben 1983). Multiple-trace memory models offer a solution as to why previously encountered instances are recognized more easily than some other member of the same category. This is because the match to a particular memory trace is much better when a previously encountered instance serves as the probe. Another feature of multiple-trace models that makes them attractive for dealing with fluent word recognition is that they can account for automaticity effects in skill learning (Logan 1988). As fluency is acquired in the production of a skill, performance reaches a point where it becomes automatic, in the sense that it is fast, effortless, and not available to consciousness. Of course, these features are particularly useful to applications, such as on-line speech recognition, where the perceiver is required to make rapid categorizations of the input under severe time constraints.

Although the present discussion has focused largely on MINERVA 2, there are other kinds of memory models that involve the storage of multiple traces that could provide alternative accounts of the organization of the lexicon. For example, some models that assume that general representations form the basis of recognition also allow for the retention of information that is specific to particular instances (Eich 1982; Murdock 1982; Pike 1984; Salasoo, Shiffrin, and Feustel 1985). Other models, such as the one proposed by Kirsner and Dunn (1985; Kirsner, Dunn, and Standen 1987), assume that abstract representations are stored in the lexicon but that perceivers also keep detailed records of the perceptual processes that were used to match each stimulus to the stored representations. The model assumes that facilitation arises whenever perceivers can use exactly the same set of perceptual operations (which is why exact repetitions show advantages).

In the end, regardless of which type of model proves most feasible, it is clear that it will have to provide some means of encoding specific information about previously experienced utterances. At present, theorizing about the storage of specific exemplars in the context of speech recognition has taken Hintzman's model as a reasonable starting point (Goldinger 1992; Jusczyk 1992, 1993a, 1994). Thus, this is one of the assumptions behind the model that is described in the next section.

WRAPSA

This model was intended as an account of the way speech-perception capacities evolve to support word recognition in continuous speech. The name of the model, WRAPSA, stands for Word Recognition and Phonetic Structure Acquisition. WRAPSA was an extension of an unnamed model that I proposed some years earlier (Jusczyk 1985b, 1986b). One major change in the new model had to do with replacing the assumption that the input was matched to abstract phonetic representations of items stored in the lexicon. Instead, in WRAPSA, I made the assumption, for reasons such as those described in the previous section, that infants store specific exemplars of sound patterns that they have heard. To be sure, the assumption that storage occurs in the form of specific instances raises some potentially thorny problems. For example, is it really the case that we store instances of everything that we experience? If so, how is the potential storage problem solved? If we do not store every instance, but only some subset of instances, what determines whether or not an instance gets stored? Is there any empirical way to determine whether and what information is likely to be stored on a given occasion?

These are hard questions to answer under any circumstances, but we cannot even begin to answer them until we have much better information about the memory and attentional capacities of infants acquiring language. Even if one were to adopt the alternative position of assuming that abstract phonetic representations are what is stored, one would still have to find some way of explaining how listeners are able to benefit from exact repetitions of previously heard stimuli. Consequently, the notion that storage in the lexicon involves exemplars, rather than abstract prototypes, remains a working assumption in the latest version of WRAPSA. In what follows, I present a brief overview of the model and its major components. Then I take a closer look at each of the components of the model and discuss any needed changes in light of more recent findings.

My aim in proposing WRAPSA was to describe the initial state of infants' speech-perception capacities and how these capacities develop and change as infants learn a native language. One assumption that I made was that as infants acquire knowledge of the sound structure of their native language, this should have an impact on how they process speech. In other words, their experience with a particular language should be incorporated into any routines that they use to process fluent speech (i.e., this information is "precompiled" into such routines, as Klatt 1979 suggested). At the same time, because speech itself provides most infants with their entry point for acquiring a native language, it seems logical to assume that the changes that go on in speech processing will also have some impact on the rest of language acquisition. In describing the components of the model, I have found it easiest to present them from the point of view of their operation during word recognition. However, the reader should keep in mind that some of these components are either not present or are only functioning in some sort of default mode during the very earliest stages of development.

Speech perception begins as the signal enters the auditory system and undergoes a preliminary analysis. In this initial phase of processing, a set of *auditory analyzers* provides a description of the spectral and temporal features present in the acoustic signal. These same analyzers are involved in the description of any acoustic input—speech or nonspeech. The features extracted at this level are ones that reflect the inherent organization of the human auditory system. Thus, the analyzers are part of the innate endowment of the infant.

At the preliminary level of analysis, then, the description that emerges is neutral with respect to the language that is spoken. This is the type of description that is attained by the infant during the first few months of life. However, once a language has been acquired, the output of the auditory analyzers is weighted to give prominence to those features that are most critical to making meaningful distinctions between words in the language. This is the next important component of the model. The weighting scheme basically amounts to routines that focus attention on the features that are critical for processing contrasts between words in a particular language. Information about the properties of sounds to which infants are exposed and their distribution in the input are likely to be critical factors in shaping the weighting scheme. One way a weighting scheme that is specific to speech, as opposed to nonspeech sounds, may develop is through the storage of contextual information that effectively tags certain kinds of acoustic signals as vocal ones. Prenatal experience could enhance any basic bias that infants have to attend to sounds with human vocal properties. Other kinds of contextual information would be required to distinguish linguistic from nonlinguistic human vocalizations (just as differences in prosodic organization apparently aid newborns in distinguishing utterances in their mothers' native language from those of a nonnative language).

The next major component of the model has to do with the pattern-extraction process that takes place on the weighted output. The pattern-extraction process refines the description of the processed signal and attempts a segmentation into word-sized units. Clearly, information from the native language regarding the kinds of cues apt to signal word boundaries affects the character of the pattern-extraction processes. The representation of the sound structure of the potential lexical items that is returned from the pattern-extraction processes is global in the sense that it provides a description that temporally groups prominent features into syllabic units. However, there is no explicit breakdown of these syllabic units into phonetic segments. The prosodic structure of these representations is also marked. The fourth component of the model involves the use of representations as probes to the mental lexicon. These are matched against existing representations of known words that have been stored away in memory. Given the assumption that traces of previously experienced instances are stored, the matching process involves a parallel activation of items in the lexicon by the probe. If a close match is obtained between the probe and some subset of stored traces corresponding to a word, then the word is recognized and its meaning, if represented, is accessed. In the event that no match is found, then the input may be reprocessed in an attempt to find a suitable match, or the representation may be stored as a new lexical item, with or without an accompanying meaning.

Given this broad overview of the WRAPSA model, it should be apparent that during the first few months of life, the preliminary analysis stage would be expected to be very active. However, at this time, only some set of defaulting weighting scheme—the same as for most other acoustic signals—would be expected to apply. Similarly, any pattern-extraction processes would be expected to be general because learners have not had sufficient input to adjust these specifically to native-language structures. It is likely that some of the patterns infants process do get stored in long-term memory. How many of such patterns get stored and how detailed they are is not clear at present. When sufficient numbers of these are stored, this will prompt the development of the weighting scheme. Let us now examine each of the main components of the model in more detail.

Preliminary Analysis of the Speech Signal
Before describing this aspect of the model, let me note that my conception of how this component of WRAPSA functions has changed little since

the model was originally proposed at the Conference on Phonological Development held at Stanford University in 1989 (see Jusczyk 1992). Most of the new findings in infant speech-perception research have more direct relevance to some of the other components of the model. Nevertheless, I have tried to provide a clearer and more detailed description here of how the auditory analyzers function during the development of speech perception.

Processing begins as speech sounds are picked up by the auditory system. The incoming information is transduced by the peripheral auditory system and passed on to auditory processing centers in the brain, where an array of analyzers provide an indication of the acoustic properties that are present in the signal. The analyzers are spectrally specific in that they are tuned to particular frequency regions (Sawusch 1986). They extract such information as the presence of noise in some region of the spectrum; whether the noise source is periodic or aperiodic; durations, bandwidths, and intensities of sounds; the presence, direction, and degree of any spectral changes that may occur, and so on. Each spectrally specific analyzer performs the feature-extraction process independently of other analyzers.

Nevertheless, there is also some temporal tagging of features that co-occur within the same syllable-sized unit. Thus, with respect to speech sounds, syllables serve as the elementary temporal slices for the input. It is worth noting that because syllable boundaries may be coarticulated in speech, boundaries between adjacent syllables may not be precisely defined. I assume that the onset of a new syllable follows an amplitude minimum, contains an amplitude peak, and is closed by the next amplitude minimum. This will most certainly mean that some syllable boundaries will be missed, and occasionally false boundaries may be registered, but in most instances these groupings will correspond to syllables. Much like the other kinds of linguistic units we have discussed earlier (e.g., words, phrases), the "syllable-like slices" are a rough approximation to what linguists typically think of as syllables. They put the learner in the right ballpark to learn the syllabic units of a particular native language.

It is important to define a temporal window over which the acoustic features are integrated. This is because the successful interpretation of any durational cues relies on the establishment of some temporal normalization of the speech signal. For example, in order to identify items that are distinguished by durational cues (such as [ba] and [wa]), the listener needs to be able to take into account the average speaking rate. As Mehler, Dupoux, and Segui (1990) have noted, averaging the duration of syllables would provide the listener with the means to arrive at an estimation of speaking rate.

The acoustic analysis at this first level yields a very fine-grained description of the speech signal. In effect, the analyzers constitute the sensory limits on our ability to resolve speech and nonspeech sounds. They are part of the infant's innate endowment and define the dimensions along which acoustic signals can be ordered and classified. The operation of these analyzers underlies the remarkable abilities that young infants display in discriminating speech contrasts during the first few months of life. Indeed, most of the findings from speech perception studies with infants less than 6 months old can be explained by reference to what the auditory analyzers pull out of the speech signal. They provide the infant with the kind of preliminary, general categorization of information that subsequently can be refined and used for distributional analyses of native-language input.

There are a number of indications that rather general auditory-processing capacities underlie speech perception during the first few months. For example, the fact that infants can discriminate phonetic contrasts not present in native-language input suggests that the basic capacities are at least general enough to function for any potential native language. Moreover, many of the interesting parallels that were noted in chapter 3 regarding infants' perception of speech and nonspeech sounds are most parsimoniously explained by the assumption that the same set of auditory analyzers are operating on both types of signals.

Of course, the auditory analyzers continue to function throughout life for all types of acoustic signals, speech or nonspeech. In speech processing, the fine-grained breakdown of information provided by these analyzers is not always obvious, because it tends to be hidden by the additional layers of processing that are more strictly tuned to the structure of the native language. It is the outputs of these higher levels of processing that listeners typically have access to (in line with what has been suggested about input systems by Fodor 1983). However, there are certain phenomena that have been observed for speech perception in adults that sometimes permit us to glimpse the operations of the auditory analyzers. For example, although the perception of certain phonemic distinctions (such as ones between stop consonants) is said to be categorical, it is also clear that this is not due to some sort of sensory limitation on the kinds of distinctions that can be detected by the auditory system.

There are situations in which the auditory system can detect these types of within category differences. For instance, Pisoni and Tash (1974) measured the time it took adults to respond "same" or "different" to pairs of items chosen either from within the same phonemic category or from two different phonemic categories. Although subjects tended to respond "same" to different items from within the same phonemic category, their reaction times to these items were significantly slower than to pairs in which the items were actually identical. Thus it is clear that the auditory system did detect some difference between the sounds, even though the listener was unable to report it. Other studies have also shown that, with special training or testing procedures, listeners can access information about within-category differences (Carney, Widin, and Veimeister 1977; Miller et al. 1983; Samuel 1977; Sawusch 1976). Consequently, although listeners are not able to access information about within-category differences in most normal speech-processing situations, that information does get into the auditory system and is detected at the level of the auditory analyzers.

The information that is extracted by the auditory analyzers decays quickly, and information that is not attended to is not available for further processing. To preserve the essential details provided by the analyzers, the information must undergo some recoding. The information that is selected for such recoding will eventually be affected by the routines that have been developed for processing a particular native language. However, prior to the acquisition of a particular language, any recoding that occurs would necessarily be language-general. As noted earlier, attentional processes are affected by one's experience in learning a native language. The kinds of differences that serve to distinguish items from within the same phonemic category will not be particularly helpful in recognizing words in the language, so they are unlikely to be attended to. Once routines have been set up to select certain kinds of information from the auditory analyzers, gaining access to unattended dimensions will be difficult. However, there are circumstances in which it may be necessary to attend to differences that are usually ignored, such as when learning a new language. Thus, when speakers of one language must learn distinctions not present in their native language, they must bypass the routines developed for attending to information relevant to native-language sounds and draw upon other sources of information provided by the auditory analyzers.

The Weighting Scheme

My thinking regarding this aspect of the model has undergone some changes in light of recent findings from studies of infant speech perception. However, the changes in my views concern not so much the weighting scheme itself but rather which elements are crucial to the formation of the weighting scheme. Initially, I placed a great deal of emphasis on the efforts of the language learner to express meaningful contrasts between words in the native language. Although I still believe that these efforts to produce meaningful contrasts do have some impact on the weighting scheme, I think that, prior to this point, sensitivity to distributional properties of the input plays a critical role in the development of this scheme. The evidence reviewed throughout this book suggests that language-learning infants are clearly tracking how sound properties are distributed in the input, at a point well before they are producing meaningful contrasts of their own. Moreover, the increases in sensitivity to information in native-language sound patterns coincides with the declines in sensitivity that have been documented for nonnative contrasts. These facts indicate that the infant's perception of speech is changing as a result of experience listening to native-language input. Tuning one's perceptual capacities to optimally pick up the kinds of differences that serve to distinguish between frequently occurring categories of sounds in the input is adaptive for developing successful word recognition procedures.

In order to successfully model how speech perception capacities develop, it is necessary to explain how infants move from a state in which they can apparently discriminate just about any kind of contrast that could possibly appear in a natural language to one in which they appear to be relatively insensitive to contrasts that do not appear in their native language. In addition, because there is evidence that adults can relearn nonnative contrasts (Caramazza et al. 1973; Flege and Eefting 1987; Flege 1989; Logan et al. 1989; Werker and Tees 1984b), it is clear that whatever changes take place in speech perception as a result of learning a particular language are not irrevocable. Rather, in line with other kinds of perceptual learning, what seems to be happening is that infants are developing strategies or schemes that focus their attention on certain aspects of speech sounds and not others.

It seems to me that this process of assigning more importance to some kinds of information in the signal is equivalent to weighting the information that is available from the auditory analyzers. Consequently, I have referred to what happens as developing a weighting scheme (Jusczyk

1985b, 1992). What I have in mind by the weighting scheme is a formula or automatic means of setting the focus of attention on properties that are relevant for recognizing words in a particular native language. For example, syllable-initial voiceless stop consonants are aspirated in English, whereas syllable-initial voiced stop consonants are not. In contrast, there is no aspiration difference accompanying the production of syllable-initial voiced and voiceless stops in French. Thus, attention to the presence of aspiration is useful for the English listener in distinguishing voiced from voiceless stops in syllable-initial positions, but it would be of no help to the French listener. Hence, by my view, information from auditory analyzers that is relevant to aspiration would receive heavy weighting in the schemes of English, but not French, listeners.

In the WRAPSA model, the consequences of directing attention to some portions of the auditory analysis and ignoring others is a distortion of the perceptual space. It is in this sense that the role of attention in weighting the output of the auditory analyzers is similar to one proposed by Nosofsky (1986, 1987; Nosofsky et al. 1989). His generalized context model claims that selectively attending to a particular dimension distorts the overall psychological space by stretching or shrinking perceptual distances (see also Smith and Heise 1992). Distances between points along an attended perceptual dimension are stretched (making them more discriminable), whereas distances along unattended perceptual dimensions are shrunk (making them less discriminable). Thus, imagine comparing two types of objects that potentially differ in size, shape, and color. If size is selected as the critical dimension for comparing the objects, then subjects will give more weight to fine gradations along this dimension and less weight to differences along the other dimensions.

The application of the weighting scheme to the output of the auditory analyzers in WRAPSA effectively stretches and shrinks dimensions in the perceptual space that relates to speech sounds. Information that is weighted most heavily is most closely attended to in categorizing the input. The listener is most sensitive to the output of these analyzers. Conversely, perceptual distinctions that are available in the output of analyzers but de-emphasized in the weighting scheme must be very large in order to be registered by the listener. Thus, although prevoicing of stops is generally not detected by English listeners because it does not contrast with voicing in the language, very exaggerated degrees of prevoicing are likely to be noticed.

The weighting scheme amounts to a way of automatically focusing attention on those analyzers that are repeatedly activated by the input. These are the ones that are most likely to provide information about properties that will be critical for recognizing and distinguishing words in a language. It is in this way that the distributional properties of the input could influence the development of the weighting scheme. Thus, one possibility is that analyzers that are frequently strongly activated by native-language input are the ones that become favored in the development of a weighting scheme. This assumes that although infants who are exposed to English input may experience some stimulation of auditory analyzers relevant to the detection of prevoicing, the frequency and intensity of such stimulation would be much less than that received by analyzers involved in registering information that is pertinent to meaningful distinctions in English. Also, the fact that certain weighted features tend to co-occur in certain situations could eventually lead to treating the relation among them as reflecting a common factor. It is in this way that the weighting scheme may evolve to pick up what Gibson (1969) has referred to as higher-level invariants.

Given the demands of fluent speech perception, such as the number of categorizations that must be made in a short timespan, it is obviously beneficial to have a way to preset attention to those portions of the signal with the highest information value. Once a language has been acquired, the weighting scheme supplies the settings used in perceptually categorizing the fluent speech input. Whenever a new language is acquired, the listener must develop a new weighting scheme to cope with utterances in that language. In general, one will have as many different weighting schemes as languages one can speak and understand fluently. There may be some overlap between the weightings used for one language and those for another, because some of the categorizations used in the languages may be the same. Whenever contrasts in the second language rely on the same weightings as those used in the listener's native language, these should be easy to discriminate. Nevertheless, although two different languages may overlap with respect to some of their weightings, there are also likely to be many differences. Consequently, learning the weighting scheme for the new language requires overcoming the tendency to fall back on those attentional settings that are used for the native language.

There is some evidence that bilingual speakers behave in a manner that is consistent with having different weighting schemes for each language. Elman, Diehl, and Buchwald (1977) reported that Spanish-English bilinguals changed the voicing category associated with a particular speech token depending on whether the carrier phrase in which it was embedded was Spanish or English. This relabeling of the token occurred despite the fact that its physical properties were exactly the same in the two situations. A reasonable explanation for these results is that subjects weighted the available acoustic information in the token differently in the Spanish and English contexts.

Although I have focused on weighting schemes relevant to language capacities, listeners may develop other kinds of weighting schemes for other types of acoustic (and for that matter nonacoustic) signals. In general, becoming an expert perceiver in some domain requires one to learn to weight the input in a way that yields the categorizations that are critical for that domain (be it birdcalls, tumblers in locks, or signals from outer space).

Extracting Patterns from the Signal

When WRAPSA was first proposed, virtually nothing was known about infants' abilities to segment words from fluent speech, let alone what sources of information they might use in segmenting speech. This picture is beginning to change. Not only do we now have some indication that infants as young as $7\frac{1}{2}$ months show the beginnings of word segmentation skills (Jusczyk and Aslin 1995), but we also have some clues as to how English-learning infants may initiate the process (Myers et al. 1996; Newsome and Jusczyk 1995). Although much remains to be discovered about how and when word-segmentation skills develop, the recent findings permit a slightly more detailed account than what was previously available regarding this aspect of the model.

Although prior to the pattern-extraction stage the speech signal has been processed to emphasize the important dimensions for word recognition in the native language, the task of actually extracting candidate words from the speech stream has not been accomplished at this point. The perceptual system still has to pull out potential word candidates from the stream of speech to either match to existing lexical items or to add new items to the lexicon. The units that are identified as a result of the pattern-extraction stage will serve as probes to the lexicon to make contact with previously stored lexical items and their meanings. An important aspect of the pattern-extraction process is to provide a potential word candidate. This candidate is an integrated description of the sound properties that have been picked out by application of the weighting scheme to the output of the auditory analyzers. For accurate word recognition, the correct time tagging of acoustic properties within the unit is important. Information relevant to determining the presence of stop closures, nasal resonances, frication, glidelike transitions, vocalic elements, and the like must be sequenced to yield an accurate description of the input. In the long run, the ordering has to be sufficient to distinguish strings like [tæp] from [pæt] and [æpt].

What kind of information is necessary to develop the correct pattern-extraction process? In my most recent descriptions of WRAPSA (e.g., Jusczyk 1993a), I considered, but dismissed, the possibility that word segmentation develops by matching patterns of words learned in isolation against whole fluent speech utterances. The basic idea behind this approach is that the child's knowledge of the word "cat" spoken in isolation might allow her to segment this word out of the string "See the cat," leaving as a possible unknown word "See–the." If on a subsequent occasion, the child learns "see," then she can apply this new information to the old unknown string to isolate "the" as a possible word. As I pointed out, relying exclusively on such an approach is fraught with a number of difficulties, including the fact that some words never occur in isolation, shorter words are often embedded in longer words, and the acoustic characteristics of words produced in isolation may differ considerably from the same words produced in sentential contexts.

Nevertheless, there are some ways that storing information about short patterns of speech (i.e., potential words) could help in the development of more general pattern-extraction processes to segment utterances into word candidates. For example, storing a number of short utterances that are potential words could help learners to detect the presence of some recurring features of native-language words, such as predominant word-stress patterns. Among the words that English-learning infants might hear with some frequency in isolation are words like "mommy," "daddy," "bottle," "doggie," "binky," and so on—all of which have the predominant strong/weak stress pattern of English bisyllabic words. Attention to this aspect of the input could be a factor in why English-learning infants' first approximations to word segmentation seem to link the onsets of words with the presence of strong syllables (see chapter 4). As I noted then, using a metrical segmentation strategy will work for a fair proportion of content words in English fluent speech, but it will also miss others, especially function words. Therefore, English learners must also use other types of information (allophonic and phonotactic cues, and distributional properties) to correctly locate word boundaries. However, the infant's first pass at word segmentation using strong syllables provides the kinds of short chunks of input that may facilitate learning about some of these other sources and how they are distributed with respect to word boundaries.

Consequently, much as the weighting scheme is shaped to conform to the nature of the input, so too must pattern-extraction routines be developed to accord with those properties that are likely to be predictive of word boundaries in the particular language that the infant is learning. What we do not know at this point is just which aspects of the development of the pattern-extraction routines are specific to particular languages and which aspects are language-general. Is there simply a general trochaic bias that all infants use when they begin to segment fluent speech into words—regardless of the nature of their particular language? Or do infants learning languages without this kind of predominant stress pattern use information from short, isolated utterances to develop other kinds of first-pass segmentation strategies? Much more information about the development of word segmentation skills in learners of languages other than English is required to have a better understanding of how and when pattern-extraction processes develop. What we have learned about such processes to this point is that they develop during the first year, and they do appear to be sensitive to the distributional frequencies of the input.

Matching and Storing the Representation

Once a candidate word representation has been extracted, it can be matched against existing words in the lexicon to see if a match can be found. In prior formulations of WRAPSA (e.g., Jusczyk 1993a), it has been assumed that the representation provided by the pattern-extraction process is not fully specified with respect to its phonetic segments. Rather, the perceiver was assumed to be operating with a more global representation. This representation is structured in terms of syllables and the salient features that they contain. Moreover, the representation includes marking of pertinent prosodic characteristics such as stress and tone. The detailed information that has the highest priority for inclusion in the representation is that which is available through the auditory analyzers that are favored by the weighting scheme. However, owing to noise, attentional demands, and the like, it is possible that some of the important features may not be encoded in the representation of a given word candidate. Finally, information that is available from other analyzers can be included in the representation, although it has a much lower priority for encoding.

The representation of any particular word candidate is the probe that is broadcast to the lexicon. As in Hintzman's MINERVA 2 Model, the lexicon includes traces of previously stored instances of words. Each memory trace will be activated in proportion to its similarity to the probe, and the combined output of all traces in response to the probe constitutes the "echo." When only a small set of traces is highly activated, presumably ones associated with the same lexical entry, the candidate word will be identified as a token of this word type. A more diffuse pattern of responding with only very weakly activated traces is likely to occur for candidates of word types that are not yet included in the lexicon (i.e., new lexical entries). Such word candidates may be stored as potential lexical items whose meaning properties are yet to be identified, or if other contextual cues are sufficient to indicate a possible meaning, that meaning (or partial meaning) will be stored along with the sound pattern of the word candidate.

I still think that this description approximates what happens during word recognition. Given the rates at which information is transmitted in speech, the most efficient representation is the one that embodies only enough detail to accurately recognize the word when it appears. Moreover, there is little evidence to suggest that listeners actually go through a stage of phoneme recognition prior to accessing lexical representations during fluent speech processing (Cutler et al. 1986; Mehler 1981; Mehler et al. 1981; Savin and Bever 1970; although see Norris and Cutler 1988). Furthermore, because their lexicons have fewer lexical items and less densely populated lexical neighborhoods, language learners could be successful at word recognition in most situations even if their representations were less detailed than those of adults (Charles-Luce and Luce 1990, 1995; Logan 1992; Walley 1993).

Nevertheless, a number of questions arise about the amount and kind of detail included in the representation of word candidates and in lexical entries that are stored in long-term memory. For example, the findings on implicit memory that were reviewed earlier (e.g., Goldinger 1992; Palmeri et al. 1993) suggest that along with a description of the word's sound pattern, listeners may encode details of a distinctly nonphonetic nature (voice characteristics, whether and what kinds of background noises may have been present, emotional tone, etc.). Indeed, the suggestion that listeners are storing specific exemplars seems to imply a rather detailed description of the acoustic characteristics of the utterance. However, data from other investigations appears to be compatible with the view that speech processing is organized around highly abstract lexical representations and that processes of phonological inference are required to adjust the interpretation of the input (e.g., Lahiri and Marslen-Wilson 1991; Marslen-Wilson 1994; Marslen-Wilson and Warren 1994; but see also Luce, Lyons, and Myers 1994). Could language learners really be encoding detailed nonlinguistic information at the same time that they are encoding a less-than-fully detailed description of the phonetic properties of the utterance? Perhaps so, if their capacities for representing the internal structure of words and syllables were not fully developed. For instance, if a coordination of perception and production capacities is what is required for deriving a phonetic representation of utterances, then the linguistic description would not be fully detailed in either the representation of word candidates or in the representations of lexical entries.

Another issue that arises has to do with the extent to which representations do get more detailed as the learner develops. One possibility is that more detail is actually encoded into new instances that are added to the lexicon as the learner develops. Hence, as more detailed traces of the same word type are added, the combination of new and old traces contributing to the echo for the same word type would eventually lead to a representation with more detail than was present at the earliest stages of lexical development. Another possibility is that an increased ability to make finer distinctions among words as the child develops could come about as a result of improvements in the on-line comparison process. For example, the number of different dimensions that are used to compare input with previously stored items could increase. This might, in turn, change the activation levels of previously stored instances, since matches or mismatches on these added dimensions could affect judgments regarding how similar the input is to previously stored items.

Viewing word recognition as involving representations of previously encountered word tokens may lead to a better account of how knowledge of the sound properties of language is modified by experience. According to WRAPSA, when a memory trace of a word is stored in the lexicon, the overall organization of properties in the derived perceptual representation are preserved. However, it is likely that not every utterance produced within range of an infant's hearing will be stored as such a trace. Some of the storage of perceived items may be random, but storing a representation as a memory trace could require that some extra effort is given to processing the input. This may take the form of rehearsing the perceptual representation, making an effort to associate it with a meaning, context, or some emotional experience, or some other such process. The traces themselves are not modified by experience, although their informational content may undergo some decay. Instead, the role of experience is to add new traces to memory. This has the effect of modifying the way that the whole memory system behaves. The more that a trace differs from the preceding ones, the greater is the change in the behavior of the system when efforts are made to identify new items. The effect that such discrepant traces have on the behavior of the system is obviously greater when there are fewer traces in memory. Thus, this property of the model fits well with the observation that during development, sometimes small alterations in the nature of the input can cause large-scaled reorganizations of categories.

WRAPSA: Then and Now

One of my original intentions in proposing WRAPSA was to provide a framework that could capture previous findings but could also be elaborated as further information was collected about the development of speech perception capacities. Although the core of the model remains the same, recent findings have helped to provide a more detailed description of some of the components of the model and to identify factors that may shape the development of these components to deal more effectively with the structure of a particular language. However, no new components have been added to the model, nor have the operations and the range of problems that they apply to changed appreciably. Thus, in the end, the view of the model presented in the previous section was more of an elaboration of the old model than one that differed substantially from it. Hence, to indicate its continuity with the previous version, and at the same time acknowledge some of the new elaborations to the model, we will designate this latest version WRAPSA '96.

Some Loose Ends to Tie

I have tried to examine what is currently known about infant speech-perception capacities and their development and to explore the implications that the development of speech perception capacities have for understanding the rest of language acquisition. Although the past 25 years have seen great gains in our understanding of basic speech perception capacities in infants, it is also clear that many issues require further exploration. Resolving these issues will not only lead to a better description of how speech perception capacities develop, but it should also help in understanding the role of these developing capacities in language acquisition. Certainly, more empirical data about the details and the course of the development of speech perception capacities are essential for evaluating models of development such as WRAPSA '96. Assumptions about the components of the model and their operations are based on our current level of understanding of how infants process and encode speech information. Should the data prove some of these assumptions wrong, the model may have to be changed in substantial ways.

For a number of years, researchers of infant speech-perception capacities focused on how infants discriminated contrasts between isolated syllables. Little attention was given to the issue of how infants segment information from fluent speech. Many early studies also employed synthetic speech sounds instead of naturally produced tokens to remove possible sources of variability that might arise from using natural speech tokens from different talkers. When voices of different talkers were used in investigations, it was for the purpose of learning about whether infants could cope with this source of variability. Whether infants actually encode and remember information about talkers' voices was not an issue that was investigated. Moreover, many of the early investigations only focused on whether infants at any age were capable of discriminating a particular phonetic contrast. It was only in the past decade that researchers really began to seriously explore the possibility that developmental changes occur in speech perception capacities during the first year.

The kinds of issues that speech researchers are addressing in studies with infants have been expanded recently. There is more interest in how speech perception capacities change as a result of experience with language. Cross-linguistic studies are beginning to yield interesting information about possible differences in the development of these capacities among infants learning different languages. The development of new procedures has also made it possible to begin to explore speech segmentation abilities and the development of word recognition. Some efforts are also underway to examine how word learning is influenced by the sound properties of novel words. More direct attempts are being made to explore how information in the speech signal affects the course of language acquisition in general. These are exciting developments in research that are likely to cause investigators to rethink some of their positions about the growth of speech perception abilities.

Nevertheless, there are still some other important areas, critical for understanding the development of speech perception, for which we have very little data at present. Chief among those areas requiring considerably more research is a more complete account of the nature of the input that language learners are receiving at the point when many changes are occurring in speech perception abilities. Huttenlocher and her colleagues (Huttenlocher et al. 1991; Smiley and Huttenlocher 1995) have conducted a detailed investigation of how information in the input affects vocabulary growth between 14 and 26 months of age. They found a significant relation between the rate of vocabulary growth and the overall amount of parental speech that the child heard. More important for the present purposes is that they also observed a relation between the frequency of different words and the age at which these words first appear in children's productions. For example, a significant correlation ($r = .77$) was found between the mother's use of object words and the child's acquisition of those same words. We need to have comparable data for younger infants with respect to how the input relates to their receptive capacities for language. For this purpose, it is first necessary to conduct systematic studies that will provide information about the frequency with which certain sound patterns occur within hearing of the learner. These data are crucial for evaluating claims that infants really are tracking the distributional frequencies of certain patterns. They are also important for understanding the development of the lexicon, including what sorts of items are likely to be among the first entries. Differences in the kinds of input that different children receive could prove helpful for understanding some of the individual differences that arise in the acquisition of native-language sound patterns.

As beneficial as it will be to have more detailed information about the input, we also need to have a much clearer view of the development of memory and attentional skills of infants. Whatever information is in the input will only have an impact on language acquisition if infants are attending to it and encoding it into memory. To explain how speech perception capacities evolve to support word recognition, we need to have a better indication of what infants are attending to and when. We also must have some indication of what kind of information they store and when they are likely to store it and how much detail they retain and for how long a period. Certainly, information about these things is required in order to evaluate claims about whether infants store specific instances or abstract prototypes of sound patterns of words.

Finally, it would be helpful to begin to explore the possibility of individual differences in the way that speech perception capacities develop. Such differences have often been noted in the development of speech production, and it would be interesting to know whether a comparable situation exists for speech perception. In fact, data about individual infants who are followed longitudinally could provide clues as to why individual differences in speech production are likely to occur. In addition, longitudinal studies of the development of speech perception capacities, when combined with input data, would help to clarify how experience affects perceptual development. Such data might allow for a better understanding of the relationship between developing speech perception capacities and other facets of language acquisition.

The first twenty-five years of research on infant speech perception have provided many surprises, especially with respect to the skills that are present during the earliest stages of infancy and the rapidity with which experience with a particular language helps to shape and refine these skills. Given the range of issues that remain to be explored, the next twenty-five years promise to be just as exciting.

Appendix

Methodology Used in Studies of Infant Speech Perception

By comparison to those researchers who are studying adults, investigators studying speech perception in infants face a special sort of problem. Namely, how does one ask nonverbal infants about their perception of speech information? Of course, this problem is not peculiar to speech research; rather, it comes up in any studies examining the cognitive and perceptual capacities of infants. Investigators studying these kinds of capacities are forced to find indirect means of posing their research questions to infants. Naturally, the answers that investigators receive to these questions are also indirect (e.g., a change in some ongoing behavior that infants are performing while speech sounds are presented). Because investigators are using changes in infants' ongoing activities to make inferences about their perceptions of speech sounds or other stimuli, they have to establish that the changes that do occur are not simply the responses to other kinds of stimuli in the environment. Fortunately, researchers today are able to rely on some testing procedures that have proven to be effective and reliable in many years of use with infants. In this section, I shall review the behavioral measures that are most frequently used in infant speech-perception studies. Although other kinds of procedures have sometimes been used in speech research with infants, such as ones based on heart rate changes or evoked potentials, I will confine my discussion to the procedures used in the vast majority of the studies reviewed in this book. In particular, these procedures are the high-amplitude sucking procedure, the operant headturning procedure, the visual-fixation procedure, and the headturn preference procedure.

The High-Amplitude Sucking Procedure

The high-amplitude sucking procedure (HAS) was originally developed by Siqueland and DeLucia (1969) for use in studies of visual perception with infants. One of their objectives was to determine whether infants would change their sucking behavior in response to visual reinforcement contingencies. They compared infants whose sucking behavior was reinforced by the presentation of visual stimuli (the experimental group) to infants whose spontaneous sucking in the absence of any visual stimulation was monitored for the same period (the control group). In contrast to infants in the control group, Siqueland and DeLucia found that infants in the experimental group significantly increased their sucking rates in response to the visual stimulation. The procedure is referred to as high-amplitude sucking because only those sucks that exceed a given sucking pressure level (usually the top third of the infant's sucking responses) are reinforced by the stimuli used in these studies.

Subsequently, Siqueland (1969) demonstrated that the procedure could be adapted for use in studying infants' discrimination of visual stimuli. To accomplish this, he reinforced infants' sucking responses with the same visual stimulus for a fixed period (e.g., 7 minutes), then he changed the reinforcement to a different visual stimulus for a fixed period thereafter. Because infants often show increased interest to novel stimuli, Siqueland hypothesized that increased sucking rates would occur to a discriminably different visual stimulus. By examining differences in sucking rates before and after the change in visual stimulation (and comparing these to the sucking rates of control subjects who received no changes in visual stimulation), Siqueland demonstrated that HAS was an effective means of testing visual discrimination.

The procedure was first used in conjunction with speech reinforcement in the study by Eimas et al. (1971). They made one important change to the procedure. Rather than present each speech stimulus for a fixed period of time, they used an individually determined habituation criterion (i.e., one that depends on the infant's own sucking rate). The problem with using a fixed period of stimulation is that because infants differ greatly in their sucking rates, the amounts of experience with the first stimulus prior to the stimulus change differs considerably. This difference in exposure to the first stimulus is potentially problematic because some infants may be disinterested in the first stimulus at the end of the fixed period, whereas other infants may not be. Adopting a criterion for shifting the stimulation that depends on changes in the sucking rate of an individual infant circumvents this problem by ensuring that all infants exhibit a similar decline in sucking prior to the change in stimulation.

Since the procedure, as Eimas et al. used it, is the model for subsequent investigations, I will describe it in some detail. Each infant (ranging in age from 1 to 4 months) is tested individually in a small laboratory room. The infant is placed in a reclining chair facing a blank wall approximately 1 meter away. A colorful slide is projected on the wall, just above a loud-speaker through which the test stimuli are played. Each infant sucks on a blind nipple (i.e., one without a hole) held in place by an experimenter who wears headphones and listens to recorded music throughout the test session. The nipple is connected by a rubber hose to a pressure transducer that is coupled to a polygraph machine in an adjacent room. The pressure transducer sends out a weak electrical charge that is amplified by the polygraph. A Schmitt trigger (or some comparable device) provides a digital output of the criterial high-amplitude sucking responses. A series of relays activates the auditory reinforcers and a counter that records the number of criterion responses on a minute-by-minute basis. The sounds are played out over an amplifier to a loudspeaker.

For each infant, the high-amplitude sucking criterion and the baseline rate of sucking are established prior to the presentation of any test stimuli. In Eimas et al.'s (1971) study, the criterion for high-amplitude sucking was adjusted to reinforce the top 33 percent of the infant's sucking responses. Following these adjustments, a 1-minute baseline period occurs in which the infant's high-amplitude sucking responses are recorded in the absence of any auditory reinforcement. After the baseline period, the presentation of stimuli is made contingent on the rate of high-amplitude sucking. Criterion sucks result in the presentation of one speech syllable. In the early studies using this procedure, the same auditory stimulus, usually a syllable, was presented throughout the preshift phase of the experiment. Depending on the durations of the auditory stimuli, the maximum stimulus presentation rate is between one and two syllables per second. If the infant produces a burst of sucking with interresponse times shorter than this, then each response resets the apparatus to provide con-tinuous auditory feedback for one second after the last suck.

The change from one stimulus to another occurs when infants meet the criterion for habituation during the preshift phase of the experiment. This criterion corresponds to some predetermined decrement in sucking rate (depending on the laboratory, a decline in sucking rate of 20 to 33 per-cent) for 2 consecutive minutes compared with the rate in the immediately preceding minute. At this point, the auditory stimulation is changed for the postshift phase of a given condition. For the experimental conditions, there is a change in the stimuli presented. By comparison, in the control conditions, infants continue to hear the same stimuli as in the preshift period. The timing of the postshift phase begins with the first high-amplitude suck after the habituation criterion is achieved. The infants' sensitivity to changes in auditory stimulation is inferred from comparisons of response rates of subjects in the experimental and control conditions during the postshift period. If the net changes in sucking rate for infants in an experimental condition are significantly greater than any spontaneous changes in sucking rates for infants in the control condition, then the stimulus difference in the experimental condition is assumed to be discriminated. The postshift period usually lasts for at least 4 minutes.

Frequently Used Variations and Extensions of This Procedure
One main modifications to the HAS procedure has been to adapt it to allow multiple stimuli to be used in the various phases of the experiment (e.g., Eilers 1977; Jusczyk and Derrah 1987; Kuhl 1983; Spring and Dale 1977). Modifications of this sort have been used to investigate either how infants handle stimulus variability (e.g., Jusczyk et al. 1992; Kuhl 1983) or the nature of early representations of speech sounds (e.g., Bertoncini et al. 1988; Jusczyk et al. 1990; Jusczyk and Derrah 1987). Thus, rather than reinforcing sucking with the presentation of a single syllable in the preshift or postshift period, any one of several different auditory stimuli may be used to reinforce a high-amplitude sucking response. For example, in Jusczyk et al.'s (1992) study investigating stimulus variability, infants heard a series of different tokens (varying in talker's voice) of the same speech syllable type. In the postshift period, a different syllable type was presented with the same kinds of variations in talker's voice. The issue was whether infants would detect the change in syllable type despite the variations in talker's voice. By comparison, in studies investigating the nature of speech categories (e.g., Jusczyk and Derrah 1987), the different stimuli used in the preshift period all included a common element, a phonetic segment (e.g., [bi], [ba], [bo], [bu]). The rationale was that if infants perceived the common phonetic segment in the different syllables, then, during the preshift period, they might habituate to the whole class of syllables beginning with [b]. In the postshift phase, a new item was added to the familiar set of items. This item either shared or did not share the common initial [b] segment. The question was whether a new syllable belonging to the familiar category [b] was treated differently than one from a different category, such as [d].

Another important extension of the HAS procedure has been to adapt it for testing what infants encode and remember about speech sounds.

This change consists of the introduction of a delay period with no auditory reinforcement between the pre- and postshift phases of the experiment. Extensive pilot testing of the procedure led Jusczyk et al. (1992) to fix the length of the delay period at 2 minutes. Obviously, it is desirable to extend the delay period as long as possible. However, a problem with delay periods longer than 2 minutes is that subjects in control conditions tend to show large increases in sucking rates in response to the reintroduction of the speech sounds. Such increases in sucking by control subjects make it difficult to pick up changes in sucking by subjects in the experimental conditions. Another problem with using too long an interval is that infants often become restless and fussy without the presence of auditory reinforcers. The 2-minute interval has proven to be the most effective of the delay periods explored.

During the delay period, infants are shown a series of colorful slides for about 5 seconds each. The pacifier is held in the infant's mouth during the delay period because pilot testing indicated that this is more effective than removing the pacifier. The problem with removing and reintroducing the pacifier is that infants in experimental and control conditions alike produce large increases in sucking as soon as the pacifier is reintroduced, regardless of what auditory stimulation occurs. Once again, this behavior tends to mask any increases attributable to changes in auditory stimulation.

The HAS delay procedure has been used successfully in a number of studies. Jusczyk et al. (1992) used it to demonstrate that talker variability affects how infants encode speech information in memory, even when it does not disrupt discrimination of speech contrasts. Mandel, Jusczyk, and Kemler Nelson (1994) employed the same procedure in their experiment investigating whether sentential prosody helps infants in encoding speech information. The advantage of using a delay period is that it provides a more powerful means of tapping infants' encoding of speech input. Subtle differences in how infants process different kinds of speech input, which are not apparent in the immediate testing situation of the standard HAS procedure, may be revealed when the HAS delay procedure is used.

The HAS procedure has been a very productive tool in speech research with infants. Modifications of the basic procedure have enabled researchers to ask about a lot more than just which contrasts between syllables are discriminated by infants. The technique has provided new information about speech categories in young infants and shows promise in studying their memory for speech. The procedure has been used successfully in research with infants from birth to about 4 months of age. One major drawback of the procedure has to do with the high subject dropout rates that typically occur. Often, only 30 to 40 percent of infants tested produce usable data. Infants may fail to complete the full test session for a variety of reasons including crying, sleeping, or failure to maintain high enough sucking rates. Still, this procedure remains the most effective one for testing infants between birth and 4 months of age (for a more extensive discussion of this procedure, see Jusczyk 1985a).

The Operant Headturn Procedure

The idea of conditioning infants to turn their heads in response to auditory stimulation originated in studies of localization by Suzuki and Ogiba (1961). However, its current usage in speech research with infants 6 to 12 months of age occurred in investigations by Moore and his colleagues (e.g., Eilers, Wilson, and Moore 1977; Moore, Thompson, and Thompson 1975; Moore, Wilson, and Thompson 1977). In the basic testing situation, an infant is seated on a caregiver's lap facing an experimenter across a table in a small test room. To the left of the infant (about 45° from midline and about 1.5 meter away) is a loudspeaker. In front of this loudspeaker, at approximately 1 meter from the infant, is a dark Plexiglas box. Concealed inside this box is a mechanical toy that is used as a visual reinforcer. During the course of the experiment, whenever infants detect a change in auditory stimulation, they are supposed to turn their heads in the direction of the Plexiglas box. If they have correctly detected a stimulus change, the box lights up, revealing an activated mechanical animal (e.g., a monkey banging cymbals, a bear playing drums). At the same time, the experimenter also responds with social reinforcement for the infant (e.g., smiling, clapping hands, using words of praise). In addition to the experimenter and the parent who are in the test room with the infant, there is an observer in an adjacent room who is monitoring the infant's headturn responses (either by looking through a one-way mirror or by watching a video monitor). This observer cannot hear the sounds that are presented to the infant (nor can the parent or the experimenter with the infant hear the sounds because they are listening to recorded music over headphones). The observer presses keys on a button box linked to a computer to indicate whenever the infant makes a headturn toward the Plexiglas reinforcer box.

The operant headturn procedure that is typically used in speech research (e.g., Kuhl 1979) includes both a conditioning phase and a discrimination phase. The basic sequence of events is similar for both these phases, so I will describe it first before discussing the differences between the conditioning and discrimination phases. At the start of a testing session, a repeating background stimulus (e.g., [a], [a], [a], ..., [a]) begins to play from the loudspeaker. At a certain point, while the infant is looking toward the experimenter (and away from the reinforcer box), the repeating sound may change for a brief interval from the background stimulus to a different "change" stimulus, and then back to the background stimulus again (e.g., ..., [a], [a], [a], [i], [i], [i], [a], [a], [a], ..., [a]). This corresponds to a "change trial." If the infant turns toward the reinforcer while the change stimulus is playing, then the Plexiglas box lights up and the reinforcer is activated. Headturning responses toward the reinforcer during change trials are recorded and scored as correct responses. A failure to turn during the interval when the change stimulus is played is recorded and scored as incorrect (i.e., a miss). In addition to change trials, test sessions also include a certain number of "no-change" control trials. During a no-change control trial, the repeating background stimulus continues to play throughout the entire period (e.g., [a], [a], [a], ..., [a], [a], [a], [a]). Any headturn responses toward the reinforcer during a no-change control trial are recorded and scored as incorrect (i.e., a false alarm). A failure to turn during a no-change control trial is scored as correct (i.e., a correct rejection). Test trials (i.e., either change or no change trials) are initiated only when the infant is looking at the experimenter. To reduce the chances of unconscious bias on the part of the observer, the exact order and occurrence of change and no change trials is under computer control and not revealed to the observer.

Only infants who have successfully completed the conditioning phase actually enter into the discrimination phase of testing. The conditioning phase is used to teach the infant the association between the change stimulus and the activation of the visual reinforcer. On the first few trials of the conditioning phase, the activation of the reinforcer is not dependent on the infant's headturning responses. Rather, the reinforcer is activated as soon as the first change stimulus occurs. Gradually, a delay is introduced between the occurrence of the change stimulus and the activation of the visual reinforcer. This delay provides the infant with the opportunity to make an anticipatory headturn toward the reinforcer. If the infant does make such an anticipatory headturning response, the reinforcer is immediately activated. To facilitate the infant's correct detection of the change stimulus, a difference in the intensity levels (e.g., 10 dB) at which the change and background stimuli are played is often used. As infants correctly detect the change stimulus, the intensity level difference between it and the background stimulus is reduced across the course of succeeding trials until both stimuli are played at equal levels. In order to advance to the discrimination phase, infants have to meet some criterion of correct responding (e.g., three consecutive correct responses on change trials when the background and change stimuli are played at the same intensity levels).

In the discrimination phase, the infant normally receives an equal number of change and no-change control trials. Successful discrimination of the change from the no-change stimulus is indexed in a number of ways. Some investigators (e.g., Kuhl 1983) have used a criterion of 9 correct out of 10 consecutive trials as an indication that an infant has discriminated a particular contrast. Other investigators, such as Werker and Lalonde (1988), used a criterion based on how many correct trials have occurred within some fixed number of trials.

Because this procedure can be used successfully with infants between 6 and 12 months of age, it has been employed to study the development of speech-perception capacities within this age period. Longitudinal and cross-sectional studies using this procedure have been instrumental in documenting the decline in sensitivity that infants show to certain non-native phonetic contrasts (Werker and Tees 1984a). In order to use the procedure in this manner, Werker and Tees (1984a) note that it is important to include a control measure to assess task performance across the different age groups that are tested. In this way, an investigator will be in a better position to distinguish between failures that relate to perceptual factors and ones that stem from factors such as boredom or indifference to the task.

Extensions of the Operant Headturn Procedure
Used in the manner described above, the operant headturn procedure provides information about how infants discriminate a pair of stimuli, such as a contrast between two syllables. However, this procedure has also been used to provide some information about the nature of infants' categorization of speech sounds. Although it is not a true categorization procedure, in the sense of requiring a forced-choice classification of new instances into one category or another, the operant headturn procedure

can furnish information about infants' tendencies to treat certain stimuli as equivalent. For instance, instead of using a single repeating background stimulus and a single change stimulus, an investigator might use a variety of different stimulus tokens as the repeating background and use multiple tokens on the change trials. Kuhl (1979) used this method to determine whether 6-month-olds would treat different talkers' productions of a particular vowel (e.g., [a]) as instances of the same vowel type. Thus, after infants succeeded in discriminating a contrast that pitted one talker's production of [a] against the same talker's production of [i], they were tested to see if they could maintain this discrimination when multiple tokens of each vowel produced by a variety of different talkers were introduced. Notice that successful discrimination in this case requires that infants treat the different instances of each vowel as equivalent with respect to the discrimination task. Thus, in order to respond correctly to the phonetic change from [a] to [i], the infants had to ignore the acoustic variability in different talkers' productions of these tokens. Had the infants simply been responding to any detectable change in the repeating stimuli, they may have turned their heads for detectable changes in talker's voice as well as to phonetic differences. In fact, it appears that the infants treat the different talkers' productions of the same vowel as equivalent because they only responded consistently to the phonetic changes.

By adding a third phase to the operant headturn procedure, Kuhl and her colleagues (e.g., Grieser and Kuhl 1989; Kuhl 1991; Kuhl et al. 1992) have been able to provide some information about the internal structure of infants' vowel categories. In the first two phases of the procedure, infants are trained to distinguish a token that is a good instance of the vowel category [i] from another token that is an atypical instance of this vowel. For half of the infants, the good instance serves as the background stimulus, whereas for the other half, the atypical instance is the background stimulus. During the generalization phase of the procedure, the perceived similarity of the background stimulus to other variants of the same vowel category is assessed. To accomplish this, on change trials, the target stimulus is a randomly selected instance of one of the other variants in the vowel category. The particular variant used as a target stimulus changes from trial to trial. Infants are expected to fail to discriminate the change stimulus whenever they perceive it to be similar to the background stimulus. In this way, Kuhl and her colleagues are able to obtain information about the internal organization of vowel categories.

They find that infants show more failures to discriminate change stimuli when the good instance, as opposed to the atypical instance, serves as the background stimulus.

Morgan (1994) devised another modification of this procedure by training infants to respond to an extraneous noise superimposed on a speech stimulus instead of to a change in the speech stimulus itself. He trained infants to respond to the occurrence of a trisyllabic string in which a 100 milliseconds buzz (12 dB more intense than the speech) occurred between two of the syllables. The duration of the buzz was shortened throughout the training phase until it was reduced to 20 milliseconds and its intensity was equal to that of the speech sounds. By varying the identity of the syllables used and their prosodic qualities, Morgan was able to use this version of the procedure to provide an indication about how infants group information in the speech signal. Specifically, he predicted that noises inserted between syllables that form a coherent perceptual unit would be harder for infants to detect than noises between syllables that were not part of the same perceptual unit (see chapter 4 for further details).

In contrast to the HAS procedure, the operant headturn procedure yields more reliable data about the performance of individual infants (i.e., instead of a single observation of an infant's response to a stimulus change, it provides multiple observations). It is also usable across a fairly wide age range and is applicable during a developmental period in which many changes in speech perception capacities have been observed. However, this procedure also has some limitations. Chief among these is the fact that the duration of the stimuli used is restricted to about the temporal length of a word. This restriction stems from the fact that it is difficult to establish a contingency between a headturn response and a change in information that unfolds over a lengthy interval. (For further details about this procedure, consult Kuhl 1985).

The Visual-Fixation Procedure

Research by Horowitz and her colleagues demonstrated that infants' visual fixation times are affected by ongoing auditory stimulation (Horowitz 1974). The observation she reported that has proven to be most important in the application of this procedure to speech research is that infants exhibit reliable increases in visual fixation times when a background auditory stimulus is changed.

In the basic procedure, an infant faces a video monitor or screen on which an image from a slide projector is displayed. The caregiver holding the infant listens to recorded music over headphones during the testing session. The screen or video monitor is surrounded by a uniformly painted surface or curtains to provide a nondistracting visual background. Sounds are presented through a hidden loudspeaker situated just above or below the visual display. In some laboratories, there is also a fixation light mounted above or below the display. This light can be flashed, if necessary, to direct the infant's attention back to the display. Hidden observers, looking through small peepholes in the vicinity of the display screen, use a button box to record when the infant is looking at the visual pattern that is displayed. The observers listen to masking music over headphones to prevent them from hearing the auditory stimuli. In other settings, a video camera may be used in place of an observer in the room with the infant. The video camera is connected to a monitor in an adjacent room, and the observer records the visual fixations without the soundtrack containing the audio stimulation.

During the course of an experimental session, the presentation of the auditory stimulus is made contingent on the infant's fixation of the visual display. In some laboratories (e.g., Polka and Werker 1994), a trial begins when the infant first looks at the display screen. At this point, the visual and auditory stimuli are simultaneously presented. In other laboratories (Best et al. 1988), the visual pattern is displayed first to initiate the infant's fixation on the screen, and when this occurs, the auditory stimulus begins to play. In both versions of the procedure, the auditory and visual stimuli continue to be displayed until the infant turns away, in which case, they are terminated simultaneously, ending a test trial. Across successive trials, the durations of the visual fixations tend to decline. When the durations of the fixations decline to some predetermined criterion level, the auditory stimulation is changed. Visual fixations are recorded for a fixed number of trials thereafter. Discrimination of the auditory stimuli is indexed by comparing the durations of fixations on the last two or three preshift trials to those on a comparable number of trials immediately following the change in auditory stimulation.

As in the HAS procedure, the habituation criterion for the visual-fixation procedure is tied to the performance of individual subjects. For example, the criterion level chosen might be a 50 percent decline in fixation duration for some number of trials (e.g., three) relative to a fixation duration on the first three trials (e.g., Eimas and Miller 1992). Other investigators have indexed the 50 percent decline in fixation times to the mean duration of the longest two consecutive trials during the preshift period (e.g., Best et al. 1988). Once again, the use of an individually determined habituation criterion helps to improve the reliability of the discrimination data by ensuring that infants' attention levels are comparable at the point when the auditory stimulus is changed.

The primary use of the visual-fixation procedure has been to study the discriminative capacities of infants. Notably, it has been used by Best and her colleagues to provide information about infants' discrimination of nonnative contrasts. One advantage in this domain that the visual-fixation procedure has over the operant headturn procedure is that the visual-fixation procedure can be used across a greater age range (from 2-month-olds to 14-month-olds). In addition, unlike the operant headturn procedure, the visual-fixation procedure allows for the presentation of speech samples of much greater duration than a single word. However, as with the other procedures considered thus far, the number of stimulus comparisons that can be tested within a single session is limited.

The Headturn Preference Procedure

This procedure was originally developed by Fernald (1985) for her investigations of infants' listening preferences for infant- versus adult-directed speech. She used a three-sided testing booth that was open on the fourth side. White curtains were hung between the ceiling and the top of the three sides of the booth in order to block the infant's view of the rest of the room. Loudspeakers were mounted into the walls of the two side panels at about the level of the infant's head. A small red light was located on each side panel in the vicinity of the loudspeaker. The center panel, which the infant faced, had a small green light mounted at the infant's eye level. Directly below this light there was a 5 centimeters hole cut into the panel for the lens of a video camera. A chair was situated in the center of the booth approximately even with the two side lights and facing the center panel. The caregiver sat on this chair and held the infant on her lap.

In her use of the headturn preference procedure, Fernald's primary dependent measure was the direction of the infant's first head turn on a trial. Experimental sessions began with a series of training trials in which infants were familiarized with four different 8-second speech samples, available on the two sides of the booth. To start a training trial, the green light on the center panel was flashed to draw the infant's attention. When a judge, viewing a video monitor in another room, decided that the infant was looking straight ahead, the green light was turned off. The judge then signaled another experimenter to turn on one of the two red side lights. The choice of whether the left or right sidelight was flashed on a trial followed a predetermined training order that was set up for a given subject. The experimenter was responsible for turning on the tape recorder that played the type of speech sample appropriate to that side (e.g., infant-directed speech samples on the left and adult-directed samples on the right). The assignment of sample types to sides was counterbalanced across subjects. When a given sample ended, the red light was extinguished and the green center light was flashed until the infant's gaze was centered. Then the next trial began. If the infant did not spontaneously look to the flashing light within the first few seconds of a training trial, the caregiver was asked to turn the infant in that direction. After four training trials, the caregiver was instructed to keep the infant centered and not to turn the infant during the remaining trials. Both the caregiver and the judge wore headphones and listened to recorded music to mask the speech samples presented during the experiment.

During the test phase, the presentation of a speech sample was made contingent upon a 30° headturn by the infant. As in the training trials, the center green light was used to attract the infant's gaze to midline. After this light was extinguished, the first 30° headturn to the left or right resulted in the presentation of a speech sample appropriate to that side accompanied by the blinking red light. Each sample was played to its completion regardless of whether the infant looked away before it finished. Infants had to complete at least 15 test trials to be included in the study. Subjects were scored as to the number of trials that they turned to a given side. Fernald (1985) found that infants turned significantly more often toward the side with the infant-directed speech samples.

For their investigations of infants' sensitivity to clausal units in fluent speech, Hirsh-Pasek et al. (1987) introduced several modifications to the procedure and apparatus. First, they enlarged the booth slightly so that each panel measured approximately 120 cm × 180 cm. Second, their booth was constructed with pegboard and backed with cardboard, except for a small area just above the center green light. The pegboard holes in this area allowed the observer to judge the direction and timing of the infant's headturns. Thus, Hirsh-Pasek and her colleagues used a live observer in the room with the infant instead of a judge viewing a video monitor in an adjoining room. Both the observer and the caregiver wore headphones and listened to recorded music to mask the sounds of the speech samples.

More recently (e.g., Jusczyk, Cutler, and Redanz 1993), a video camera has been used in addition to the live observer to permit reliability checks and to provide a permanent record of each test session. Reliability checks are made by having a second observer view and score the video tapes of each session with the sound turned off. This second observer uses the same type of response box as the live observer. Reliability in judging the direction and timing of the headturns has proved to be quite high, with agreement between observers ranging between .92 and .96, and on 72 percent of the trials in one study (Jusczyk, Cutler and Redanz 1993), the discrepancies in the timing of trials between the live and videotape observers was less than 0.5 seconds.

One key difference between Fernald's use of this procedure and most subsequent uses has to do with the primary dependent measure that is used. Hirsh-Pasek et al. (1987) believed that infants' sensitivity to differences in their stimuli might be reflected in the amount of time that a subject listened to each type of sample. For this reason, they recorded both the direction of the headturns and the amount of time that an infant actually oriented in the direction of a speech sample on a given trial. Hirsh-Pasek and coworkers also made several other changes in the procedure, including

1. using a greater number of training trials (eight instead of four);
2. terminating a trial when infants turned away for 2 seconds or more;
3. using a silent moving hand puppet occasionally in addition to the flashing center light to attract the infant's fixation to the center;
4. changing the way the blinking sidelights functioned during an experimental session; and
5. putting the presentation and selection of samples during the experiment under computer control (in experiment 2 of their first study and in all subsequent studies).

The last two changes were the most significant ones, so I will comment on these further. First, with respect to the sidelights, in the training phase the sidelight blinked only until the infant oriented to the loudspeaker and the sounds began, then it was turned off for the remainder of the trial.[1] When the green center light was extinguished at the start of the test trials, both sidelights began to blink simultaneously. Once the infant turned toward one of the sidelights, the other one was extinguished. Turning toward a sidelight caused the sample associated with that particular side to play. The blinking light on that side remained on until the trial ended.

By using a computer to control various aspects of the test procedure, Hirsh-Pasek and coworkers were able to use a single individual to conduct the test session. In this modified version of HPP, the speech stimuli are digitized and stored on a computer. A computer program controls the presentation of the stimuli, initiates the blinking lights at the appropriate times, records looking times, and terminates the test trials. A single observer sits behind the center panel and presses a series of buttons on a response box tethered to the computer. Loudness levels for the stimuli on each side are set and measured on a sound level meter by a second assistant (not involved in the testing). The pairing of sample type and side of presentation is determined for each subject by the computer and not revealed to the experimenter until the completion of the test session. Because of this as well as the masking music played over the headphones during testing, the experimenter is blind to the pairing of sample type and side of presentation. The experimenter presses a button on the response box whenever the infant orients by 30° degrees in the direction of the blinking light. A different button press indicates when the infant fails to maintain the headturn, and if 2 seconds pass without an indication that the infant is once again oriented toward the blinking light, the trial is terminated.

The training phase of this modification of the HPP remains unchanged. However, in the test phase, after the center green light is extinguished, the red light on only one of the two side panels begins to blink. When the infant makes a 30° headturn in this direction, the experimenter presses a response button that initiates the speech sample and begins the timing of the trial. Since the program keeps a record of how long the infant actually orients toward the blinking light on each trial, this potentially more sensitive measure (instead of total trial duration) is used to assess infant's preferences for the different types of speech samples. Switching to the use of durational measure permits other changes that improve the overall sensitivity of the procedure. For example, on different trials, both versions of a particular sample are played during the course of testing. Not only does this provide infants with the opportunity to listen to both of the different sample types, but it also permits within-subject comparisons for the different versions of each sample.

In their investigation, Hirsh-Pasek and her colleagues presented 9-month-olds with speech samples that contained artificial 1-second pauses inserted either at boundaries between different clauses or between words in the middle of clauses. Analysis of the direction of the first headturn provided no indication that infants turned more to the side associated with one type of sample than to the other. However, the durational measure (i.e., how long the infants oriented toward the loudspeaker playing each type of sample) indicated that infants listened longer to the samples with the pauses inserted at the clause boundaries.

Several changes have further strengthened the standard version of HPP. When it was determined that the duration of listening times was a more sensitive index, it became clear that it is unnecessary to play all of the samples of a given type to the same side. If the duration of the headturn has to do with the properties of a particular type of stimulus, then the infant's behavior should be mediated by those properties regardless of whether the stimulus changes sides during the course of the experiment. One methodological advantage of this procedure is that the link between sample type and presentation side is determined randomly from trial to trial; this makes it even less likely that an observer could anticipate the type of sample that is presented on a given trial.

Variations and Extensions of the Headturn Preference Procedure
One strength of the headturn preference procedure is that it allows the presentation of long samples of continuous speech (samples with durations as long as 30 seconds have been used). Procedures like HAS or operant headturning typically allow the presentation of only brief samples of speech (usually four or five syllables). Thus, HPP is very useful for investigating cues distributed over long stretches of speech. Moreover, the procedure can also be used for other types of stimuli. Krumhansl and Jusczyk (1990; Jusczyk and Krumhansl 1993) used it to investigate infants' perception of musical phrase structure.

Jusczyk and his colleagues (Jusczyk, Cutler, and Redanz 1993; Jusczyk, Friederici et al. 1993) have also adapted the procedure to investigate infants' sensitivity to properties associated with native-language word structure. This was accomplished by using auditory stimuli that consisted of lists of spoken items instead of fluent speech passages. Thus, on training and test trials alike, the infants hear lists of words or nonsense words. Across the various investigations using these kinds of materials, the lengths of the lists have varied between 12 and 15 items. Typically, two types of lists are tested in a given experiment. The items on each type of list are chosen to be similar in some way, such as following a particular word stress pattern (Jusczyk, Cutler, and Redanz 1993) or phonotactic structure (Jusczyk, Friederici et al. 1993). Depending on their age and the linguistic property that is varied across the lists, infants have been shown to listen significantly longer to one type of list over another. For example, Jusczyk, Cutler, and Redanz (1993) found that at 9 months, but not at 6 months, American infants listen significantly longer to lists following the predominant strong/weak stress pattern of English words.

Another important variant of the HPP is the version that has been used to study infants' abilities to detect words in fluent speech (e.g., Jusczyk and Aslin 1995). Unlike the earlier versions of the procedure in which the stimuli used during the training phase are of the same type as those used in the test phase, Jusczyk and Aslin's version uses different kinds of stimuli in each phase. Their modified procedure begins with a "familiarization phase." For example, in their first experiment, $7\frac{1}{2}$-month-olds were exposed to repetitions of two different words (e.g., "cup" and "bike") on alternating trials in the familiarization phase. The samples on a given familiarization trial consisted of 15 different tokens of the same word produced by a single talker. The familiarization phase ended when the infants had listened to each word for at least 30 seconds.

In the same experiment, the test phase consisted of four blocks of trials, with four trials in each block. However, the speech samples used in the test phase differed considerably from those used in the familiarization phase. Specifically, each test trial stimulus consisted of a fluent speech passage that was six sentences long. In each of these passages, there was one word that appeared in every sentence (e.g., "dog"). The repeated word in two of the passages was one of the words heard in the training phase. The repeated words in the other two passages were ones not previously heard. Different infants were familiarized with different pairs of words. Infants listened significantly longer to the passages with the familiar words. Jusczyk and Aslin interpreted this finding as an indication that infants remembered the words and recognized them when they occurred in sentences. In another experiment in the same study, Jusczyk and Aslin used two passages during the familiarization phase. During the test phase, on a given trial, infants heard tokens of a particular word that was repeated up to 15 times. For two of the four test trials that occurred within a block of trials, the word corresponded to one that appeared in one of the passages that had been presented during the familiarization phase. For the other two trials, the repeated words were ones that had not occurred in the passages used during the familiarization phase. As in the earlier experiment, the $7\frac{1}{2}$-month-olds listened significantly longer to those test trials containing the words that had occurred during the familiarization phase. Hence, this particular variant of the HPP appears to be effective whether passages or isolated words are used during the familiarization period.

The HPP has proven useful in investigating infant speech perception and its development as language is acquired. It has been used successfully in studies with children ranging between 4 and 11 months of age. Most recently, in my laboratory, we have had success in extending the upper end of the age range to 18-month-olds. Depending on the age of the infants being tested and the kinds of stimulus materials presented, the success rate of the procedure is high compared to other methods used in infant speech perception. The drop-out rate for subjects is typically only 15 to 20 percent, and very rarely higher than 40 percent. Moreover, the procedure has proven adaptable to posing a wide range of experimental questions. (For a more detailed treatment of the HPP, see Kemler Nelson et al. 1995.)

Notes

Chapter 2

1. Note that this particular assumption is similar to one that has been included in the WRAPSA Model and its forerunners (Jusczyk 1985b, 1986b, 1993a), namely that during development, infants learn to weight information in the speech signal to optimize it for processing the sound structure of their native language.

2. Pinker (1987) admits that the fulfillment of these background assumptions is problematic and questions whether semantic bootstrapping accounts will provide an adequate account of language acquisition. He suggests that a constraint-satisfaction model that incorporates insights from semantic, prosodic, and syntactic bootstrapping may yield a better account. It should be evident from the ensuing discussion that I concur with him on this point.

3. As we shall see in chapter 4, there is some reason to believe that this kind of information actually does play a role in word segmentation.

Chapter 4

1. In general, there is considerable controversy about the role of induction in developmental change. Some, such as Fodor (1975, 1981), have argued that the only model that we have of learning new categories or concepts is one in which we use evidence from experience to assess some internally represented hypothesis about the content of the concept. However, this implies that the learner is already in possession of the concept because any hypothesis about the concept must already contain the concept. Nevertheless, some recent efforts with connectionist paradigms hold some promise of modeling how new structures may emerge in the course of development (Elman 1993, 1995; Nolfi, Elman, and Parisi, in press; Plunkett and Sinha 1992; and for a general discussion of this issue see A. Clark 1993).

2. A language spoken by people in a tribe indigenous to the Pacific Northwest.

3. A recent finding reported by Pegg (1995) is interesting with respect to this issue. Pegg tested 6- to 8-month-olds and 10- to 12-month-olds from English-speaking homes on a speech contrast that corresponds to an allophonic difference in English. She found that the younger infants discriminated this contrast, but the

older group did not. This finding is interesting because both allophones appear in speech input directed to the infants. Hence, Pegg notes that the decline in sensitivity in the older infants cannot be attributed to their lack of experience with these sounds. Rather, she argues that the reorganization may be due to infants' learning about the way that these allophones map to phonemic categories in English. Another possibility is that infants' sensitivity to phonotactic patterns in the language may have affected their performance with the particular stimuli that Pegg used. Either way, there is some indication here that the 10- to 12-month-olds' knowledge of the organization of native-language sound patterns is affecting their discrimination performance.

4. It should be noted that the preference that the infants displayed was for the *novel* trochaic pattern in this study. This is contrary to the tendency that is typically observed with the headturn preference procedure in my laboratory and others (e.g., Friederici and Wessels 1993). In most instances, infants display a preference for what is familiar. Our interpretation of this preference for the familiar is that it occurs for two reasons. First, unlike many infant test procedures like HAS and the operant headturn procedure, the HPP is not a habituation procedure. The stimuli vary considerably from trial to trial (e.g., new lists are presented, or new passages with sentences containing many words). Hence, what is "familiar" often occurs in a novel context. Second, infants at this age appear to be engaged in learning about regularities, rather than exceptions, in native-language input. Obviously, at some point, they will also need to learn about the exceptions or less frequently occurring patterns in their language, but perhaps not until they first master the regularly occurring features. In this regard, Echols et al.'s finding is a little puzzling. However, one possible reason that a novelty preference occurred has to do with the nature of the stimuli used in the test phase of their experiment. The test stimuli were excised from the longer strings used in familiarization. Consequently, they were physically identical to those heard in familiarization. By comparison, in the studies described in the next section (i.e., Jusczyk and Aslin 1995; Newsome and Jusczyk 1995) the targets in fluent speech were physically different from the isolated versions of these targets (which were recorded in citation form).

Chapter 5

1. As is noted in the discussion of the WRAPSA model in chapter 8, these units are containers of acoustic and phonetic features, that is, the kind of information that is provided by auditory analyzers. However, at least at this stage of development, there is no indication that these features are organized into distinct phonetic segments.

2. Note that in a separate experiment Jusczyk and his colleagues showed that the infants could discriminate the isolated syllables [ba] and [bʌ] from each other.

Chapter 6

1. As noted in chapter 4, infants tested with the HPP tended to display preferences for what is familiar, presumably because the stimuli vary from trial to trial. One question that is often raised about the pattern of results in these studies with inserted pauses is whether infants listen longer to the coincident versions of the

samples because they find the noncoincident versions of the samples aversive. However, as Kemler Nelson (1989) has argued, inspection of the pattern of responding across a number of studies with infants of different ages (e.g., Hirsh-Pasek et al. 1987; Jusczyk et al. 1992; Kemler Nelson et al. 1989) is not consistent with the view that infants listen longer to the coincident versions because they perceive the noncoincident versions aversive. In particular, developmentally prior to the point that the infants manifest a preference for the coincident versions, they tend to listen equally long to both versions of the samples. When a significant preference is found, it tends to show up as an *increase* in listening time for the coincident versions as opposed to a *decrease* in listening time for the non-coincident versions (as might be expected if they found the latter to be aversive). Hence, the longer listening times to the coincident versions seem to be the result of infants being more positively attracted to these samples. Perhaps infants are drawn to these kinds of samples because they appear to provide exceptionally clear marking of units (i.e., they are, in effect, superstimuli).

Chapter 7

1. Boysson-Bardies et al. argued that this index of the distribution of consonants in the adult language was a more appropriate one than simply using counts drawn from average media speech (such as radio and television broadcasts). They view the latter as not representative of the speech in the child's environment because it includes uncommon words, as well as function words (which they argue are "acoustically less salient and pragmatically less relevant for infants.") For this reason, they made their comparisons of distributional properties in the infants' productions to ones in adult words that served as targets for the infants.

Chapter 8

1. Of course, constraints involved in language learning extend beyond ones pertinent to learning a spoken system of communication. Research by Bellugi and others (e.g., Bellugi 1980, 1988; Klima and Bellugi 1979; Newport and Meier 1986) has shown that signed languages embody the same complexities as do spoken languages. Moreover, there are marked similarities in the kind of specialization of brain functions that have been observed between native users of signed and spoken languages (Poizner, Klima, and Bellugi 1987). Critical periods have been observed for the acquisition of sign, just as for spoken languages (e.g., Mayberry and Fisher 1989; Newport 1991). In addition, as observed in chapter 7, there is even evidence that hearing and nonhearing infants exposed to sign language engage in manual babbling (Pettito and Marentette 1991).

Appendix

1. Extensive pilot testing revealed that leaving the lights blinking during the training trials often led to very short looking times on the test trials. Turning the blinking lights off during the training trials, but leaving them on for the duration of the test trials, better maintains the infants' interest in the samples during the test trials.

References

Abrams, K., and T. G. Bever. 1969. Syntactic structure modifies attention during speech perception and recognition. *Quarterly Journal of Experimental Psychology* 21, 280–290.

Abramson, A. S., and L. Lisker. 1967. Discriminability along the voice continuum: Cross language tests. Paper presented at the Sixth International Congress of Phonetic Sciences, Prague.

Ament, W. 1899. *Die entwicklung von sprechen und denken beim kinde.* Leipzig: Wunderlich.

Anderson, J. R. 1983. *The architecture of cognition.* Cambridge, Mass.: Harvard University Press.

Anderson, S. R. 1981. Why phonology isn't "natural." *Linguistic Inquiry* 12, 493–539.

Armitage, S. E., B. A. Baldwin, and M. A. Vince. 1980. The fetal sound environment of sheep. *Science* 208, 1173–1174.

Aslin, R. N. 1981. Experiential differences and sensitive periods in perceptual development: A unified model. In R. N. Aslin, J. R. Alberts, and M. R. Petersen, eds., *Development of perception: Psychobiological perspectives.* New York: Academic Press.

Aslin, R. N., P. W. Jusczyk, and D. B. Pisoni. In press. Speech and auditory processing during infancy: Constraints on and precursors to language. In R. Siegler, ed., *Mussen's handbook of child psychology.* New York: Wiley.

Aslin, R. N., and D. B. Pisoni. 1980. Some developmental processes in speech perception. In G. H. Yeni-Komshian, J. F. Kavanagh, and C. A. Ferguson, eds., *Child phonology.* New York: Academic Press.

Aslin, R. N., D. B. Pisoni, B. L. Hennessy, and A. J. Perey. 1981. Discrimination of voice onset time by human infants: New findings and implications for the effects of early experience. *Child Development* 52, 1135–1145.

Aslin, R. N., D. B. Pisoni, and P. W. Jusczyk. 1983. Auditory development and speech perception in infancy. In M. M. Haith and J. J. Campos, eds., *Infancy and the biology of development.* New York: Wiley.

Atkinson, K., B. MacWhinney, and C. Stoel. 1968. An experiment on the recognition of babbling 14, University of California, Berkeley, Language Behavior Research Laboratory Working Paper.

Bahrick, L. E., and J. N. Pickens. 1988. Classification of bimodal English and Spanish language passages by infants. *Infant Behavior and Development* 11, 277–296.

Balaban, M. T., and S. R. Waxman. 1995. An examination of the factors underlying the facilitative effect of word phrases in object categorization in 9-month-olds. Paper presented at the Boston University Conference on Language Development, Boston, Mass., November 1995.

Barton, D. 1976. Phonemic discrimination and the knowledge of words in children under three years. *Papers and Reports on Child Language Development* 11, 61–68.

Baru, A. V. 1975. Discrimination of synthesized vowels [a] and [i] with varying parameters in dog. In G. Fant and M. A. A. Tatham, eds., *Auditory analysis and the perception of speech.* London: Academic Press.

Bates, E., and B. MacWhinney. 1982. Functionalist approaches to grammar. In E. Wanner and L. Gleitman, eds., *Language acquisition: The state of the art.* New York: Cambridge University Press.

Bates, E., and B. MacWhinney. 1987. Competition, variation and language learning. In B. MacWhinney, ed., *Mechanisms of language acquisition.* Hillsdale, NJ: Erlbaum.

Bates, E., and B. MacWhinney. 1989. Functionalism and the competition model. In B. MacWhinney and E. Bates, eds., *The crosslinguistic study of sentence processing.* New York: Cambridge University Press.

Bauman, A., M. Goodman, and P. W. Jusczyk. 1995. Infants' sensitivity to sound similarities within words. Paper presented at the Boston University Conference on Language Development, Boston, Mass., November 1995.

Beckman, M., and J. Edwards. 1990. Lengthening and shortening and the nature of prosodic constituency. In J. Kingston and M. E. Beckman, eds., *Papers in laboratory phonology I: Between the grammar and physics of speech.* Cambridge: Cambridge University Press.

Bellugi, U. 1980. The structuring of language: Clues from the similarities between signed and spoken language. In U. Bellugi and M. Studdert-Kennedy, eds., *Signed and spoken language: Biological constraints on linguistic form.* Dahlem Konferenzen. Weinheim/Deerfield Beach, Fla.: Verlag Chemie.

Bellugi, U. 1988. The acquisition of a spatial language. In F. Kessell, ed., *The development of language and language researchers: Essays in honor of Roger Brown.* Hillsdale, N.J.: Erlbaum.

Bellugi, U., and R. Brown. 1964. The acquisition of language. *Monographs for the Society for Research in Child Development* 29.

Benedict, H. 1979. Early lexical development: Comprehension and production. *Journal of Child Language* 6, 183–201.

Berko, J., and R. Brown. 1960. Psycholinguistic research methods. In P. H. Mussen, eds., *Handbook of research methods in child development.* New York: Wiley.

Bernstein Ratner, N. 1986. Durational cues which mark clause boundaries in mother–child speech. *Phonetics* 14, 303–309.

Bertoncini, J. 1993. Infants' perception of speech units: Primary representational capacities. In B. B. de Boysson-Bardies, S. de Schonen, P. Jusczyk, P. MacNeilage, and J. Morton, eds., *Developmental neurocognition: Speech and face processing in the first year of life.* Dordrecht: Kluwer.

Bertoncini, J., R. Bijeljac-Babic, S. E. Blumstein, and J. Mehler. 1987. Discrimination in neonates of very short CV's. *Journal of the Acoustical Society of America* 82, 31–37.

Bertoncini, J., R. Bijeljac-Babic, P. W. Jusczyk, L. J. Kennedy, and J. Mehler. 1988. An investigation of young infants' perceptual representations of speech sounds. *Journal of Experimental Psychology: General* 117, 21–33.

Bertoncini, J., and J. Mehler. 1981. Syllables as units in infant speech perception. *Infant Behavior and Development* 4, 247–260.

Best, C. T. 1991. Phonetic influences on the peception of non-native speech contrasts by 6–8 and 10–12 month olds. Paper presented at Biennial meeting of the Society for Research in Child Development, Seattle, Wash., April 1991.

Best, C. T. 1993. Emergence of language-specific constraints in perception of native and non-native speech: A window on early phonological development. In B. de Boysson-Bardies, S. de Schonen, P. Jusczyk, P. MacNeilage, and J. Morton, eds., *Developmental neurocognition: Speech and face processing in the first year of life.* Dordrecht: Kluwer.

Best, C. T. 1995. Learning to perceive the sound patterns of English. In C. Rovee-Collier and L. P. Lipsitt, eds., *Advances in infancy research.* Norwood, N.J.: Ablex.

Best, C. T., and G. W. McRoberts. 1989. Phonological influences on the perception of native and non-native speech contrasts. Paper presented at Biennial Meeting of the Society for Research in Child Development, Kansas City, Mo., April 1989.

Best, C. T., G. W. McRoberts, and N. M. Sithole. 1988. Examination of the perceptual re-organization for speech contrasts: Zulu click discrimination by English-speaking adults and infants. *Journal of Experimental Psychology: Human Perception and Performance* 14, 345–360.

Best, C. T., B. Morrongiello, and R. Robson. 1981. Perceptual equivalence of acoustic cues in speech and nonspeech perception. *Perception and Psychophysics* 29, 191–211.

Bever, T. G. 1970. The cognitive basis for linguistic structures. In J. R. Hayes, ed., *Cognition and language learning.* New York: Wiley.

Bever, T. G. 1975. Psychologically real grammar emerges because of its role in language acquisition. In D. P. Dato, ed., *Developmental psycholinguistics: Theory and applications.* Georgetown University Roundtable on Languages and Linguistics. Washington, D.C.: Georgetown University Press.

Bever, T. G., ed. 1981. Normal acquisition processes explain the critical period for language learning. K. C. Diller, ed., *Individual differences and universals in language learning aptitude.* Rowley, Mass.: Newbury House.

Bijeljac-Babic, R., J. Bertoncini, and J. Mehler. 1993. How do four-day-old infants categorize multisyllabic utterances? *Developmental Psychology* 29, 711–721.

Birnholz, J. C., and B. B. Benacerraf. 1983. The development of human fetal hearing. *Science* 222, 516–518.

Blake, R., and H. V. B. Hirsch. 1975. Deficits in binocular depth perception in cats after alternating monocular deprivation. *Science* 190, 1114–1116.

Blakemore, C. 1976. The conditions required for the maintenance of binocularity in the kitten's visual cortex. *Journal of Physiology (London)* 261, 423–444.

Blasdell, R., and P. Jensen. 1970. Stress and word position as determinants of imitation in first language learners. *Journal of Speech and Hearing Research* 13, 193–202.

Blount, B. G. 1969. Acquisition of language by Luo children. Ph.D. dissertation, University of California, Berkeley.

Blumstein, S. E., E. Isaacs, and J. Mertus. 1982. The role of gross spectral shape as a perceptual cue to place of articulation in initial stop consonants. *Journal of the Acoustical Society of America* 72, 43–50.

Blumstein, S. E., and K. N. Stevens. 1978. Acoustic invariance for place of articulation in stops and nasals across syllabic context. *Journal of the Acoustical Society of America* 62, S26.

Bolinger, D. L. 1978. Intonation across languages. In J. P. Greenberg, C. A. Ferguson, and E. A. Moravcsik, eds., *Universals of human language.* Stanford: Stanford University Press.

Bolinger, D. L., and L. J. Gerstman. 1957. Disjuncture as a cue to constraints. *Word* 13, 246–255.

Bomba, P. C., and E. R. Siqueland. 1983. The nature and structure of infant form categories. *Journal of Experimental Child Psychology* 35, 294–328.

Bornstein, M. H., W. Kessen, and S. Weiskopf. 1976. Color vision and hue categorization in young human infants. *Journal of Experimental Psychology: Human Perception and Performance* 2, 115–129.

Bowerman, M. 1982. Reorganizational processes in lexical and syntactic development. In E. Wanner and L Gleitman, eds., *Language acquisition: State of the art.* Cambridge: Cambridge University Press.

Boyle, M. K., and L. A. Gerken. In press. Effects of familiarity on children's function morpheme omissions. Journal of Memory and Language.

Boysson-Bardies, B. de. 1993. Ontogeny of language-specific syllabic productions. In B. de Boysson-Bardies, S. de Schonen, P. Jusczyk, P. MacNeilage, and J.

Morton, eds., *Developmental neurocognition: Speech and face processing in the first year of life.* Dordrecht: Kluwer.

Boysson-Bardies, B. de, P., Halle, L. Sagart, and C. Durand. 1989. A cross-linguistic investigation of vowel formants in babbling. *Journal of Child Language* 16, 1–17.

Boysson-Bardies, B. de, and M. M. Vihman. 1991. Adaptation to language: Evidence from babbling and first words in four languages. *Language* 67, 297–319.

Boysson-Bardies, B. de, L. Sagart, and C. Durand. 1984. Discernible differences in the babbling of infants according to target language. *Journal of Child Language* 11, 1–15.

Boysson-Bardies, B. de, M. M. Vihman, L. Roug-Hellichius, C. Durand, I. Landberg, and F. Arao. 1992. Material evidence of selection from the target language. In C. A. Ferguson, L. Menn, and C. Stoel-Gammon, eds., *Phonological development: Models, research, implications.* Timonium, Md.: York Press.

Braine, M. D. S. 1963. The ontogeny of English phrase structure. *Language* 39, 1–13.

Braine, M. D. S. 1976. Review of *The acquisition of phonology* by N. V. Smith. *Language* 52, 489–498.

Brent, M. R., and T. A. Cartwright. In press. Distributional regularity and phonotactic constraints are useful for segmentation. *Cognition.*

Bretherton, I., S. McNew, L. Snyder, and E. Bates. 1983. Individual differences at 20 months: Analytic and holistic strategies in language acquisition. *Journal of Child Language* 10, 293–320.

Bricker, P. D., and S. Pruzansky. 1966. Effects of stimulus context and stimulus duration on talker identification. *Journal of the Acoustical Society of America* 40, 1441–1449.

Broadbent, D. E. 1952. Listening to two synchronous messages. *Journal of Experimental Psychology* 44, 51–55.

Broen, P. 1972. The verbal environment of the language learning child. *ASHA Monograph* 17.

Brown, R. 1958. *Words and things.* Glencoe, Ill.: Free Press.

Brown, R. 1964. Three processes in the acquisition of syntax. *Harvard Educational Review* 34, 133–151.

Brown, R. 1973. *A first language.* Cambridge, Mass.: Harvard University Press.

Brown, R. 1977. Introduction. In C. E. Snow and C. A. Ferguson, eds., *Talking to children.* Cambridge: Cambridge University Press.

Brown, R., C. Cazden, and U. Bellugi. 1969. The child's grammar from I to III. In J. P. Hill, eds., *Minnesota Symposium on Child Psychology* Minneapolis: University of Minnesota Press.

Brown, R., and C. Fraser. 1964. The acquisition of syntax. *Monographs of the Society for Research in Child Development* 29, 9–34.

Buhr, R. D. 1980. The emergence of vowels in an infant. *Journal of Speech and Hearing Research* 23, 62–94.

Caramazza, A., G. Yeni-Komshian, E. Zurif, and E. Carbone. 1973. The acquisition of a new phonological contrast: The case of stop consonants in French-English bilinguals. *Journal of the Acoustical Society of America* 54, 421–428.

Carden, G., A. Levitt, P. W. Jusczyk, and A. C. Walley. 1981. Evidence for phonetic processing of cues to place of articulation: Perceived manner affects perceived place. *Perception and Psychophysics* 29, 26–36.

Carney, A. E., G. P. Widin, and N. F. Veimeister. 1977. Noncategorical perception of stop consonants differing in VOT. *Journal of the Acoustical Society of America* 62, 961–970.

Carterette, E. C., and A. Barneby. 1975. Recognition memory for voices. In A. Cohen and S. G. Nooteboom, eds., *Structure and process in speech perception.* New York: Springer-Verlag.

Cassidy, K. W., and M. H. Kelly. 1991. Phonological information for grammatical category assignments. *Journal of Memory and Language* 30, 348–369.

Changeux, J. P., T. Heidmann, and P. Patte. 1984. Learning by selection. In P. Marler and H. S. Terrace, eds., *The biology of learning.* Berlin: Springer-Verlag.

Charles-Luce, J., and P. Luce. 1995. An examination of similarity neighborhoods in young children's receptive vocabularies. *Journal of Child Language* 22, 727–735.

Charles-Luce, J., and P. A. Luce. 1990. Similarity neighborhoods of words in young children's lexicons. *Journal of Child Language* 17, 205–215.

Cherry, E. C. 1953. Some experiments on the recognition of speech, with one and with two ears. *Journal of the Acoustical Society of America* 25, 975–979.

Chiat, S. 1979. The role of the word in phonological development. *Linguistics* 17, 591–610.

Chomsky, N. 1959. A review of B. F. Skinner's *Verbal Behavior. Language* 35, 26–58. Reprinted in J. A. Fodor and J. J. Katz, eds. 1964. *The structure of language.* Englewood Cliffs, N.J.: Prentice-Hall.

Chomsky, N. 1961. Some methodological remarks on generative grammar. *Word* 17, 219–239.

Chomsky, N. 1965. *Aspects of a theory of syntax.* Cambridge, Mass.: MIT Press.

Chomsky, N. 1980. *Rules and representations.* New York: Columbia University Press.

Chomsky, N. 1981. *Lectures on Government and Binding.* Dordrecht: Foris.

Chomsky, N. 1986. *Knowledge of language: Its nature, origin, and use.* London: Praeger.

Chomsky, N., and M. Halle. 1968. *The sound pattern of English.* New York: Harper and Row.

Christophe, A., E. Dupoux, J. Bertoncini, and J. Mehler. 1994. Do infants perceive word boundaries? An empirical approach to the bootstrapping problem for lexical acquisition. *Journal of the Acoustical Society of America* 95, 1570–1580.

Church, K. 1987. Phonological parsing and lexical retrieval. *Cognition* 25, 53–69.

Clark, A. 1993. *Associative engines.* Cambridge, Mass.: Bradford Books/MIT Press.

Clark, E. V. 1973. What's in a word? On the child's acquisition of semantics in his first language. In T. E. Moore, eds., *Cognitive development and the acquisition of language.* New York: Academic Press.

Clark, E. V. 1983. Meanings and concepts. In J. H. Flavell and E. M. Markman, eds., *Cognitive Development.* New York: Wiley.

Clark, E. V. 1993. *The lexicon in acquisition.* Cambridge: Cambridge University Press.

Clifford, B. R. 1983. Memory for voices: The feasibility and quality of earwitness evidence. In S. M. A. Bostock and B. R. Clifford, eds., *Evaluating witness evidence.* New York: John Wiley and Sons.

Cohen, L. B., and M. S. Strauss. 1979. Concept acquisition in the human infant. *Child Development* 50, 419–424.

Cole, R. A., and J. Jakimik. 1980. A model of speech perception. In R. A. Cole, ed., *Perception and production of fluent speech.* Hillsdale, N.J.: Erlbaum.

Collier, R., and J. t'Hart. 1975. The role of intonation in speech perception. In A. Cohen and S. G. Nooteboom, eds., *Structure and process in speech perception.* Heidelberg: Springer Verlag.

Colombo, J., and R. S. Bundy. 1981. A method for the measurement of infant auditory selectivity. *Infant Behavior and Development* 4, 219–223.

Cooper, R. P., and R. N. Aslin. 1990. Preference for infant-directed speech in the first month after birth. *Child Development* 61, 1584–1595.

Cooper, R. P., and R. N. Aslin. 1994. Developmental differences in infant attention to the spectral properties of infant-directed speech. *Child Development* 65, 1663–1677.

Cooper, W. E., and J. Paccia-Cooper. 1980. *Syntax and speech.* Cambridge, Mass.: Harvard University Press.

Craik, F. I. M., and K. Kirsner. 1974. The effect of speaker's voice on word recognition. *Quarterly Journal of Experimental Psychology* 26, 274–284.

Creelman, C. D. 1957. Case of the unkown talker. *Journal of the Acoustical Society of America* 29, 655.

Crelin, E. 1987. *The human vocal tract.* New York: Vantage Press.

Cruttenden, A. 1970. A phonetic study of babbling. *British Journal of Disorders of Communication* 5, 110–117.

Cruttenden, A. 1986. *Intonation.* Cambridge: Cambridge University Press.

Crystal, T. H., and A. S. House. 1988. Segmental durations in connected speech signals: Current Results. *Journal of the Acoustical Society of America* 83, 1553–1573.

Cutler, A. 1990. Exploiting prosodic probabilities in speech segmentation. In G. T. M. Altmann, ed., *Cognitive models of speech processing: psycholinguistic and computational perspectives.* Cambridge: MIT Press.

Cutler, A. 1994. Segmentation problems, rhythmic solutions. *Lingua* 92, 81–104.

Cutler, A., and S. Butterfield. 1992. Rhythmic cues to speech segmentation: Evidence from juncture misperception. *Journal of Memory and Language* 31, 218–236.

Cutler, A., and D. M. Carter. 1987. The predominance of strong initial syllables in the English vocabulary. *Computer Speech and Language* 2, 133–142.

Cutler, A., J. McQueen, and K. Robinson. 1990. Elizabeth and John: Sound patterns of men's and women's names. *Journal of Linguistics* 26, 471–482.

Cutler, A., J. Mehler, D. G. Norris, and J. Segui. 1983. A language-specific comprehension strategy. *Nature* 304, 159–160.

Cutler, A., J. Mehler, D. G. Norris, and J. Segui. 1986. The syllable's differing role in the segmentation of French and English. *Journal of Memory and Language* 25, 385–400.

Cutler, A., and D. G. Norris. 1988. The role of strong syllables in segmentation for lexical access. *Journal of Experimental Psychology: Human Perception and Performance* 14, 113–121.

Cutting, J. E., and B. S. Rosner. 1974. Categories and boundaries in speech and music. *Perception and Psychophysics* 16, 564–570.

Davis, B. L., and P. F. MacNeilage. 1994. Organization of babbling: A case study. *Language and Speech* 37, 341–355.

DeCasper, A. J., and W. P. Fifer. 1980. Of human bonding: Newborns prefer their mothers' voices. *Science* 208, 1174–1176.

DeCasper, A. J., and M. J. Spence. 1986. Prenatal maternal speech influences newborns' perception of speech sounds. *Infant Behavior and Development* 9, 133–150.

Delattre, P. C., A. M. Liberman, and F. S. Cooper. 1955. Acoustic loci and transitional cues for consonants. *Journal of the Acoustical Society of America* 27, 769–773.

Demany, L. 1982. Auditory stream segregation in infancy. *Infant Behavioral Development* 5, 261–276.

D'Entremont, B., and P. J. Dunham. 1992. The noun-category bias phenomenon in 3-year-olds: Taxonomic constraint or translation? *Cognitive Development* 7, 47–62.

Dirks, D. D., and R. H. Wilson. 1969. The effect of spatially separated sound sources on speech intelligibility. *Journal of Speech and Hearing Research* 12, 5–38.

Dodd, B. 1975. Children's understanding of their own phonological forms. *Quarterly Journal of Psychology* 27, 165–173.

Dollaghan, C. A. 1994. Children's phonological neighborhoods: Half empty or half full? *Journal of Child Language* 21, 257–273.

Duquesnoy, A. J. 1983. The intelligibility of sentences in quiet and in noise in aged listeners. *Journal of the Acoustical Society of America* 74, 1136–1144.

Echols, C. H. 1993. A perceptually based model of children's earliest productions. *Cognition* 46, 245–296.

Echols, C. H., M. J. Crowhurst, and J. B. Childers. In press. The perception of rhythmic units in speech by infants and adults. *Journal of Memory and Language.*

Echols, C. H., and E. L. Newport. 1992. The role of stress and position in determining first words. *Language Acquisition* 2, 189–220.

Edelman, G. M. 1987. *Neural Darwinism.* New York: Basic Books.

Edwards, M. L. 1974. Perception and production in child phonology: The testing of four hypotheses. *Journal of Child Language* 1, 205–215.

Eich, J. M. 1982. A composite holographic associative recall model. *Psychological Review* 89, 627–661.

Eilers, R. E. 1977. Context sensitive perception of naturally produced stop and fricative consonants by infants. *Journal of the Acoustical Society of America* 61, 1321–1336.

Eilers, R. E., W. R. Wilson, and J. M. Moore. 1977. Developmental changes in speech discrimination in infants. *Journal of Speech and Hearing Research* 20, 766–780.

Eilers, R. E., W. R. Wilson, and J. M. Moore. 1979. Speech discrimination in the language-innocent and language-wise: A study in the perception of voice onset time. *Journal of Child Language* 6, 1–18.

Eimas, P. D. 1974. Auditory and linguistic processing of cues for place of articulation by infants. *Perception and Psychophysics* 16, 513–521.

Eimas, P. D. 1975a. Auditory and phonetic coding of the cues for speech: Discrimination of the [r-l] distinction by young infants. *Perception and Psychophysics* 18, 341–347.

Eimas, P. D. 1975b. Speech perception in early infancy. In L. B. Cohen and P. Salapatek, eds., *Infant perception: From sensation to cognition* New York: Academic Press.

Eimas, P. D. 1985. The equivalence of cues for the peception of speech by infants. *Infant Behavior and Development* 8, 125–138.

Eimas, P. D. 1991. Comment: Some effects of language acquisition on speech perception. In I. G. Mattingly and M. Studdert-Kennedy, eds., *Modularity and the motor theory of speech perception.* Hillsdale, N.J.: Erlbaum.

Eimas, P. D. 1996. The perception and representation of speech by infants. In J. L. Morgan and K. Demuth, eds., *Signal to syntax.* Mahwah, N.J.: Erlbaum.

Eimas, P. D., and J. L. Miller. 1980a. Contextual effects in infant speech perception. *Science* 209, 1140–1141.

Eimas, P. D., and J. L. Miller. 1980b. Discrimination of the information for manner of articulation. *Infant Behavior and Development* 3, 367–375.

Eimas, P. D., and J. L. Miller. 1981. Organization in the perception of segmental and suprasegmental information by infants. *Infant Behavior and Development* 4, 395–399.

Eimas, P. D., and J. L. Miller. 1991. A constraint on the discrimination of speech by young infants. *Language and Speech* 34, 251–263.

Eimas, P. D., and J. L. Miller. 1992. Organization in the perception of speech by young infants. *Psychological Science* 3, 340–345.

Eimas, P. D., J. L. Miller, and P. W. Jusczyk. 1987. On infant speech perception and the acquisition of language. In S. Harnad, eds., *Categorical Perception.* New York: Cambridge University Press.

Eimas, P. D., E. R. Siqueland, P. W. Jusczyk, and J. Vigorito. 1971. Speech perception in infants. *Science* 171, 303–306.

Elbers, L. 1982. Operating principles in repetitive babbling: A case study. *Cognition* 12, 45–64.

Elbers, L. 1985. A tip-of-the-tongue experience at the age of two? *Journal of Child Language* 12, 353–365.

Elbers, L., and J. Ton. 1985. Play pen monologues: The interplay of words and babbles in the first words period. *Journal of Child Language* 12, 551–564.

Elman, J. L. 1993. Learning and development in neural networks: The importance of starting small. *Cognition* 48, 71–99.

Elman, J. L. 1995. Language as a dynamical system. In R. E. Port and T. van Gelder, eds., *Mind as motion.* Cambridge, Mass.: MIT Press.

Elman, J. L., R. L. Diehl, and S. E. Buchwald. 1977. Perceptual switching in bilinguals. *Journal of the Acoustical Society of America* 62, 971–974.

Ervin, S. 1964. Imitation and structural change in children's language. In E. Lenneberg, ed., *New directions in the study of language* Cambridge, Mass.: MIT Press.

Estes, W. K. 1994. *Classification and cognition.* New York: Oxford University Press.

Fairbanks, G., and W. Pronovost. 1939. An experimental study of the pitch characteristics of the voice during the expression of emotions. *Speech monographs* 6, 87–194.

Feldman, H., S. Goldin-Meadow, and L. R. Gleitman. 1977. Beyond Herodotus: The creation of language by linguistically deprived deaf children. In A. Lock, eds., *Action, symbol, and gesture: The emergence of language.* New York: Academic Press.

Ferguson, C. A. 1977. Baby talk as a symplified register. In C. E. Snow and C. A. Ferguson, eds., *Talking to children.* Cambridge: Cambridge University Press.

Ferguson, C. A. 1979. Phonology as an individual access system: Some data from language acquisition. In C. J. Fillmore, D. Kempler, and W. S.-Y. Wang, eds.,

Individual differences in language ability and language behavior. New York: Academic Press.

Ferguson, C. A. 1986. Discovering sound units and constructing sound systems: It's child's play. In J. Perkell and D. H. Klatt, eds., *Invariance and variability in speech processes.* Hillsdale, N. J.: Erlbaum.

Ferguson, C. A., and C. B. Farwell. 1975. Words and sounds in early language acquisition. *Language* 51, 419–439.

Ferguson, C. A., and O. K. Garnica. 1975. Theories of phonological development. In E. H. Lenneberg and E. Lenneberg, eds., *Foundations of language development* New York: Academic Press.

Ferguson, C. A., and M. A. Macken. 1983. The role of play in phonological development. In K. E. Nelson, ed., *Children's language.* Hillsdale, N.J.: Erlbaum.

Fernald, A. 1985. Four-month-old infants prefer to listen to motherese. *Infant Behavior and Development* 8, 181–195.

Fernald, A., and P. K. Kuhl. 1987. Acoustic determinants of infant preference for motherese speech. *Infant Behavior and Development* 10, 279–293.

Fernald, A., and T. Simon. 1984. Expanded intonation contours in mothers' speech to newborns. *Developmental psychology* 20, 104–113.

Fernald, A., T. Taeschner, J. Dunn, M. Papousek, B. de Boysson-Bardies, and I. Fukui. 1989. A cross-language study of prosodic modifications in mothers' and fathers' speech to preverbal infants. *Journal of Child Language* 16, 477–501.

Fisher, C. In press-a. From form to meaning: A role for structural analogy in the acquisition of language. In H. W. Reese, ed., *Advances in child development and behavior.* New York: Academic Press.

Fisher, C. In press-b. Structure and meaning in the verb lexicon: Input for syntax-aided verb learning procedure. *Language and Cognitive Processes.*

Fisher, C., G. Hall, S. Rakowitz, and L. Gleitman. 1994. When it is better to receive than give: Syntactic and conceptual constraints on vocabulary growth. *Lingua* 92, 333–375.

Fisher, C., and H. Tokura. 1996. Prosody in speech to infants: Direct and indirect acoustic cues to syntactic structure. In J. L. Morgan and K. Demuth, eds., *Signal to syntax.* Mahwah, N.J.: Erlbaum.

Fitch, H. L., T. Halwes, D. M. Erickson, and A. M. Liberman. 1980. Perceptual equivalence of two acoustic cues for stop-consonant manner. *Perception and Psychophysics* 27, 343–350.

Flege, J., and W. Eefting. 1987. The production and perception of English stops by Spanish speakers of English. *Journal of Phonetics* 15, 67–83.

Flege, J. E. 1989. Chinese subjects' perception of the word-final English /t/–/d/ contrast: Before and after training. *Journal of the Acoustical Society of America* 86, 1684–1697.

Flege, J. E. 1991. Perception and production: The relevance of phonetic input to L2 phonological learning. In C. A. Ferguson and T. Heubner, eds., *Crosscurrents in second language acquisition and linguistic theories.* Philadelphia: John Benjamins.

Flege, J. E. 1995. Second language speech learning: Theory, findings, and problems. In W. Strange, ed., *Speech perception and linguistic experience: Theoretical and methodological issues.* Timonium, Md.: York Press.

Flege, J. E., N. Takagi, and V. Mann. 1995. Japanese adults can learn to produce English /ɹ/ and /l/ accurately. *Language and Speech* 38, 25–56.

Fodor, J. A. 1966. How to learn to talk: Some simple ways. In F. Smith and G. A. Miller, eds., *The genesis of language.* Cambridge, Mass.: MIT Press.

Fodor, J. A. 1975. *The language of thought.* New York: Thomas Y. Crowell.

Fodor, J. A. 1981. *Representations: Philosophical essays on the foundations of cognitive science.* Cambridge, Mass.: MIT Press.

Fodor, J. A. 1983. *The modularity of mind.* Cambridge, Mass.: MIT Press.

Forster, K. I., and E. S. Bednall. 1976. Terminating and exhaustive search in lexical access. *Memory and Cognition* 43, 53–61.

Fowler, C. A. 1986. An event approach to the study of speech perception from a direct-realist perspective. *Journal of Phonetics* 14, 3–28.

Fowler, C. A., C. T. Best, and G. W. McRoberts. 1990. Young infants' perception of liquid coarticulatory influences following stop consonants. *Perception and Psychophysics* 48, 559–570.

Friederici, A. D., and J. M. I. Wessels. 1993. Phonotactic knowledge and its use in infant speech perception. *Perception and Psychophysics* 54, 287–295.

Friedlander, B. Z., and S. S. Wisdom. 1971. Preverbal infants' selective operant responses for different levels of auditory complexity and language redundancy. Paper presented at Annual General Meeting of the Eastern Psychological Association, New York.

Fry, D. B. 1966. The development of the phonological system in the normal and deaf child. In F. Smith and G. A. Miller, eds., *The genesis of language.* Cambridge, Mass.: MIT Press.

Fry, D. B., A. S. Abramson, P. D. Eimas, and A. M. Liberman. 1962. The identification and discrimination of synthetic vowels. *Language and Speech* 5, 171–189.

Fujisaki, H., and T. Kawashima. 1970. Some experiments on speech perception and a model for the perceptual mechanism 29, University of Tokyo, Faculty of Engineering, Tokyo, *Annual Report of the Engineering Institute.*

Fujisaki, H., and T. Kawashima. 1969. On the modes and mechanisms of speech perception 28, University of Tokyo, Faculty of Engineering, Tokyo, *Annual Report of the Engineering Institute.*

Garnica, O. 1973. The development of phonemic speech perception. In T. E. Moore, ed., *Cognitive development and the acquisition of language.* New York: Academic Press.

Garnica, O. K. 1977. Some prosodic and paralinguistic features of speech to young children. In C. Snow and C. A. Ferguson, eds., *Talking to children: Language input and acquisition.* Cambridge: Cambridge University Press.

Gathercole, S. E., and A. D. Baddeley. 1993. *Working memory and language.* Hove, U.K.: Lawrence Erlbaum Associates, Ltd.

Geiselman, R. E., and F. S. Bellezza. 1976. Long-term memory for speaker's voice and source location. *Memory and Cognition* 4, 483–489.

Gelfand, S. A., N. Piper, and S. Silman. 1986. Consonant recognition in quiet and in noise with aging among normal hearing listeners. *Journal of the Acoustical Society of America* 80, 1589–1598.

Gelman, S. A., and E. M. Markman. 1985. Implicit contrast in adjectives vs. nouns: Implications for word-learning in preschoolers. *Journal of Child Language* 12, 124–143.

Gelman, S. A., and M. Taylor. 1984. How two-year-old children interpret proper and common names for unfamiliar objects. *Child Development* 55, 1535–1540.

Gerken, L. A. 1991. The metrical basis for children's subjectless sentences. *Journal of Memory and Language* 30, 431–451.

Gerken, L. A. 1994a. Child phonology: Past research, present questions, future directions. In M. A. Gernsbacher, ed., *Handbook of psycholinguistics.* New York: Academic Press.

Gerken, L. A. 1994b. Young children's representation of prosodic phonology: evidence from English-speakers' weak syllable omissions. *Journal of Memory and Language* 33, 19–38.

Gerken, L. A. 1996. Phonological and distributional information in syntax acquisition. In J. L. Morgan and K. Demuth, eds., *Signal to syntax.* Mahwah, N.J.: Erlbaum.

Gerken, L. A. In press. Prosody's role in language acquisition and adult parsing. *Journal of Psycholinguistic Research* 25, 341–352.

Gerken, L. A. In press. Prosodic structure in young children's language production. *Language.*

Gerken, L. A., P. W. Jusczyk, and D. R. Mandel. 1994. When prosody fails to cue syntactic structure: Nine-month-olds' sensitivity to phonological vs. syntactic phrases. *Cognition* 51, 237–265.

Gerken, L. A., B. Landau, and R. E. Remez. 1990. Function morphemes in young children's speech perception and production. *Developmental Psychology* 25, 204–216.

Gerken, L. A., and B. J. McIntosh. 1993. Interplay of function morphemes and prosody in early language. *Developmental Psychology* 29, 448–457.

Gerken, L. A., W. D. Murphy, and R. N. Aslin. 1995. Three- and four-year-olds' perceptual confusions for spoken words. *Perception and Psychophysics* 57, 475–486.

Gibson, E. J. 1969. *Principles of perceptual learning and development.* New York: Appleton.

Gilbert, J. H. V. 1982. Babbling and the deaf child: A commentary on Lenneberg et al. (1965) and Lenneberg (1965). *Journal of Child Language* 9, 511–515.

Givón, T. 1979. *On understanding grammar.* New York: Academic Press.

Gleitman, L. R. 1990. The structural sources of verb meanings. *Language Acquisition* 1, 1–55.

Gleitman, L. R. 1994. A picture is worth a thousand words, but that's the problem. In B. Lust, M. Suner, and J. Whitman, eds., *Syntactic theory and first language acquisition. Crosslinguistic perspectives. Vol. 1: Heads, projections, and learnability.* Hillsdale, N.J.: Erlbaum.

Gleitman, L., H. Gleitman, B. Landau, and E. Wanner. 1988. Where the learning begins: Initial representations for language learning. In F. Newmeyer, ed., *The Cambridge Linguistic Survey,* vol. 3. Cambridge, Mass.: Harvard University Press.

Gleitman, L., and B. Landau, ed. 1994. *The acquisition of the lexicon.* Cambridge, Mass.: MIT Press.

Gleitman, L., and E. Wanner. 1982. The state of the state of the art. In E. Wanner and L. Gleitman, eds., *Language acquisition: The state of the art.* Cambridge: Cambridge University Press.

Glenn, S. M., C. C. Cunningham, and P. F. Joyce. 1981. A study of auditory preferences in non handicapped infants and infants with Down's Syndrome. *Child Development* 52, 1303–1307.

Gold, E. M. 1967. Language identification in the limit. *Information and Control* 10, 447–474.

Goldin-Meadow, S., and H. Feldman. 1977. The development of language-like communication without a language model. *Science* 197, 401–403.

Goldin-Meadow, S., and C. Mylander. 1984. Gestural communication in deaf children: The effects and noneffects of parental input on early language development. *Monographs of the Society for Research in Child Development,* Serial No. 207, 49, Nos. 3–4.

Goldinger, S. D. 1992. Words and voices: Implicit and explicit memory for spoken words. *Research on Speech Perception Technical Report* 7, Indiana University.

Goldinger, S. D., D. B. Pisoni, and J. S. Logan. 1991. On the locus of talker variability effects on the recall of spoken word lists. *Journal of Experimental Psychology: Learning, Memory, and Cognition* 17, 152–162.

Golinkoff, R., K. Hirsh-Pasek, K. Cauley, and L. Gordon. 1987. The eyes have it: Lexical and syntactic comprehension in a new paradigm. *Journal of Child Language* 14, 23–45.

Golinkoff, R., K. Hirsh-Pasek, L. M. Bailey, and N. R. Wenger. 1992. Young children and adults use lexical prinicples to learn new nouns. *Developmental Psychology* 28, 99–108.

Goodsitt, J. V., J. L. Morgan, and P. K. Kuhl. 1993. Perceptual strategies in prelingual speech segmentation. *Journal of Child Lanaguage* 20, 229–252.

Goodsitt, J. V., P. A. Morse, J. N. Ver Hoove, and N. Cowan. 1984. Infant speech perception in multisyllabic contexts. *Child Development* 55, 903–910.

Gould, J. L., and P. Marler. 1987. Learning by instinct. *Scientific American* 256, 62–73.

Greenberg, J. H. 1966. Some universals of grammar with particular reference to the order of meaningful elements. In J. H. Greenberg, ed., *Universals of language.* Cambridge, Mass.: MIT Press.

Gregoire, A. 1933. L'apprentissage de la parole pendant les deux premieres annees de l'enfance. *Journal de Psychologie* 30, 375–389.

Gregoire, A. 1937. *L'apprentissage du langage.* Liège: Bibliotheque de la Faculte de Philosophie et Lettres de l'Universite de Liège.

Grewel, F. 1959. How do children acquire the use of language. *Phonetica* 3, 193–202.

Grieser, D., and P. K. Kuhl. 1989. The categorization of speech by infants: Support for speech-sound prototypes. *Developmental Psychology* 25, 577–588.

Grieser, D. I., and P. K. Kuhl. 1988. Maternal speech to infants in a tonal language: Support for universal prosodic features in motherese. *Developmental Psychology* 24, 14–20.

Grimshaw, J. 1981. Form, function, and the language acquisition device. In C. L. Baker and J. J. McCarthy, eds., *The logical problem of language acquisition.* Cambridge, Mass.: MIT Press.

Grosjean, F., and J. P. Gee. 1987. Prosodic structure and spoken word recognition. *Cognition* 25, 135–155.

Hall, D. G., S. R. Waxman, and W. R. Hurwitz. 1993. How two- and four-year-old children interpet adjectives and count nouns. *Child Development* 64, 1651–1664.

Hallé, P., and B. de Boysson-Bardies. 1994a. Early receptive lexicons: Representations of word sounds. Paper presented at the International Conference on Infant Studies, Paris, June 1994.

Hallé, P., and B. de Boysson-Bardies. 1994b. Emergence of an early receptive lexicon: Infants' recognition of words. *Infant Behavior and Development* 17, 119–129.

Hamburger, H., and K. Wexler. 1975. A mathematical theory of learning transformational grammar. *Journal of Mathematical Psychology* 12, 137–177.

Harris, K. S., H. S. Hoffman, A. M. Liberman, P. C. Delattre, and F. S. Cooper. 1958. Effect of third-formant transitions on the perception of voiced stop consonants. *Journal of the Acoustical Society of America* 30, 122–126.

Haugen, E., and M. Joos. 1972. Tone and intonation in East Norwegian. In D. Bolinger, ed., *Intonation.* Harmondsworth, England: Penguin, Ltd.

Hayes, B. 1982. Extrametricality and English stress. *Linguistic Inquiry* 13, 227–276.

Hayes, B. 1989. The prosodic hierarchy in meter. In P. Kiparsky and G. Youmans, eds., *Phonetics and phonology: Rhythm and meter* San Diego, Calif.: Academic Press.

Henry, L. A. 1991. The effects of word length and phonemic similarity in young children's short-term memory. *Quarterly Journal of Experimental Psychology* 43a, 35–52.

Hillenbrand, J. 1983. Perceptual organization of speech sounds by infants. *Journal of Speech and Hearing Research* 26, 268–282.

Hillenbrand, J. 1984. Speech perception by infants: Categorization based on nasal consonant place of articulation. *Journal of the Acoustical Society of America* 75, 1613–1622.

Hillenbrand, J. M., F. D. Minifie, and T. J. Edwards. 1979. Tempo of spectrum change as a cue in speech sound discrimination by infants. *Journal of Speech and Hearing Research* 22, 147–165.

Hintzman, D. L. 1986. "Schema Abstraction" in a multiple-trace memory model. *Psychological Review* 93, 411–428.

Hintzman, D. L. 1988. Judgments of frequency and recognition memory in a multiple-trace memory model. *Psychological Review* 95, 528–551.

Hintzman, D. L., R. A. Block, and N. R. Inskeep. 1972. Memory for the mode of input. *Journal of Verbal Learning and Verbal Behavior* 11, 741–749.

Hirsh-Pasek, K., D. G. Kemler Nelson, P. W. Jusczyk, K. Wright Cassidy, B. Druss, and L. Kennedy. 1987. Clauses are perceptual units for young infants. *Cognition* 26, 269–286.

Hirsh-Pasek, K., M. Tucker, and R. Golinkoff. 1996. Dynamic systems theory: Reinterpreting "prosodic bootstrapping" and its role in language acquisition. In J. L. Morgan and K. Demuth, eds., *Signal to syntax*. Mahwah, N.J.: Erlbaum.

Hockett, C. A. 1954. Two models of grammatical description. *Word* 10, 210–31.

Hohne, E. A., A. M. Jusczyk, and N. J. Redanz. 1994. Do infants remember words from stories? Paper presented at the meeting of the Acoustical Society of America, Cambridge, Mass., June 1994.

Hohne, E. A., and P. W. Jusczyk. 1994. Two-month-old infants' sensitivity to allophonic differences. *Perception and Psychophysics* 56, 613–623.

Holmberg, T. L., K. A. Morgan, and P. K. Kuhl. 1977. Speech perception in early infancy: Discrimination of fricative consonants. Paper presented at the meeting of the Acoustical Society of America, Miami Beach, Fla., December 1977.

Hubel, D. H., and T. N. Wiesel. 1970. The period of susceptibility to the physiological effects of unilateral eye closure in kittens. *Journal of Physiology* 206, 419–436.

Huttenlocher, J. 1974. The origins of language comprehension. In R. L. Solso, ed., *Theories in cognitive psychology*. New York: Wiley.

Huttenlocher, J., W. Haight, A. Bryk, M. Seltzer, and T. Lyons. 1991. Early vocabulary growth: Relation to language input and gender. *Developmental Psychology* 27, 236–248.

Hyams, N. 1986. *Language acquisition and the theory of parameters*. Dordrecht: D. Reidel.

Hyman, L. M. 1977. On the nature of linguistic stress. In L. M. Hyman, ed., *Studies in stress and accent*. Los Angeles: University of Southern California.

Ingram, D. 1974a. Fronting in child phonology. *Journal of Child Language* 1, 233–241.

Ingram, D. 1974b. Phonological rules in young children. *Journal of Child Language* 1, 49–64.

Ingram, D. 1976. *Phonological disability in children*. New York: Elsevier.

Ingram, D. 1978. Phonological patterns in the speech of young children. In P. Fletcher and M. Garman, eds., *Language acquisition: Studies in first language development*. New York: Cambridge University Press.

Ingram, D., L. Christensen, S. Veach, and B. Webster. 1980. The acquisition of word-initial fricatives and affricates in English by children between two and six years. In G. H. Yeni-Komshian, J. F. Kavanagh, and C. A. Ferguson, eds., *Child phonology, I: Production*. New York: Academic Press.

Irwin, O. C. 1947. Infant speech: Consonantal sounds according to place of articulation. *Journal of Speech Disorders* 12, 397–401.

Irwin, O. C., and H. P. Chen. 1947. Infant speech: Vowel and consonant frequency. *Journal of Speech and Hearing Disorders* 13, 123–125.

Jacoby, L. L. 1983. Perceptual enhancement: Persistent effects of an experience. *Journal of Experimental Psychology: Learning, Memory and Cognition* 9, 21–38.

Jacoby, L. L., and M. Dallas. 1981. On the relationship between autobiographical memory and perceptual learning. *Journal of Experimental Psychology: General* 110, 306–340.

Jakobson, R. 1941. *Child language, aphasia and phonological universals*. The Hague: Mouton (English translation 1968).

Jakobson, R. 1971. *Selected writings*. The Hague: Mouton.

Jakobson, R., and L. R. Waugh. 1987. *The sound shape of language*. Berlin: Mouton de Gruyter.

Johnson, M. K., and L. Hasher. 1987. Human learning and memory. *Annual Review of Psychology* 38, 631–668.

Jusczyk, P. W. 1977. Perception of syllable-final stops by two-month-old infants. *Perception and Psychophysics* 21, 450–454.

Jusczyk, P. W. 1985a. The high amplitude sucking procedure as a methodological tool in speech perception research. In G. Gottlieb and N. A. Krasnegor, eds.,

Measurement of audition and vision in the first year of postnatal life: A methodological overview. Norwood, N.J.: Ablex.

Jusczyk, P. W. 1985b. On characterizing the development of speech perception. In J. Mehler and R. Fox, eds., *Neonate cognition: Beyond the blooming, buzzing confusion.* Hillsdale, N.J.: Erlbaum.

Jusczyk, P. W. 1986a. Some further reflections on how speech perception develops. In J. Perkell and D. H. Klatt, eds., *Invariance and variability in speech processes.* Hillsdale, N.J.: Erlbaum.

Jusczyk, P. W. 1986b. Towards a model for the development of speech perception. In J. Perkell and D. H. Klatt, eds., *Invariance and variability in speech processes.* Hillsdale, N.J.: Erlbaum.

Jusczyk, P. W. 1989. Perception of cues to clausal units in native and non-native languages. Paper presented at the biennial meeting of the Society for Research in Child Development, Kansas City, Mo., April 1989.

Jusczyk, P. W. 1992. Developing phonological categories from the speech signal. In C. A. Ferguson, L. Menn, and C. Stoel-Gammon, eds., *Phonological development: Models, research, implications.* Timonium, Md.: York Press.

Jusczyk, P. W. 1993a. From general to language specific capacities: The WRAPSA model of how speech perception develops. *Journal of Phonetics* 21, 3–28.

Jusczyk, P. W. 1993b. Sometimes it pays to look back before you leap ahead. In B. de Boysson-Bardies, S. de Schonen, P. Jusczyk, P. MacNeilage, and J. Morton, eds., *Developmental neurocognition: Speech and face processing in the first year of life.* Dordrecht: Kluwer.

Jusczyk, P. W. 1994. The development of word recognition. Paper presented at the International Conference on Spoken Language Processing, Yokohama, Japan.

Jusczyk, P. W., and R. N. Aslin. 1995. Infants' detection of sound patterns of words in fluent speech. *Cognitive Psychology* 29, 1–23.

Jusczyk, P. W., and J. Bertoncini. 1988. Viewing the development of speech perception as an innately guided learning process. *Language and Speech* 31, 217–238.

Jusczyk, P. W., J. Bertoncini, R. Bijeljac-Babic, L. J. Kennedy, and J. Mehler. 1990. The role of attention in speech perception by infants. *Cognitive Development* 5, 265–286.

Jusczyk, P. W., H. Copan, and E. Thompson. 1978. Perception by two-month-olds of glide contrasts in multisyllabic utterances. *Perception and Psychophysics* 24, 515–520.

Jusczyk, P. W., A. Cutler, and N. Redanz. 1993. Preference for the predominant stress patterns of English words. *Child Development* 64, 675–687.

Jusczyk, P. W., and C. Derrah. 1987. Representation of speech sounds by young infants. *Developmental Psychology* 23, 648–654.

Jusczyk, P. W., A. D. Friederici, J. Wessels, V. Y. Svenkerud, and A. M. Jusczyk. 1993a. Infants' sensitivity to the sound patterns of native language words. *Journal of Memory and Language* 32, 402–420.

Jusczyk, P. W., L. A. Gerken, and E. Turk. A. In preparation. How prosodic and phonotactic patterns interact in infants' perception of native language word patterns.

Jusczyk, P. W., K. Hirsh-Pasek, D. G. Kemler Nelson, L. Kennedy, A. Woodward, and J. Piwoz. 1992. Perception of acoustic correlates of major phrasal units by young infants. *Cognitive Psychology* 24, 252–293.

Jusczyk, P. W., E. A. Hohne, and A. Bauman. In preparation. An investigation of infants' use of allophonic cues to word boundaries in fluent speech contexts.

Jusczyk, P. W., E. A. Hohne, A. M. Jusczyk, and N. J. Redanz. 1993b. Do infants remember voices? *Journal of the Acoustical Society of America* 93, 2373.

Jusczyk, P. W., A. M. Jusczyk, L. J. Kennedy, T. Schomberg, and N. Koenig. 1995. Young infants' retention of information about bisyllabic utterances. *Journal of Experimental Psychology: Human Perception and Performance* 21, 822–836.

Jusczyk, P. W., and D. G. Kemler Nelson. 1996. Syntactic units, prosody, and psychological reality during infancy. In J. L. Morgan and K. Demuth, eds., *Signal to syntax*. Mahwah, N.J.: Erlbaum.

Jusczyk, P. W., L. J. Kennedy, and A. M. Jusczyk. 1995. Young infants' retention of information about syllables. *Infant Behavior and Development* 18, 27–42.

Jusczyk, P. W., and C. L. Krumhansl. 1993. Pitch and rhythmic patterns affecting infants' sensitivity to musical phrase structure. *Journal of Experimental Psychology: Human Perception and Performance* 19, 627–640.

Jusczyk, P. W., P. A. Luce, and J. Charles-Luce. 1994. Infants' sensitivity to phonotactic patterns in the native language. *Journal of Memory and Language* 33, 630–645.

Jusczyk, P. W., R. Mazuka, D. R. Mandel, S. Kiritani, and A. Hayashi. 1993c. A cross-linguistic study of American and Japanese infants' perception of acoustic correlates to clausal units. Paper presented at the biennial Meeting of the Society for Research in Child Development, New Orleans, La., March 1993.

Jusczyk, P. W., M. Newsome, and D. Houston. In preparation. The beginnings of word segmentation in English-learning infants.

Jusczyk, P. W., D. B. Pisoni, and J. Mullennix. 1992. Some consequences of stimulus variability on speech processing by 2-month old infants. *Cognition* 43, 253–291.

Jusczyk, P. W., D. B. Pisoni, M. Reed, A. Fernald, and M. Myers. 1983. Infants' discrimination of the duration of a rapid spectrum change in nonspeech signals. *Science* 222, 175–177.

Jusczyk, P. W., D. B. Pisoni, A. C. Walley, and J. Murray. 1980. Discrimination of the relative onset of two-component tones by infants. *Journal of the Acoustical Society of America* 67, 262–270.

Jusczyk, P. W., B. S. Rosner, J. E. Cutting, F. Foard, and L. B. Smith. 1977. Categorical perception of non-speech sounds by two-month old infants. *Perception and Psychophysics* 21, 50–54.

Jusczyk, P. W., B. S. Rosner, M. Reed, and L. J. Kennedy. 1989. Could temporal order differences underlie 2-month-olds' discrimination of English voicing contrasts? *Journal of the Acoustical Society of America* 85, 1741–1749.

Jusczyk, P. W., and E. J. Thompson. 1978. Perception of a phonetic contrast in multisyllabic utterances by two-month-old infants. *Perception and Psychophysics* 23, 105–109.

Karzon, R. G. 1985. Discrimination of a polysyllabic sequence by one- to four-month-old infants. *Journal of Experimental Child Psychology* 39, 326–342.

Katz, J. J. 1966. *The philosophy of language.* New York: Harper.

Katz, N., E. Baker, and J. Macnamara. 1974. What's in a name? A study of how children learn common and proper nouns. *Child Development* 45, 469–473.

Kelly, M. H. 1992. Using sound to solve syntactic problems: The role of phonology in grammatical category assignments. *Psychological Review* 99, 349–364.

Kelly, M. H., and J. K. Bock. 1988. Stress in time. *Journal of Experimental Psychology: Human Perception and Performance* 14, 389–403.

Kemler Nelson, D. G. 1989. Developmental trends in infants' sensitivity to prosodic cues correlated with linguistic units. Paper presented at the biennial meeting of the Society for Research in Child Development, April, Kansas City.

Kemler Nelson, D. G., K. Hirsh-Pasek, P. W. Jusczyk, and K. Wright-Cassidy. 1989. How prosodic cues in motherese might assist language learning. *Journal of Child Language* 16, 55–68.

Kemler Nelson, D. G., P. W. Jusczyk, D. R. Mandel, J. Myers, A. Turk, and L. A. Gerken. 1995. The headturn preference procedure for testing auditory perception. *Infant Behavior and Development* 18, 111–116.

Kenstowicz, M. 1994. *Phonology in generative grammar.* Cambridge, Mass.: Blackwell.

Kent, R. D. 1992. The developmental biology of phonological acquisition. In C. A. Ferguson, L. Menn, and C. Stoel-Gammon, eds., *Phonological development: Models, research, and implications.* Timonium, Md.: York Press.

Kent, R. D., and G. Miolo. 1995. Phonetic abilities in the first year of life. In P. Fletcher and B. MacWhinney, eds., *Handbook of child language.* Cambridge, Mass.: Basil Blackwell.

Kent, R. D., and A. D. Murray. 1982. Acoustic features of infant vocalic utterances at 3, 6, and 9 months. *Journal of the Acoustical Society of America* 72, 353–365.

Kewley-Port, D. 1983. Time-varying features as correlates of place of articulation in stop consonants 3, Indiana University, Bloomington, Ind., *Research on Speech Perception: Technical Report.*

Kiparsky, P. 1982. From cyclic phonology to lexical phonology. In H. v. d. Hulst and N. Smith, eds., *The structure of phonological representations.* Dordrecht: Foris.

Kiparsky, P., and L. Menn. 1977. On the acquisition of phonology. In J. Macnamara, ed., *Language, learning, and thought.* New York: Academic Press.

Kirsner, K., and J. C. Dunn. 1985. The perceptual record: A common factor in repetition priming and attribute retention? In M. I. Posner and O. M. Marin, eds., *Attention and performance XI.* Hillsdale, N.J.: Erlbaum.

Kirsner, K., J. C. Dunn, and P. Standen. 1987. Record-based word recognition. In M. Coltheart, eds., *Attention and Performance XII: The psychology of reading.* Hillsdale, N.J.: Erlbaum.

Klatt, D. H. 1975. Vowel lengthening is syntactically determined in connected discourse. *Journal of Phonetics* 3, 129–140.

Klatt, D. H. 1976. Linguistic uses of segment duration in English: Acoustic and perceptual evidence. *Journal of the Acoustical Society of America* 59, 1208–1221.

Klatt, D. H. 1979. Speech perception: A model of acoustic-phonetic analysis and lexical access. *Journal of Phonetics* 7, 279–312.

Klatt, D. H. 1989. Review of selected models of speech perception. In W. Marslen-Wilson, ed., *Lexical representation and process.* Cambridge: MIT Press.

Klein, H. 1978. The relationship between perceptual strategies and production strategies in the learning of early lexical items. Indiana University Linguisitics Club.

Klima, E. S., and U. Bellugi. 1979. *The signs of language.* Cambridge, Mass.; Harvard University Press.

Kluender, K. R., R. L. Diehl, and P. R. Killeen. 1987. Japanese quail can learn phonetic categories. *Science* 237, 1195–1197.

Koopmans van Beinum, F. J., and J. M. van der Stelt. 1986. Early stages in the development of speech movements. In B. Lindblom and R. Zetterstrom, eds., *Precursors of early speech.* New York: Stockton.

Krumhansl, C. L., and P. W. Jusczyk. 1990. Infants' perception of phrase structure in music. *Psychological Science* 1, 70–73.

Krumholz, A., J. K. Felix, P. J. Goldstein, and E. McKenzie. 1985. Maturation of the brain-stem auditory evoked potential in premature infants. *Electroencephalography and Clinical Neurophysiology* 62, 124–134.

Kuhl, P. K. 1976. Speech perception in early infancy: The acquisiton of speech sound categories. In S. K. Hirsh, D. H. Eldridge, I. J. Hirsh, and S. R. Silverman, eds., *Hearing and Davis: Essays honoring Hallowell Davis.* St. Louis: Washington University Press.

Kuhl, P. K. 1979. Speech perception in early infancy: Perceptual constancy for spectrally dissimilar vowel categories. *Journal of the Acoustical Society of America* 66, 1668–1679.

Kuhl, P. K. 1981. Discrimination of speech by nonhuman animals: Basic auditory sensitivities conducive to the perception of speech-sound categories. *Journal of the Acoustical Society of America* 70, 340–349.

Kuhl, P. K. 1983. Perception of auditory equivalence classes for speech in early infancy. *Infant Behavior and Development* 6, 263–285.

Kuhl, P. K. 1985. Methods in the study of infant speech perception. In G. Gottlieb and N. A. Krasnegor, eds., *Measurement of audition and vision in the first year of postnatal life.* Norwood, N.J.: Ablex.

Kuhl, P. K. 1991. Human adults and human infants show a "perceptual magnet effect" for the prototypes of speech categories, monkeys do not. *Perception and Psychophysics* 50, 93–107.

Kuhl, P. K. 1993. Innate predispositions and the effects of experience in speech perception: The native language magnet theory. In B. de Boysson-Bardies, S. de Schonen, P. Jusczyk, P. McNeilage, and J. Morton, eds., *Developmental neurocognition: Speech and face processing in the first year of life.* Dordrecht: Kluwer.

Kuhl, P. K., and P. Iverson. 1995. Linguistic experience and the perceptual magnet effect. In W. Strange, ed., *Speech perception and linguistic experience.* Timonium, Md.: York Press.

Kuhl, P. K., and A. N. Meltzoff. 1982. The bimodal perception of speech in infancy. *Science* 218, 1138–1141.

Kuhl, P. K., and A. N. Meltzoff. 1984. The intermodal representation of speech in infants. *Infant Behavior and Development* 7, 361–381.

Kuhl, P. K., and J. D. Miller. 1975. Speech perception by the chinchilla: voiced–voiceless distinction in alveolar plosive consonants. *Science* 190, 69–72.

Kuhl, P. K., and J. D. Miller. 1978. Speech perception by the chinchilla: Identification functions for synthetic VOT stimuli. *Journal of the Acoustical Society of America* 63, 905–917.

Kuhl, P. K., and J. D. Miller. 1982. Discrimination of auditory target dimensions in the presence or absence of variation in a second dimension by infants. *Perception and Psychophysics* 31, 279–292.

Kuhl, P. K., and D. M. Padden. 1982. Enhanced discriminability at the phonetic boundaries for the voicing feature in macaques. *Perception and Psychophysics* 32, 542–550.

Kuhl, P. K., and D. M. Padden. 1983. Enhanced discriminability at the phonetic boundaries for the place feature in macaques. *Journal of the Acoustical Society of America* 73, 1003–1010.

Kuhl, P. K., K. A. Williams, F. Lacerda, K. N. Stevens, and B. Lindblom. 1992. Linguistic experiences alter phonetic perception in infants by 6 months of age. *Science* 255, 606–608.

Labov, W., and T. Labov. 1978. The phonetics of cat and mama. *Language* 54, 816–852.

Lachter, J., and T. G. Bever. 1988. The relation between linguistic structure and associative language learning: A constructive critique of some connectionist learning models. *Cognition* 28, 195–247.

Ladefoged, P. 1975. *A course in phonetics.* New York: Harcourt, Brace, Jovanovich.

Ladefoged, P., and D. E. Broadbent. 1957. Information conveyed by vowels. *Journal of Acoustical Society of America* 29, 98–104.

Ladefoged, P., and D. E. Broadbent. 1960. Perception of sequence in auditory events. *Quarterly Journal of Experimental Psychology* 12, 162–170.

Ladefoged, P., and J. Ladefoged. 1980. The ability of listeners to identify voices, 49, UCLA, *Working Papers in Linguistics.*

Lahiri, A., and W. Marslen-Wilson. 1991. The mental representation of lexical form: A phonological approach to the recognition lexicon. *Cognition* 38, 245–294.

Landau, B., and L. R. Gleitman. 1985. *Language and experience: Evidence from a blind child.* Cambridge, Mass.: Harvard University Press.

Landau, B., and E. Shipley. 1995. Object naming and category boundaries. Paper presented at the Boston University Conference on Language Development. Boston, Mass., November 1995.

Lasky, R. E., A. Syrdal-Lasky, and R. E. Klein. 1975. VOT discrimination by four to six and a half month old infants from Spanish environments. *Journal of Experimental Child Psychology* 20, 215–225.

Lecanuet, J.-P., and C. Granier-Deferre. 1993. Speech stimuli in the fetal environment. In B. de Boysson-Bardies, S. de Schonen, P. Jusczyk, P. MacNeilage, and J. Morton, eds., *Developmental neurocognition: Speech and face processing in the first year of life.* Dordrecht: Kluwer Academic.

Lederer, A., and M. H. Kelly. 1991. Prosodic correlates to the adjunct/complement distinction in motherese. In Papers and Reports on Child Language Development. Vol. 30. Stanford, Calif.

Lederer, A. H., H. Gleitman, and L. R. Gleitman. 1995. The syntactic contexts of maternal verb use. In M. Tomasello and W. Merriman, eds., *Beyond names for things: Young children's acquisition of verbs.* Hillsdale, N.J.: Erlbaum.

Lehiste, I. 1960. *An acoustic-phonetic study of internal open juncture.* New York: S. Karger.

Lehiste, I., J. P. Olive, and L. Streeter. 1976. The role of duration in disambiguating syntactically ambiguous sentences. *Journal of the Acoustical Society of America* 60, 1199–1202.

Lenneberg, E. 1967. *Biological foundations of language.* New York: Wiley.

Leonard, L. B., M. Newhoff, and L. Mesalam. 1980. Individual differences in early child phonology. *Applied Linguistics* 1, 7–30.

Leonard, L. B., L. Rowan, B. Morris, and M. Fey. 1982. Intra-word variability in young children. *Journal of Child Language* 9, 55–70.

Leopold, W. F. 1939. *Speech development of a bilingual child, 1: Vocabulary growth in the first two years.* Evanston: Northwestern University.

Leopold, W. F. 1947. *Speech development of a bilingual child, 2: Sound learning in the first two years.* Evanston: Northwestern University.

Levelt, W. J. M. 1975. *What became of LAD?* Lisse, Netherlands: Peter de Ridder Press.

Levitt, A., P. W. Jusczyk, J. Murray, and G. Carden. 1988. The perception of place of articulation contrasts in voiced and voiceless fricatives by two-month-old infants. *Journal of Experimental Psychology: Human Perception and Performance* 14, 361–368.

Levitt, A. G. 1993. The acquisition of prosody: Evidence from French- and English-learning infants. In B. de Boysson-Bardies, S. de Schonen, P. Jusczyk, P. McNeilage, and J. Morton, eds., *Developmental neurocognition: Speech and face processing in the first year of life.* Dordrecht: Kluwer.

Levitt, A. G., J. Utman, and J. Aydelott. 1992. From babbling towards the sound systems of English and French: A longitudinal two-case study. *Journal of Child Language* 19, 19–49.

Liberman, A. M. 1970. The grammars of speech and language. *Cognitive Psychology* 1, 301–323.

Liberman, A. M. 1996. *Speech: A special code.* Cambridge, Mass.: Bradford Books/MIT Press.

Liberman, A. M., F. S. Cooper, D. P. Shankweiler, and M. G. Studdert-Kennedy. 1967. Perception of the speech code. *Psychological Review* 74, 431–461.

Liberman, A. M., P. C. Delattre, L. J. Gerstman, and F. S. Cooper. 1956. Tempo of frequency change as a cue for distinguishing classes of speech sounds. *Journal of Experimental Psychology* 52, 127–137.

Liberman, A. M., P. D. DeLattre, and F. S. Cooper. 1952. The role of selected stimulus variables in the perception of unvoiced stop consonants. *American Journal of Psychology* 65, 497–516.

Liberman, A. M., P. D. Delattre, and F. S. Cooper. 1958. Some cues for the distinction between voiced and unvoiced stops in initial position. *Language and Speech* 1, 153–167.

Liberman, A. M., K. S. Harris, J. A. Kinney, and H. L. Lane. 1961. The discrimination of relative-onset time of the components of certain speech and non-speech patterns. *Journal of Experimental Psychology* 61, 379–388.

Liberman, A. M., D. Isenberg, and B. Rakerd. 1981. Duplex perception of cues for stop consonants: Evidence for a phonetic mode. *Perception and Psychophysics* 30, 133–143.

Liberman, A. M., and I. G. Mattingly. 1985. The motor theory of speech perception revised. *Cognition* 21, 1–36.

Liberman, A. M., and M. G. Studdert-Kennedy. 1978. Phonetic perception. In R. Held, H. Leibowitz, and H. L. Teuber, eds., *Handbook of sensory physiology: Perception.* Berlin: Springer-Verlag.

Lieberman, P. 1961. Perturbations in vocal pitch. *Journal of the Acoustical Society of America* 33, 597–603.

Lieberman, P. 1963. Some effects of semantic and grammatical context on the production and perception of speech. *Language and Speech* 6, 172–179.

Lieberman, P. 1965. On the acoustic basis of the perception of intonation by linguists. *Word* 21, 40–54.

Lieberman, P. 1977. *Speech physiology and acoustic phonetics.* New York: Macmillan.

Lieberman, P. 1984. *The biology and evolution of language.* Cambridge, Mass.: Harvard University Press.

Lieberman, P., E. S. Crelin, and D. H. Klatt. 1972. Phonetic ability and related anatomy of the newborn and adult human, Neanderthal man, and the chimpanzee. *American Anthropologist* 74, 287–307.

Light, L. L., C. Stansbury, C. Rubin, and S. Linde. 1973. Memory for the modality of presentation: Within-modality discrimination. *Memory and Cognition* 1, 395–400.

Lightfoot, D. 1989. The child's trigger experience: Degree-0 learnability. *Behavioral and Brain Sciences* 12, 321, 375.

Lindblom, B. 1986. On the origin and purpose of discreteness and invariance in sound patterns. In J. Perkell and D. H. Klatt, eds., *Invariance and variability in speech processes.* Hillsdale, N.J.: Erlbaum.

Lindblom, B. 1992. Phonological units as adaptive emergents of lexical development. In C. A. Ferguson, L. Menn, and C. Stoel-Gammon, eds., *Phonological development: Models, research, implications.* Timonium, Md.: York Press.

Lindblom, B., P. MacNeilage, and M. Studdert-Kennedy. 1983. Self-organizing processes and the explanation of phonological universals. In B. Butterworth, B. Comrie, and O. Dahl, eds., *Explanations of linguistic universals.* The Hague: Mouton Press.

Lisker, L. 1975. Is it VOT or a first-formant transition detector? *Journal of the Acoustical Society of America* 57, 1547–1551.

Lisker, L. 1986. "Voicing" in English: A catalog of acoustic features signalling /b/ versus /p/ in trochees. *Language and Speech* 29, 3–11.

Lisker, L., and A. S. Abramson. 1964. A cross language study of voicing in initial stops: Acoustical measurements. *Word* 20, 384–422.

Lisker, L., and A. S. Abramson. 1967. The voicing dimension: some experiments in comparative phonetics. Paper presented at the International Congress of Phonetic Sciences, Prague.

Lisker, L., A. M. Liberman, D. M. Erickson, D. Dechovitz, and R. Mandler. 1977. On pushing the voice-onset-time (VOT) boundary about. *Language and Speech* 20, 209–220.

Lively, S., and D. B. Pisoni. 1993. An examination of the "perceptual magnet" effect. *Journal of the Acoustical Society of America* 93, 2423.

Locke, J. L. 1983. *Phonological acquisition and change.* New York: Academic Press.

Locke, J. L. 1988. The sound shape of early lexical representations. In M. D. Smith and J. L. Locke, eds., *The emergent lexicon: The child's development of a linguistic vocabulary.* San Diego, Calif.: Academic Press.

Logan, G. D. 1988. Toward an instance theory of automatization. *Psychological Review* 95, 492–527.

Logan, J. S. 1992. A computational analysis of young children's lexicons. *Research on Spoken Language Processing: Technical Report* 8, Indiana University.

Logan, J. S., S. E. Lively, and D. B. Pisoni. 1989. Training Japanese listeners to identify /r/ and /l/. *Journal of the Acoustical Society of America* 85, 137–138.

Luce, P. A., and J. Charles-Luce. 1983. Contextual effects on the consonant/vowel ratio in speech production. Paper presented at the meeting of the Acoustical Society of America, Cincinnati, May 1983.

Luce, P. A., E. A. Lyons, and J. Myers. 1994. The abstractness and specificity of lexical representations in memory: Implications for models of spoken word recognition. In *Proceedings of the 1994 International Conference on Spoken Language Processing* (Addendum). Yokohama: Acoustical Society of Japan.

Luce, P. A., D. B. Pisoni, and S. D. Goldinger. 1990. Similarity neighborhoods of spoken words. In G. T. M. Altman, ed., *Cognitive models of speech perception: Psycholinguistic and computational perspectives.* Cambridge, Mass.: MIT Press.

MacKain, K., M. Studdert-Kennedy, S. Spieker, and D. Stern. 1983. Infant intermodal speech perception is a left-hemisphere function. *Science* 219, 1347–1349.

MacKain, K. S. 1982. Assessing the role of experience on infants' speech discrimination. *Journal of Child Language* 9, 527–542.

Macken, M. A. 1978. Permitted complexity in phonological development: One child's acquisition of Spanish consonants. *Lingua* 44, 219–253.

Macken, M. A. 1979. Developmental reorganization of phonology: A hierarchy of basic units of acquisition. *Lingua* 49, 11–49.

Macken, M. A. 1980a. Aspects of the acquisition of stop systems: A cross linguistic perspective. In G. H. Yeni-Komshian, J. F. Kavanagh, and C. A. Ferguson, eds., *Child Phonology* New York: Academic Press.

Macken, M. A. 1980b. The child's lexical representation: The "puzzle–puddle–pickle" evidence. *Journal of Linguistics* 16, 1–19.

Macken, M. A., and D. Barton. 1980. The acquisition of the voicing contrast in English: A study of voice onset time in word-initial stop consonants. *Journal of Child Language* 7, 41–74.

Macnamara, J. 1972. Cognitive basis of language learning in infants. *Psychological Review* 79, 1–13.

Macnamara, J. 1982. *Names for things: a study of child language.* Cambridge, Mass.: Bradford Books/MIT Press.

MacNeilage, P. F., and B. L. Davis. 1990. Acquisition of speech production: The achievement of segmental independence. In W. J. Hardcastle and A. Marchal, eds., *Speech production and speech modelling.* Dordrecht: Kluwer.

MacNeilage, P. F., and B. L. Davis. 1991. Vowel–consonant relations in babbling. Paper presented at the International Congress of Phonetic Sciences, Aix-en-Provence, France.

MacWhinney. 1987. The competition model. In B. MacWhinney, ed., *The mechanisms of language acquisition.* Hillsdale, N.J.: Erlbaum.

MacWhinney, B. 1991. *The CHILDES project: Tools for analyzing talk.* Hillsdale, N.J.: Erlbaum.

MacWhinney, B., and J. Leinbach. 1991. Implementations are not conceptualizations: Revising the verb learning model. *Cognition* 40, 121–157.

Mandel, D. R., P. W. Jusczyk, and D. G. Kemler Nelson. 1994. Does sentential prosody help infants to organize and remember speech information? *Cognition* 53, 155–180.

Mandel, D. R., P. W. Jusczyk, and R. Mazuka. 1992. Perception of Japanese clauses by American $4\frac{1}{2}$ month olds. Paper presented at Workshop on cross-language speech perception, Tampa, Fla.

Mandel, D. R., P. W. Jusczyk, and D. B. Pisoni. 1995. Infants' recognition of the sound patterns of their own names. *Psychological Science* 6, 315–318.

Mandel, D. R., D. G. Kemler Nelson, and P. W. Jusczyk. 1996. Infants remember the order of words in a spoken sentence. *Cognitive Development.*

Mann, V. A. 1980. Influence of preceding liquid on stop-consonant perception. *Perception and Psychophysics* 28, 407–412.

Manzini, M. R., and K. Wexler. 1987. Parameters, binding theory, and learnability. *Linguistic Inquiry* 18, 413–444.

Marcus, G. F. 1995. The acquisition of the English past tense in children and multilayered connectionist networks. *Cognition* 56, 271–279.

Marcus, G. F., S. Pinker, M. Ullman, M. Hollander, T. J. Rosen, and F. Xu. 1992. Overregularization in language acquisition. *Monographs of the Society for Research in Child Development,* Serial No. 228 57, No. 4.

Marcus, S. M. 1984. Recognizing speech: On the mapping from sound to word. In H. Bouma and D. G. Bouwhuis, eds., *Attention and Performance: Control of language processes.* Hillsdale, N.J.: Erlbaum.

Markman, E. M. 1989. *Categorization and naming in children.* Cambridge, Mass.: MIT Press.

Markman, E. M. 1991. The whole-object, taxonomic, and mutual exclusivity assumptions as initial constraints on word meanings. In S. A. Gelman and J. P. Byrnes, eds., *Perspectives on language and thought.* Cambridge: Cambridge University Press.

Markman, E. M., and J. E. Hutchinson. 1984. Children's sensitivity to constraints on word meaning: Taxonomic vs. thematic relations. *Cognitive Psychology* 20, 121–157.

Marks, L., and G. A. Miller. 1964. The role of semantic and syntactic constraints in the memorization of English sentences. *Journal of Verbal Learning and Verbal Behavior* 3, 1–5.

Marler, P. 1990. Innate learning preferences: Signals for communication. *Developmental Psychobiology* 23, 557–569.

Marler, P., ed. 1991. *The instinct to learn.* Hillsdale, N.J.: Erlbaum.

Marler, P., and S. Peters. 1981. Birdsong and speech: Evidence for special processing. In P. D. Eimas and J. L. Miller, eds., *Perspectives on the Study of speech.* Hillsdale, N.J.: Erlbaum.

Marslen-Wilson, W. 1994. Speech perception as a cognitive process: The role of abstractness and inference. In *Proceedings of the 1994 International Conference on Spoken Language Processing* (Addendum). Yokohama: Acoustical Society of Japan.

Marslen-Wilson, W., and P. Warren. 1994. Levels of perceptual representation and process in lexical access: Words, phonemes, and features. *Psychological Review* 101, 653–675.

Marslen-Wilson, W., and A. Welsh. 1978. Processing interactions and lexical access during word recognition in continuous speech. *Cognitive Psychology* 10, 29–63.

Martin, C. S., J. W. Mullennix, D. B. Pisoni, and W. V. Summers. 1989. Effects of talker variability on recall of spoken word lists. *Journal of Experimental Psychology Learning, Memory, and Cognition* 15, 676–684.

Martin, J. G. 1970. On judging pauses in simultaneous speech. *Journal of Verbal Learning and Verbal Behavior* 9, 75–78.

Matthei, E. H. 1989. Crossing boundaries: More evidence for phonological constraints on early multi-word utterances. *Journal of Child Language* 16, 41–54.

Mattingly, I. G., A. M. Liberman, A. K. Syrdal, and T. Halwes. 1971. Discrimination in speech and non-speech modes. *Cognitive Psychology* 2, 131–157.

Mayberry, R., and S. Fisher. 1989. Looking through phonological shape to lexical meaning: The bottleneck of non-native sign language processing. *Memory and Cognition* 17, 740–754.

Mazuka, R. 1996. Can a parameter be set before the first word? Prosodic contributions to early setting of a grammatical parameter. In J. L. Morgan and K. Demuth, eds., *Signal to syntax.* Mahwah, N.J.: Erlbaum.

McClelland, J. L., and J. L. Elman. 1986. The TRACE model of speech perception. *Cognitive Psychology* 18, 1–86.

McGhee, F. 1937. The reliability of the identification of the human voice. *Journal of General Psychology* 17, 249–271.

McNeill, D. 1966. Developmental psycholinguistics. In F. Smith and G. A. Miller, eds., *The genesis of language.* Cambridge, Mass.: MIT Press.

Medin, D. L., and M. M. Shaffer. 1978. Context theory of classification learning. *Psycholgical Review* 85, 207–238.

Mehler, J. 1981. The role of syllables in speech processing: Infant and adult data. *Philosophical Transactions of the Royal Society (London)* B295, 333–352.

Mehler, J., J. Y. Dommergues, U. Frauenfelder, and J. Segui. 1981. The syllable's role in speech segmentation. *Journal of Verbal Learning and Verbal Behavior* 20, 298–305.

Mehler, J., E. Dupoux, T. Nazzi, and G. Dehaene-Lambertz. 1996. Coping with linguistic diversity: The infant's point of view. In J. L. Morgan and K. Demuth, eds., *Signal to syntax.* Mahwah, N.J.: Erlbaum.

Mehler, J., E. Dupoux, and J. Segui. 1990. Constraining models of lexical access: The onset of word recognition. In G. T. M. Altmann, ed., *Cognitive models of speech processing.* Hillsdale, N.J.: Erlbaum.

Mehler, J., P. W. Jusczyk, G. Lambertz, N. Halsted, J. Bertoncini, and C. Amiel-Tison. 1988. A precursor of language acquisition in young infants. *Cognition* 29, 144–178.

Menn, L. 1976. Pattern, control and contrast in beginning speech: A case study of word form and word function. Ph.D. dissertation, University of Illinois.

Menn, L. 1978. Phonological units in beginning speech. In J. B. Hooper, eds., *Syllables and segments.* Amsterdam: North Holland.

Menn, L. 1980. Phonological theory and child phonology. In G. H. Yeni-Komshian, J. F. Kavanagh, and C. A. Ferguson, eds., *Child phonology, vol. 1: Production.* New York: Academic Press.

Menn, L. 1983. Development of articulatory, phonetic, and phonological capabilities. In B. Butterworth, ed., *Language production.* New York: Academic Press.

Menn, L. and E. Matthei. 1992. The "two-lexicon" account of child phonology: Looking back and looking ahead. In C. A. Ferguson, L. Menn, and C. Stoel-Gammon, eds., *Phonological development: Models, research, implications.* Timonium, Md.: York Press.

Menyuk, P., and L. Menn. 1979. Early strategies for the perception and production of words and sounds. In P. Fletcher and M. Garman, eds., *Studies in language acquisition.* Cambridge: Cambridge University Press.

Mervis, C. B. 1989. Child-basic object categories and lexical development. In U. Neisser, ed., *Concepts and conceptual development: Ecological and intellectual factors in categorization.* Cambridge: Cambridge University Press.

Miller, C. L., B. A. Younger, and P. A. Morse. 1982. Categorization of male and female voices in infancy. *Infant Behavior and Development* 5, 143–159.

Miller, G. A. 1956. The magical number seven, plus or minus two: Some limits on our capacity for processing information. *Psychological Review* 63, 81–96.

Miller, G. A., and S. Isard. 1963. Some perceptual consequences of linguistic rules. *Journal of Verbal Learning and Verbal Behavior* 2, 217–228.

Miller, J. D., C. C. Weir, L. Pastore, W. J. Kelly, and R. J. Dooling. 1976. Discrimination and labeling of noise-buzz sequences with varying noise-lead times: An example of categorical perception. *Journal of the Acoustical Society of America* 60, 410–417.

Miller, J. L., C. M. Connine, T. Schermer, and K. R. Kluender. 1983. A possible auditory basis for internal structure of phonetic categories. *Journal of the Acoustical Society of America* 73, 2124–2133.

Miller, J. L., and P. D. Eimas. 1979. Organization in infant speech perception. *Canadian Journal of Psychology* 33, 353–367.

Miller, J. L., and P. D. Eimas. 1983. Studies on the categorization of speech by infants. *Cognition* 13, 135–165.

Miller, J. L., and A. M. Liberman. 1979. Some effects of later-occurring information on the perception of stop consonant and semivowel. *Perception and Psychophysics* 25, 457–465.

Mills, C. B. 1980. Effects of the match between listener expectancies and coarticulatory cues on the perception of speech. *Journal of Experimental Psychology: Human Perception and Performance* 6, 528–535.

Mitchell, D. E. 1981. Sensitive periods in visual development. In R. N. Aslin, J. R. Alberts, and M. R. Petersen, eds., *Development of perception: Psychobiological perspectives. Vol. 2: The visual system.* New York: Academic.

Miyawaki, K., W. Strange, R. Verbrugge, A. M. Liberman, J. J. Jenkins, and O. Fujimura. 1975. An effect of linguistic experience: The discrimination of /r/ and /l/ by native speakers of Japanese and English. *Perception and Psychophysics* 18, 331–340.

Moffitt, A. R. 1971. Consonant cue perception by twenty-to-twenty-four-week old infants. *Child Development* 42, 717–731.

Mohanon, K. P. 1986. *Lexical phonology.* Dordrecht: Reidel.

Moon, C., R. P. Cooper, and W. P. Fifer. 1993. Two-day old infants prefer their native language. *Infant Behavior and Development* 16, 495–500.

Moore, J. M., G. Thompson, and M. Thompson. 1975. Auditory localization in infants as a function of reinforcement conditions. *Journal of Speech and Hearing Disorders* 40, 29–34.

Moore, J. M., W. R. Wilson, and G. Thompson. 1977. Visual reinforcement of head-turn responses in infants under 12 months of age. *Journal of Speech and Hearing Disorders* 42, 328–334.

Morgan, J. L. 1986. *From simple input to complex grammar.* Cambridge, Mass.: MIT Press.

Morgan, J. L. 1990. Input, innateness, and induction in language acquisition. *Developmental Psychobiology* 23, 661–678.

Morgan, J. L. 1994. Converging measures of speech segmentation in prelingual infants. *Infant Behavior and Development* 17, 387–400.

Morgan, J. L. In press. A rhythmic bias in preverbal speech segmentation. *Journal of Memory and Language.*

Morgan, J. L., P. Allopenna, and R. Shi. 1996. Perceptual bases of rudimentary grammatical categories: Toward a broader conception of bootstrapping. In J. L. Morgan and K. Demuth, eds., *Signal to syntax.* Mahwah, N.J.: Erlbaum.

Morgan, J. L., and K. Demuth, ed. 1996. *Signal to syntax.* Mahwah, N.J.: Erlbaum.

Morgan, J. L., R. P. Meier, and E. L. Newport. 1987. Structural packaging in the input to language learning: Contributions of prosodic and morphological marking of phrases to the acquisition of language? *Cognitive Psychology* 19, 498–550.

Morgan, J. L., R. P. Meier, and E. L. Newport. 1989. Facilitating the acquisition of syntax with transformational cues to phrase structure. *Journal of Memory and Language* 28, 360–374.

Morgan, J. L., and J. R. Saffran. 1995. Emerging integration of sequential and suprasegmental information in preverbal speech segmentation. *Child Development* 66, 911–936.

Morgan, J. L., D. Swingley, and K. Miritai. 1993. Infants listen longer to speech with extraneous noises inserted at clause boundaries. Paper presented at the biennial Meeting of the Society for Research in Child Development, New Orleans, La., March 1993.

Morse, P. A. 1972. The discrimination of speech and nonspeech stimuli in early infancy. *Journal of Experimental Child Psychology* 13, 477–492.

Morse, P. A., and C. T. Snowdon. 1975. An investigation of categorical speech discrimination by rhesus monkeys. *Perception and Psychophysics* 17, 9–16.

Morton, J. 1969. The interaction of information in word recognition. *Psychological Review* 76, 165–178.

Moskowitz, A. 1970. The two-year-old stage in the acquisition of English phonology. *Language* 46, 426–441.

Mullennix, J. W., D. B. Pisoni, and C. S. Martin. 1989. Some effects of talker variability on spoken word recognition. *Journal of the Acoustical Society of America* 85, 365–378.

Murdock, B. B. J. 1982. A theory of storage and retrieval of item and associative information. *Psychological Review* 89, 609–626.

Myers, J., P. W. Jusczyk, D. G. Kemler Nelson, J. Charles Luce, A. Woodward, and K. Hirsh-Pasek. 1996. Infants' sensitivity to word boundaries in fluent speech. *Journal of Child Language* 23, 1–30.

Naigles, L. 1990. Children use syntax to learn verb meanings. *Journal of Child Language* 17, 357–374.

Naigles, L., H. Gleitman, and L. R. Gleitman. 1993. Children acquire word meaning components from syntactic evidence. In E. Dromi, ed., *Language and development*. Norwood, N.J.: Ablex.

Naigles, L., and E. Kako. 1993. First contact: Biases in verb learning with and without syntactic information. *Child Development* 64, 1665–1687.

Nakatani, L., and K. Dukes. 1977. Locus of segmental cues for word juncture. *Journal of the Acoustical Society of America* 62, 714–719.

Nelson, K. 1988. Constraints on word learning? *Cognitive Development* 3, 221–246.

Nespor, M., and I. Vogel. 1986. *Prosodic phonology*. Dordrecht: Foris.

Newman, R. S., and P. W. Jusczyk. In press. The cocktail party effect in infants. *Perception and Psychophysics*.

Newport, E. 1988. Constraints on learning and their role in language acquisition: Studies of the acquisition of American Sign Language. *Language Sciences* 10, 147–172.

Newport, E. 1990. Maturational constraints on language learning. *Cognitive Science* 14, 11–28.

Newport, E. 1991. Contrasting conceptions of the critical period for language. In S. Carey and R. Gelman, eds., *The epigenesis of mind: Essays on biology and cognition*. Hillsdale, N.J.: Erlbaum.

Newport, E., H. Gleitman, and L. Gleitman. 1977. Mother, I'd rather do it myself: Some effects and non-effects of maternal speech style. In C. E. Snow and C. A. Ferguson, eds., *Talking to children: Language input and acquisition*. Cambridge: Cambridge University Press.

Newport, E. and R. Meier. 1986. The acquisition of American Sign Language. In D. Slobin, ed., *The cross-linguistic study of language acquisition*. Hillsdale Meier, N.J.: Erlbaum.

Newsome, M., and P. W. Jusczyk. 1995. Do infants use stress as a cue for segmenting fluent speech? In D. MacLaughlin and S. McEwen, ed., *19th Annual Boston University Conference on Language Development,* 2. Somerville, Mass.: Cascadilla Press.

Nolfi, S., J. L. Elman, and D. Parisi. In press. Learning and evolution in neural networks. *Adaptive Behavior*.

Norris, D., and A. Cutler. 1988. The relative accessibility of phonemes and syllables. *Perception and Psychophysics* 43, 541–550.

Nosofsky, R. M. 1986. Attention, similarity, and the identification-categorization relationship. *Journal of Experimental Psychology: General* 115, 39–57.

Nosofsky, R. M. 1987. Attention and learning processes in the identification and categorization of integral stimuli. *Journal of Experimental Psychology: Learning, Memory and Cognition* 14, 700–708.

Nosofsky, R. M. 1988. Similarity, frequency, and category representations. *Journal of Experimental Psychology: Learning, Memory and Cognition* 14, 54–65.

Nosofsky, R. M. 1991. Tests of an exemplar model for relating perceptual classi-fication and recognition memory. *Journal of Experimental Psychology: Human Perception and Performance* 17, 3–27.

Nosofsky, R. M., S. E. Clark, and H. J. Shin. 1989. Rules and exemplars in cat-egorization, identification and recognition. *Journal of Experimental Psychology: Learning, Memory and Cognition* 15, 282–304.

Nozza, R. J., S. L. Miller, R. N. F. Rossman, and L. C. Bond. 1991. Reliability and validity of infant-speech discrimination-in-noise thresholds. *Journal of Speech and Hearing Research* 34, 643–650.

Nozza, R. J., R. N. F. Rossman, L. C. Bond, and S. L. Miller. 1990. Infant speech sound discrimination in noise. *Journal of the Acoustical Society of America* 87, 339–350.

Nozza, R. J., E. F. Wagner, and M. A. Crandell. 1988. Binaural release from masking for a speech sound in infants, preschool children, and adults. *Journal of Speech and Hearing Research* 31, 212–218.

Nozza, R. J., and W. R. Wilson. 1984. Masked and unmasked pure-tone thresh-olds of infants and adults. *Journal of Speech and Hearing Research* 27, 613–622.

Nusbaum, H. C., and T. M. Morin. 1992. Paying attention to differences among talkers. In Y. Tohkura, E. Vatikiotis-Bateson, and Y. Sagisaka, eds., *Speech per-ception, production, and linguistic structure.* Tokyo: IOS Press.

Nusbaum, H. C., E. C. Schwab, and J. R. Sawusch. 1983. The role of the "chirp" identification in duplex perception. *Perception and Psychophysics* 33, 323–332.

Oden, G. C., and D. W. Massaro. 1978. Integration of featural information in speech perception. *Psychological Review* 85, 172–191.

Oller, D. K. 1980. The emergence of speech sounds in infancy. In G. H. Yeni-Komshian, J. F. Kavanagh, and C. A. Ferguson, eds., *Child phonology.* New York: Academic.

Oller, D. K., and R. E. Eilers. 1988. The role of audition in infant babbling. *Child Development* 59, 441–449.

Olmsted, D. L. 1971. *Out of the mouths of babes: Earliest stages in language learning.* The Hague: Mouton.

Olney, R. K., and E. K. Scholnick. 1974. Adult judgments of age and linguistic differences in infant vocalization. *Journal of Child Language* 3, 145–155.

Osgood, C. E., and R. Hoosain. 1974. Salience of the word as a unit in the per-ception of language. *Perception and Psychophysics* 15, 168–192.

Osherson, D. N., M. Stob, and S. Weinstein. 1986. *Systems that learn.* Cambridge, Mass.: MIT Press.

Osherson, D. N., and T. Wasow. 1976. Task-specificity and species-specificity in the study of language: A methodological note. *Cognition* 4, 203–214.

Otake, T., G. Hatano, A. Cutler, and J. Mehler. 1993. Mora or syllable? Speech segmentation in Japanese. *Journal of Memory and Language* 32, 258–278.

Packwood, J., and B. Gordon. 1975. Stereopsis in normal domestic cat, Siamese cat, and cat raised with alternating monocular occlusion. *Journal of Neurophysiology* 38, 1485–1499.

Palmeri, T. J., S. D. Goldinger, and D. B. Pisoni. 1993. Episodic encoding of voice attributes and recognition memory for spoken words. *Journal of Experimental Psychology: Learning, Memory, and Cognition* 19, 309–328.

Papcun, G., J. Kreiman, and A. Davis. 1989. Long-term memory for unfamiliar voices. *Journal of the Acoustical Society of America* 85, 913–925.

Papousek, M., H. Papousek, and M. Haekel. 1987. Didactic adjustments in fathers' and mothers' speech to their three-month-old infants. *Journal of Psycholinguistic Research* 16, 491–516.

Pasman, R. L., R. Näätman, and K. Alho. 1991. Auditory evoked responses in prematures. *Infant Behavior and Development* 14, 129–135.

Pastore, R. E., W. A. Ahroon, K. A. Buffuto, C. J. Friedman, J. S. Puleo, and E. A. Fink. 1977. Common factor model of categorical perception. *Journal of Experimental Psychology: Human Perception and Performance* 4, 686–696.

Pegg, J. E. 1995. Adult and infant perception of an English phonetic distinction. Ph.D. dissertation, University of British Columbia, Vancouver.

Peters, A. 1983. *The units of language acquisition.* Cambridge, England: Cambridge University Press.

Peters, A. In press. Language typology, individual differences and the acquisition of grammatical morphemes. In D. Slobin, ed., *Cross-linguistic perspectives in language acquisition, Vol. 4.* Hillsdale, N.J.: Erlbaum.

Peters, A., and L. Menn. 1993. False starts and filler syllables: Ways to learn grammatical morphemes. *Language* 69, 742–747.

Peters, A. M. 1977. Language learning strategies: Does the whole equal the sum of the parts? *Language* 53, 560–573.

Peters, A. M. 1985. Language segmentation: Operating principles for the perception and analysis of language. In D. I. Slobin, eds., *The cross-linguistic study of language acquisition, Vol. 2, Theoretical Issues.* Hillsdale, N.J.: Erlbaum.

Peterson, G. E., and H. L. Barney. 1952. Control methods used in a study of the vowels. *Journal of the Acoustical Society of America* 24, 175–184.

Petitto, L. A. 1993. On the ontogenetic requirements for early language acquisition. In B. de Boysson-Bardies, S. de Schonen, P. Jusczyk, P. MacNeilage, and J. Morton, eds., *Developmental neurocognition: Speech and face processing in the first year of life.* Dordrecht: Kluwer.

Petitto, L. A., and P. F. Marentette. 1991. Babbling in the manual mode: Evidence for the ontogeny of language. *Science* 251, 1493–1496.

Pierce, J. E., and I. V. Hanna. 1974. *The development of a phonological system in English speaking American children.* Portland Ore.: HaPi Press.

Pike, R. 1984. Comparison of convolution and matrix distributed memory systems for associative recall and recognition. *Psychological Review* 91, 281–294.

Pilon, R. 1981. Segmentation of speech in a foreign language. *Journal of Psycholinguistic Research* 10, 113–121.

Pinker, S. 1982. A theory of acquisition of lexical-interpretive grammars. In J. W. Bresnan, ed., *The mental representation of grammatical relations.* Cambridge, Mass.: MIT Press.

Pinker, S. 1984. *Language learnability and language development.* Cambridge, Mass.: Harvard University Press.

Pinker, S. 1987. The bootstrapping problem in language acquisition. In B. MacWhinney, ed., *Mechanisms of language acquisition.* Hillsdale, N.J.: Erlbaum.

Pinker, S. 1989. *Learnability and cognition.* Cambridge, Mass.: MIT Press.

Pinker, S. 1994. How could a child use verb syntax to learn verb semantics? *Lingua* 93, 377–410.

Pinker, S., and A. Prince. 1988. On language and connectionism: Analysis of a parallel distributed processing model of language acquisition. *Cognition* 28, 73–192.

Pisoni, D. B. 1971. On the nature of categorization of speech sounds, SR–27, Haskins Laboratories, New Haven, Conn., *Supplement to Status Report on Speech Research.*

Pisoni, D. B. 1973. Auditory and phonetic memory codes in the discrimination of consonants and vowels. *Perception and Psychophysics* 13, 253–260.

Pisoni, D. B. 1977. Identification and discrimination of the relative onset of two component tones: Implications for voicing perception in stops. *Journal of the Acoustical Society of America* 61, 1352–1361.

Pisoni, D. B., T. D. Carrell, and S. J. Gans. 1983. Perception of the duration of rapid spectrum changes: Evidence for context effects with speech and nonspeech signals. *Perception and Psychophysics* 34, 314–322.

Pisoni, D. B., and J. Tash. 1974. Reaction times to comparisons within and across phonetic categories. *Perception and Psychophysics* 15, 285–290.

Plomp, R., and A. M. Mimpen. 1979. Speech-reception threshold for sentences as a function of age and noise. *Journal of the Acoustical Society of America* 66, 1333–1342.

Plunkett, K. 1993. Lexical segmentation and vocabulary growth in early language acquisition. *Journal of Child Language* 20, 43–60.

Plunkett, K. 1995. Connectionist approaches to language acquisition. In P. Fletcher and B. MacWhinney, eds., *The handbook of child language.* Cambridge, Mass.: Basil Blackwell, Inc.

Plunkett, K., and V. Marchman. 1991. U-shaped learning and frequency effects in a multi-layered perceptron: Implications for child language acquisition. *Cognition* 38, 43–102.

Plunkett, K., and V. Marchman. 1993. From rote learning to system building: Acquiring verb morphology in children and connectionist nets. *Cognition* 48, 21–69.

Plunkett, K., and C. Sinha. 1992. Connectionism and developmental theory. *British Journal of Developmental Psychology* 10, 209–254.

Poizner, H., E. S. Klima, and U. Bellugi. 1987. *What the hands reveal about the brain* Cambridge, Mass.: Bradford Books/MIT Press.

Polka, L. 1991. Cross-language speech perception in adults: phonemic, phonetic, and acoustic contributions. *Journal of the Acoustical Society of America* 89, 2961–2977.

Polka, L., P. W. Jusczyk, and S. Rvachew. 1995. Methods for studying speech perception in infants and children. In W. Strange, ed., *Speech perception and linguistic experience: Theoretical and methodological issues in cross-language speech research.* Timonium, Md.: York Press.

Polka, L., and J. F. Werker. 1994. Developmental changes in perception of non-native vowel contrasts. *Journal of Experimental Psychology: Human Perception and Performance* 20, 421–435.

Pollack, I. 1952. The information in elementary auditory displays. *Journal of the Acoustical Society of America* 24, 745–749.

Pollack, I., and J. M. Pickett. 1964. The intelligibility of excerpts from conversation. *Language and Speech* 6, 161–171.

Potter, M. C., and B. A. Faulconer. 1979. Understanding noun phrases. *Journal of Verbal Learning and Verbal Behavior* 18, 509–521.

Price, P. J., M. Ostendorf, S. Shattuck-Hufnagel, and C. Fong. 1991. The use of prosody in syntactic disambiguation. *Journal of the Acoustical Society of America* 90, 2956–2970.

Priestly, T. M. S. 1976. One idiosyncratic strategy in the acquistion of phonology. *Journal of Child Language* 4, 45–66.

Pujol, R., and A. Uziel. 1986. Auditory development: Peripheral aspects. In P. F. Timiras and E. Meisami, eds., *Handbook of human biologic development.* Boca Raton, Fla.: C. R. C. Press.

Pye, C. 1983. Mayan telegraphese: Intonational determinants of inflectional development in Quiché Mayan. *Language* 59, 583–604.

Read, C., and P. Schreiber. 1982. Why short subjects are hard to find. In E. Wanner and L. R. Gleitman, eds., *Language acquisition: The state of the art.* Cambridge: Cambridge University Press.

Reddy, R. 1976. Speech recognition by machine: A review. *Proceedings of the IEEE* 64, 501–531.

Reitveld, A. C. M. 1988. Woordklemtoon inn spraak. In M. P. R. v. d. Broeke, eds., *Ter spraake.* Dordrecht: Foris.

Reitveld, A. C. M., and F. J. Koopmans-van Beinum. 1987. Vowel reduction and stress. *Speech communication* 6, 217–229.

Remez, R. E., J. M. Fellowes, and P. E. Rubin. In press. Voice identification based on phonetic information. *Journal of Experimental Psychology: Human Perception and Performance.*

Remez, R. E., P. E. Rubin, S. M. Burns, J. S. Pardo, and J. M. Lang. 1994. On the perceptual organization of speech. *Psychological Review* 101, 129–156.

Remez, R. E., P. E. Rubin, L. C. Nygaard, and W. A. Howell. 1987. Perceptual normalization of vowels produced by sinusoidal voices. *Journal of Experimental Psychology: Human Perception and Performance* 13, 40–61.

Remez, R. E., P. E. Rubin, D. B. Pisoni, and T. D. Carrell. 1981. Speech perception without traditional cues. *Science* 212, 947–950.

Repp, B. H. 1982. Phonetic trading relations and context effects: New experimental evidence for a speech mode of perception. *Psychological Bulletin* 92, 81–110.

Rosen, S. M., and P. Howell. 1981. Plucks and bows are not categorically perceived. *Perception and Psychophysics* 30, 156–168.

Roth, E. M., and E. J. Schoben. 1983. The effect of context on the structure of categories. *Cognitive Psychology* 15, 346–378.

Roug, L., I. Landberg, and L. Lundberg. 1989. Phonetic developments in early infancy: A study of four Swedish children during the first eighteen months of life. *Journal of Child Language* 16, 19–40.

Rubel, E. W. 1985. Auditory system development. In G. Gottlieb and N. A. Krasnegor, eds., *Measurement of audition and vision in the first year of postnatal life.* Norwood, N.J.: Ablex.

Ruben, R. J. 1992. The ontogeny of human hearing. *Acta Otolaryngologica* 112, 192–196.

Rumelhart, D., and J. McClelland. 1986. On learning the past tenses of English verbs: Implicit rules or parallel distributed processing? In J. McClelland and D. Rumelhart and the PDP Research Group, eds., *Parallel distributed processing: Explorations of the microstructure of cognition,* vol. 2, *Psychological and biological models.* Cambridge, Mass.: MIT Press.

Salasoo, A., R. M. Shiffrin, and T. C. Feustel. 1985. Building permanent memory codes: Codification and repetition effects in word identification. *Journal of Experimental Psychology: General* 114, 50–77.

Samuel, A. G. 1977. The effect of discrimination training on speech perception: Noncategorical perception. *Perception and Psychophysics* 22, 321–330.

Savin, H. B., and T. G. Bever. 1970. The nonperceptual reality of the phoneme. *Journal of Verbal Learning and Verbal Behavior* 9, 295–302.

Sawusch, J. R. 1976. Selective adaptation effects on end-point stimuli in a speech series. *Perception and Psychophysics* 20, 61–65.

Sawusch, J. R. 1986. Auditory and phonetic coding of speech. In E. C. Schwab and H. C. Nusbaum, eds., *Pattern recognition by humans and machines.* New York: Academic Press.

Sawusch, J. R. 1992. Auditory metrics for speech perception. In M. E. H. Schouten, ed., *The auditory processing of speech.* New York: Mouton de Gruyter.

Sawusch, J. R., and D. A. Gagnon. 1995. Auditory coding, cues, and coherence in phonetic perception. *Journal of Experimental Psychology: Human Perception and Performance* 21, 635–652.

Schacter, D. L. 1987. Implicit memory: History and current status. *Journal of Experimental Psychology: Learning, Memory and Cognition* 13, 501–518.

Schacter, D. L., B. Church, and J. Treadwell. 1994. Implicit memory in amnesic patients: Evidence for spared auditory priming. *Psychological Science* 5, 20–25.

Schacter, D. L., and B. A. Church. 1992. Auditory priming: Implicit and explicit memory for words and voices. *Journal of Experimental Psychology: Learning, Memory and Cognition* 18, 915–930.

Schwartz, R., and M. Folger. 1977. Sensorimotor development and descriptions of child phonology: A preliminary view of phonological analysis for Stage I speech. *Papers and Reports on Child Language Development* 13, 8–15.

Schwartz, R., and L. Leonard. 1982. Do children pick and choose? An examination of phonological selection and avoidance in early lexical acquisition. *Journal of Child Language* 9, 319–336.

Schwartz, R. G. 1988. Phonological factors in early lexical acquisition. In M. D. Smith and J. L. Locke, eds., *The emergent lexicon: The child's development of a linguistic vocabulary.* New York: Academic Press.

Scott, D. R. 1982. Duration as a cue to the perception of a phrase boundary. *Journal of the Acoustical Society of America* 71, 996–1007.

Scott, D. R., and A. Cutler. 1984. Segmental phonology and the perception of syntactic structure. *Journal of Verbal Learning and Verbal Behavior* 23, 450–466.

Scupin, E., and G. Scupin. 1907. *Bubis erste kindheit.* Leipzig: Grieben.

Searle, C. L., J. Z. Jacobson, and S. G. Rayment. 1979. Phoneme recognition based on human audition. *Journal of the Acoustical Society of America* 65, 799–809.

Seidenberg, M., and J. McClelland. 1989. A distributed, developmental model of word recognition and naming. *Psychological Review* 97, 447–452.

Selkirk, E. 1980. The role of prosodic categories in English word stress. *Linguistic Inquiry* 11, 563–605.

Selkirk, E. 1981. On the nature of phonological representation. In T. Myers, J. Laver, and J. Anderson, eds., *The cognitive representation of speech.* Amsterdam: North Holland.

Selkirk, E. O. 1984. *Phonology and syntax: The relation between sound and structure.* Cambridge, Mass.: MIT Press.

Sereno, J. A., and A. Jongman. 1995. Acoustic correlates of grammatical class. *Language and Speech* 38, 57–76.

Shady, M., L. A. Gerken, and P. W. Jusczyk. 1995. Prosody serves as a linguistic marker to local co-occurrence patterns in ten-month-olds. In D. MacLaughlin and S. McEwen, ed., *19th Annual Boston University Conference on Language Development,* 2. Somerville, Mass.: Cascadilla Press.

Shafer, V., L. A. Gerken, J. Shucard, and D. Shucard. 1992. "The" and the brain: An electrophysiological study of infants' sensitivity to English function morphemes. Paper presented at the Boston University Conference on Language Development, Boston, Mass., October 1992.

Shepard, R. N. 1972. Psychological representation of speech sounds. In E. E. David and P. B. Denes, eds., *Human communication: A unified view.* New York: McGraw-Hill.

Shipley, E. F., C. S. Smith, and L. R. Gleitman. 1969. A study in the acquisition of language: Free responses to commands. *Language* 45, 322–342.

Shvachkin, N. K. 1973. The development of phonemic speech perception in early childhood. In C. A. Ferguson and D. I. Slobin, eds., *Studies of child language development.* New York: Holt, Rinehart, and Winston.

Sinnott, J. M., M. D. Beecher, D. B. Moody, and W. C. Stebbins. 1976. Speech sound discrimination by monkeys and humans. *Journal of the Acoustical Society of America* 60, 687–695.

Sinnott, J. M., D. B. Pisoni, and R. N. Aslin. 1983. A comparison of pure tone auditory thresholds in human infants and adults. *Infant Behavior and Development* 6, 3–17.

Siqueland, E. R. 1969. The development of instrumental exploratory behavior during the first year of human life. Paper presented at the Biennial Meeting of the Society for Research in Child Development, Santa Monica, Calif., March 1969.

Siqueland, E. R., and DeLucia, C. A. 1969. Visual reinforcement of non-nutritive sucking in human infants. *Science* 165, 1144–1146.

Skinner, B. F. 1957. *Verbal behavior.* New York: Appleton-Century-Crofts.

Slobin, D. I. 1966. The acquisition of Russian as a native language. In F. Smith and G. A. Miller, eds., *The genesis of language: A psycholinguistic approach.* Cambridge, Mass.: MIT Press.

Slobin, D. I. 1973. Cognitive prerequisites for the development of grammar. In C. A. Ferguson and D. I. Slobin, eds., *Studies of child language development.* New York: Holt, Rinehart and Winston.

Slobin, D. I. 1982. Universal and particular in the acquisition of language. In E. Wanner and L. R. Gleitman, eds., *Language acquisition: The state of the art.* Cambridge: Cambridge University Press.

Slobin, D. I. 1985a. Cross-linguistic evidence for the language-making capacity. In D. I. Slobin, ed., *The cross-linguistic study of language acquisition, volume 2: Theoretical issues.* Hillsdale, N.J.: Erlbaum.

Slobin, D. I. 1985b. Why study language crosslinguistically. In D. I. Slobin, ed., *The crosslinguistic study of language acquisition.* Hillsdale, N.J.: Erlbaum.

Slobin, D. I., and T. G. Bever. 1982. Children use canonical sentence schemas: A cross-linguistic study of word order and inflections. *Cognition* 12, 229–265.

Smiley, P., and J. Huttenlocher. 1995. Conceptual development and the child's early words for events, objects, and persons. In M. Tomasello and W. Merriman, eds., *Beyond names for things.* Hillsdale, N.J.: Erlbaum.

Smith, L. B., and D. Heise. 1992. Perceptual similarity and conceptual structure. In B. Burns, eds., *Percepts, concepts, and categories: The representation and processing of information.* Amsterdam: Elsevier.

Smith, L. B., Jones, S., and Landau, B. (1992). Count nouns, adjectives and perceptual properties in novel word interpretations. *Developmental Psychology* 28, 273–288.

Smith, N. V. 1973. *The acquisition of phonology.* London: Cambridge University Press.

Soja, N., S. Carey, and E. Spelke. 1991. Ontological categories guide young children's inductions about word meaning: Object and substance terms. *Cognition* 38, 179–211.

Spelke, E. S. 1994. Initial knowledge: Six suggestions. *Cognition* 50, 431–445.

Spelke, E. S., K. Breinlinger, J. Macomber, and K. Jacobson. 1992. Origins of knowledge. *Psychological Review* 99, 605–632.

Spence, M. J., and A. D. DeCasper. 1987. Prenatal experience with low-frequency maternal-voice sounds influence neonatal perception of maternal voice samples. *Infant Behavior and Development* 10, 133–142.

Spencer, A. 1986. Toward a theory of phonological development. *Lingua* 68, 3–38.

Spring, D. R., and P. S. Dale. 1977. Discrimination of linguistic stress in early infancy. *Journal of Speech and Hearing Research* 20, 224–232.

Stampe, D. K. 1969. The acquisition of phonetic representation. Paper presented at the fifth Regional Meeting, Chicago Linguistics Society, Chicago, Ill.

Stark, R. E. 1980. Stages of speech development durign the first year of life. In G. H. Yeni-Komshian, J. F. Kavanagh, and C. A. Ferguson, eds., *Child phonology.* New York: Academic.

Starr, A., R. N. Amlie, W. H. Martin, and S. Sanders. 1977. Development of auditory function in newborn infants revealed by auditory brainstem potentials. *Pediatrics* 60, 831–839.

Stemberger, J. P. 1992. A connectionist view of child phonology: Phonological processing without phonological processes. In C. A. Ferguson, L. Menn, and C. Stoel-Gammon, eds., *Phonological development: Models, research, implications.* Timonium, Md.: York Press.

Stern, D. N., S. Spieker, R. K. Barnett, and K. MacKain. 1983. The prosody of maternal speech: Infant age and context related changes. *Journal of Child Language* 10, 1–15.

Stern, W., and C. Stern. 1928. *Die kindersprache.* Leipzig: Barth.

Stevens, K. N., and S. E. Blumstein. 1978. Invariant cues for place of articulation in stop consonants. *Journal of the Acoustical Society of America* 64, 1358–1368.

Stevens, K. N., and S. E. Blumstein. 1981. The search for invariant acoustic cor-relates for phonetic features. In P. D. Eimas and J. L. Miller, eds., *Perspectives on the study of speech.* Hillsdale, N J: Erlbaum.

Stevens, K. N., and D. H. Klatt. 1974. Role of formant transitions in the voiced-voiceless distinction for stops. *Journal of the Acoustical Society of America* 55, 653–659.

Stevens, K. N., A. M. Liberman, M. G. Studdert-Kennedy, and S. E. G. Ohman. 1969. Cross-language study of vowel perception. *Language and Speech* 12, 1–23.

Stoel-Gammon, C., and J. A. Cooper. 1984. Patterns of early lexical and phono-logical development. *Journal of Child Language* 11, 247–271.

Stoel-Gammon, C., and K. Otomo. 1986. Babbling development of hearing impaired and normally hearing subjects. *Journal of Speech and Hearing Disorders* 51, 33–41.

Strange, W., and P. A. Broen. 1981. The relationship between perception and production of /w/, /r/, and /l/ by three-year-old children. *Journal of Experimental Child Psychology* 31, 81–102.

Strange, W., and J. J. Jenkins. 1978. Role of linguistic experience in the perception of speech. In R. D. Walk and H. L. Pick, eds., *Perception and experience.* New York: Plenum.

Streeter, L. A. 1976. Language perception of 2-month old infants shows effects of both innate mechanisms and experience. *Nature* 259, 39–41.

Streeter, L. A. 1978. Acoustic determinants of phrase boundary perception. *Jour-nal of the Acoustical Society of America* 64, 1582–1592.

Stryker, M. P., H. Sherk, A. G. Leventhal, and H. V. B. Hirsch. 1978. Physio-logical consequences for the cat's visual cortex of effectively restricting experience with oriented contours. *Journal of Neurophysiology* 41, 896–909.

Studdert-Kennedy, M. 1986. Sources of variability in early speech development. In J. Perkell and D. H. Klatt, eds., *Invariance and variability in speech processes.* Hillsdale, N.J.: Erlbaum.

Studdert-Kennedy, M. 1991a. Comment: The emergent gesture. In I. G. Mat-tingly and M. Studdert-Kennedy, eds., *Modularity and the motor theory of speech perception.* Hillsdale, N.J.: Erlbaum.

Studdert-Kennedy, M. 1991b. Learning to speak: A note on the units of speech production and speech perception. *Perilus* 14, 173–183.

Suci, G. 1967. The validity of pause as an index of units in language. *Journal of Verbal Learning and Verbal Behavior* 6, 26–32.

Summerfield, Q., and M. P. Haggard. 1973. Vocal tract normalisation as demon-strated by reaction times. *Report of Speech Research in Progress* 2, The Queen's University of Belfast, Belfast, Ireland.

Suomi, K. 1993. An outline of a developmental model of adult phonological organization and behavior. *Journal of Phonetics* 21, 29–60.

Sussman, H. M., H. A. McCaffrey, and S. A. Matthews. 1991. An investigation of locus equations as a source of relational invariance for stop place categorization. *Journal of the Acoustical Society of America* 90, 1309–1325.

Sussman, J. E., and V. J. Lauckner-Morano. 1995. Further tests of the "perceptual magnet effect" in the perception of [i]: Identification and change/no change discrimination. *Journal of the Acoustical Society of America* 97, 539–552.

Suzuki, T., and Y. Ogiba. 1961. Conditioned orientation of reflex audiometry. *Archives of Otolaryngology* 74, 192–198.

Swoboda, P., J. Kass, P. A. Morse, and L. A. Leavitt. 1978. Memory factors in infant vowel discrimination of normal and at-risk infants. *Child Development* 49, 332–339.

Swoboda, P., P. A. Morse, and L. A. Leavitt. 1976. Continuous vowel discrimination in normal and at-risk infants. *Child Development* 47, 459–465.

Tanenhaus, M. K., J. E. Boland, G. A. Mauner, and G. N. Carlson. 1993. More on combinatory lexical information: Thematic structure in parsing and interpretation. In G. T. M. Altmann and R. Shillcock, eds., *Cognitive models of speech processing: The second Sperlonga meeting.* Hillsdale, N.J.: Erlbaum.

Taylor, M., and S. A. Gelman. 1988. Adjectives and nouns: Children's strategies for learning new words. *Child Development* 59, 411–419.

Templin, M. 1957. Certain language skills in children. In *Institute of Child Welfare Monographs.* Minneapolis: University of Minnesota Press.

Thelen, E., and L. B. Smith. 1994. *A dynamic systems approach to the development of cognition and action.* Cambridge, Mass.: Bradford Books/MIT Press.

Trehub, S. E. 1973. Infants' sensitivity to vowel and tonal contrasts. *Developmental Psychology* 9, 91–96.

Trehub, S. E. 1976. The discrimination of foreign speech contrasts by infants and adults. *Child Development* 47, 466–472.

Trehub, S. E., D. Bull, and B. A. Schneider. 1981. Infants' detection of speech in noise. *Journal of Speech and Hearing Research* 24, 202–206.

Trehub, S. E., D. Bull, and L. A. Thorpe. 1984. Infants' perception of melodies: The role of melodic contour. *Child Development* 55, 821–830.

Trehub, S. E., and L. A. Thorpe. 1989. Infants' perception of rhythm: Categorization of auditory sequences by temporal structure. *Canadian Journal of Psychology* 43, 217–229.

Trehub, S. E., L. A. Thorpe, and B. A. Morrongiello. 1985. Infants' perception of melodies: Changes in a single tone. *Infant Behavior and Development* 8, 213–223.

Tsushima, T., O. Takizawa, M. Sasaki, S. Siraki, K. Nishi, M. Kohno, P. Menyuk, and C. Best. 1994. Discrimination of English /r-l/ and /w-y/ by Japanese infants at 6–12 months: Language specific developmental changes in speech perception abilities. Paper presented at International Conference on Spoken Language Processing, 4. Yokohama, Japan.

Turk, A. E., P. W. Jusczyk, and L. A. Gerken. 1995. Do English-learning infants use syllable weight to determine stress? *Language and Speech* 38, 143–158.

Van Lancker, D., J. Kreiman, and K. Emmorey. 1985. Familiar voice recognition: Patterns and parameters. Part I: Recognition of backwards voices. *Journal of Phonetics* 13, 19–38.

Van Lancker, D., J. Kreiman, and T. D. Wickens. 1985. Familiar voice recognition: Patterns and parameters: Part II: Recognition of rate-altered voices. *Journal of Phonetics* 13, 39–52.

Vassiere, J. 1981. Speech recognition programs as models of speech perception. In T. Myers, J. Laver, and J. Anderson, eds., *The cognitive representation of speech.* Amsterdam: North Holland.

Velten, H. V. 1943. The growth of phonemic and lexical patterns in infant language. *Language* 19, 281–292.

Verbrugge, R. R., W. Strange, D. P. Shankweiler, and T. R. Edman. 1976. What information enables a listener to map a talker's vowel space? *Journal of the Acoustical Society of America* 60, 198–212.

Vihman, M. 1982. A note on children's lexical representations. *Journal of Child Language* 9, 249–253.

Vihman, M. M. 1980. Sound change and child language. *Current Issues in Linguistic Theory* 14, 304–320.

Vihman, M. M. 1986. Individual differences in babbling and early speech: Predicting to age three. In B. Lindblom and R. Zetterstrom, eds., *Precursors of early speech.* New York: Stockton Press.

Vihman, M. M. 1991. Ontogeny of phonetic gestures: Speech production. In I. G. Mattingly and M. Studdert-Kennedy, eds., *Modularity and the motor theory of speech perception.* Hillsdale, N.J.: Erlbaum.

Vihman, M. M. 1992. Early syllables and the construction of phonology. In C. A. Ferguson, L. Menn, and C. Stoel-Gammon, eds., *Phonological development: Models, research, implications.* Timonium, Md.: York Press.

Vihman, M. M. 1993a. The construction of a phonological system. In B. de Boysson-Bardies, S. de Schonen, P. Jusczyk, P. McNeilage, and J. Morton, eds., *Developmental neurocognition: Speech and face perception in the first year of life.* Dordrecht: Kluwer.

Vihman, M. M. 1993b. Variable paths to early word production. *Journal of Phonetics* 21, 61–82.

Vihman, M. M. (1996). *Phonological development: The origins of language in the child.* Cambridge MA: Blackwell Publishers.

Vihman, M. M., and M. Elbert. 1987. Phonological development. In J. E. Berenthal and N. W. Bankson, eds., *Articulation Disorders.* Englewood Cliffs, N.J.: Prentice Hall.

Vihman, M. M., M. A. Macken, R. Miller, H. Simmons, and J. Miller. 1985. From babbling to speech: A reassessment of the continuity issue. *Language* 61, 397–445.

Vihman, M. M., and R. Miller. 1988. Words and babble at the threshold of language acquisition. In M. D. Smith and J. L. Locke, eds., *The emergent lexicon*. New York: Academic.

Waibel, A. 1986. Suprasegmentals in very large vocabulary word recognition speech perceptions. In E. C. Schwab and H. C. Nusbaum, eds., *Pattern recognition by humans and machines*. New York: Academic Press.

Wakefield, J. R., E. B. Doughtie, and L. Yom. 1974. Identification of structural components of an unknown language. *Journal of Psycholinguistic Research* 3, 262–269.

Walley, A. C. 1993. The role of vocabulary development in children's spoken word recognition and segmentation ability. *Developmental Review* 13, 286–350.

Waters, R. S., and W. A. Wilson. 1976. Speech perception by rhesus monkeys: The voicing distinction in synthesized labial and velar stop consonants. *Perception and Psychophysics* 19, 285–289.

Waterson, N. 1971. Child phonology: A prosodic view. *Journal of Linguistics* 7, 179–211.

Waterson, N. 1978. The growth of complexity in phonological development. In N. Waterson and C. Snow, eds., *The development of communication*. Chicester: Wiley.

Waterson, N. 1981. A tentative developmental model of phonological representation. In T. Myers, J. Laver, and J. Anderson, eds., *The cognitive representation of speech*. Amsterdam: North Holland.

Waxman, S. R. 1991. Convergence between semantic and conceptual organization in preschool years. In *Perspectives on language and thought*. Cambridge: Cambridge University Press.

Waxman, S. R., and R. Gelman. 1986. Preschoolers' use of superordinate relations in classification and language. *Cognitive Development* 1, 139–156.

Waxman, S. R., and T. D. Kosowski. 1990. Nouns mark category relations: Toddlers' and pre-schoolers' word-learning biases. *Child Development* 61, 1461–1473.

Waxman, S. R., and D. B. Markow. 1995. Words as invitations to form categories: Evidence from 12- to 13-month-old infants. *Cognitive Psychology* 29, 257–302.

Weir, R. 1966. Some questions on the child's learning of phonology. In F. Smith and G. A. Miller, eds., *The genesis of language*. Cambridge, Mass.: MIT Press.

Werker, J. F. 1991. The ontogeny of speech perception. In I. G. Mattingly and M. Studdert-Kennedy, eds., *Modularity and the motor theory of speech perception*. Hillsdale, N.J.: Erlbaum.

Werker, J. F. 1994. Changing input, changing perceptual abilities, and changing cognitive skills: toward a more comprehensive account of age-related changes in cross-language speech perception. Paper presented at the International Conference on Infant Studies, Paris, June 1994.

Werker, J. F., J. H. Gilbert, K. Humphrey, and R. C. Tees. 1981. Developmental aspects of cross-language speech perception. *Child Development* 52, 349–355.

Werker, J. F., and C. E. Lalonde. 1988. Cross-language speech perception: Initial capabilities and developmental change. *Developmental Psychology* 24, 672–683.

Werker, J. F., and P. J. McLeod. 1989. Infant preference for both male and female infant-directed talk: A developmental study of attentional and affective responsiveness. *Canadian Journal of Psychology* 43, 230–246.

Werker, J. F., and J. E. Pegg. 1992. Infant speech perception and phonological acquisition. In C. A. Ferguson, L. Menn, and C. Stoel-Gammon, eds., *Phonological development: Models, research, implications.* Timonium, Md.: York Press.

Werker, J. F., and R. C. Tees. 1983. Developmental changes across childhood in the perception of non-native speech sounds. *Canadian Journal of Psychology* 37, 278–286.

Werker, J. F., and R. C. Tees. 1984a. Cross-language speech perception: Evidence for perceptual reorganization during the first year of life. *Infant Behavior and Development* 7, 49–63.

Werker, J. F., and R. C. Tees. 1984b. Phonemic and phonetic factors in adult cross-language speech perception. *Journal of the Acoustical Society of America* 75, 1866–1878.

Wexler, K., and P. Culicover. 1980. *Formal principles of language acquisition.* Cambridge, Mass.: MIT Press.

Whalen, D. H., A. Levitt, and Q. Wang. 1991. Intonational differences between the reduplicative babbling of French- and English-learning infants. *Journal of Child Language* 18, 501–506.

Wheeler, D., and G. Iverson. 1976. Hierarchical structures in child phonology. Paper presented at *Annual Meeting of the Linguistic Society of America.*

Wightman, C. W., S. Shattuck-Hufnagel, M. Ostendorf, and P. J. Price. 1992. Segmental durations in the vicinity of prosodic phrase boundaries. *Journal of the Acoustical Society of America* 91, 1707–1717.

Wijnen, F., E. Krikhaar, and E. den Os. 1994. The (non)realization of unstressed elements in children's utterances: a rhythmic constraint? *Journal of Child Language* 21, 59–84.

Williams, C. E., and K. N. Stevens. 1972. Emotions and speech: Some acoustical correlates. *Journal of the Acoustical Society of America* 52, 233–248.

Williams, E. 1987. Introduction. In T. Roeper and E. Williams, eds., *Parameter setting.* Dordrecht: D. Reidel.

Williams, L. 1977a. The effects of phonetic environment and stress placement on infant discrimination of place of stop consonant articulation. Paper presented at the Boston University Conference on Language Development, Boston, Mass., October 1977.

Williams, L. 1977b. The perception of stop consonant voicing by Spanish-English bilinguals. *Perception and Psychophysics* 21, 289–297.

Woodward, J. Z., and R. N. Aslin. 1990. Segmentation cues in maternal speech to infants. Paper presented at the meeting of the International Conference on Infant Studies, Montreal, Quebec.

Young, L. L., C. Parker, and R. Carhart. 1975. Effectiveness of speech and noise maskers on numbers embedded in continuous discourse. *Journal of the Acoustical Society of America* 58, S35.

Name Index

Subject Index

Acoustic invariants, 43, 45–46, 48
Acquired distinctiveness, 49
Adult-directed speech, 69, 141–144, 244
Allophones
  and study by Pegg, 251–252
  and word boundaries, 9, 93–95, 104–106,
    157, 203, 224
Analytic style, 31
American sign language, 201
Aphasia, 170
Artificial grammars, 139
Articulatory
  gestures, 191–193, 205
  rehearsal, 195–196
  representations, 194
Assimilation, 185
Attention, 116, 118–120, 134, 199–200, 203,
    215, 221–222
  attentional capacities, 15, 123–124, 134,
    193, 203, 214, 230
  attentional demands, 225
  attentional focus, 117, 189
  attentional processes, 116, 133, 219
  attentional resources, 116, 122, 133
  attentional shifts, 121
  to onsets, 120
  selective, 121, 123
  for words, 192
Attenuation, 74, 81
Auditory
  capacities, 56, 70
  mechanisms, 59, 61
  threshold, 121
  analyzers, 215, 218–222, 224–225, 252
Automatic speech recognition, 8

Babbling, 15, 49, 171–172, 175–176, 191–
    192, 197
  Brown's view, 18–19
  canonical, 173–174

and cross-linguistic studies, 177–179
in deaf infants, 171–174
drifts, 19, 176–177, 205
Jakobson's view, 168–169
manual, 174, 253
reduplicated, 174–176
variegated, 174–176
and word production, 172, 180–181
Bilingual speakers, 222–223
Biological endowment for language, 50,
    51
Bootstrapping
  general, 27, 31, 35, 160, 162
  models, 35
  prosodic, 15, 37–40, 138–139, 152, 156–
    157, 251
  semantic, 37, 41, 251
  syntactic, 35, 251
Boundary cues, 31
Broadening, 74, 75

Capacities
  auditory, 56, 70
  cognitive, 233
  general perceptual, 38
    mechanisms, 78
  innate, 20, 22
  linguistic, 14, 20, 23, 25, 38, 41, 56, 139
    specialized, 26
  memory, 134, 193, 202–203, 214, 230
  perceptual, 20, 137, 208, 227, 233
  productive, 208, 227
Categorical discrimination, 52, 53, 59
Categorical perception, 46–51, 57–58
Categorization
  formulaic, 184
  word-oriented, 184
Child-directed speech, 141–145, 148. *See
  also* Infant-directed speech
Chinchillas, 57